エスカフローネ

ESCAFLOWNE

2

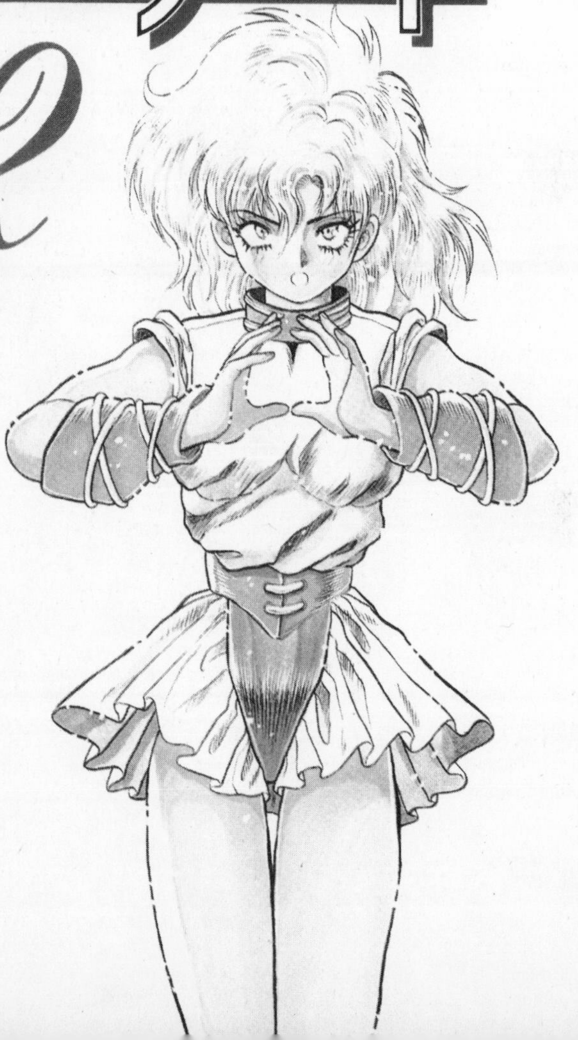

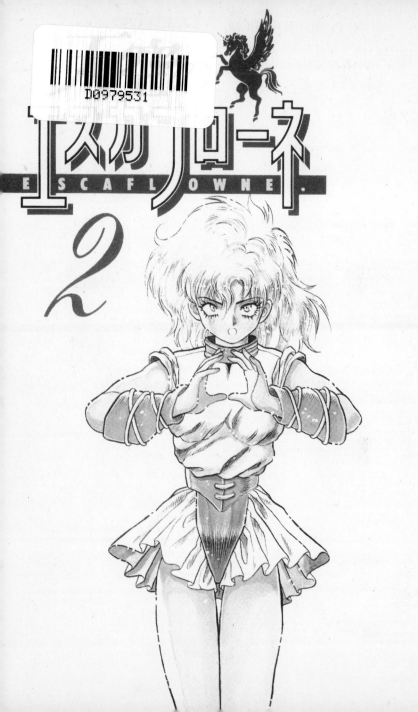

ALSO AVAILABLE FROM 🐱 TOKYOPOP®

MANGA

.HACK//LEGEND OF THE TWILIGHT
@LARGE (October 2003)
ANGELIC LAYER*
BABY BIRTH*
BATTLE ROYALE*
BRAIN POWERED*
BRIGADOON*
CARDCAPTOR SAKURA
CARDCAPTOR SAKURA: MASTER OF THE CLOW*
CHOBITS*
CHRONICLES OF THE CURSED SWORD
CLAMP SCHOOL DETECTIVES*
CLOVER
CONFIDENTIAL CONFESSIONS*
CORRECTOR YUI
COWBOY BEBOP*
COWBOY BEBOP: SHOOTING STAR*
CYBORG 009*
DEMON DIARY
DIGIMON*
DRAGON HUNTER
DRAGON KNIGHTS*
DUKLYON: CLAMP SCHOOL DEFENDERS*
ERICA SAKURAZAWA*
FAKE*
FLCL*
FORBIDDEN DANCE*
GATE KEEPERS*
G GUNDAM*
GRAVITATION*
GTO*
GUNDAM WING
GUNDAM WING: BATTLEFIELD OF PACIFISTS
GUNDAM WING: ENDLESS WALTZ*
GUNDAM WING: THE LAST OUTPOST*
HAPPY MANIA*
HARLEM BEAT
I.N.V.U.
INITIAL D*
ISLAND
JING: KING OF BANDITS*
JULINE
KARE KANO*
KINDAICHI CASE FILES, THE*
KING OF HELL
KODOCHA: SANA'S STAGE*
LOVE HINA*
LUPIN III*
MAGIC KNIGHT RAYEARTH*

MAGIC KNIGHT RAYEARTH II* (COMING SOON)
MAN OF MANY FACES*
MARMALADE BOY*
MARS*
MIRACLE GIRLS
MIYUKI-CHAN IN WONDERLAND* (October 2003)
MONSTERS, INC.
PARADISE KISS*
PARASYTE
PEACH GIRL
PEACH GIRL: CHANGE OF HEART*
PET SHOP OF HORRORS*
PLANET LADDER*
PLANETES* (October 2003)
PRIEST
RAGNAROK
RAVE MASTER*
REALITY CHECK
REBIRTH
REBOUND*
RISING STARS OF MANGA
SABER MARIONETTE J*
SAILOR MOON
SAINT TAIL
SAMURAI DEEPER KYO*
SAMURAI GIRL: REAL BOUT HIGH SCHOOL*
SCRYED*
SHAOLIN SISTERS*
SHIRAHIME-SYO: SNOW GODDESS TALES* (Dec. 2003)
SHUTTERBOX (November 2003)
SORCERER HUNTERS
THE SKULL MAN*
THE VISION OF ESCAFLOWNE
TOKYO MEW MEW*
UNDER THE GLASS MOON
VAMPIRE GAME*
WILD ACT*
WISH*
WORLD OF HARTZ (COMING SOON)
X-DAY*
ZODIAC P.I. *

For more information visit www.TOKYOPOP.com

*INDICATES 100% AUTHENTIC MANGA (RIGHT-TO-LEFT FORMAT)

CINE-MANGA™

CARDCAPTORS
JACKIE CHAN ADVENTURES (November 2003)
JIMMY NEUTRON
KIM POSSIBLE
LIZZIE MCGUIRE
POWER RANGERS: NINJA STORM
SPONGEBOB SQUAREPANTS
SPY KIDS 2

NOVELS

KARMA CLUB (April 2004)
SAILOR MOON

TOKYOPOP KIDS

STRAY SHEEP

ART BOOKS

CARDCAPTOR SAKURA*
MAGIC KNIGHT RAYEARTH*

ANIME GUIDES

COWBOY BEBOP ANIME GUIDES
GUNDAM TECHNICAL MANUALS
SAILOR MOON SCOUT GUIDES

062703

THE · VISION · OF
ESCAFLOWNE

Volume 2

By

KATSU AKI

Original concept
by
HAJIME YATATE
SHOJI KAWAMORI
(STUDIO NUE)

TOKYOPOP®

LOS ANGELES · TOKYO · LONDON

Translation - Jeremiah Bourque
English Adaptation - Lianne Sentar
Associate & Copy Editor - Tim Beedle
Retouch & Lettering - Eric Botero
Cover Design - Raymond Makowski
Editors - Mark Paniccia & Rob Tokar

Managing Editor - Jill Freshney
Production Coordinator - Antonio DePietro
Production Manager - Jennifer Miller
Art Director - Matt Alford
Director of Editorial - Jeremy Ross
VP of Production - Ron Klamert
President & C.O.O. - John Parker
Publisher & C.E.O. - Stuart Levy

Email: editor@TOKYOPOP.com
Come visit us online at www.TOKYOPOP.com

A  Manga

TOKYOPOP Inc.
5900 Wilshire Blvd. Suite 2000
Los Angeles, CA 90036

THE VISION OF ESCAFLOWNE volume 2 © SUNRISE•TV TOKYO ©KATSU AKI 1995.
First published in Japan in 1995 by KADOKAWA SHOTEN PUBLISHING, CO., LTD., Tokyo.
English translation rights arranged with KADOKAWA SHOTEN PUBLISHING CO., LTD., Tokyo
through TUTTLE-MORI AGENCY, INC., Tokyo.

English text copyright ©2003 TOKYOPOP Inc.

ISBN: 1-59182-367-6

First TOKYOPOP printing: September 2003

10 9 8 7 6 5 4 3 2 1
Printed in the USA

THE · VISION · OF
ESCAFLOWNE

INTRODUCTION

"Tenkuu no Escaflowne" ("Escaflowne of the Heavens," or "The Vision of Escaflowne" in North America) began as a story in the minds of Hajime Yatate and Shoji Kawamori, two brilliant creators who planned Hitomi's epic tale to appear as an animated television series. While most anime series begin as manga, Escaflowne's two manga series were built off the ideas developed for the anime. Yuzuru Yashiro's shoujo, or "girl's" manga, is two volumes in length. In contrast, Katsu Aki's shonen, or "boy's" manga, is much longer and happens to be the version you now hold in your hands.

Aki-sensei handled both the art and writing for this title, and it was actually the first version of Escaflowne to reach the public. While based on the concept of the anime, it began its serialization before the anime was complete. This version of the Escaflowne tale has a different flavor than the television series, with more action, tweaked character design, and an altered story. As a result, it is difficult to closely compare the two—they are simply two different versions of Hitomi's adventures. Escaflowne's versatility has always fetched great praise over the years. Its manga counterparts only expand the work's reach and deepen its universe. With that in mind, please put aside all preconceptions you may have as you sit back, relax, and enjoy this new look at the world of Escaflowne like you've never seen it before.

Lianne Sentar, April 2003

Special thanks to Egan Loo and his Escaflowne Compendium (http://www.anime.net/escaflowne/).

ESCAFLOWNE VOL.2
CONTENTS

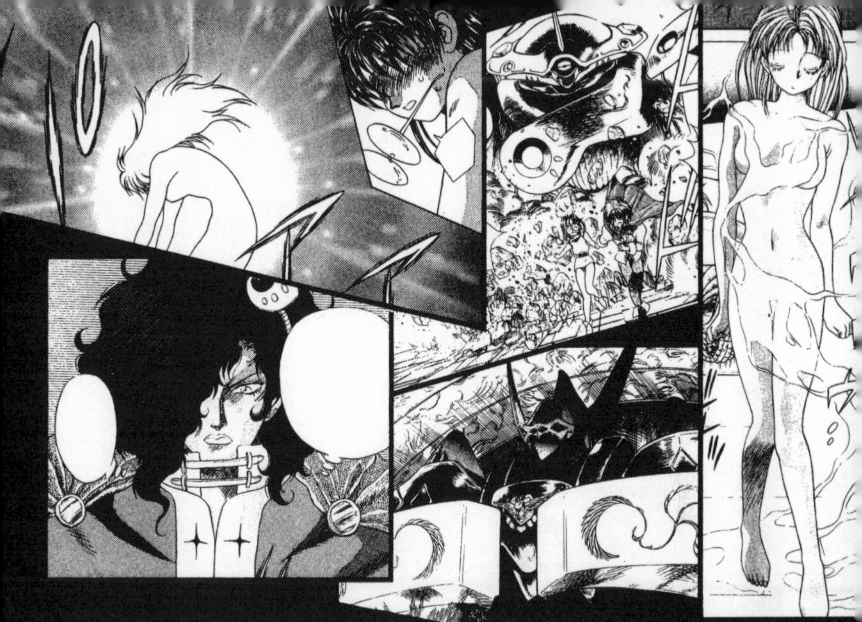

Hitomi Hoshino's interest in fortune-telling was both simple and innocent—until she started having strange, recurring visions of a prince and a jewel. A routine reading resulted in Hitomi's soul being snatched from her body and, when she awoke, she found herself in the strange land of Gaea—the very place that she had seen in her visions! The beautiful jewel Energist formed her body and left her panting on a mysterious temple's floor.

But not everything was quite so poetic. The prince she'd seen in her dreams turned out to be a rash, hot-headed, and rather short teenager named Van. The magic of his country (Fanelia) had selected Hitomi to be the Energist power of their mechanical god Escaflowne. As Van tried to push Hitomi into her new role of robot fuel, Fanelia was attacked by the aggressive Zaibach Empire. Hitomi managed to power Escaflowne to save her life and Van's, but the Zaibach warrior Dilandau killed Captain Balgus, kidnapped Queen Escalina and flattened Fanelia.

During some dangerous run-ins with Zaibach and Dilandau, Hitomi and Van gained the aid of the Asturian knight Allen Schezar. It was decided that, in order to save Van's mother and stop Zaibach's ruthless attacks on their nations, Hitomi's power needed to be better utilized. In an attempt to do this, Hitomi, Van, and Allen set out on a dangerous journey to the Holy Spring Ubdo to ask its inhabitants the secret of the Energist...

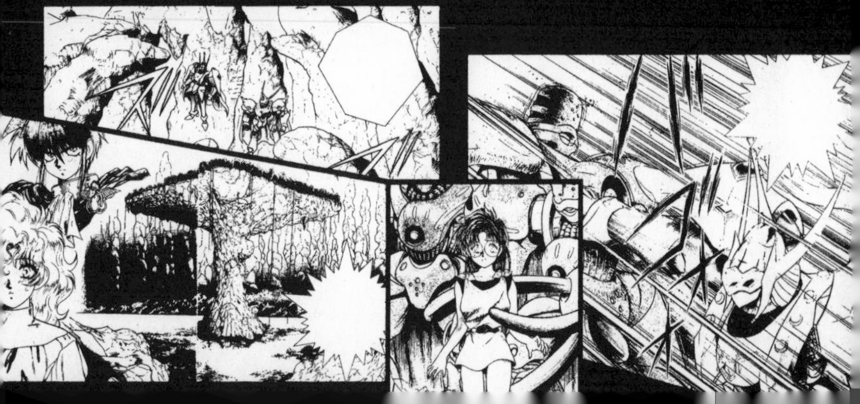

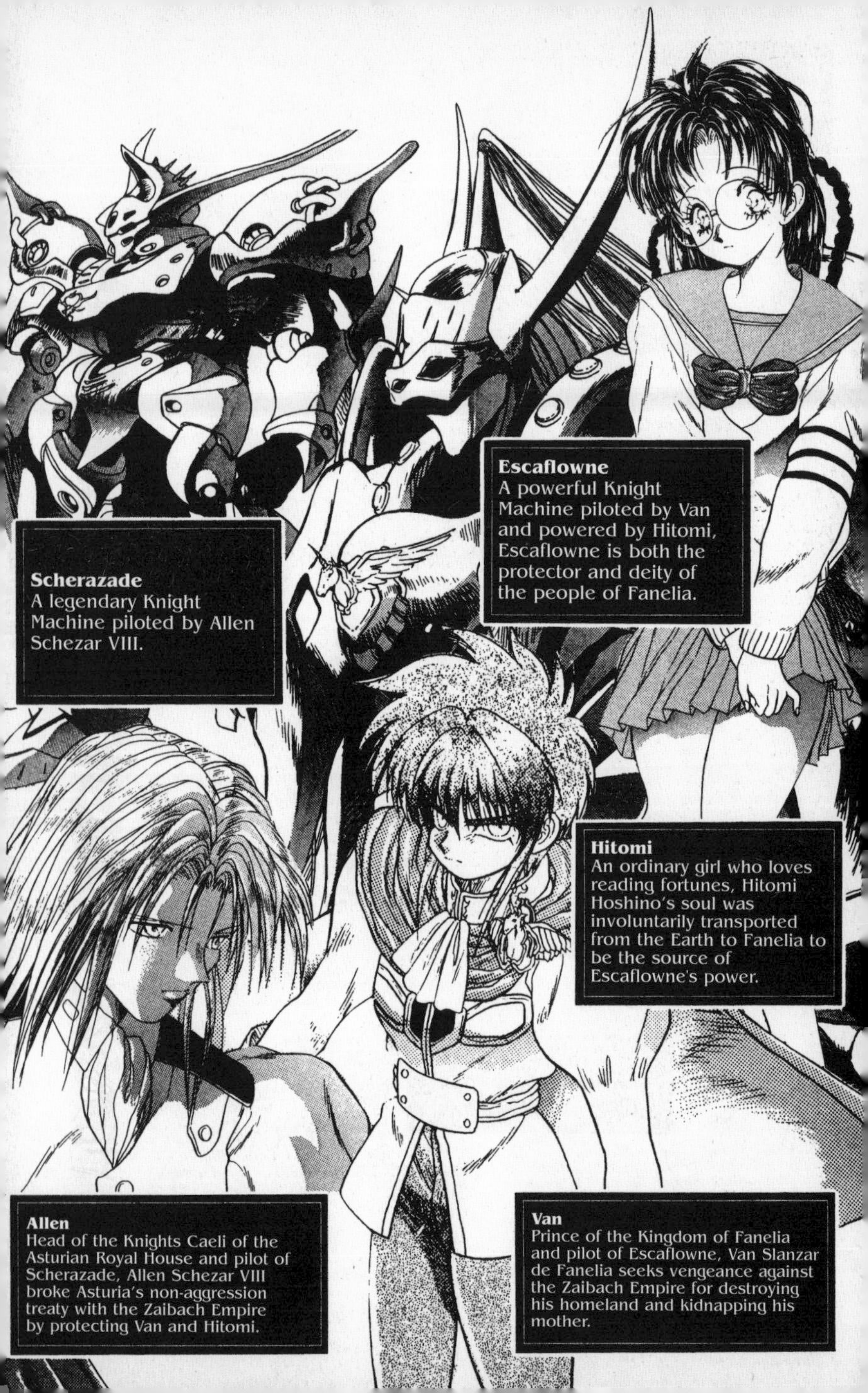
Escaflowne
A powerful Knight Machine piloted by Van and powered by Hitomi, Escaflowne is both the protector and deity of the people of Fanelia.
Scherazade
A legendary Knight Machine piloted by Allen Schezar VIII.
Hitomi
An ordinary girl who loves reading fortunes, Hitomi Hoshino's soul was involuntarily transported from the Earth to Fanelia to be the source of Escaflowne's power.
Van
Prince of the Kingdom of Fanelia and pilot of Escaflowne, Van Slanzar de Fanelia seeks vengeance against the Zaibach Empire for destroying his homeland and kidnapping his mother.
Allen
Head of the Knights Caeli of the Asturian Royal House and pilot of Scherazade, Allen Schezar VIII broke Asturia's non-aggression treaty with the Zaibach Empire by protecting Van and Hitomi.

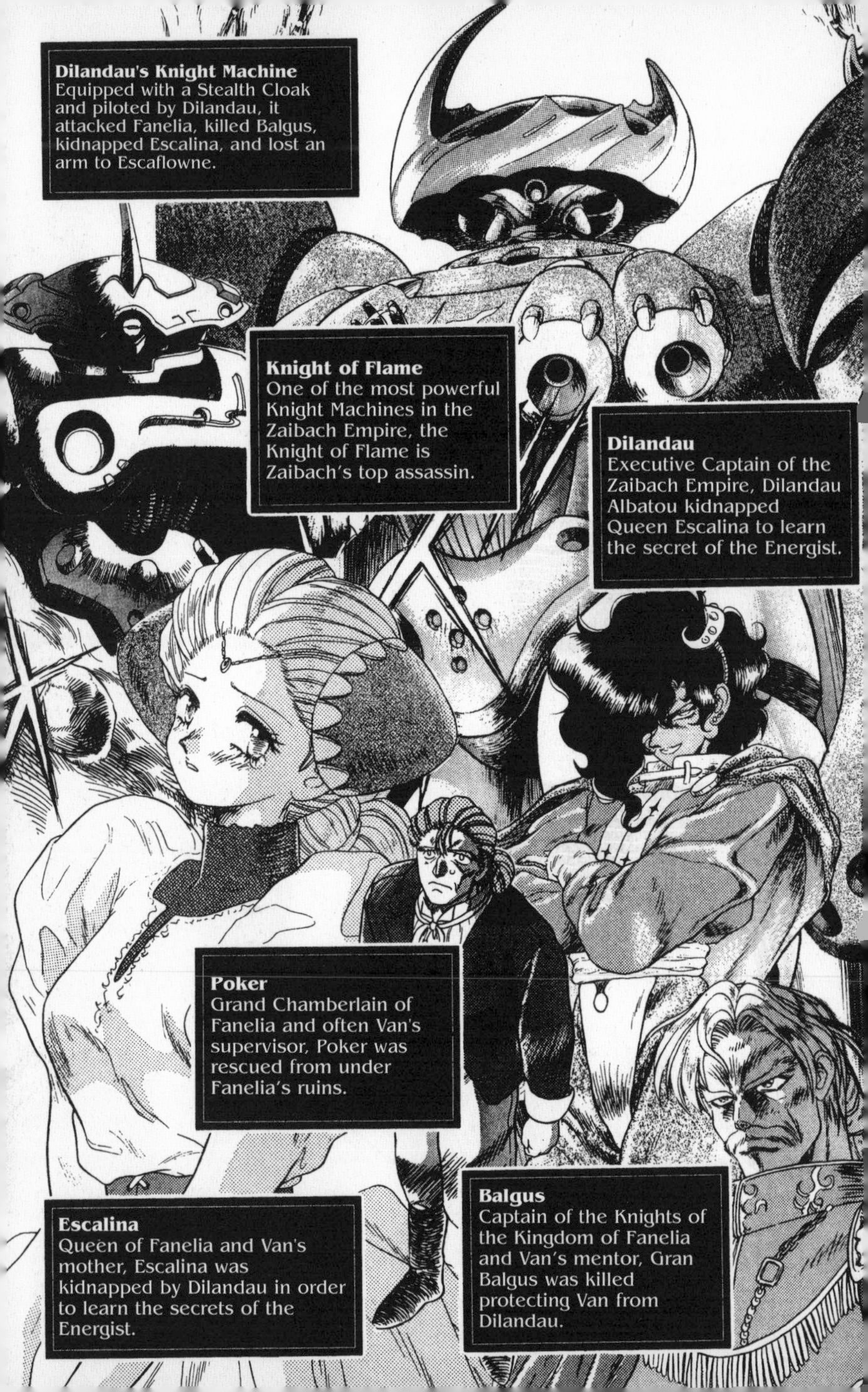
Dilandau's Knight Machine
Equipped with a Stealth Cloak and piloted by Dilandau, it attacked Fanelia, killed Balgus, kidnapped Escalina, and lost an arm to Escaflowne.
Knight of Flame
One of the most powerful Knight Machines in the Zaibach Empire, the Knight of Flame is Zaibach's top assassin.
Dilandau
Executive Captain of the Zaibach Empire, Dilandau Albatou kidnapped Queen Escalina to learn the secret of the Energist.
Poker
Grand Chamberlain of Fanelia and often Van's supervisor, Poker was rescued from under Fanelia's ruins.
Balgus
Captain of the Knights of the Kingdom of Fanelia and Van's mentor, Gran Balgus was killed protecting Van from Dilandau.
Escalina
Queen of Fanelia and Van's mother, Escalina was kidnapped by Dilandau in order to learn the secrets of the Energist.

VISION 5: SECRETS OF THE HOLY SPRING

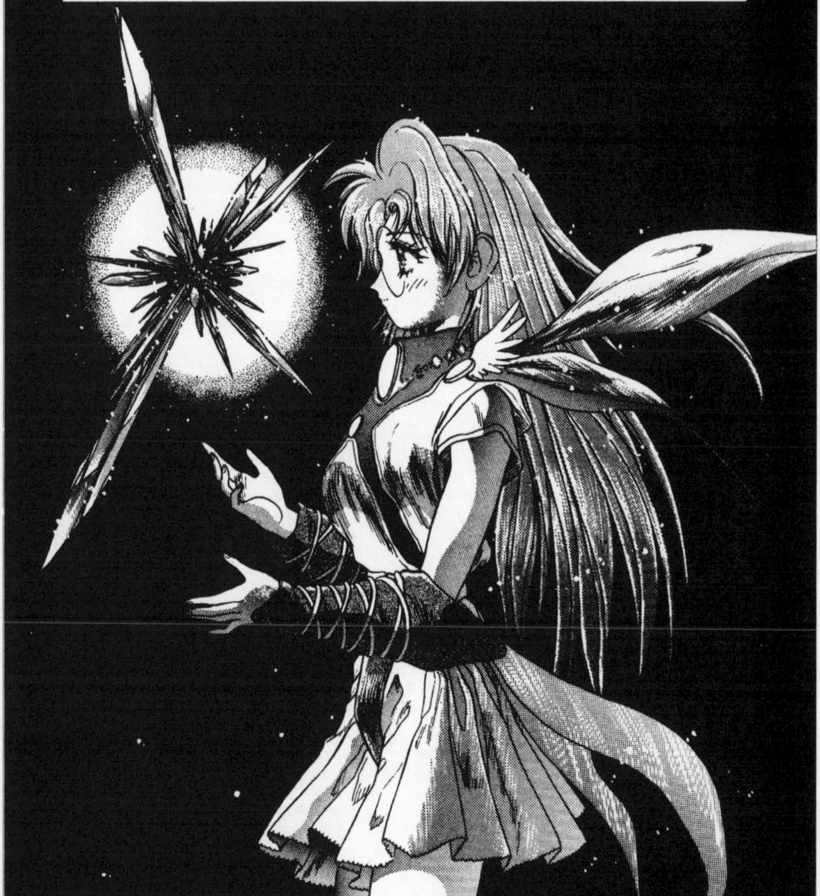

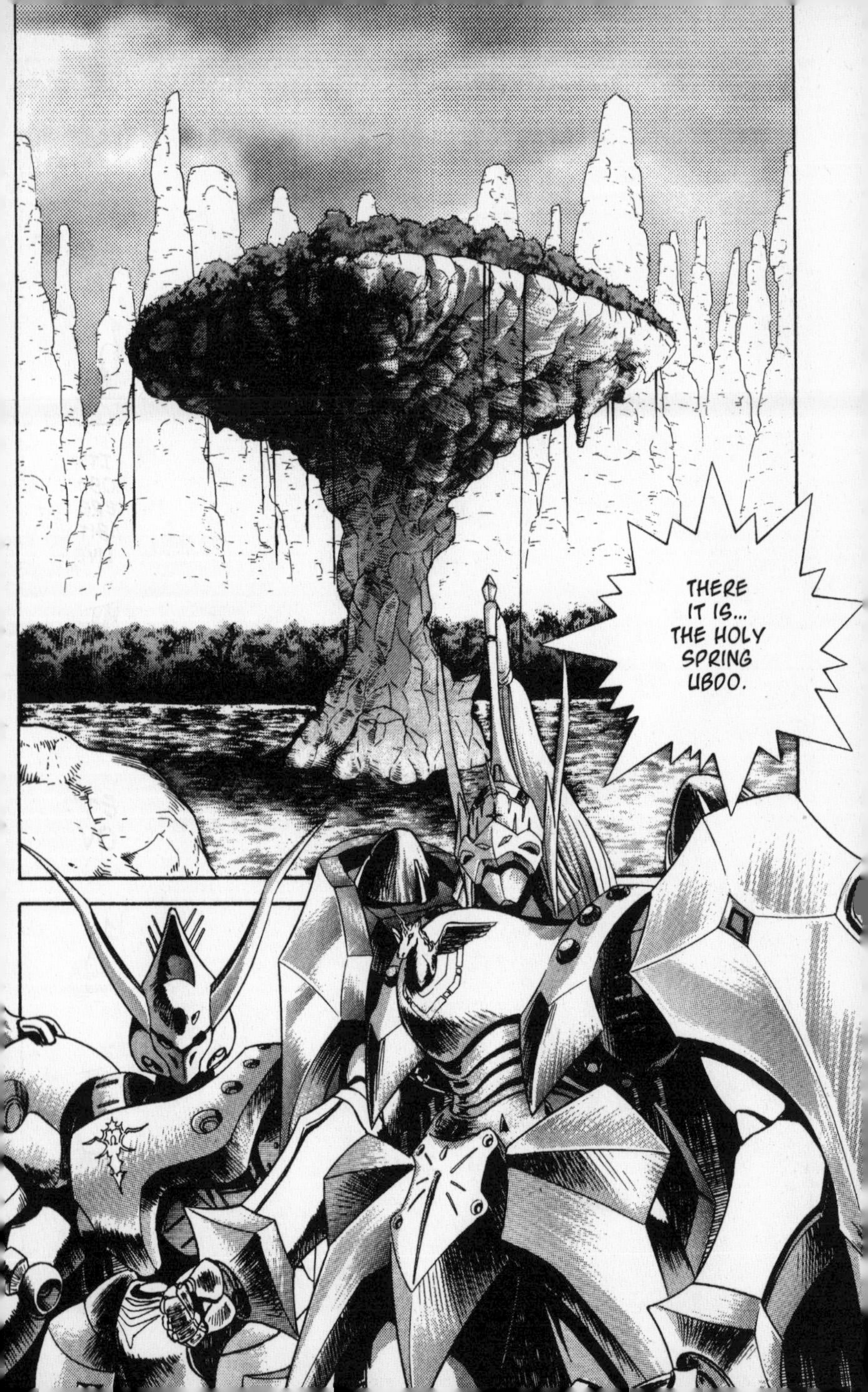
THERE IT IS... THE HOLY SPRING UBDO.

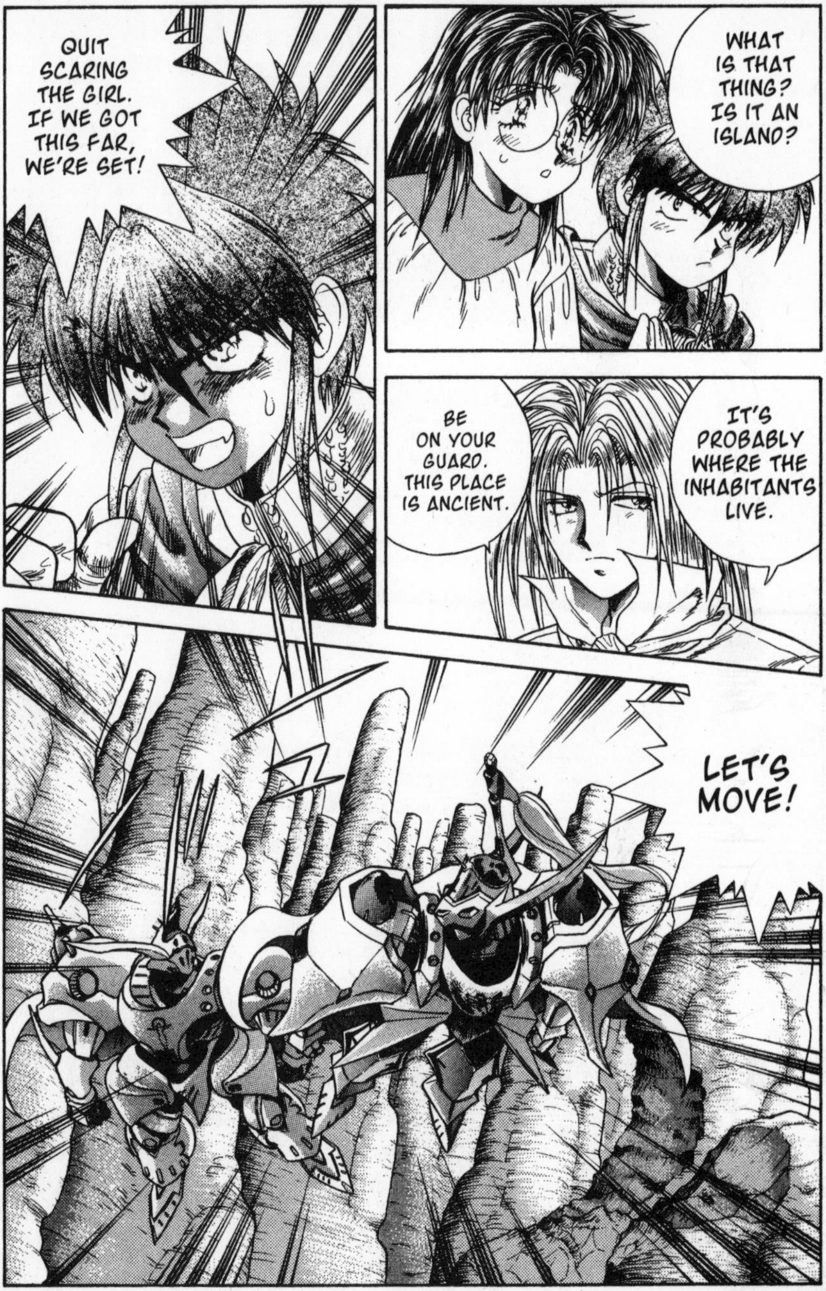
WHAT IS THAT THING? IS IT AN ISLAND?
IT'S PROBABLY WHERE THE INHABITANTS LIVE.
BE ON YOUR GUARD. THIS PLACE IS ANCIENT.
QUIT SCARING THE GIRL. IF WE GOT THIS FAR, WE'RE SET!
LET'S MOVE!

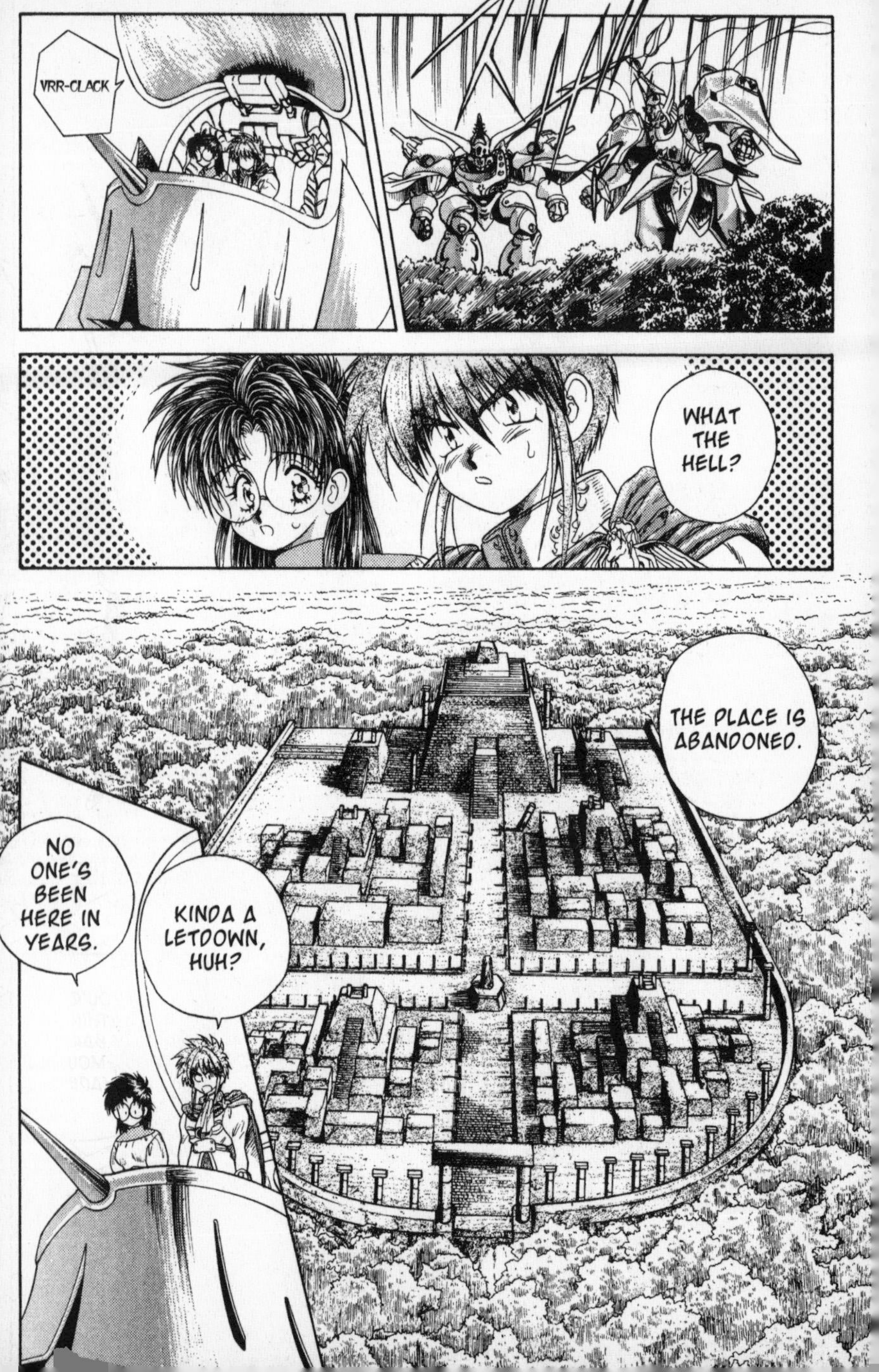
VRR-CLACK
WHAT THE HELL?
THE PLACE IS ABANDONED.
KINDA A LETDOWN, HUH?
NO ONE'S BEEN HERE IN YEARS.

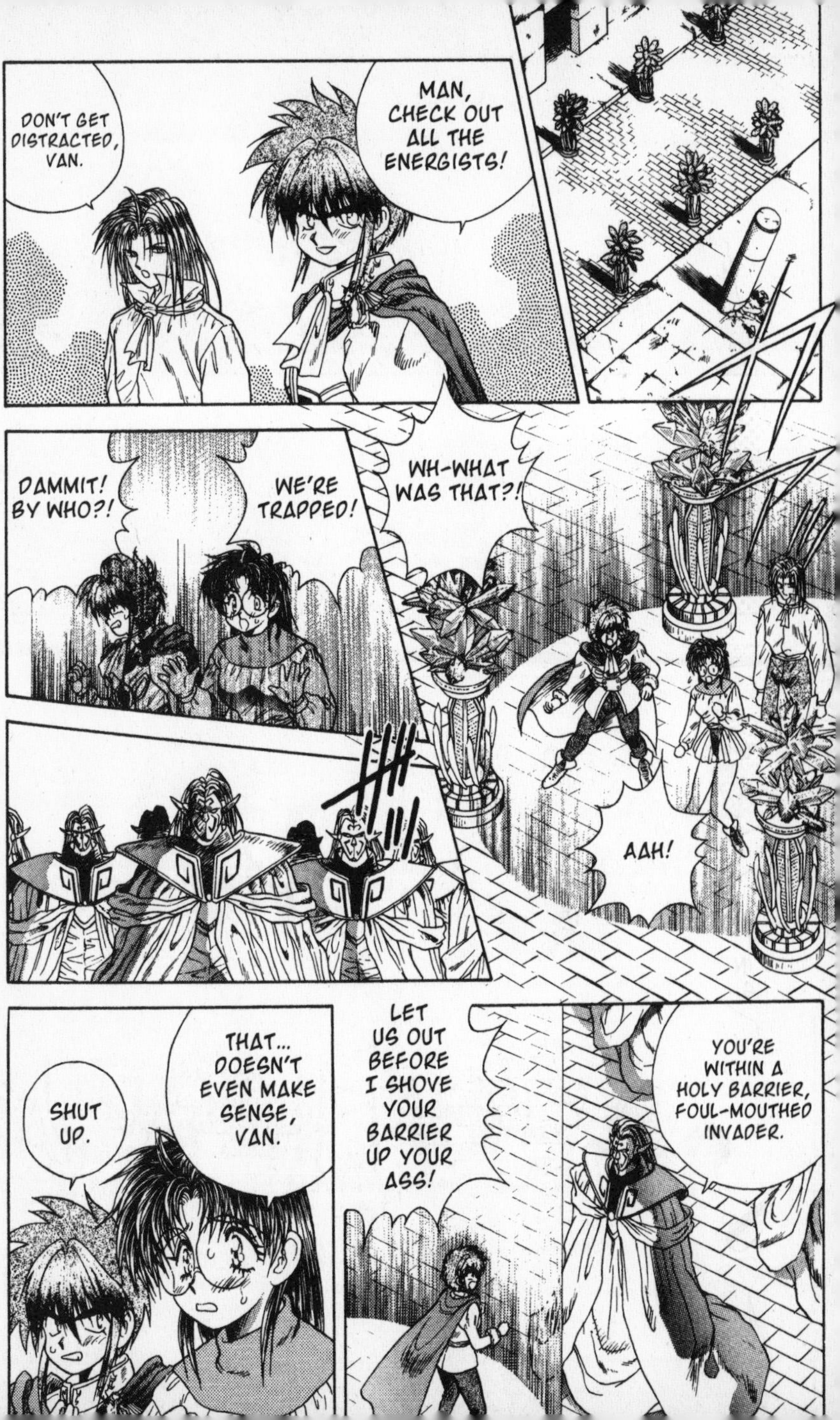
MAN, CHECK OUT ALL THE ENERGISTS!
DON'T GET DISTRACTED, VAN.
WH-WHAT WAS THAT?!
AAH!
WE'RE TRAPPED!
DAMMIT! BY WHO?!
YOU'RE WITHIN A HOLY BARRIER, FOUL-MOUTHED INVADER.
LET US OUT BEFORE I SHOVE YOUR BARRIER UP YOUR ASS!
THAT... DOESN'T EVEN MAKE SENSE, VAN.
SHUT UP.

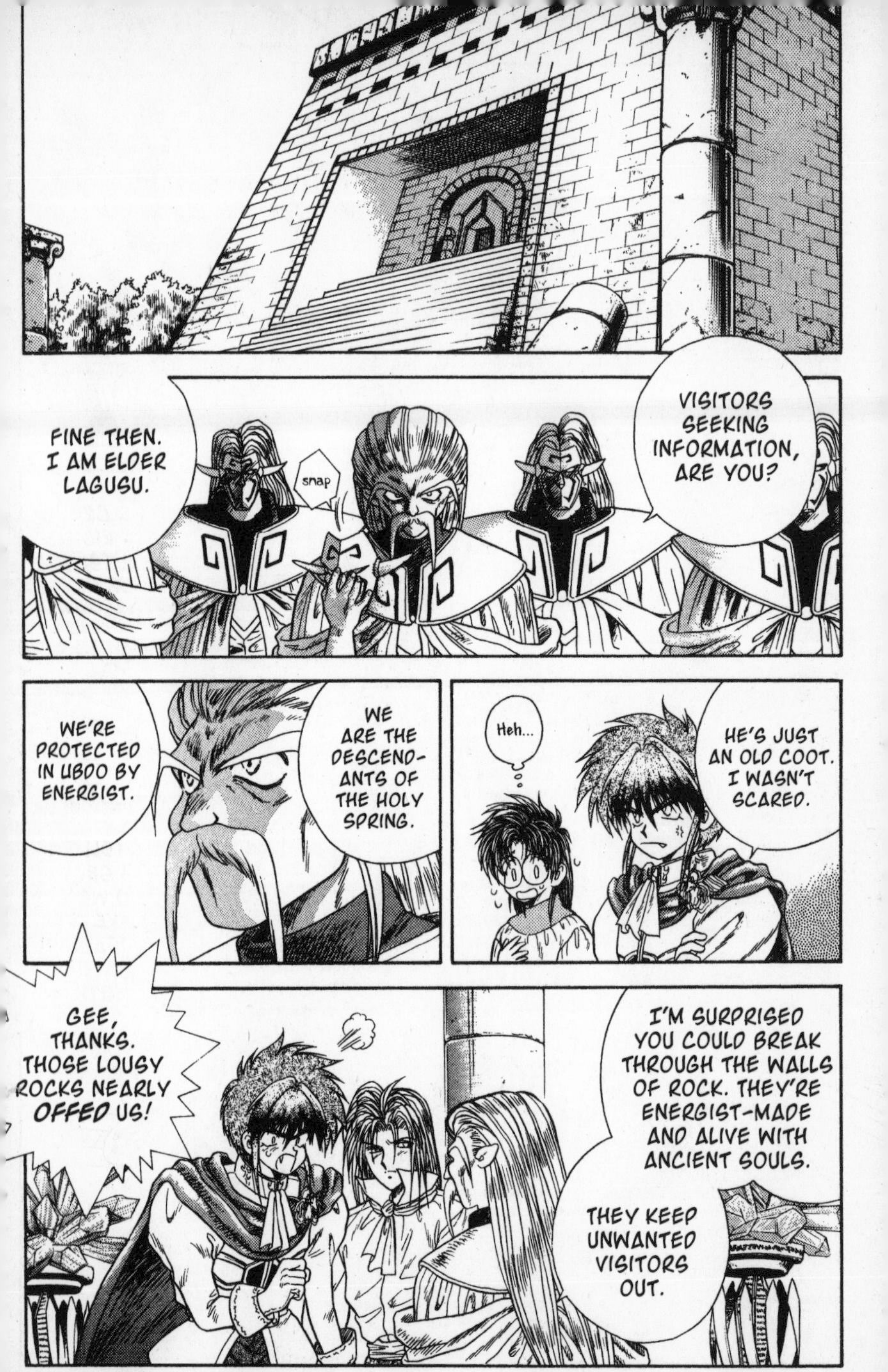
VISITORS SEEKING INFORMATION, ARE YOU?
snap
FINE THEN. I AM ELDER LAGUSU.
HE'S JUST AN OLD COOT. I WASN'T SCARED.
Heh...
WE ARE THE DESCEND-ANTS OF THE HOLY SPRING.
WE'RE PROTECTED IN UBDO BY ENERGIST.
I'M SURPRISED YOU COULD BREAK THROUGH THE WALLS OF ROCK. THEY'RE ENERGIST-MADE AND ALIVE WITH ANCIENT SOULS.
THEY KEEP UNWANTED VISITORS OUT.
GEE, THANKS. THOSE LOUSY ROCKS NEARLY *OFFED* US!

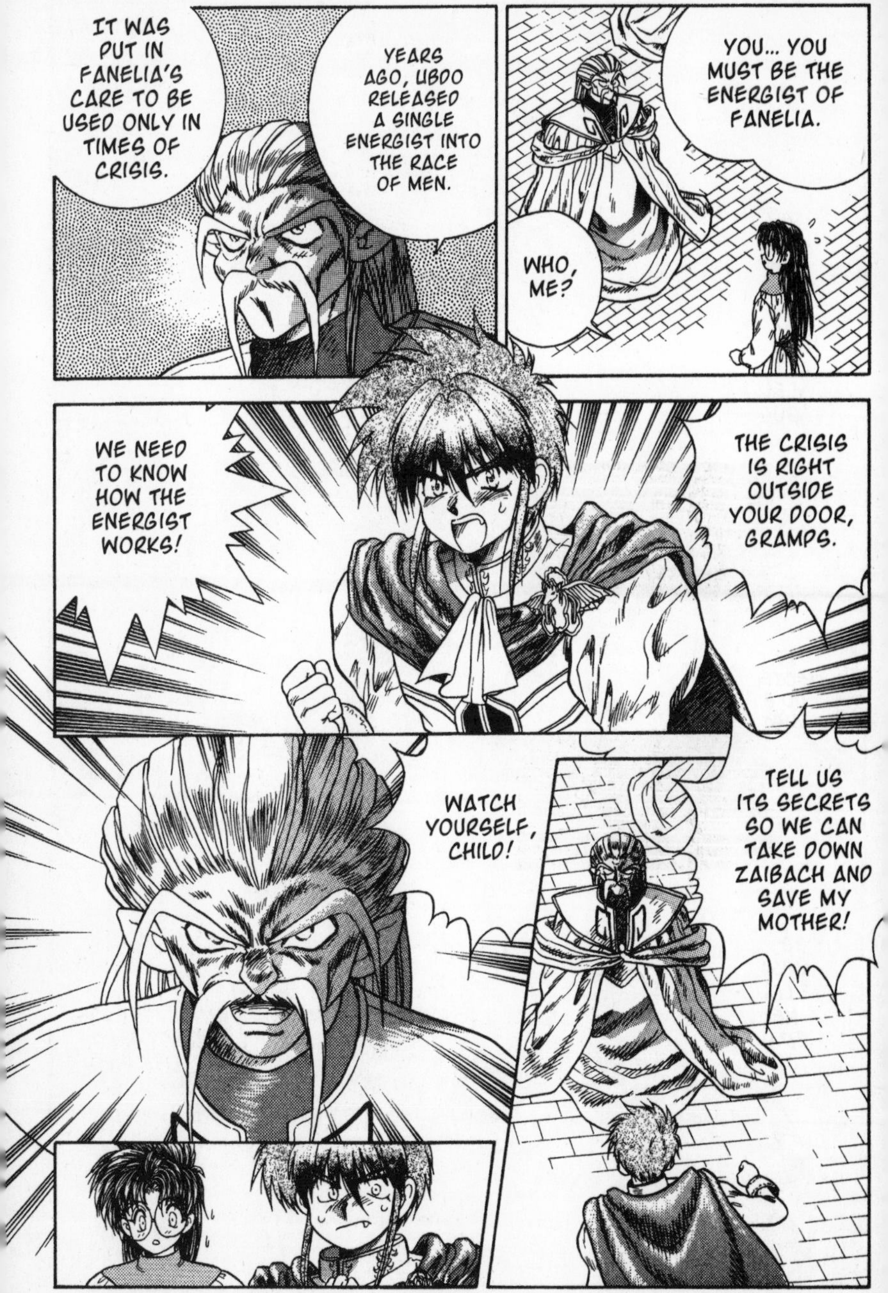
YOU... YOU MUST BE THE ENERGIST OF FANELIA.
WHO, ME?
YEARS AGO, UBOO RELEASED A SINGLE ENERGIST INTO THE RACE OF MEN.
IT WAS PUT IN FANELIA'S CARE TO BE USED ONLY IN TIMES OF CRISIS.
THE CRISIS IS RIGHT OUTSIDE YOUR DOOR, GRAMPS.
WE NEED TO KNOW HOW THE ENERGIST WORKS!
TELL US ITS SECRETS SO WE CAN TAKE DOWN ZAIBACH AND SAVE MY MOTHER!
WATCH YOURSELF, CHILD!

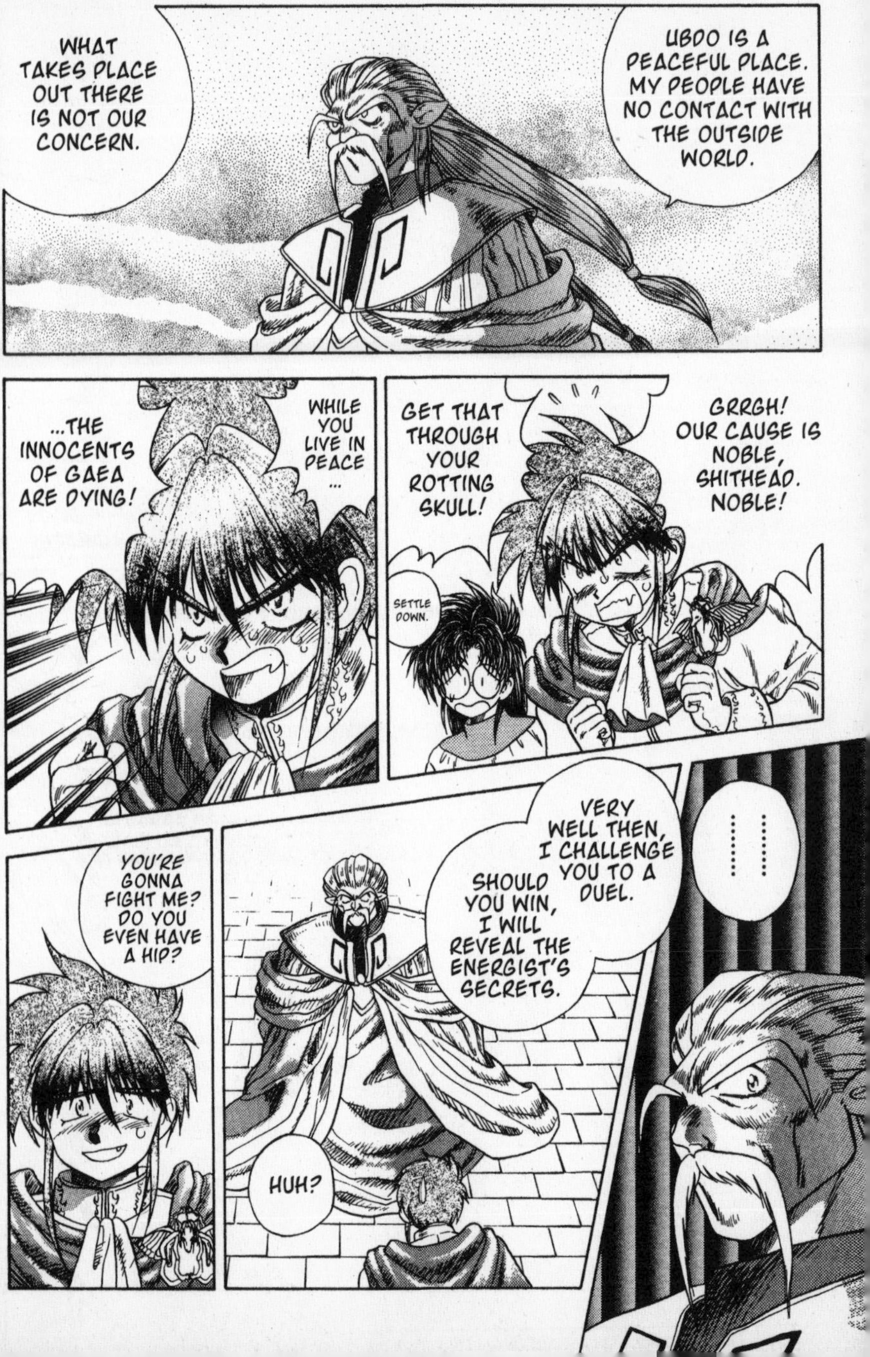
UBOO IS A PEACEFUL PLACE. MY PEOPLE HAVE NO CONTACT WITH THE OUTSIDE WORLD.
WHAT TAKES PLACE OUT THERE IS NOT OUR CONCERN.
GRRGH! OUR CAUSE IS NOBLE, SHITHEAD. NOBLE!
GET THAT THROUGH YOUR ROTTING SKULL!
SETTLE DOWN.
WHILE YOU LIVE IN PEACE ...
...THE INNOCENTS OF GAEA ARE DYING!
......
VERY WELL THEN, I CHALLENGE YOU TO A DUEL.
SHOULD YOU WIN, I WILL REVEAL THE ENERGIST'S SECRETS.
HUH?
YOU'RE GONNA FIGHT ME? DO YOU EVEN HAVE A HIP?

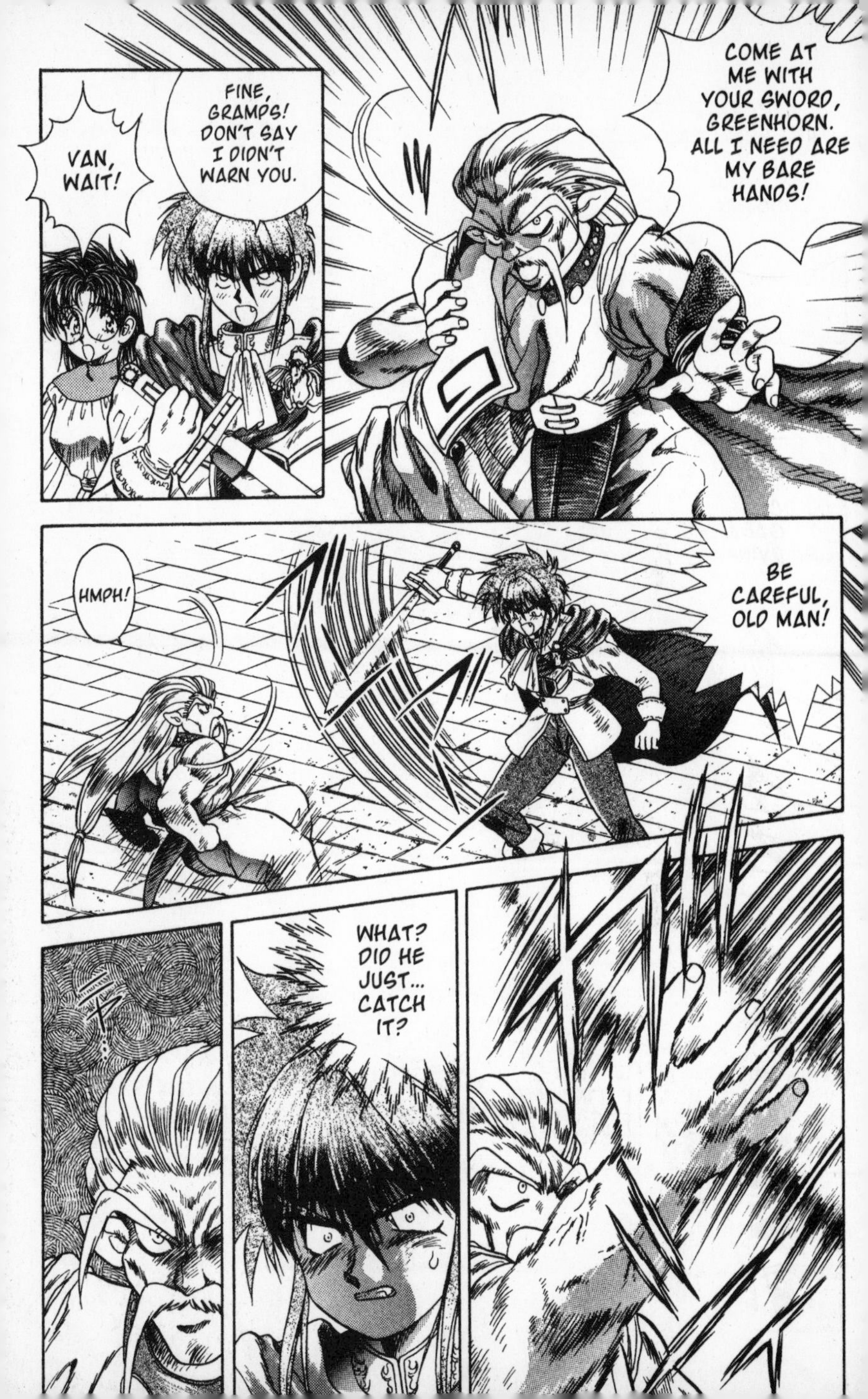
COME AT ME WITH YOUR SWORD, GREENHORN. ALL I NEED ARE MY BARE HANDS!
FINE, GRAMPS! DON'T SAY I DIDN'T WARN YOU.
VAN, WAIT!
BE CAREFUL, OLD MAN!
HMPH!
WHAT? DID HE JUST... CATCH IT?

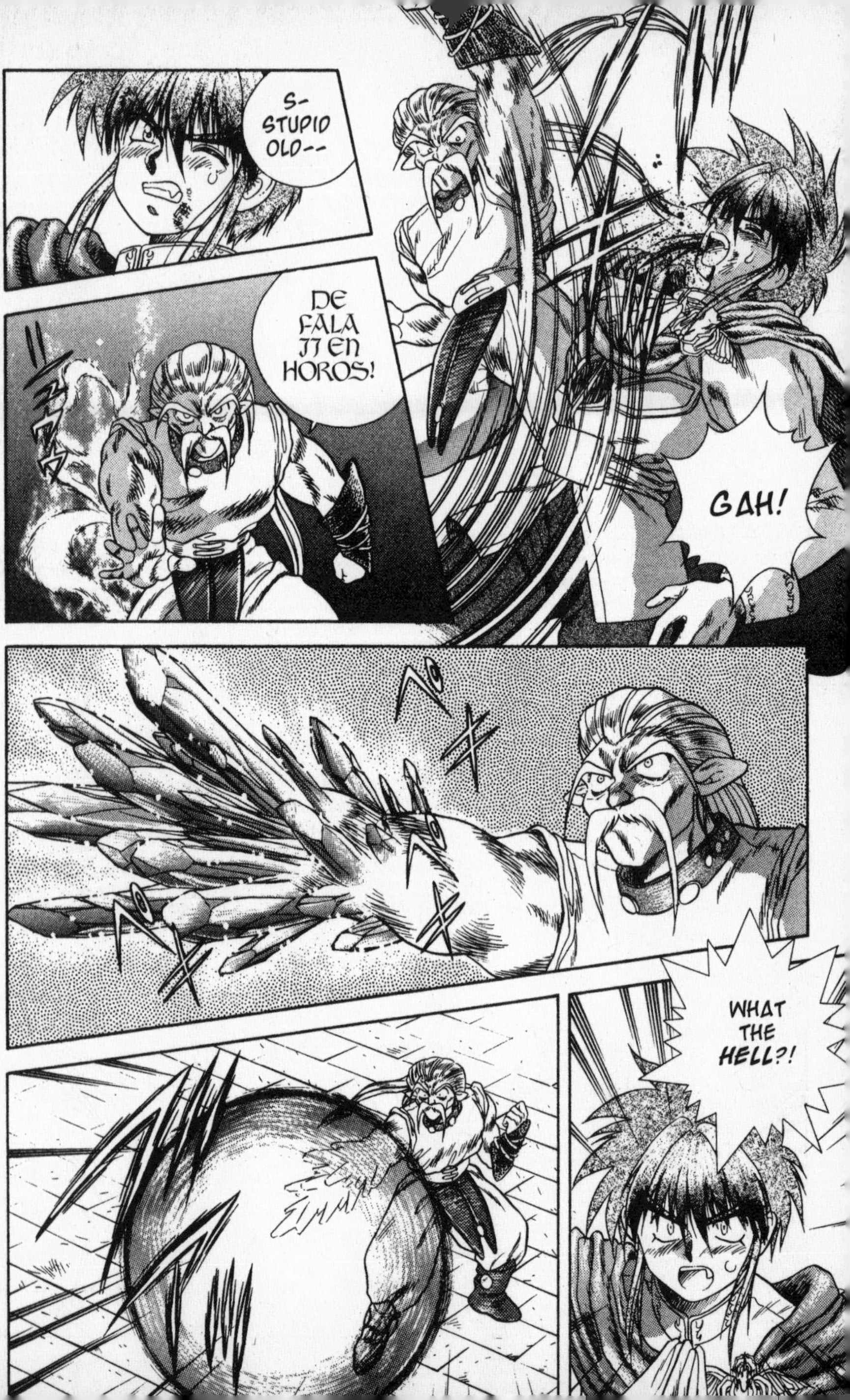
GAH!
S-STUPID OLD--
DE FALA JJ EN HOROS!
WHAT THE HELL?!

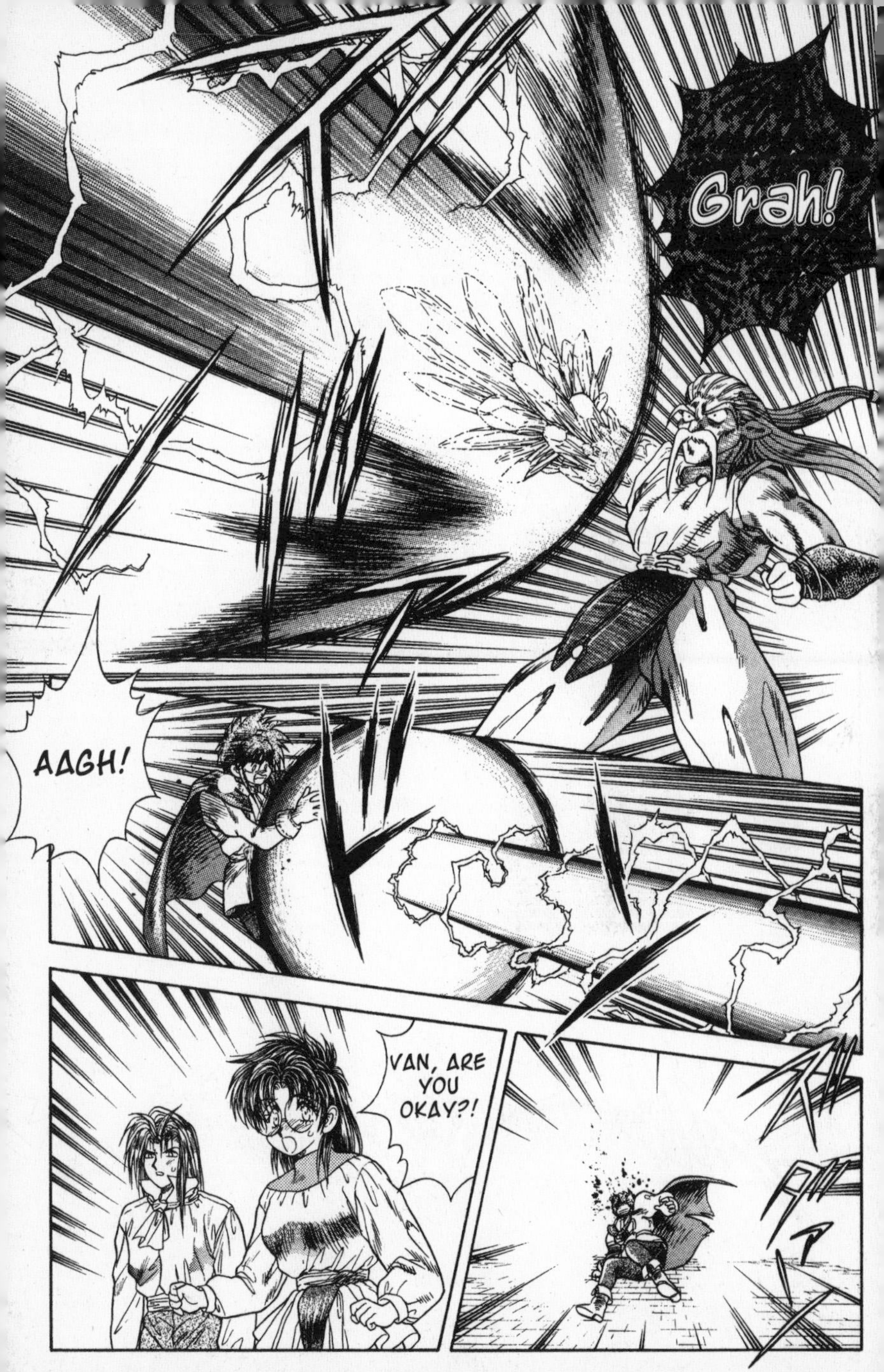
Grah!
AAGH!
VAN, ARE YOU OKAY?!

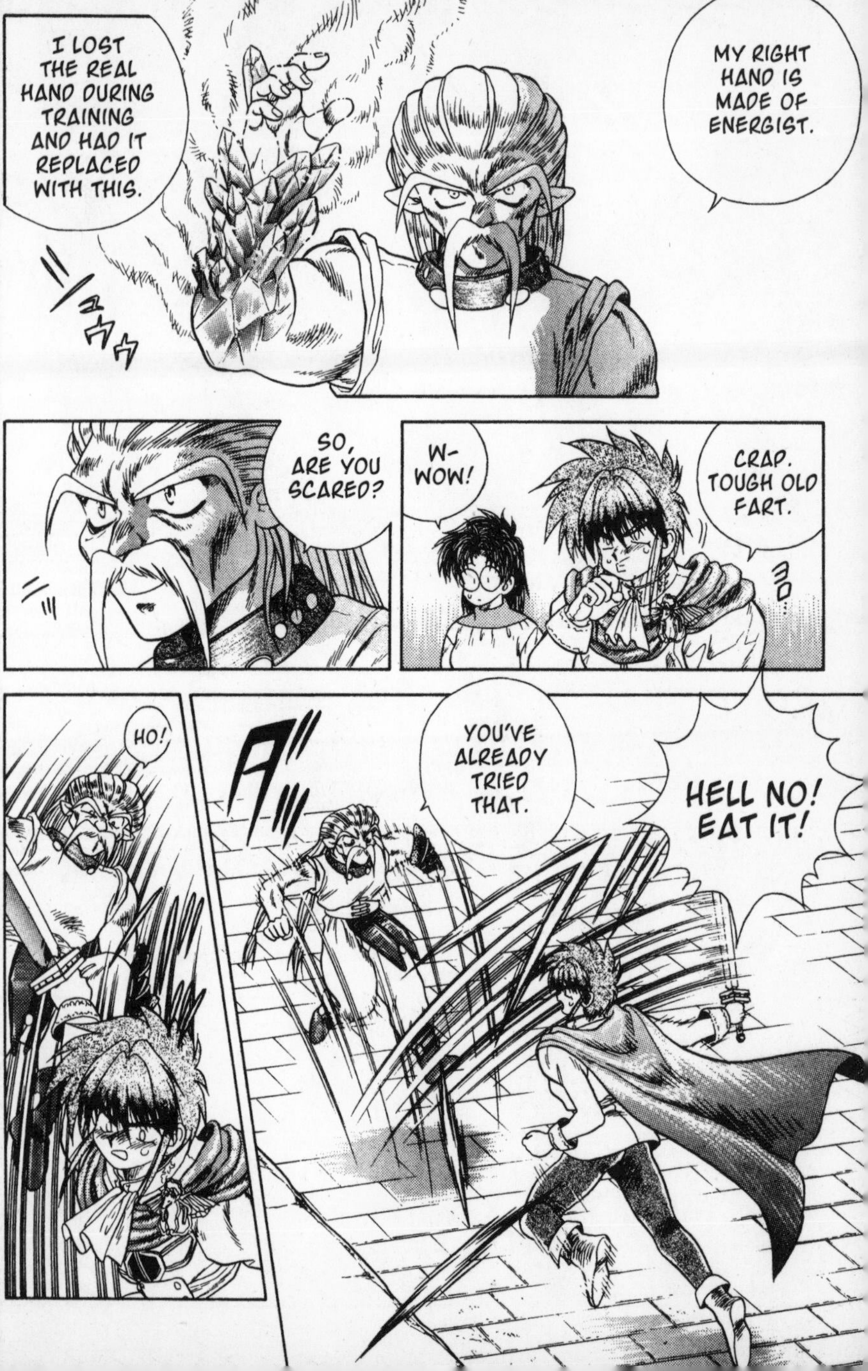
MY RIGHT HAND IS MADE OF ENERGIST.
I LOST THE REAL HAND DURING TRAINING AND HAD IT REPLACED WITH THIS.
CRAP. TOUGH OLD FART.
W-WOW!
SO, ARE YOU SCARED?
HELL NO! EAT IT!
YOU'VE ALREADY TRIED THAT.
HO!

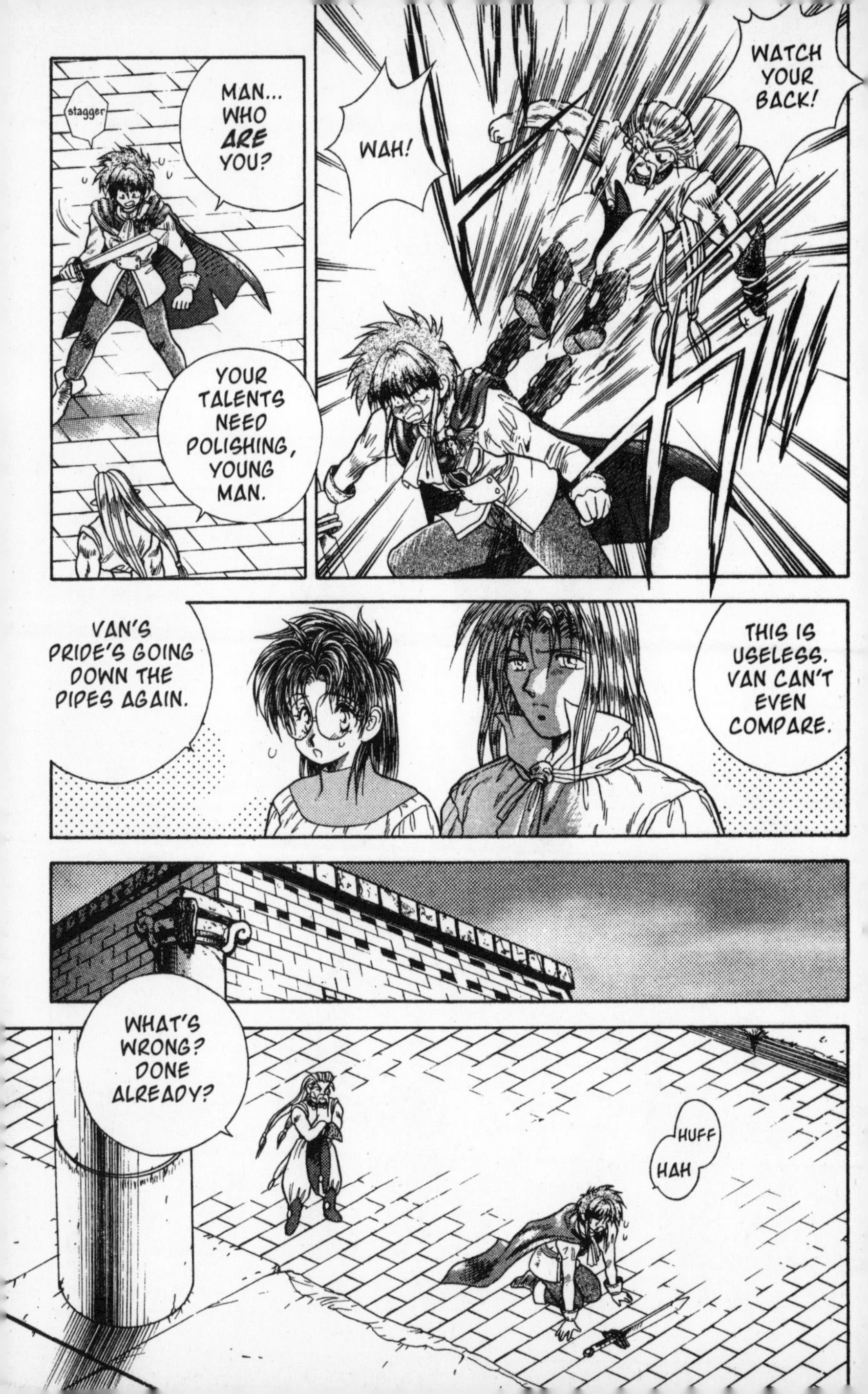
WATCH YOUR BACK!
WAH!
MAN... WHO ARE YOU?
stagger
YOUR TALENTS NEED POLISHING, YOUNG MAN.
THIS IS USELESS. VAN CAN'T EVEN COMPARE.
VAN'S PRIDE'S GOING DOWN THE PIPES AGAIN.
WHAT'S WRONG? DONE ALREADY?
HUFF
HAH

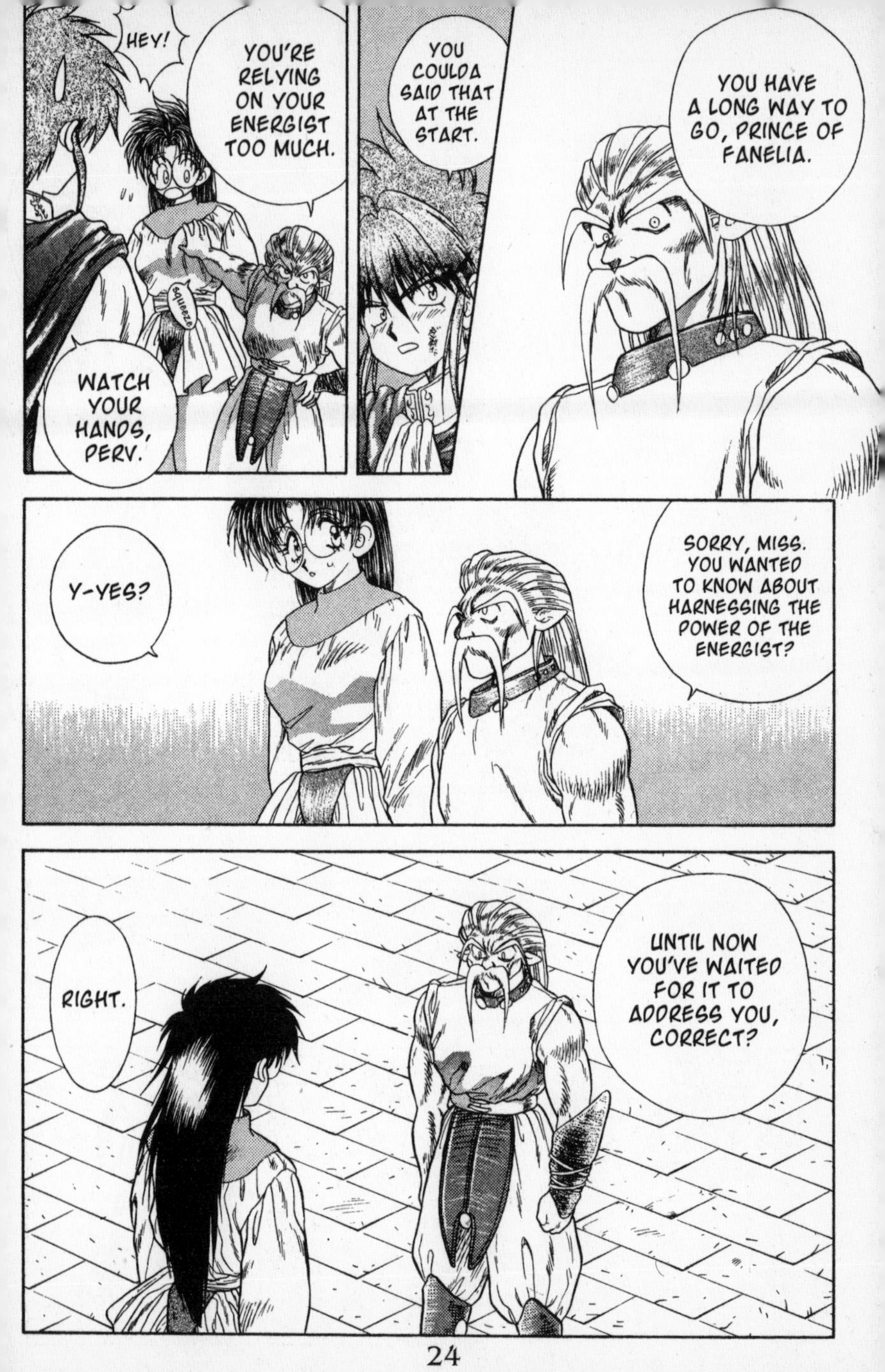
YOU HAVE A LONG WAY TO GO, PRINCE OF FANELIA.
YOU COULDA SAID THAT AT THE START.
YOU'RE RELYING ON YOUR ENERGIST TOO MUCH.
HEY!
squeeze
WATCH YOUR HANDS, PERV.
SORRY, MISS. YOU WANTED TO KNOW ABOUT HARNESSING THE POWER OF THE ENERGIST?
Y-YES?
UNTIL NOW YOU'VE WAITED FOR IT TO ADDRESS YOU, CORRECT?
RIGHT.

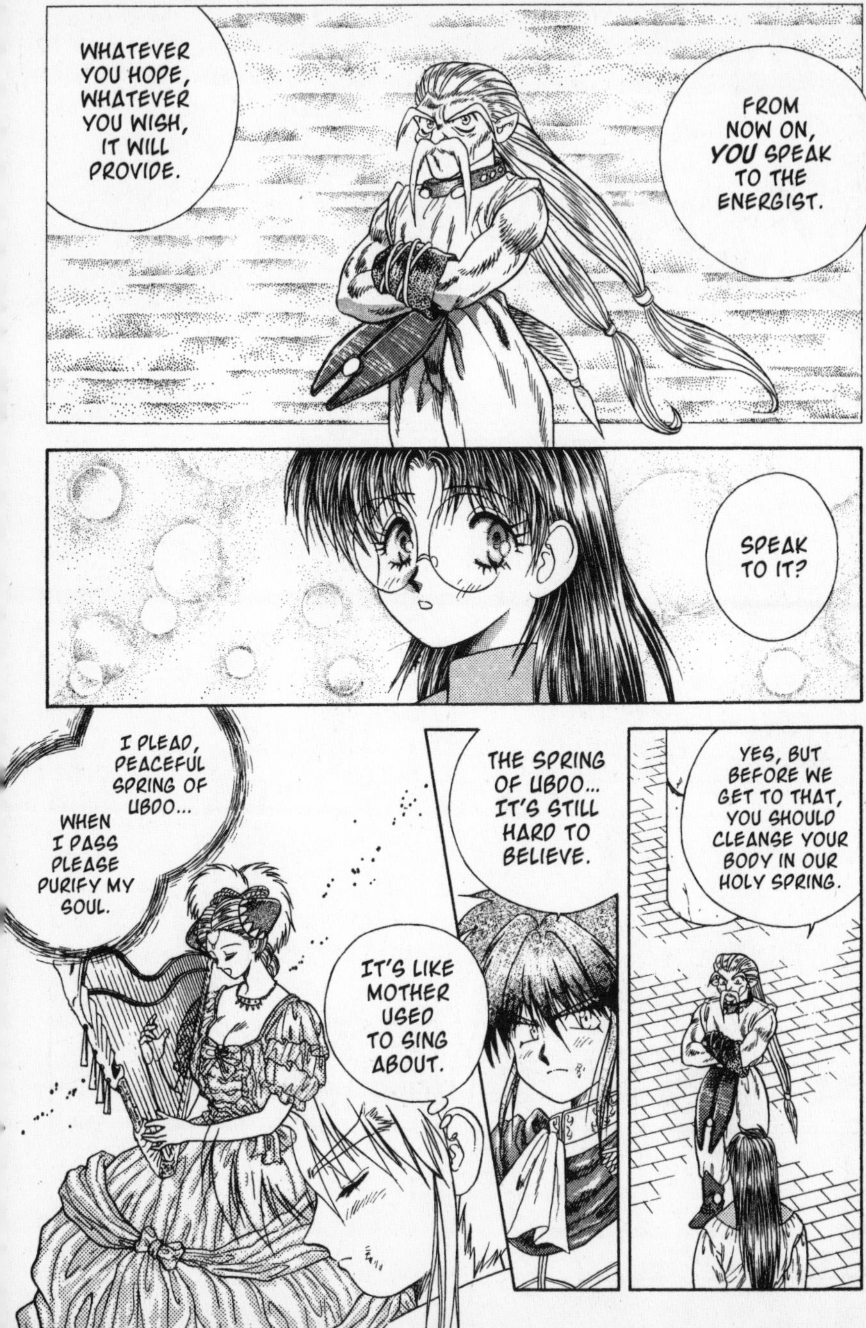
FROM NOW ON, YOU SPEAK TO THE ENERGIST.
WHATEVER YOU HOPE, WHATEVER YOU WISH, IT WILL PROVIDE.
SPEAK TO IT?
YES, BUT BEFORE WE GET TO THAT, YOU SHOULD CLEANSE YOUR BODY IN OUR HOLY SPRING.
THE SPRING OF UBOO... IT'S STILL HARD TO BELIEVE.
IT'S LIKE MOTHER USED TO SING ABOUT.
I PLEAD, PEACEFUL SPRING OF UBOO...
WHEN I PASS PLEASE PURIFY MY SOUL.

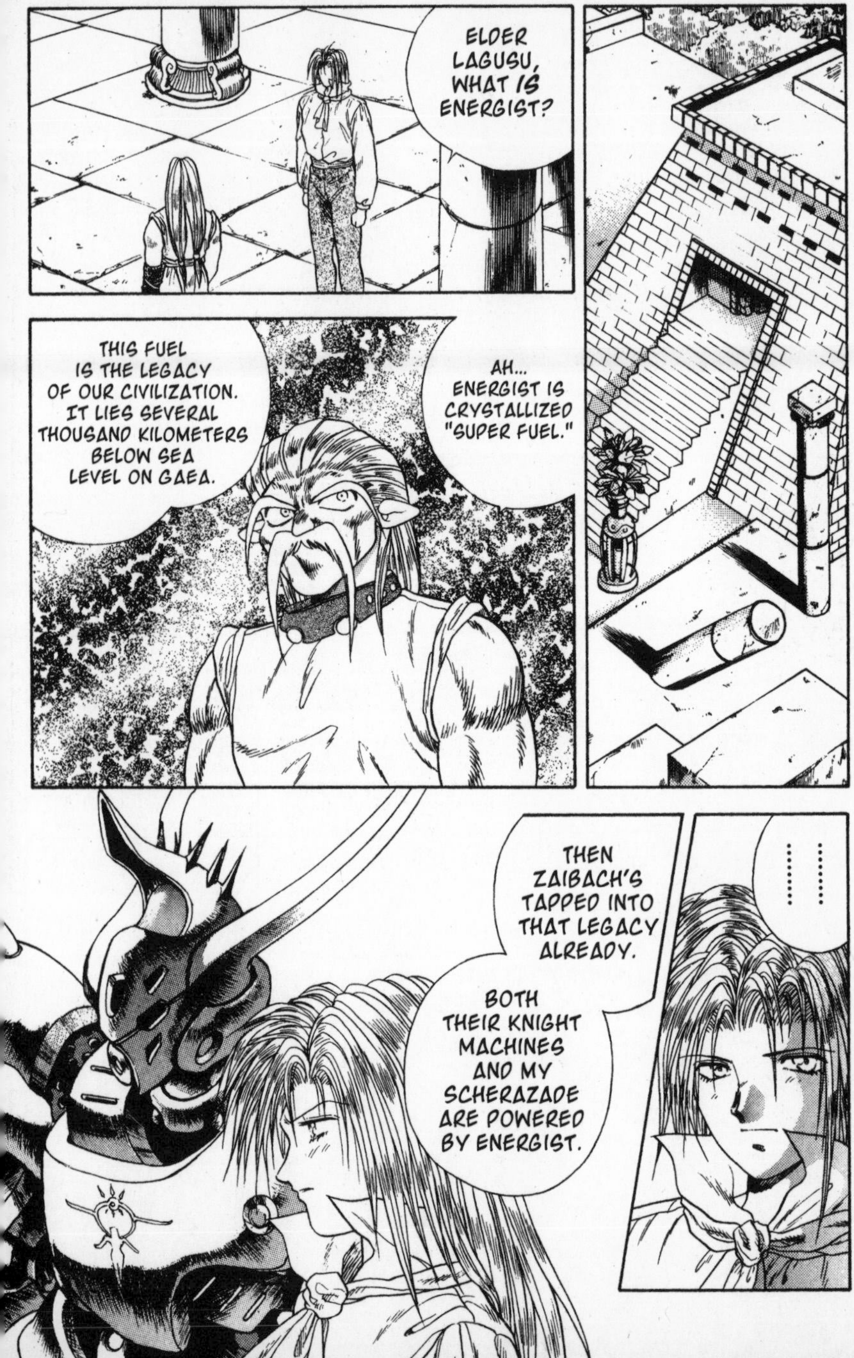
ELDER LAGUSU, WHAT IS ENERGIST?
AH... ENERGIST IS CRYSTALLIZED "SUPER FUEL."
THIS FUEL IS THE LEGACY OF OUR CIVILIZATION. IT LIES SEVERAL THOUSAND KILOMETERS BELOW SEA LEVEL ON GAEA.
......
THEN ZAIBACH'S TAPPED INTO THAT LEGACY ALREADY.
BOTH THEIR KNIGHT MACHINES AND MY SCHERAZADE ARE POWERED BY ENERGIST.

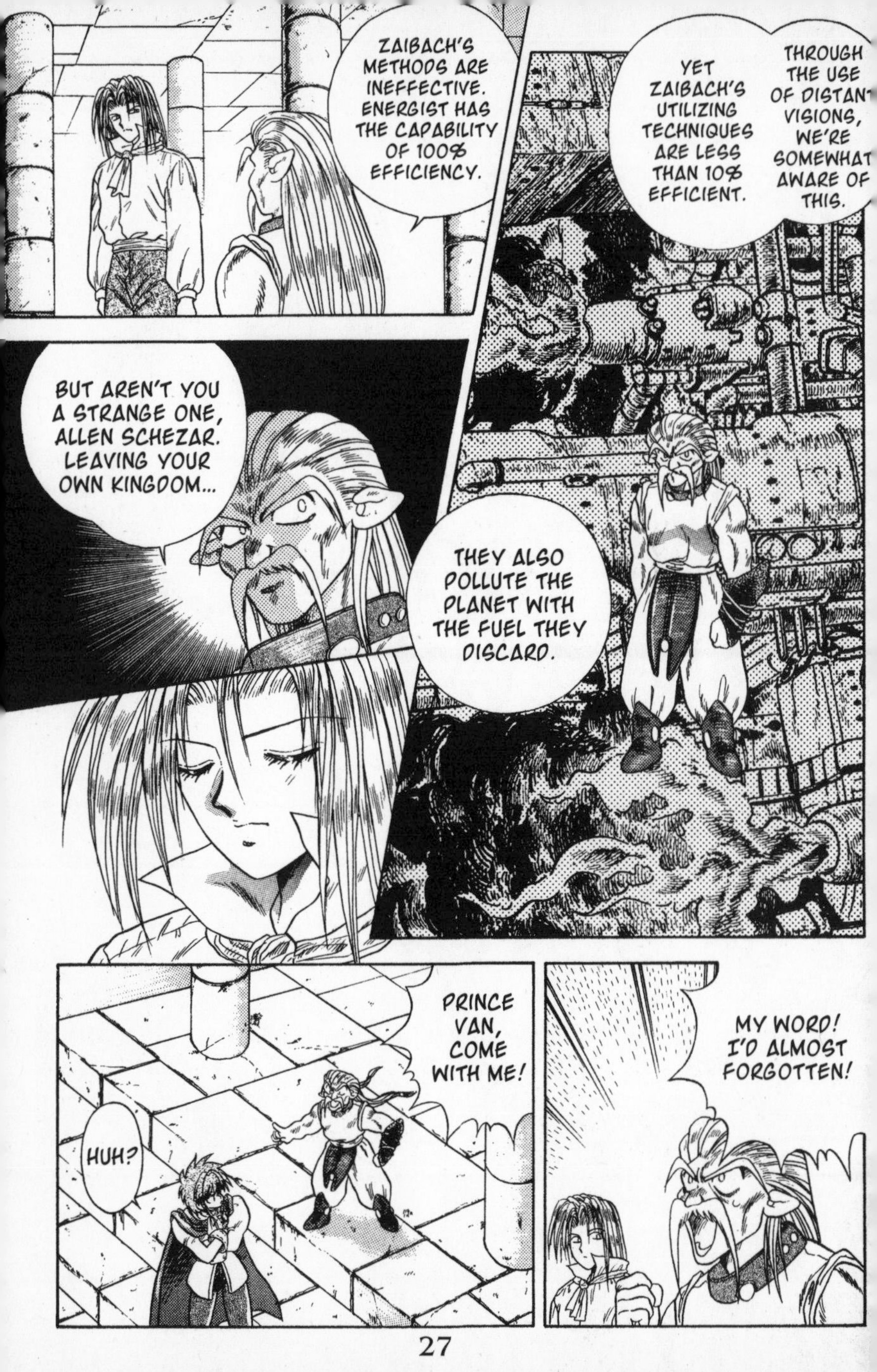
THROUGH THE USE OF DISTANT VISIONS, WE'RE SOMEWHAT AWARE OF THIS.
YET ZAIBACH'S UTILIZING TECHNIQUES ARE LESS THAN 10% EFFICIENT.
THEY ALSO POLLUTE THE PLANET WITH THE FUEL THEY DISCARD.
ZAIBACH'S METHODS ARE INEFFECTIVE. ENERGIST HAS THE CAPABILITY OF 100% EFFICIENCY.
BUT AREN'T YOU A STRANGE ONE, ALLEN SCHEZAR. LEAVING YOUR OWN KINGDOM...
MY WORD! I'D ALMOST FORGOTTEN!
PRINCE VAN, COME WITH ME!
HUH?

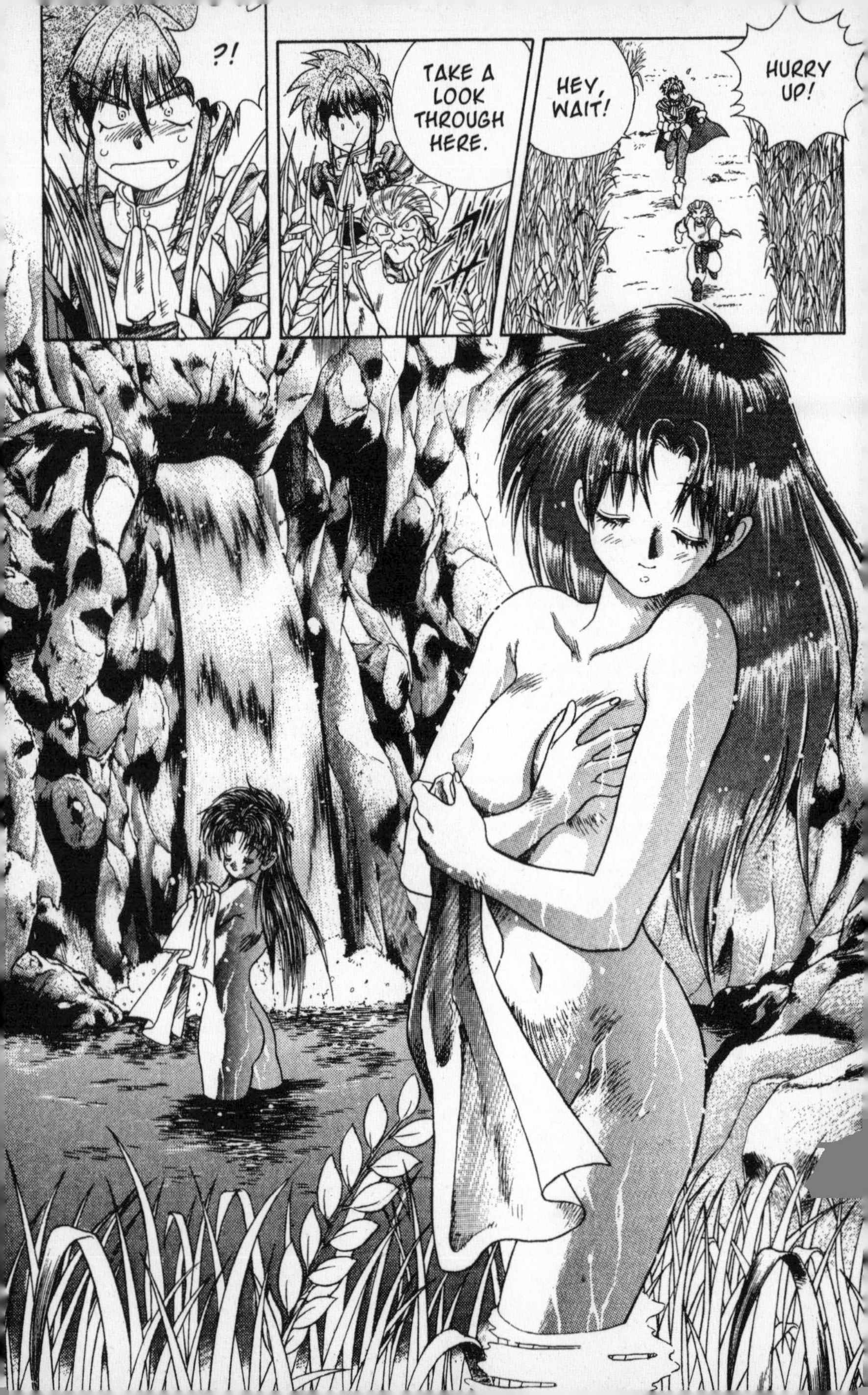
HURRY UP!
HEY, WAIT!
TAKE A LOOK THROUGH HERE.
?!

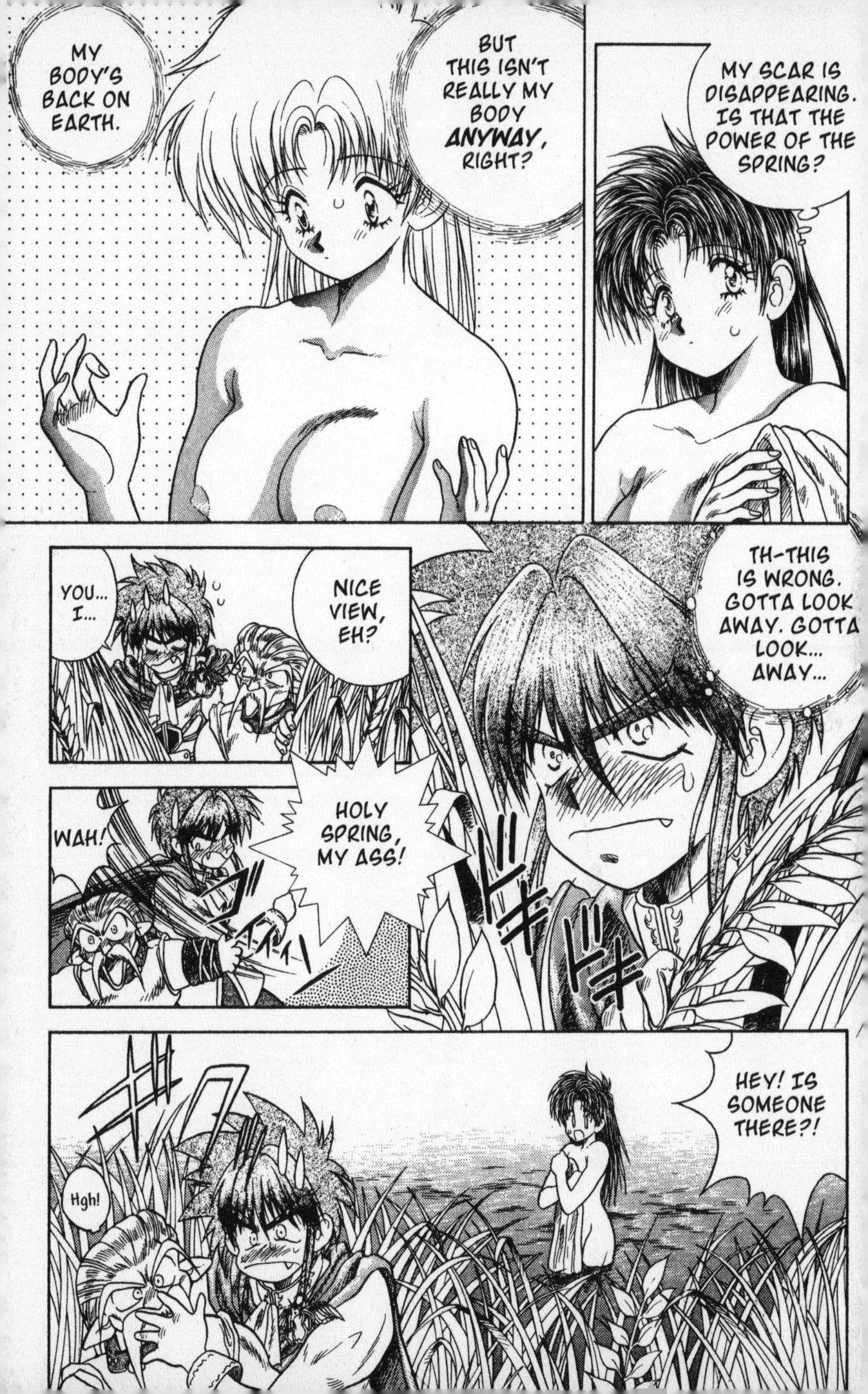
MY SCAR IS DISAPPEARING. IS THAT THE POWER OF THE SPRING?
MY BODY'S BACK ON EARTH.
BUT THIS ISN'T REALLY MY BODY **ANYWAY**, RIGHT?
TH-THIS IS WRONG. GOTTA LOOK AWAY. GOTTA LOOK... AWAY...
ドキ
ドキ
NICE VIEW, EH?
YOU... I...
HOLY SPRING, MY ASS!
WAH!
HEY! IS SOMEONE THERE?!
Hgh!

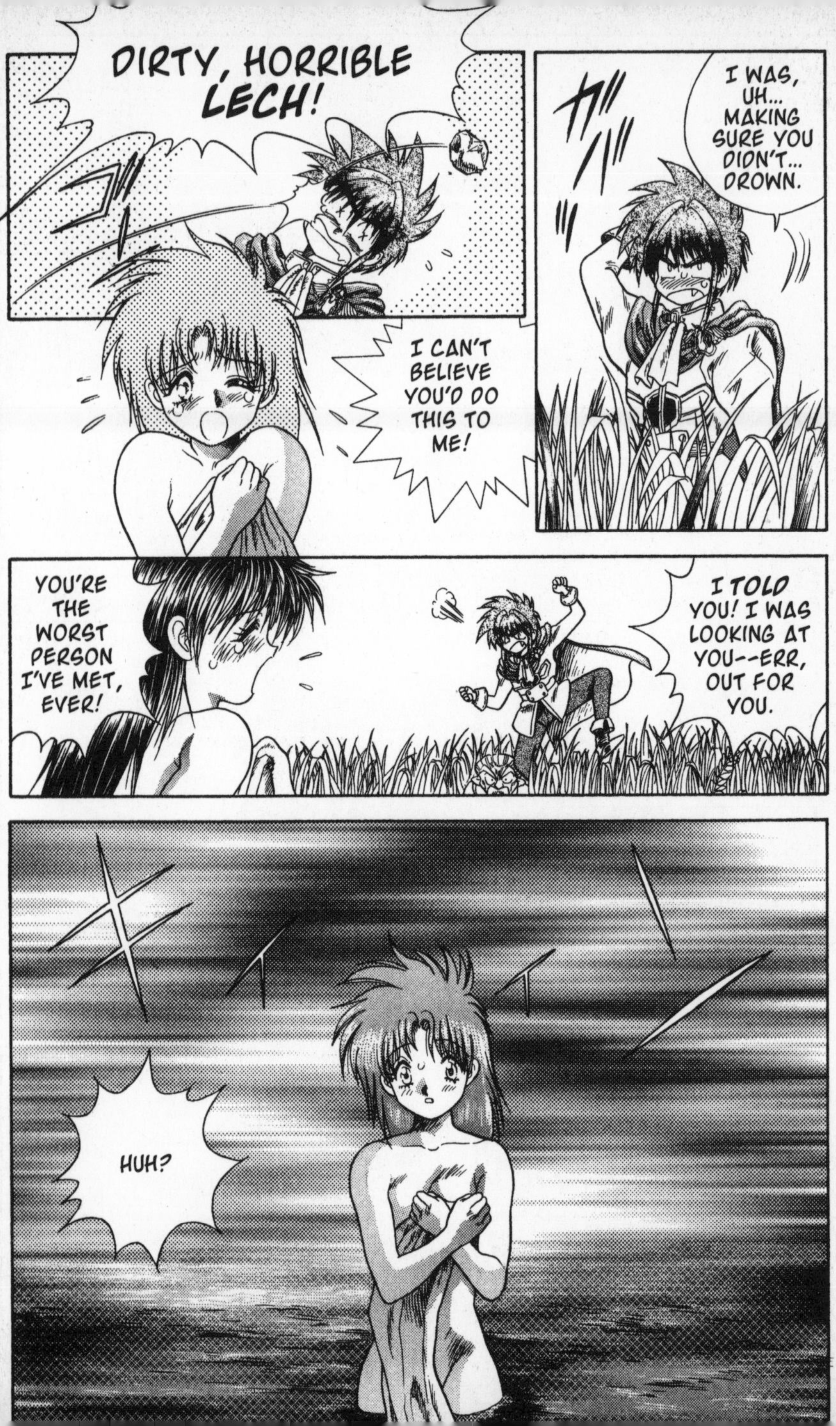
I WAS, UH... MAKING SURE YOU DIDN'T... DROWN.
DIRTY, HORRIBLE LECH!
I CAN'T BELIEVE YOU'D DO THIS TO ME!
I TOLD YOU! I WAS LOOKING AT YOU--ERR, OUT FOR YOU.
YOU'RE THE WORST PERSON I'VE MET, EVER!
HUH?

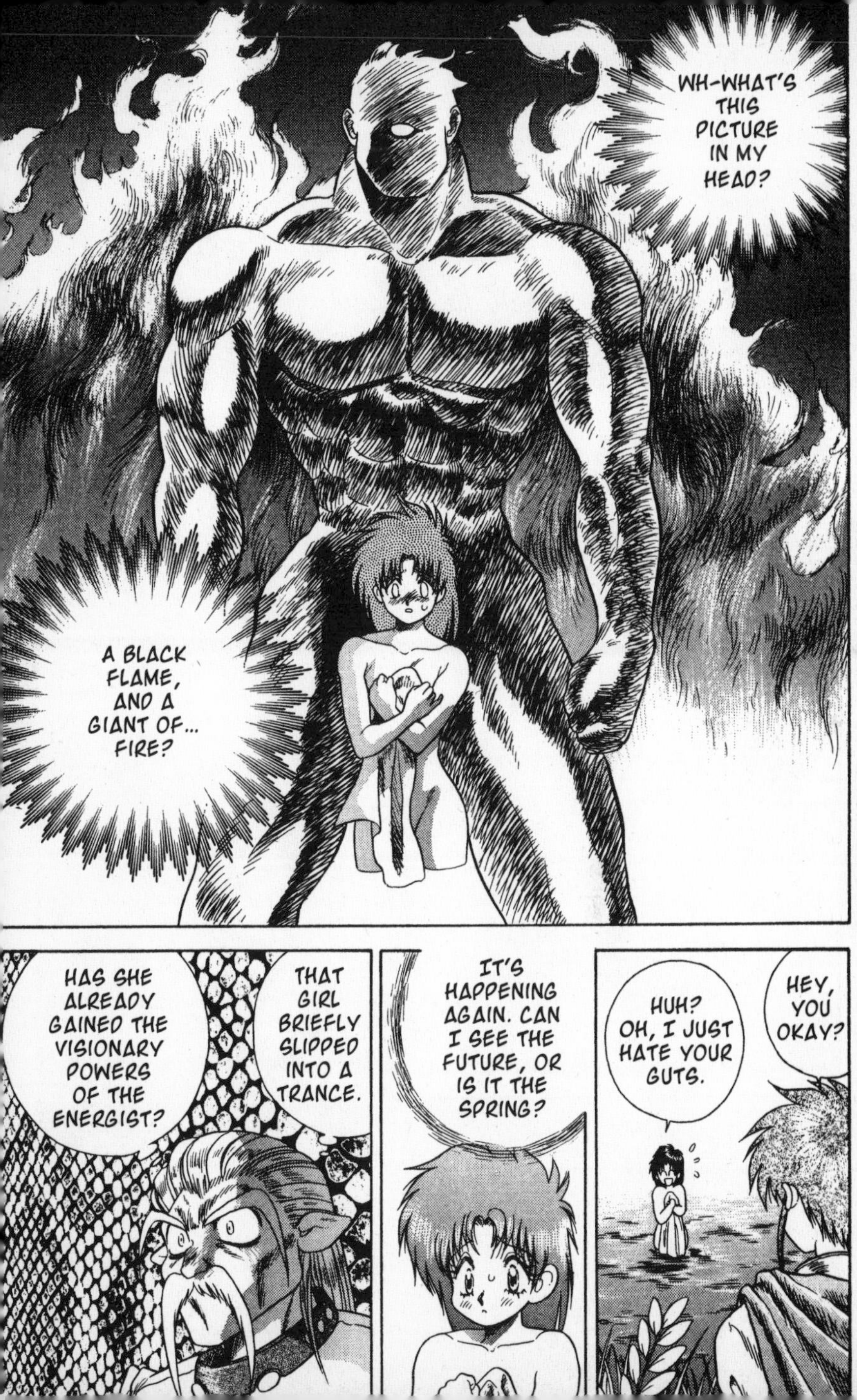
WH-WHAT'S THIS PICTURE IN MY HEAD?
A BLACK FLAME, AND A GIANT OF... FIRE?
HEY, YOU OKAY?
HUH? OH, I JUST HATE YOUR GUTS.
IT'S HAPPENING AGAIN. CAN I SEE THE FUTURE, OR IS IT THE SPRING?
THAT GIRL BRIEFLY SLIPPED INTO A TRANCE.
HAS SHE ALREADY GAINED THE VISIONARY POWERS OF THE ENERGIST?

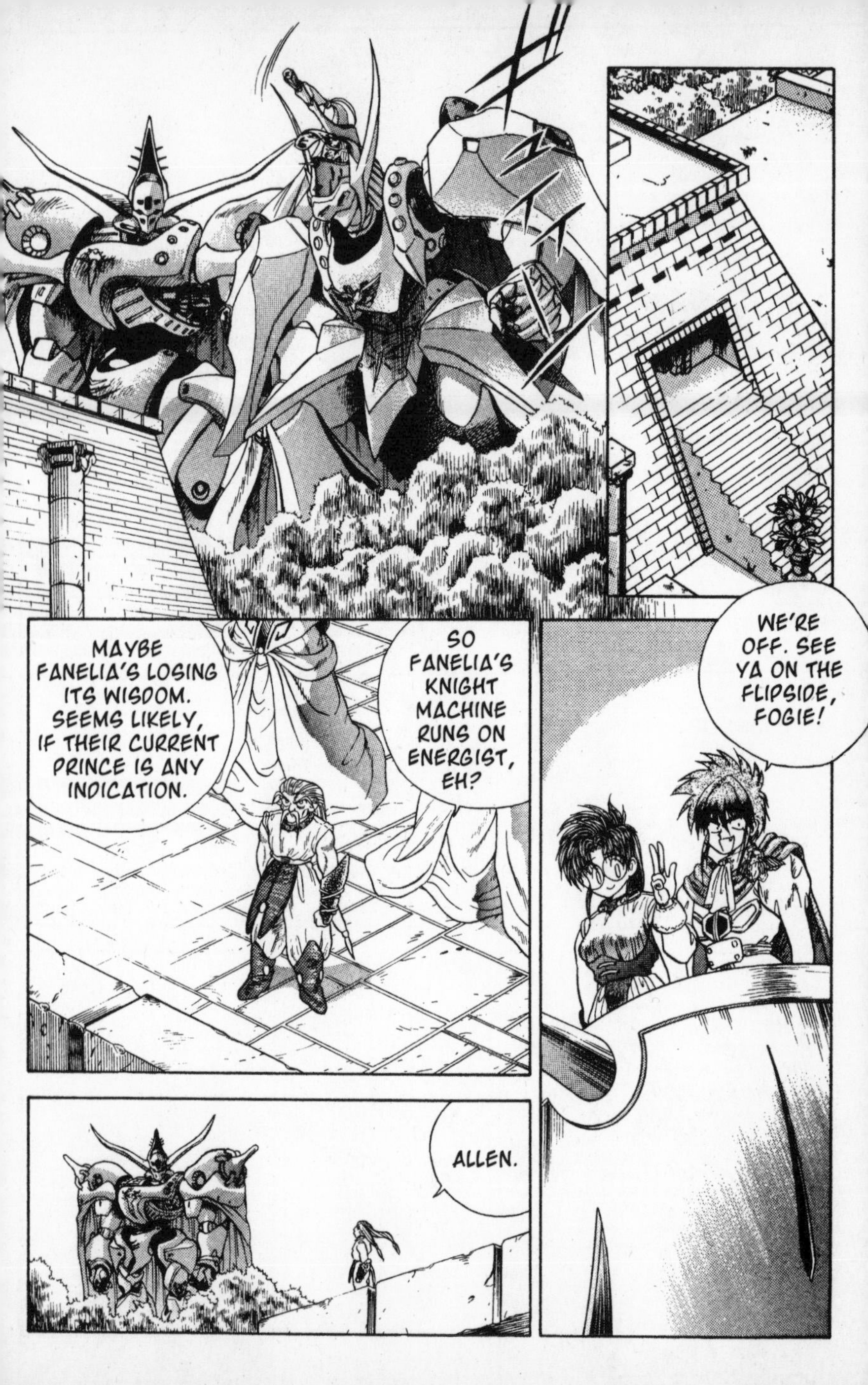
WE'RE OFF. SEE YA ON THE FLIPSIDE, FOGIE!
SO FANELIA'S KNIGHT MACHINE RUNS ON ENERGIST, EH?
MAYBE FANELIA'S LOSING ITS WISDOM. SEEMS LIKELY, IF THEIR CURRENT PRINCE IS ANY INDICATION.
ALLEN.

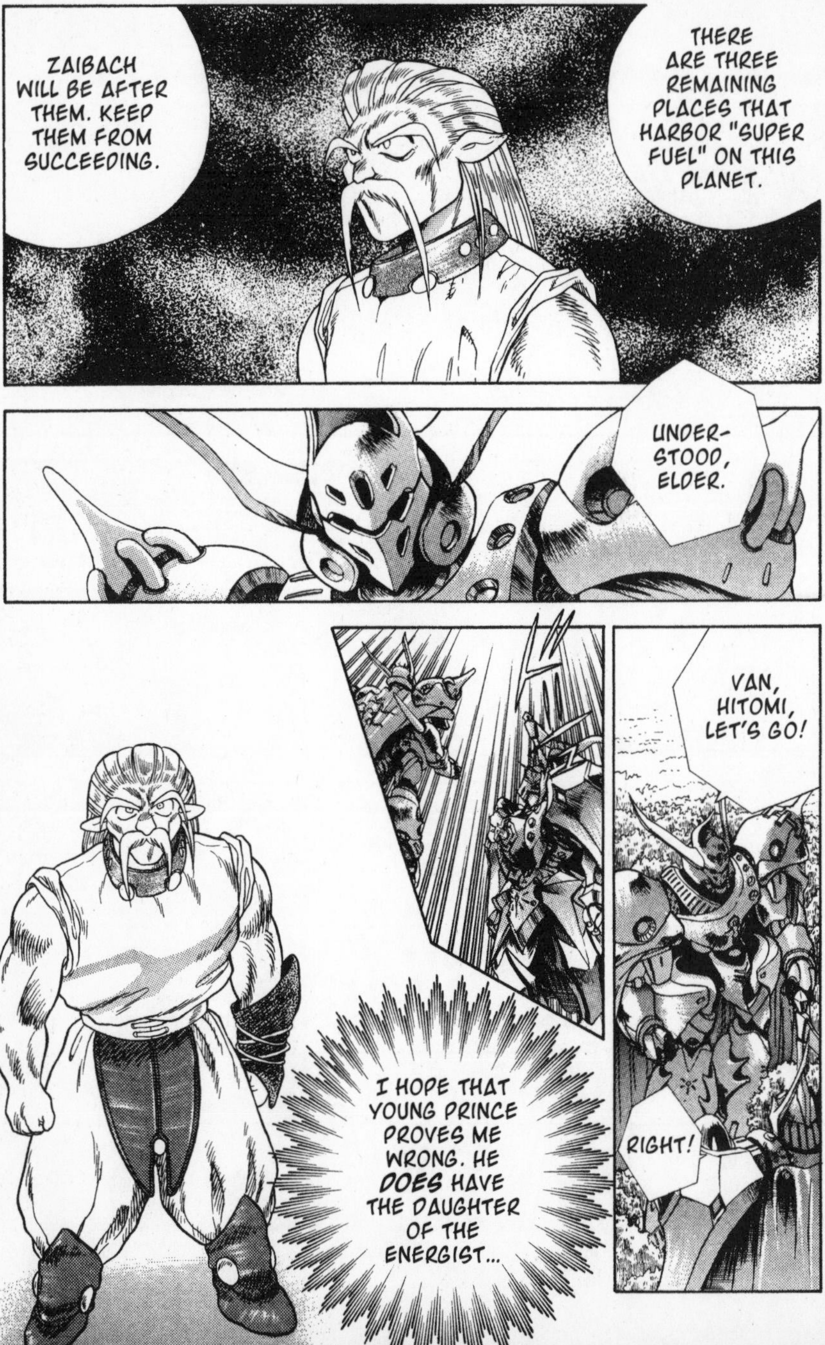
THERE ARE THREE REMAINING PLACES THAT HARBOR "SUPER FUEL" ON THIS PLANET.
ZAIBACH WILL BE AFTER THEM. KEEP THEM FROM SUCCEEDING.
UNDER-STOOD, ELDER.
VAN, HITOMI, LET'S GO!
RIGHT!
I HOPE THAT YOUNG PRINCE PROVES ME WRONG. HE ***DOES*** HAVE THE DAUGHTER OF THE ENERGIST...

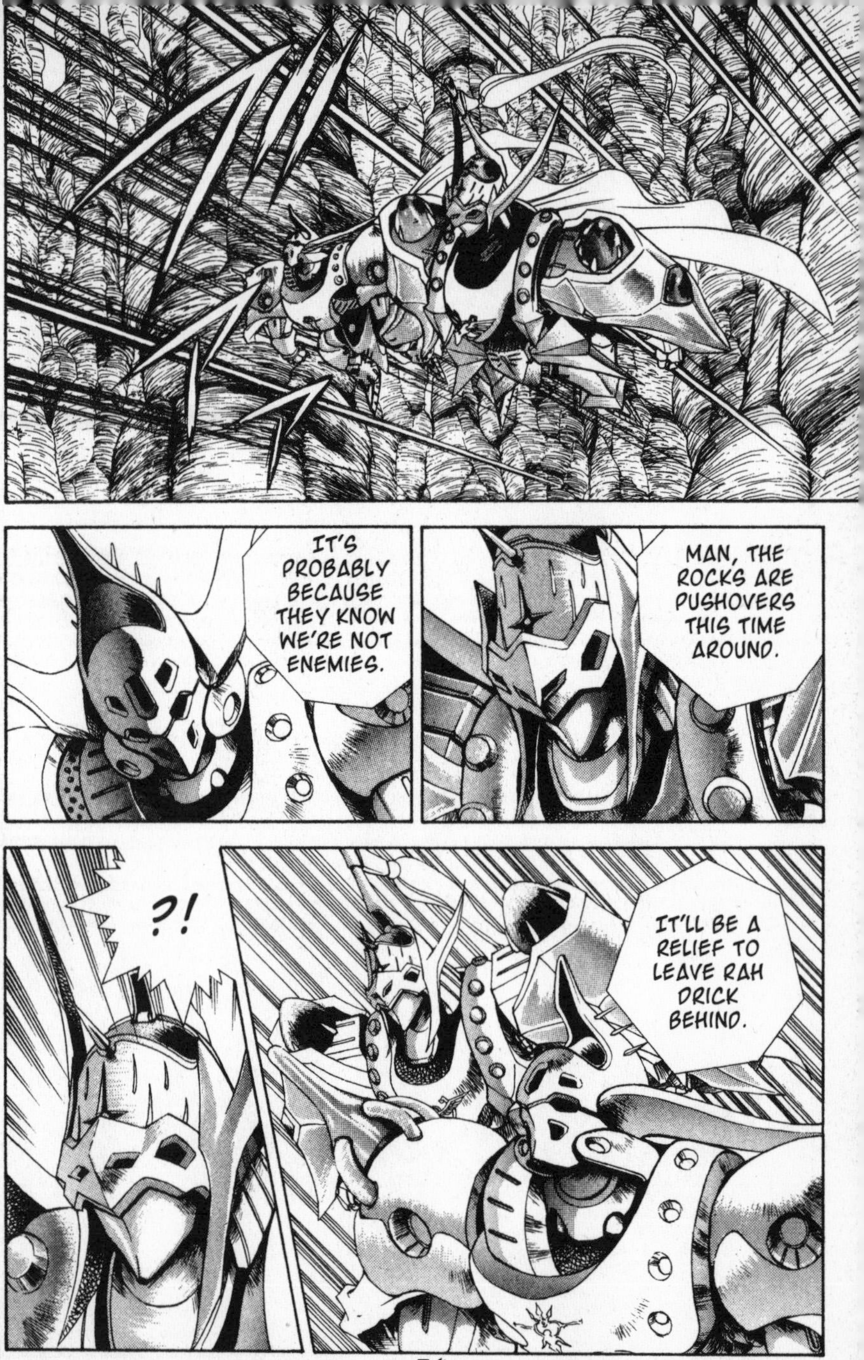
MAN, THE ROCKS ARE PUSHOVERS THIS TIME AROUND.
IT'S PROBABLY BECAUSE THEY KNOW WE'RE NOT ENEMIES.
IT'LL BE A RELIEF TO LEAVE RAH DRICK BEHIND.
?!

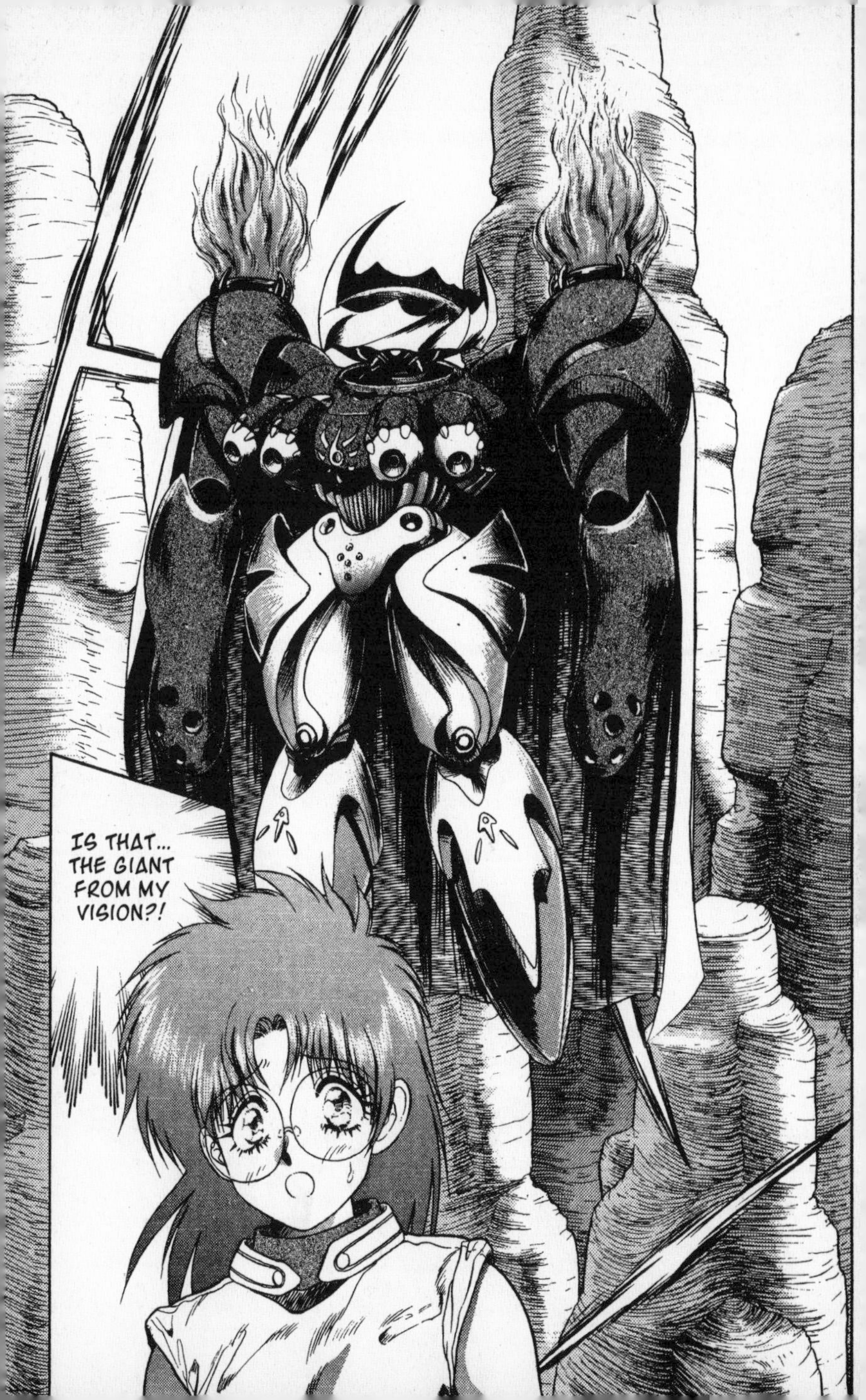
IS THAT... THE GIANT FROM MY VISION?!

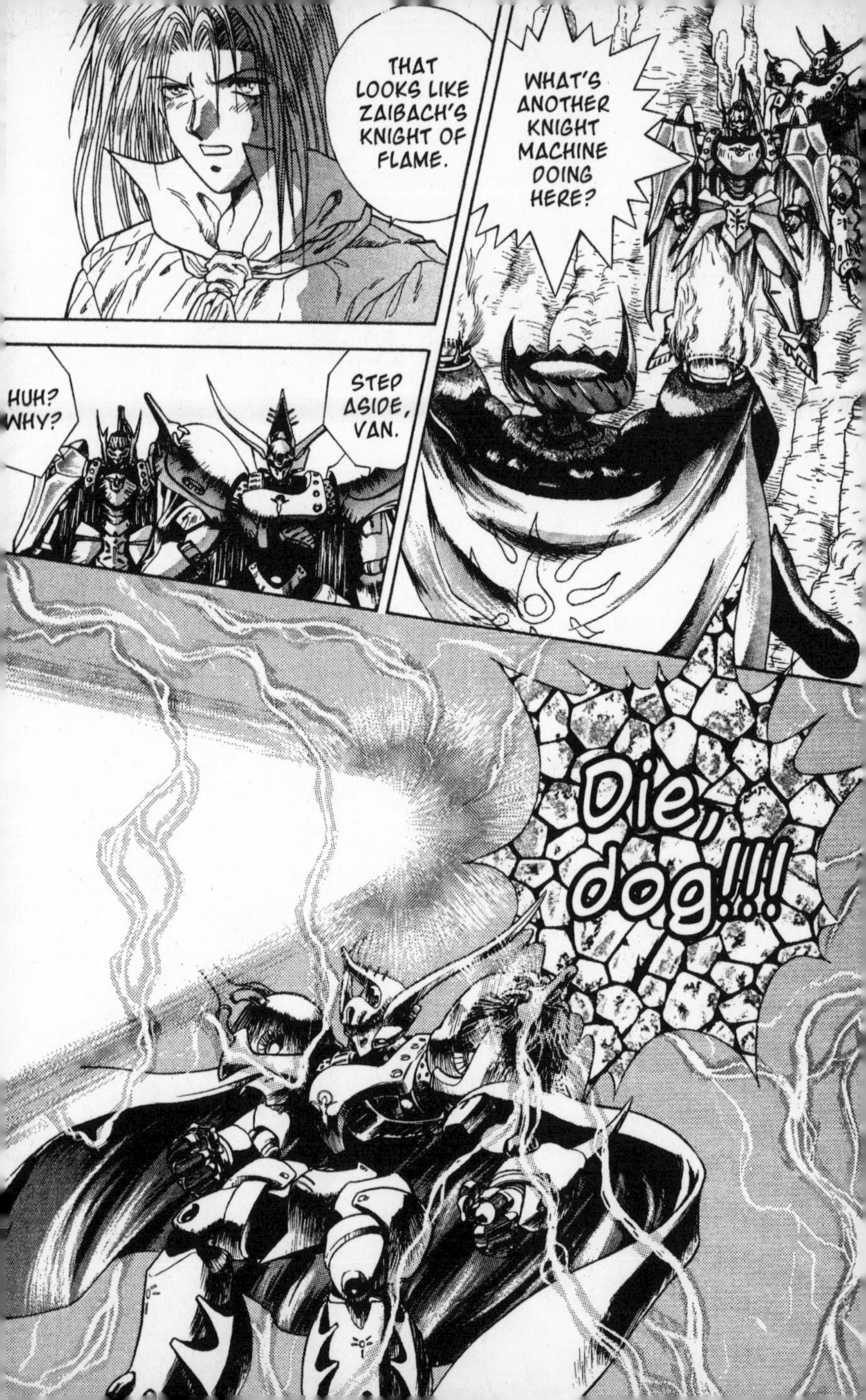
WHAT'S ANOTHER KNIGHT MACHINE DOING HERE?
THAT LOOKS LIKE ZAIBACH'S KNIGHT OF FLAME.
STEP ASIDE, VAN.
HUH? WHY?
Die, dog!!!!

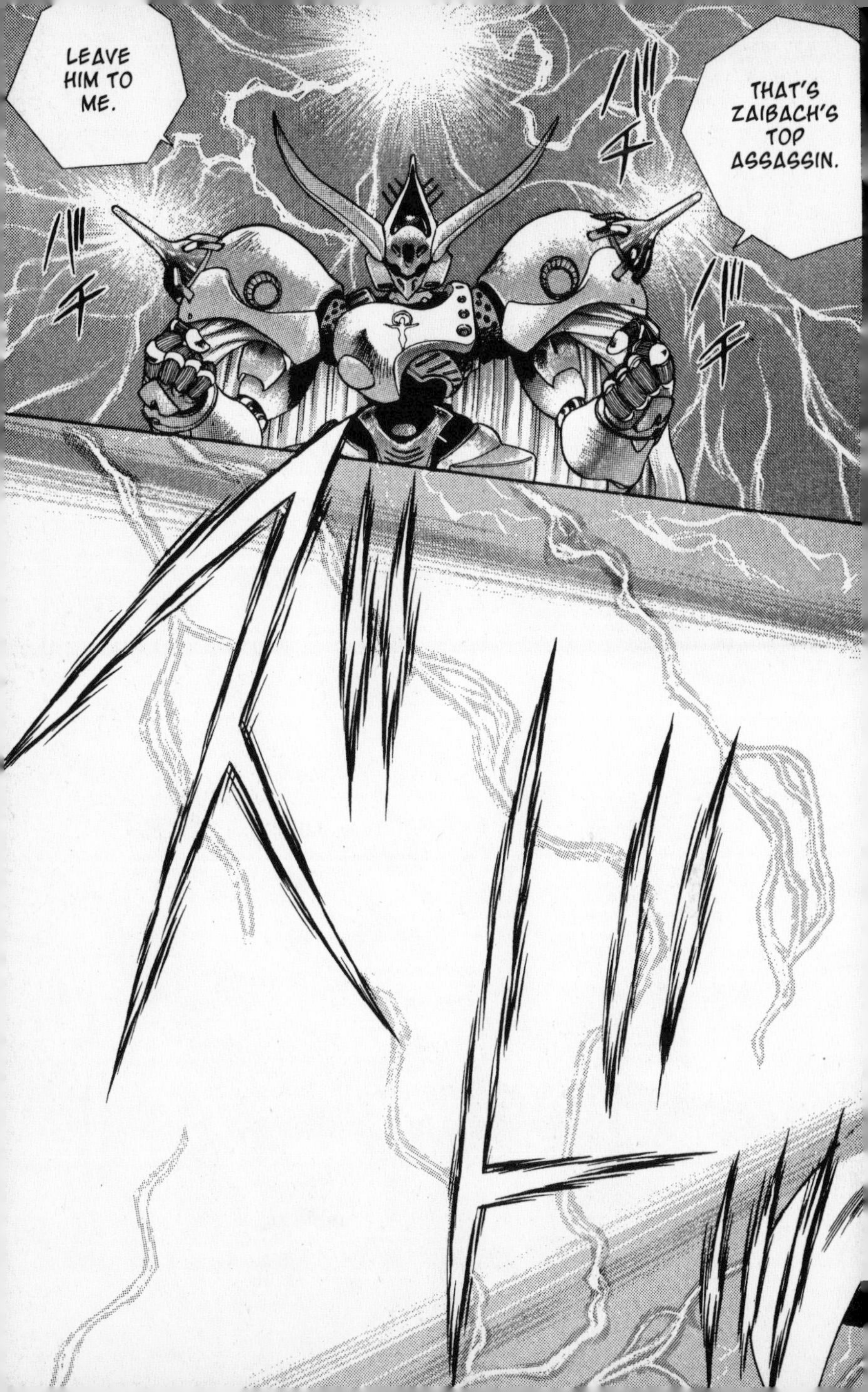
THAT'S ZAIBACH'S TOP ASSASSIN.
バチ
バチ
LEAVE HIM TO ME.
バチ

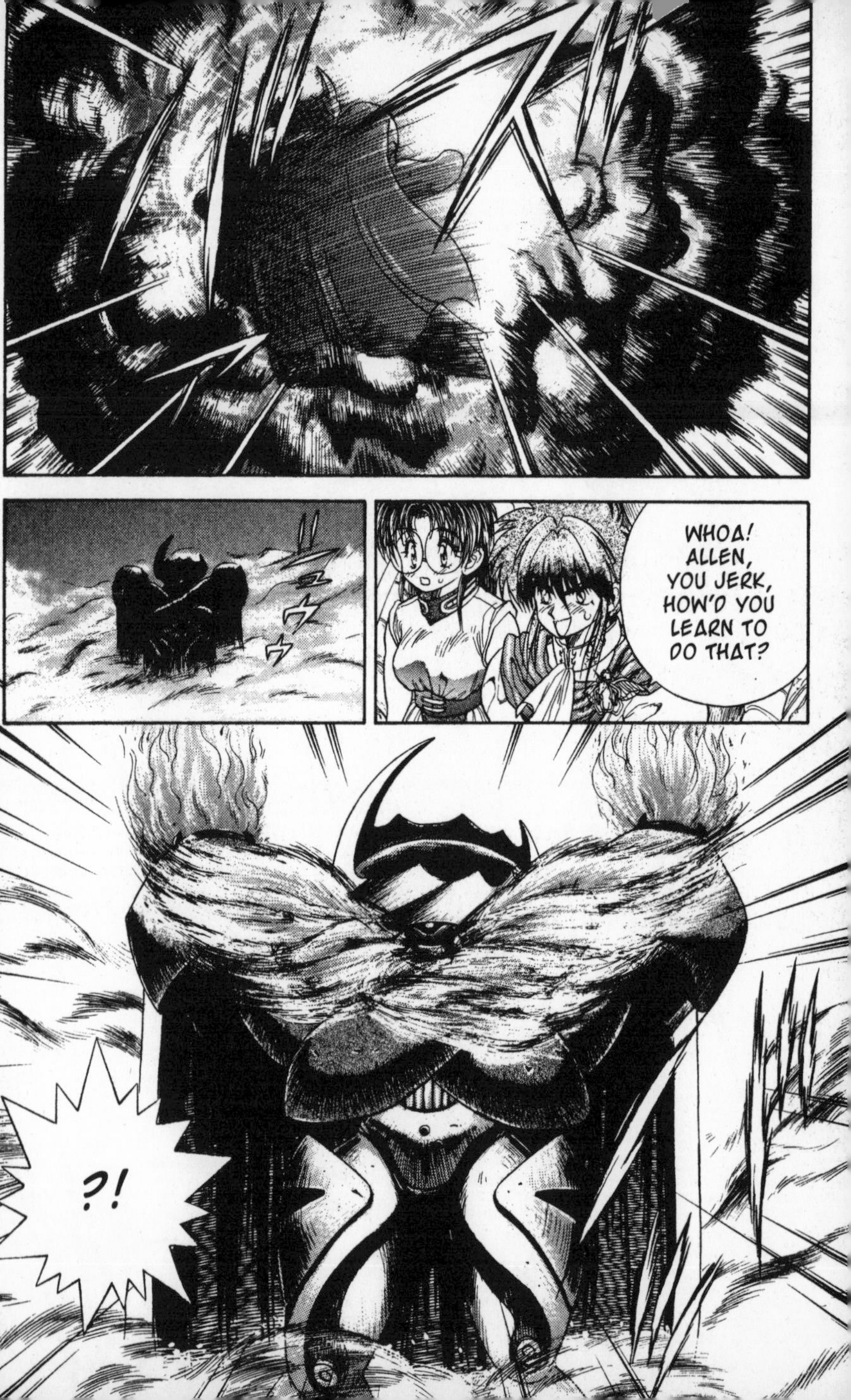
WHOA! ALLEN, YOU JERK, HOW'D YOU LEARN TO DO THAT?
?!

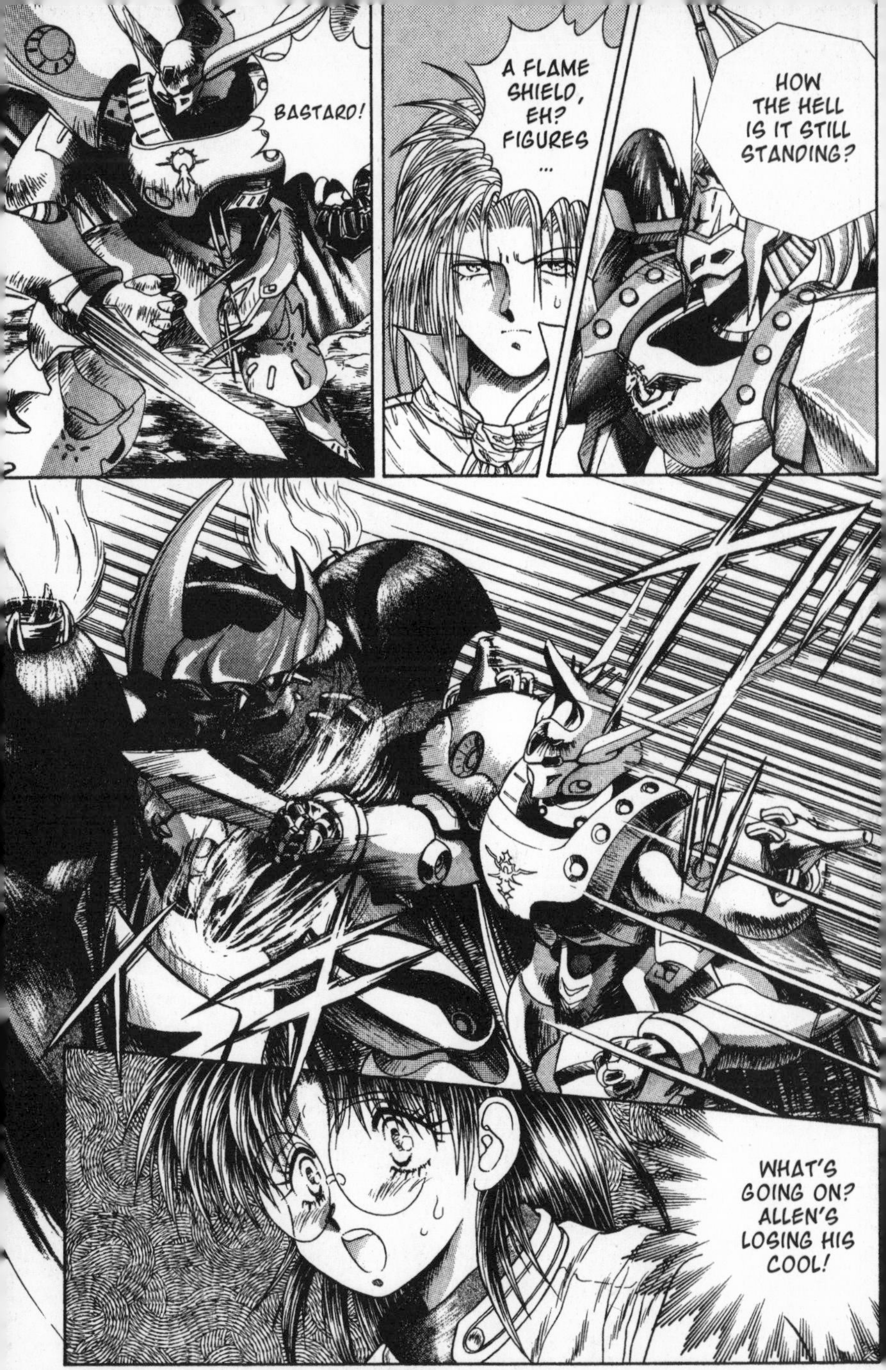
HOW THE HELL IS IT STILL STANDING?
A FLAME SHIELD, EH? FIGURES ...
BASTARD!
WHAT'S GOING ON? ALLEN'S LOSING HIS COOL!

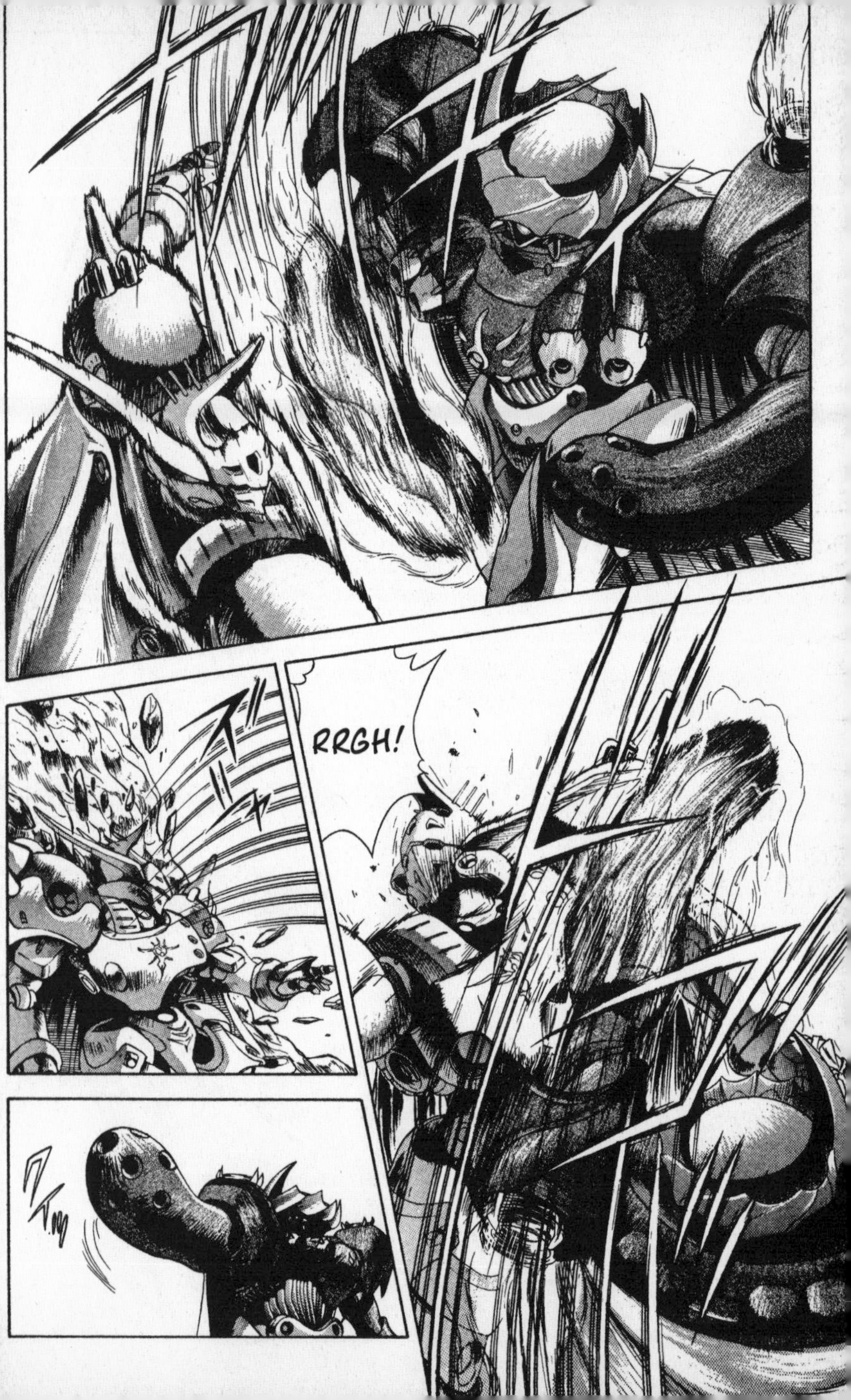
RRGH!

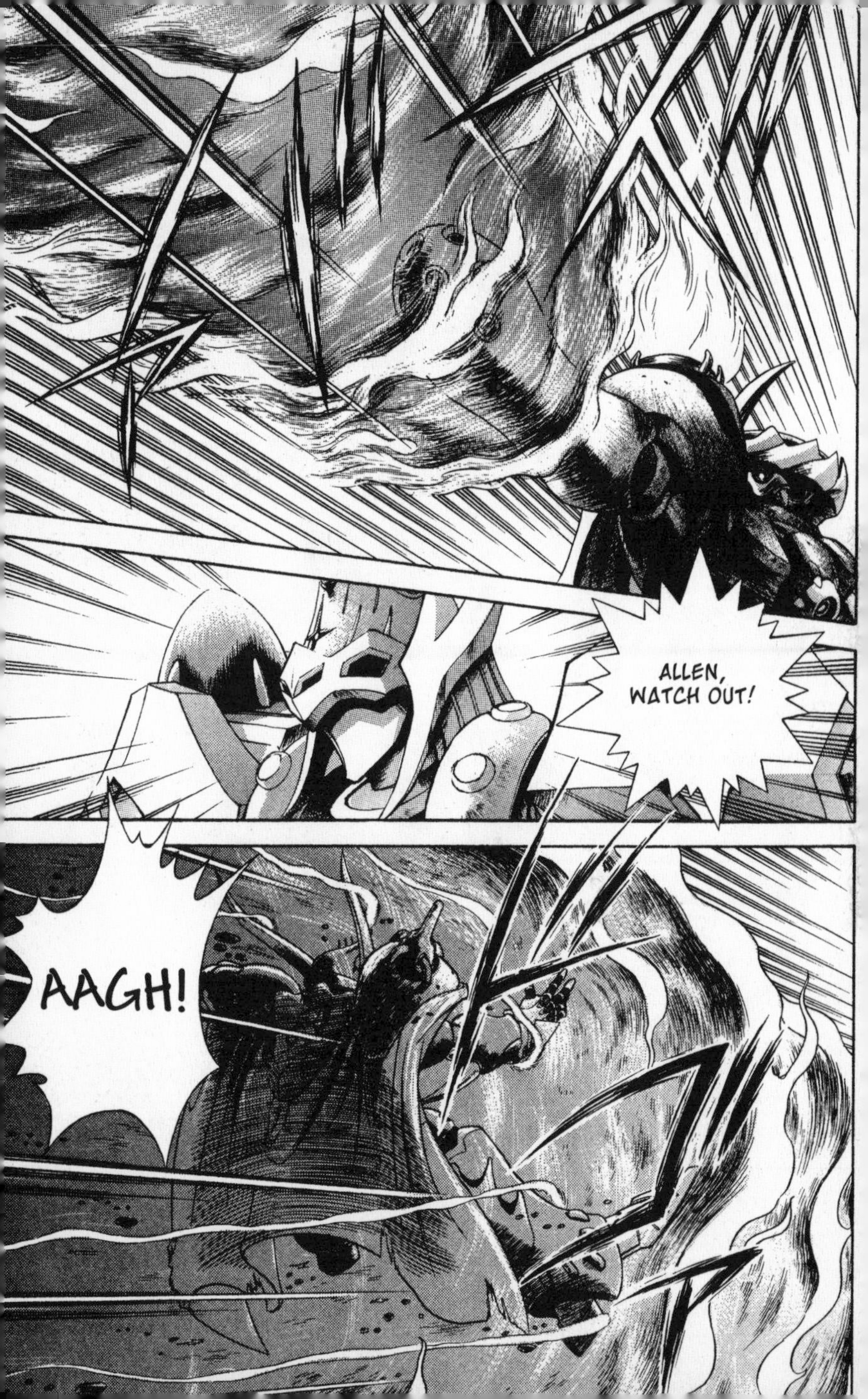
ALLEN, WATCH OUT!
AAGH!

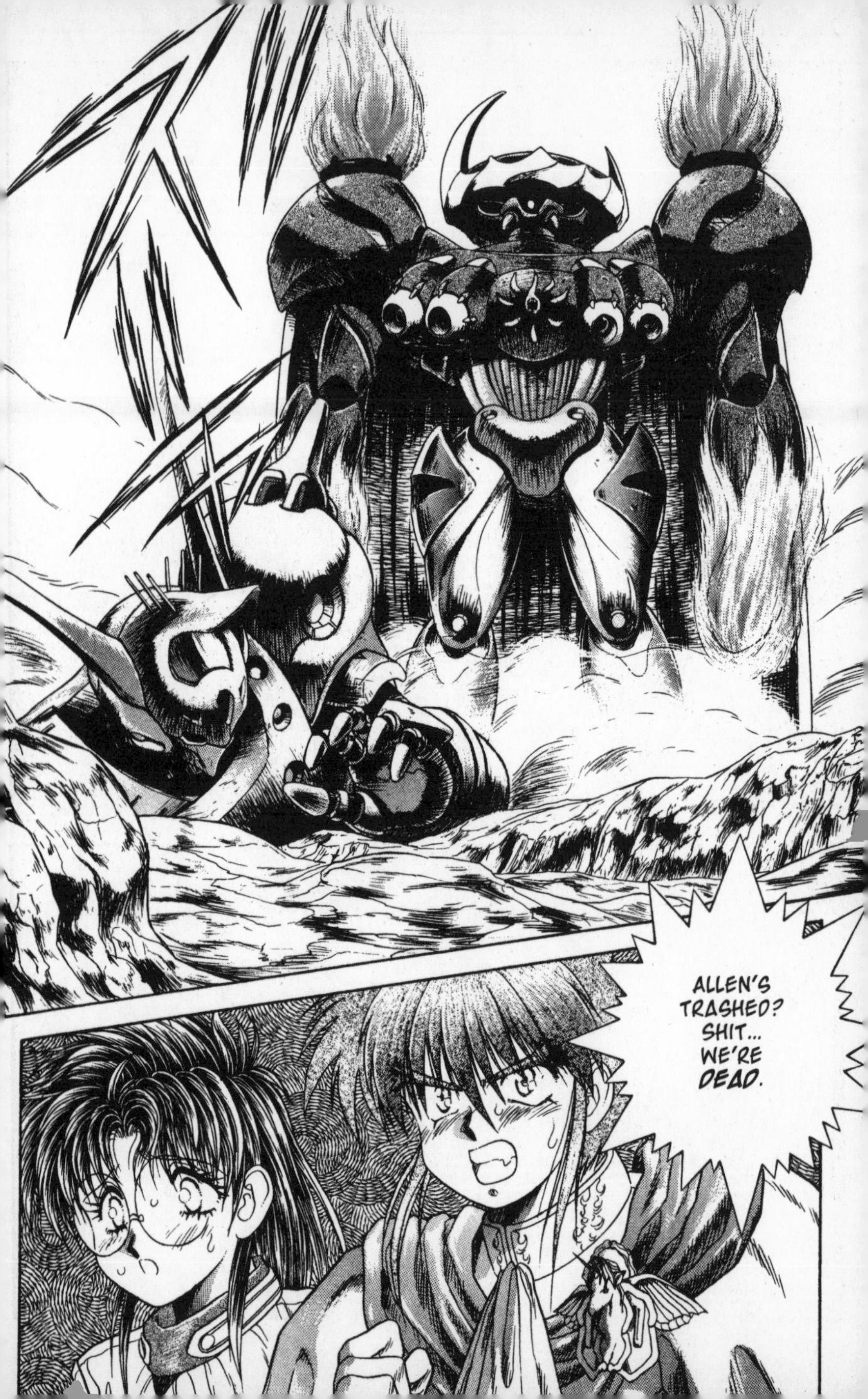
ALLEN'S TRASHED? SHIT... WE'RE DEAD.

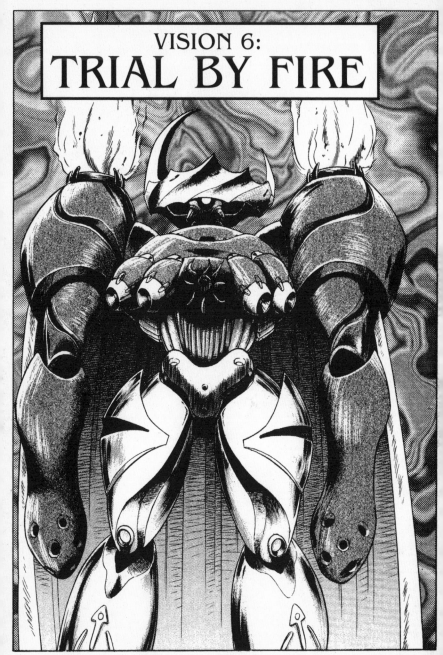

VISION 6:
TRIAL BY FIRE

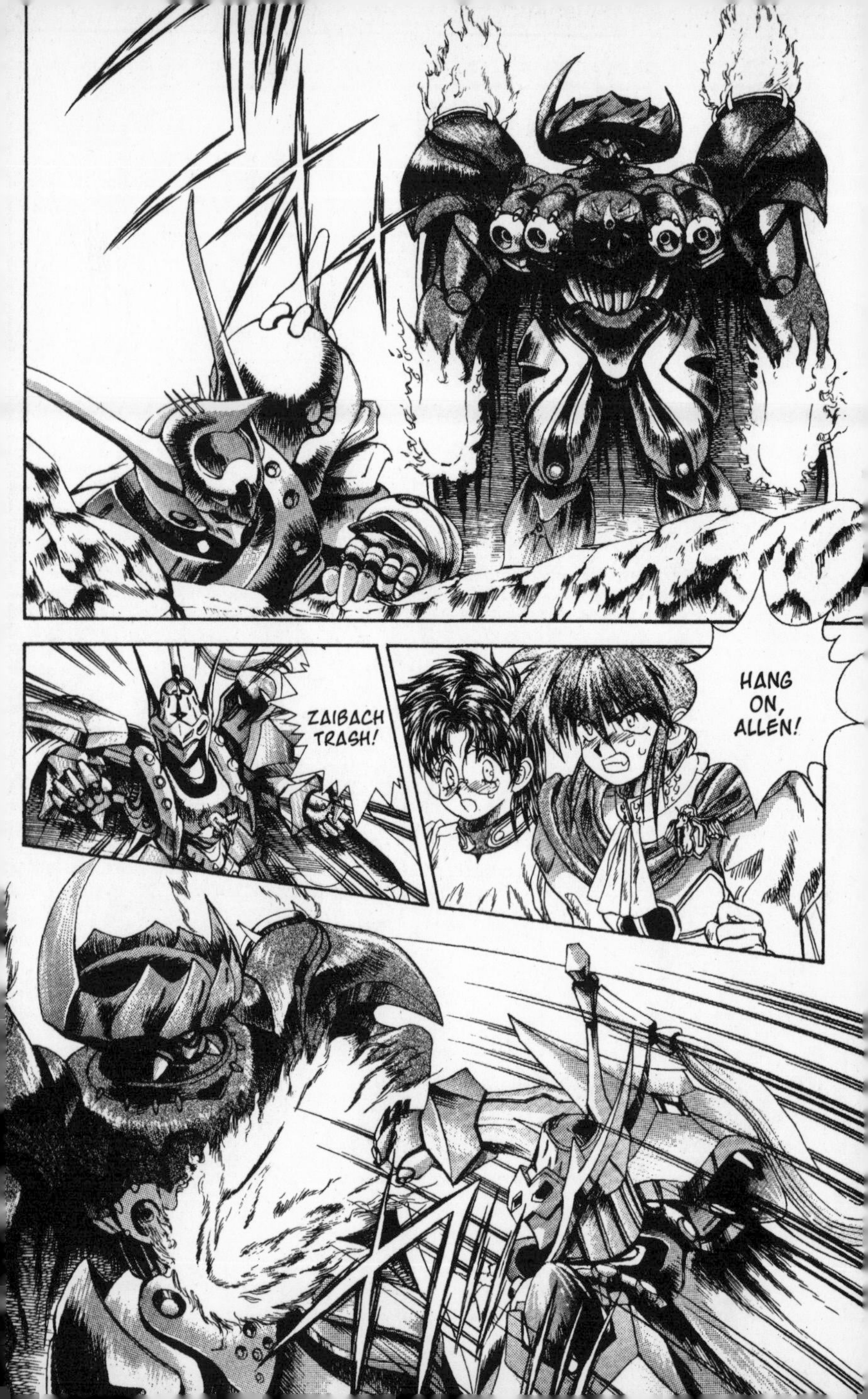
HANG ON, ALLEN!
ZAIBACH TRASH!

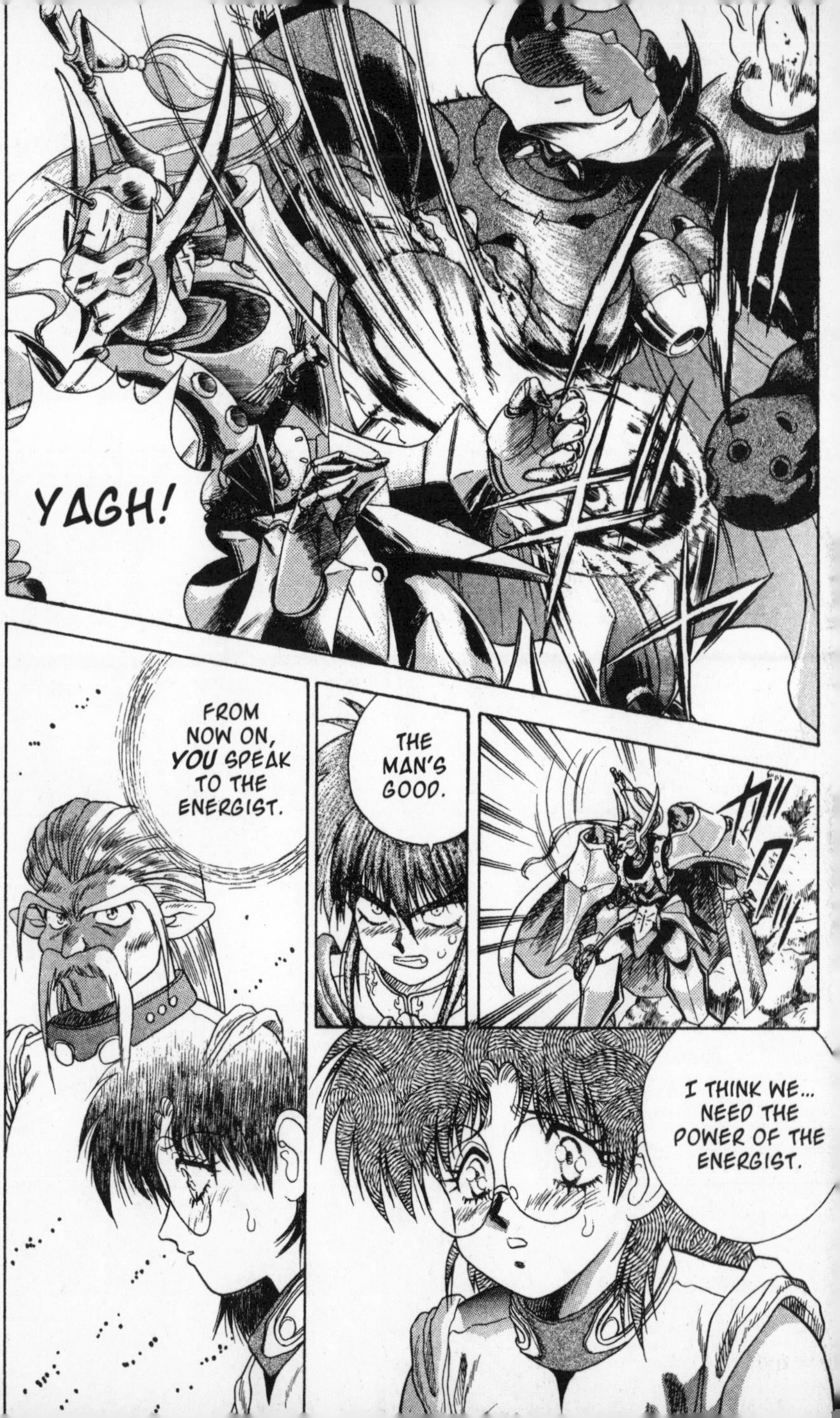
YAGH!
THE MAN'S GOOD.
I THINK WE... NEED THE POWER OF THE ENERGIST.
FROM NOW ON, YOU SPEAK TO THE ENERGIST.

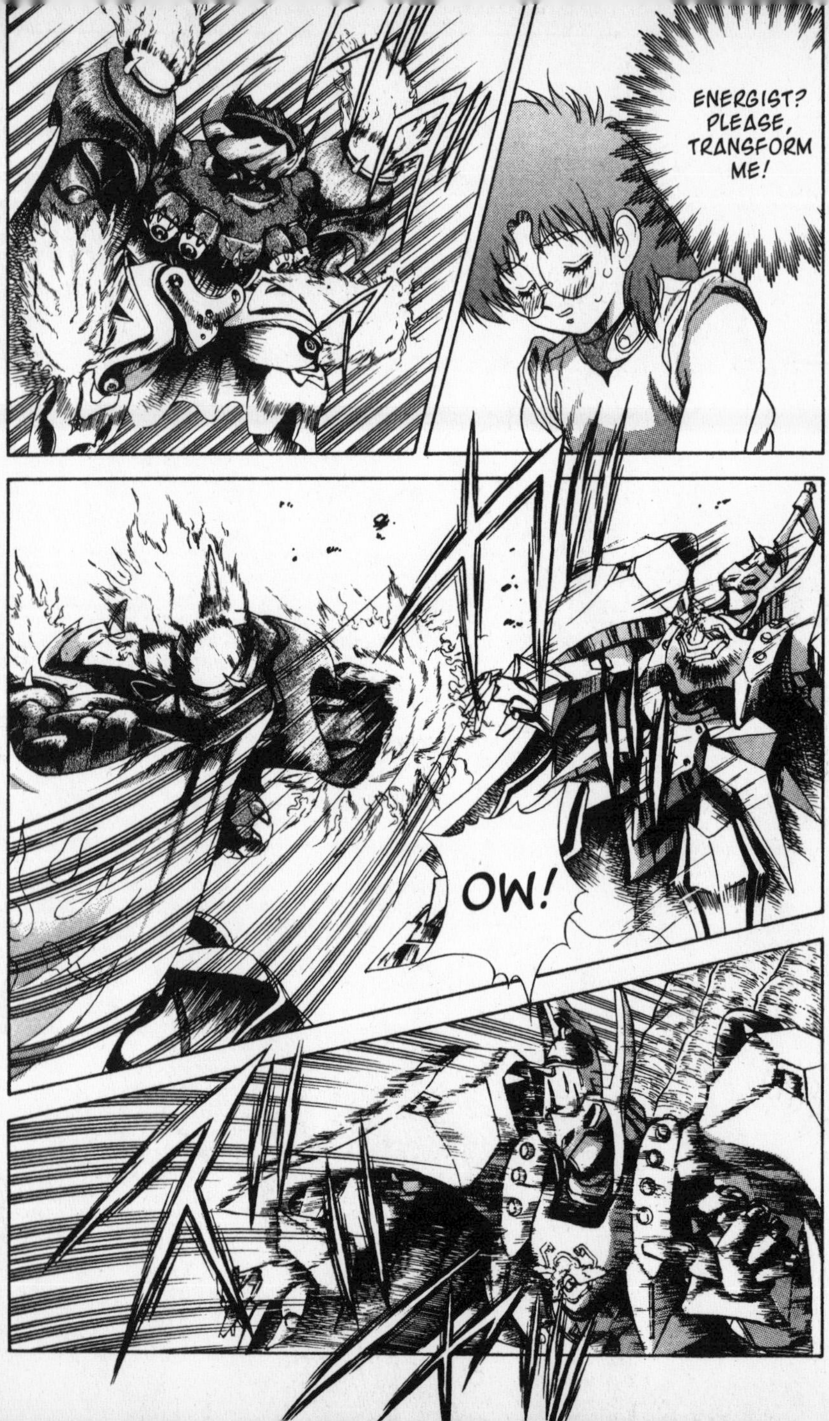
ENERGIST? PLEASE, TRANSFORM ME!
OW!

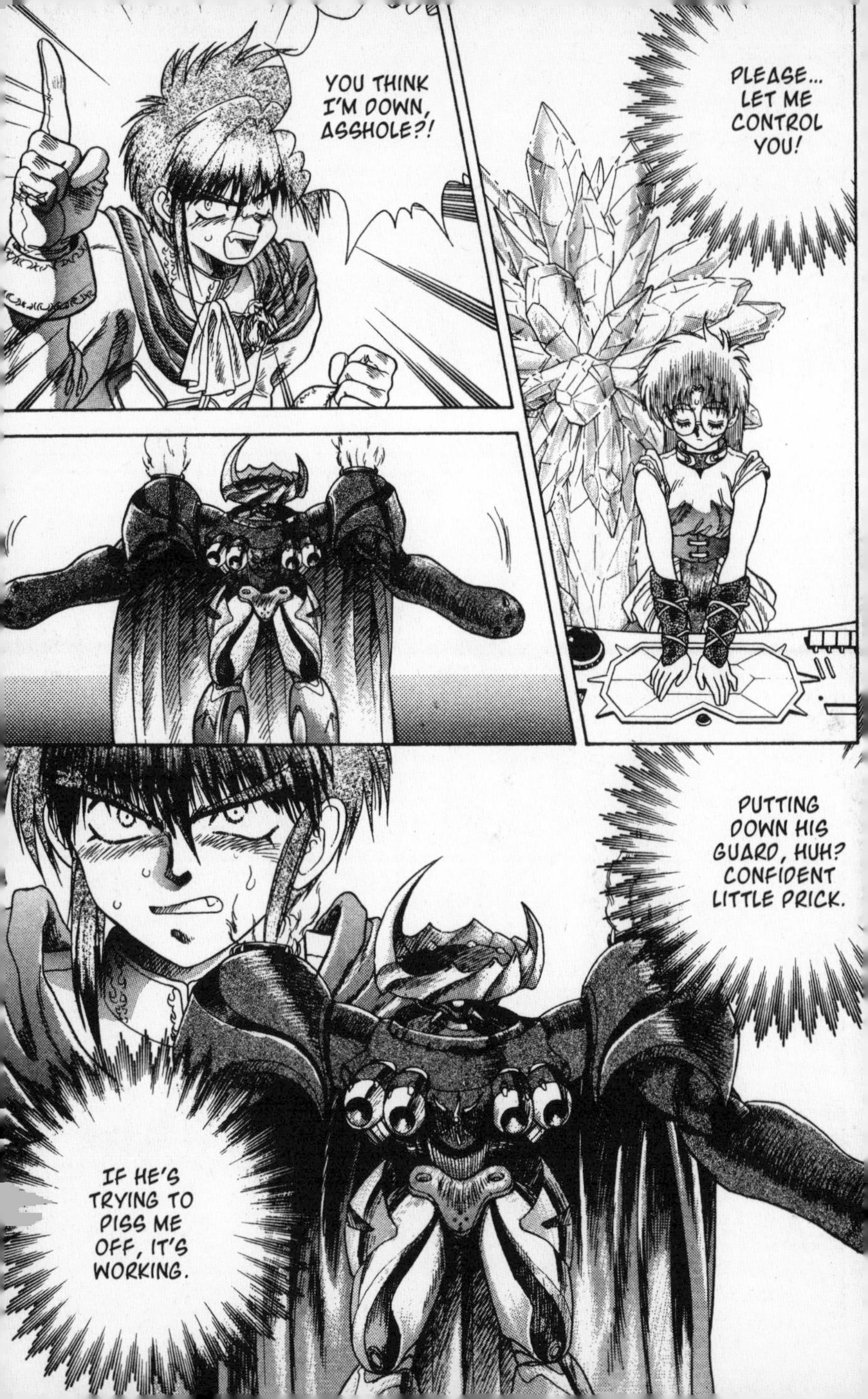
PLEASE... LET ME CONTROL YOU!
YOU THINK I'M DOWN, ASSHOLE?!
PUTTING DOWN HIS GUARD, HUH? CONFIDENT LITTLE PRICK.
IF HE'S TRYING TO PISS ME OFF, IT'S WORKING.

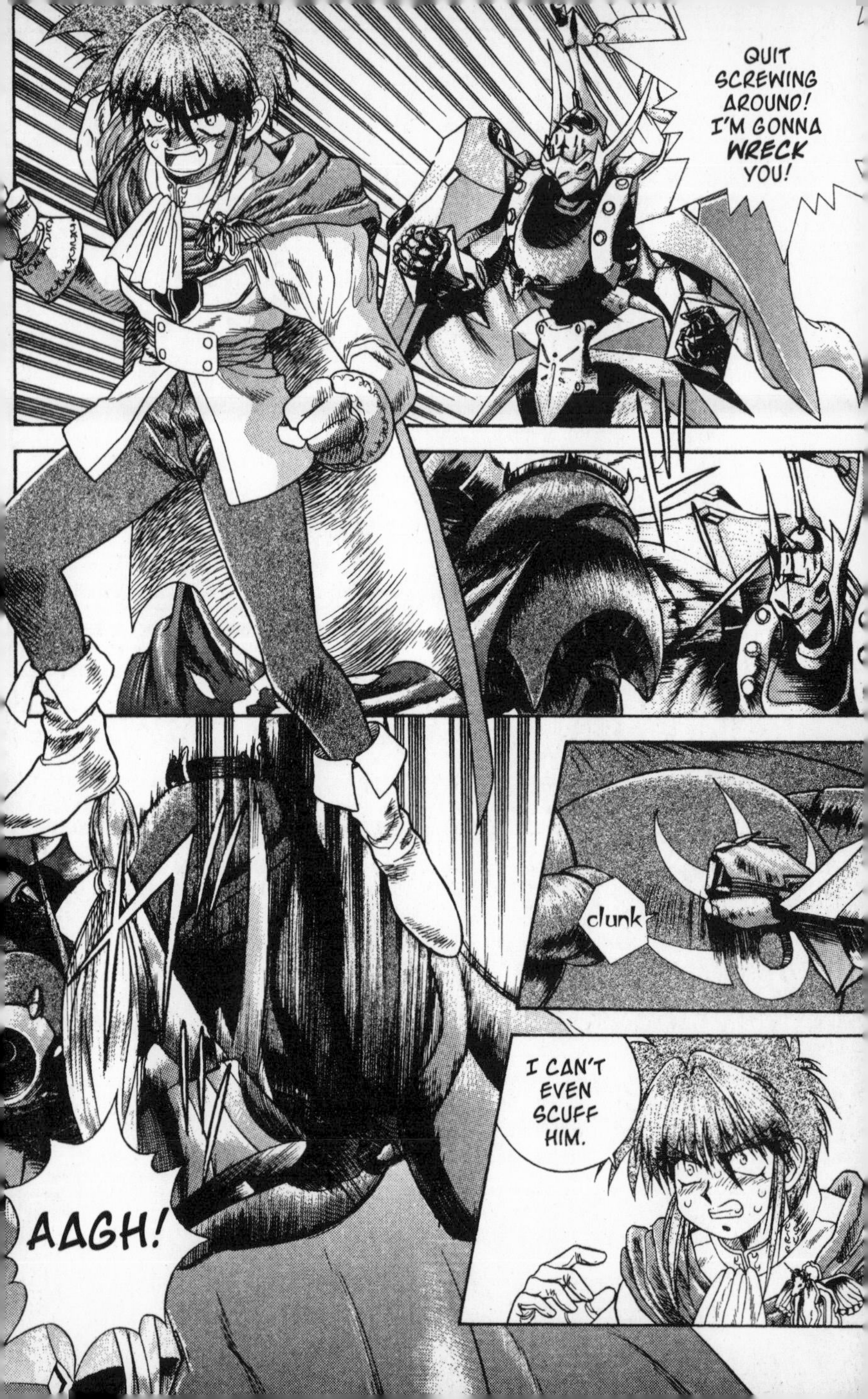
QUIT SCREWING AROUND! I'M GONNA **WRECK** YOU!
clunk
I CAN'T EVEN SCUFF HIM.
AAGH!

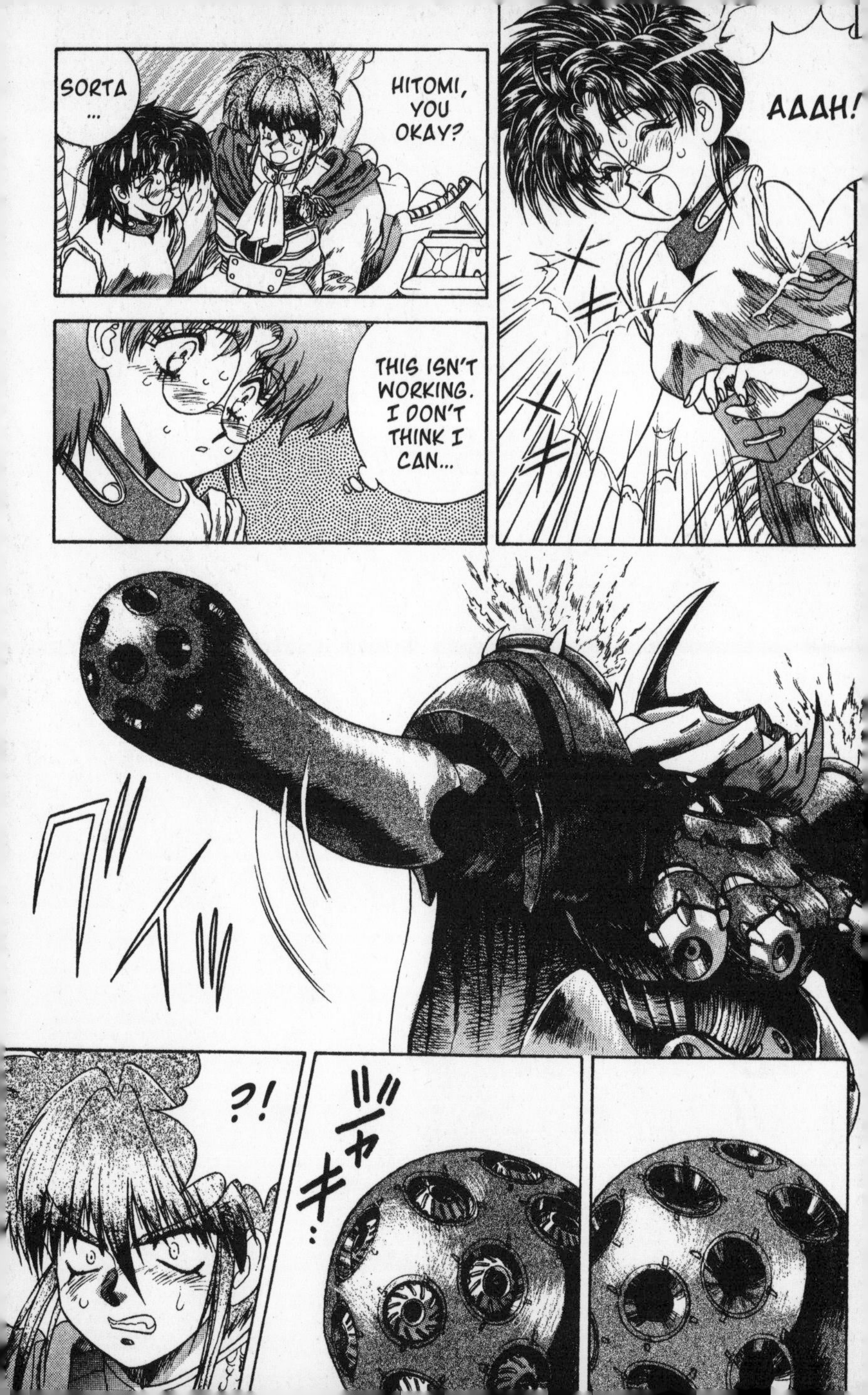
AAAH!
HITOMI, YOU OKAY?
SORTA ...
THIS ISN'T WORKING. I DON'T THINK I CAN...
?!

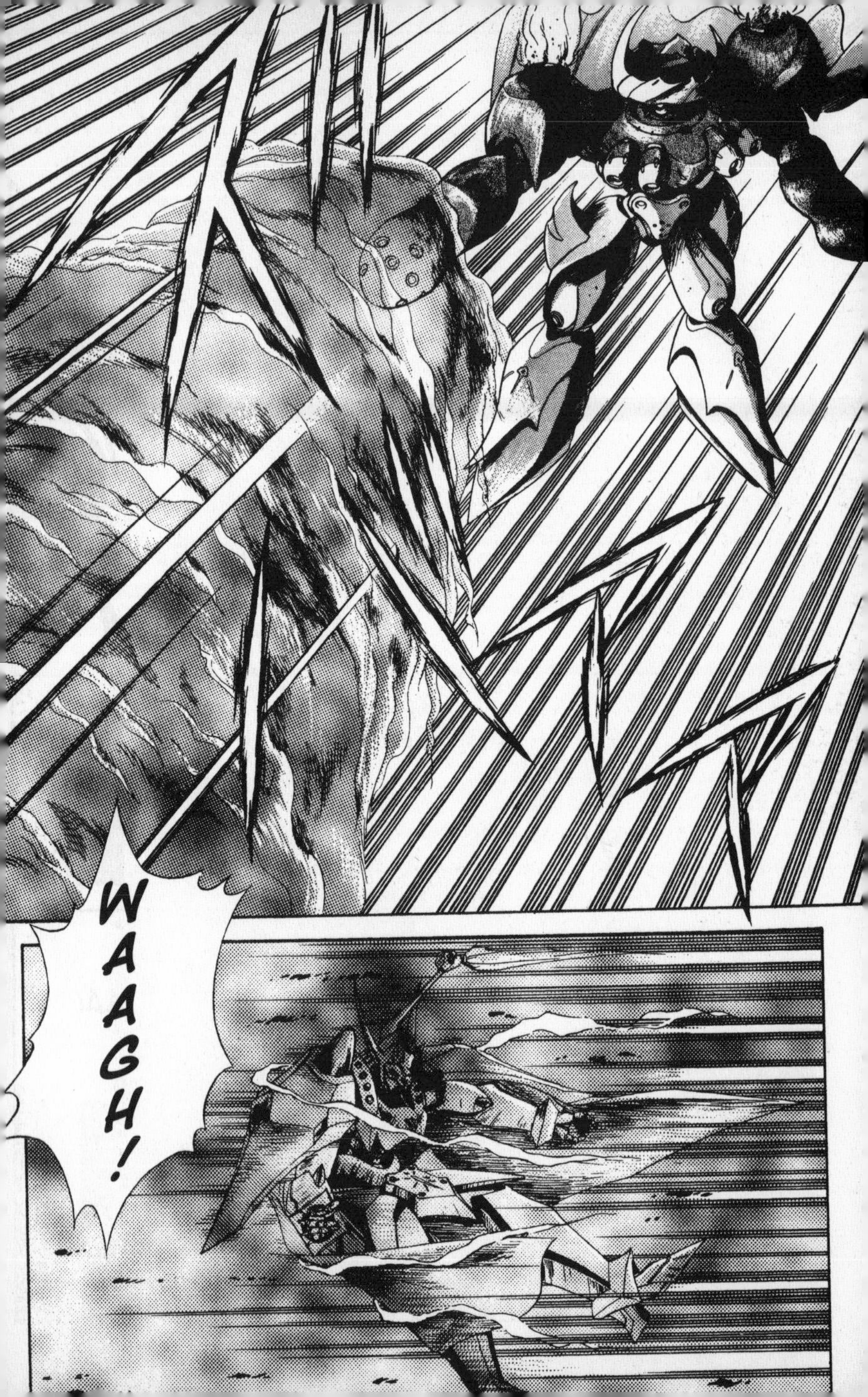
WAAGH!

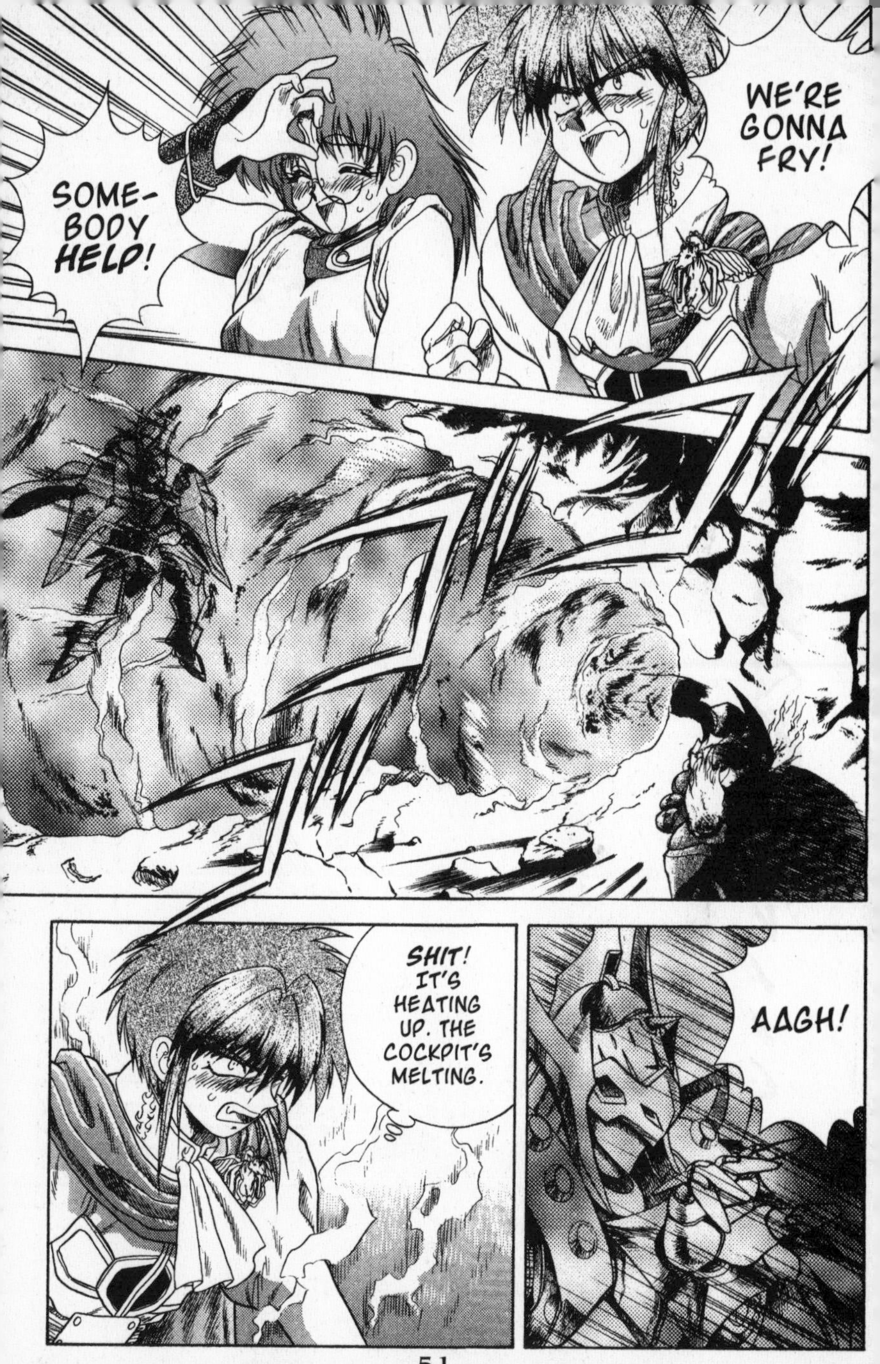
WE'RE GONNA FRY!
SOME-BODY HELP!
AAGH!
SHIT! IT'S HEATING UP. THE COCKPIT'S MELTING.

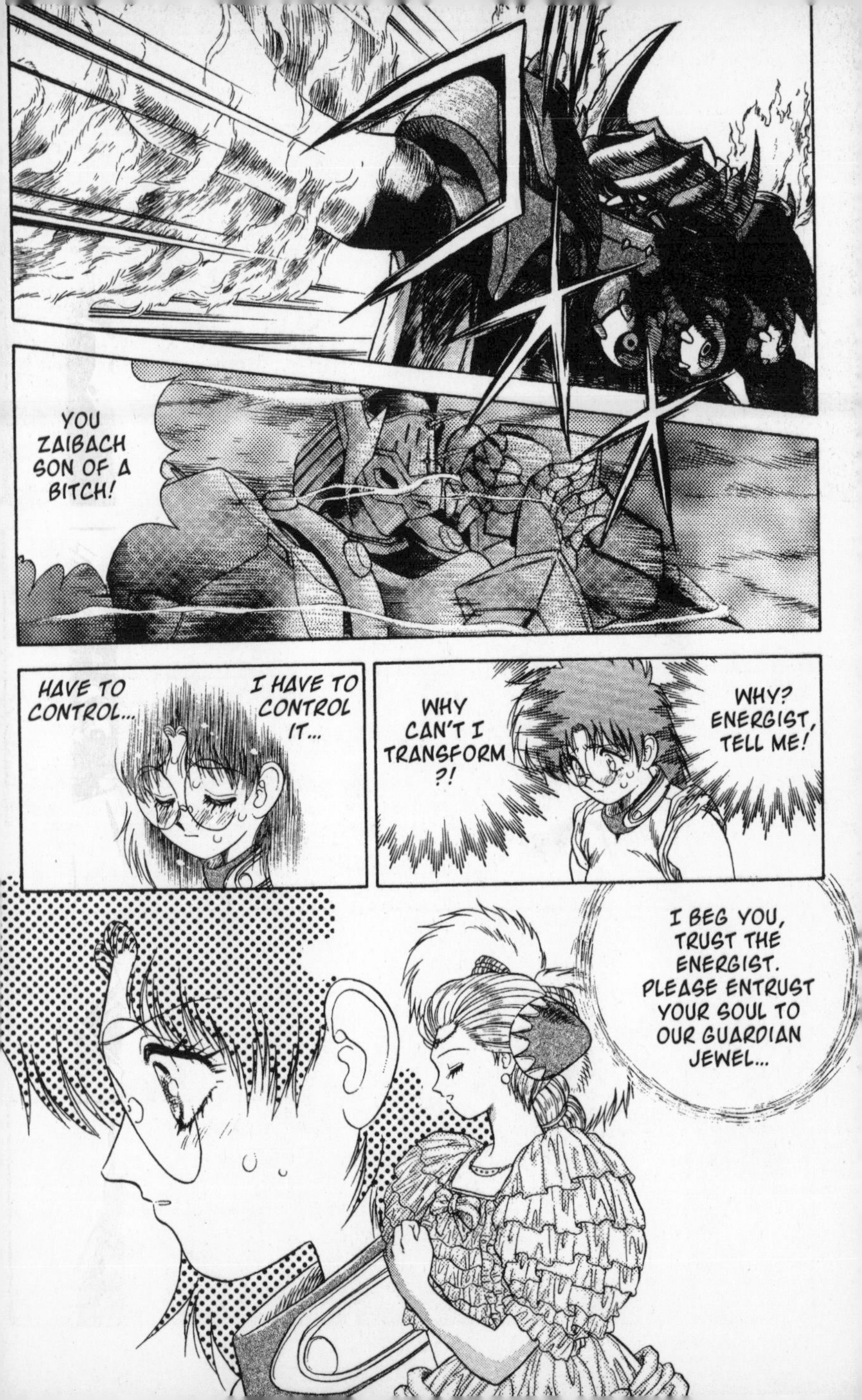
YOU ZAIBACH SON OF A BITCH!
WHY? ENERGIST, TELL ME!
WHY CAN'T I TRANSFORM ?!
I HAVE TO CONTROL IT...
HAVE TO CONTROL...
I BEG YOU, TRUST THE ENERGIST. PLEASE ENTRUST YOUR SOUL TO OUR GUARDIAN JEWEL...

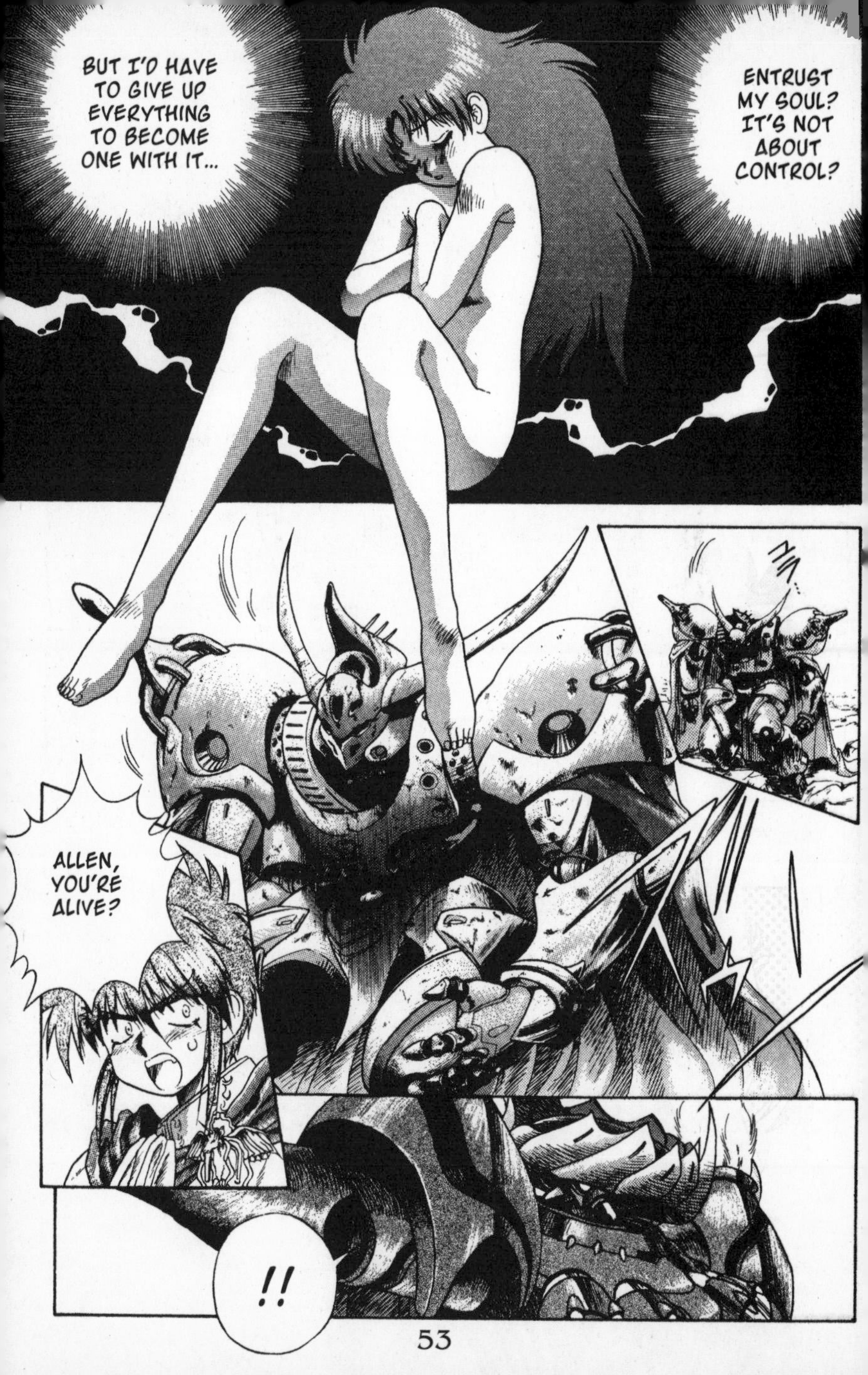
ENTRUST MY SOUL? IT'S NOT ABOUT CONTROL?
BUT I'D HAVE TO GIVE UP EVERYTHING TO BECOME ONE WITH IT...
ALLEN, YOU'RE ALIVE?
!!

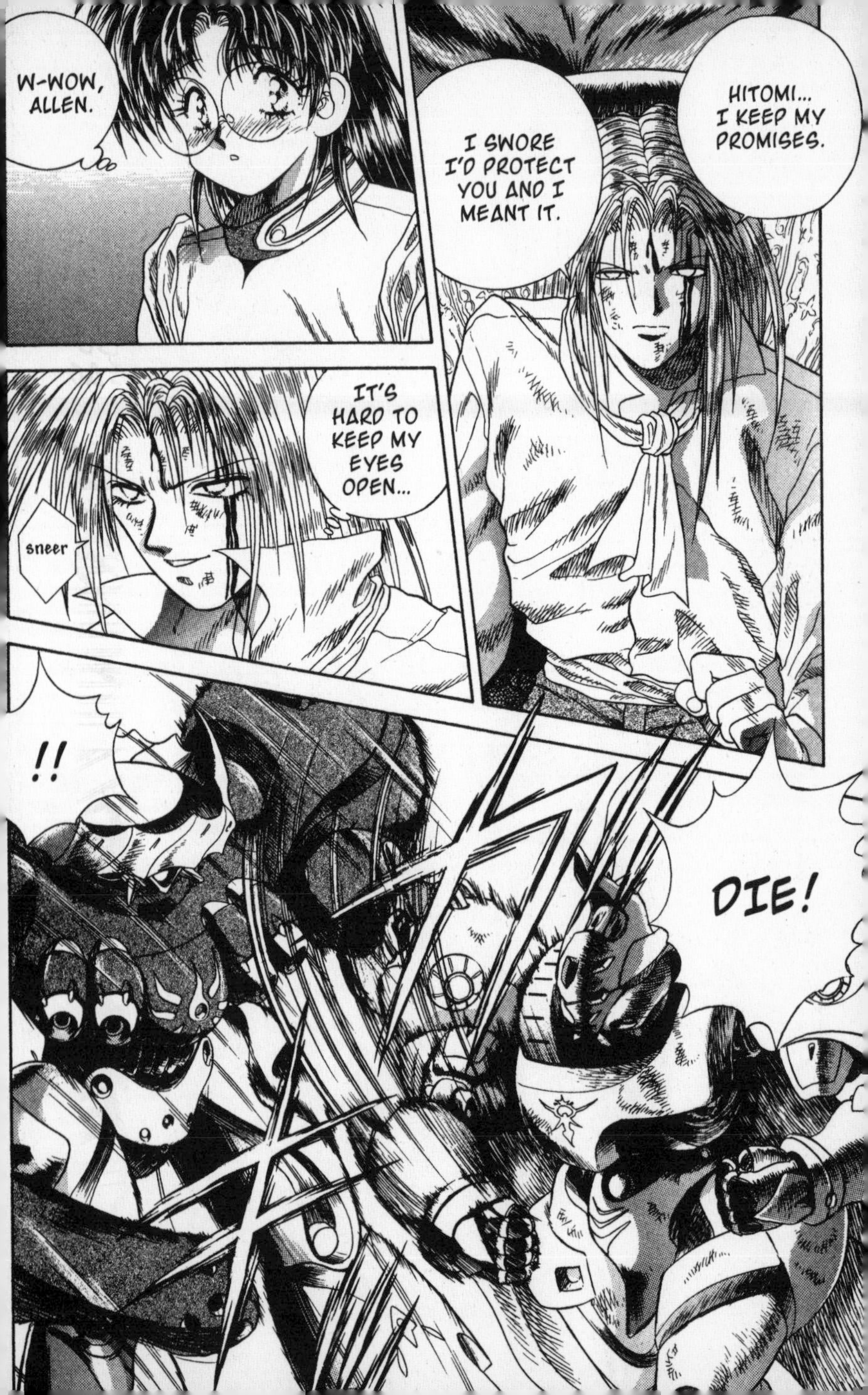
HITOMI... I KEEP MY PROMISES.
I SWORE I'D PROTECT YOU AND I MEANT IT.
W-WOW, ALLEN.
IT'S HARD TO KEEP MY EYES OPEN...
sneer
DIE!
!!

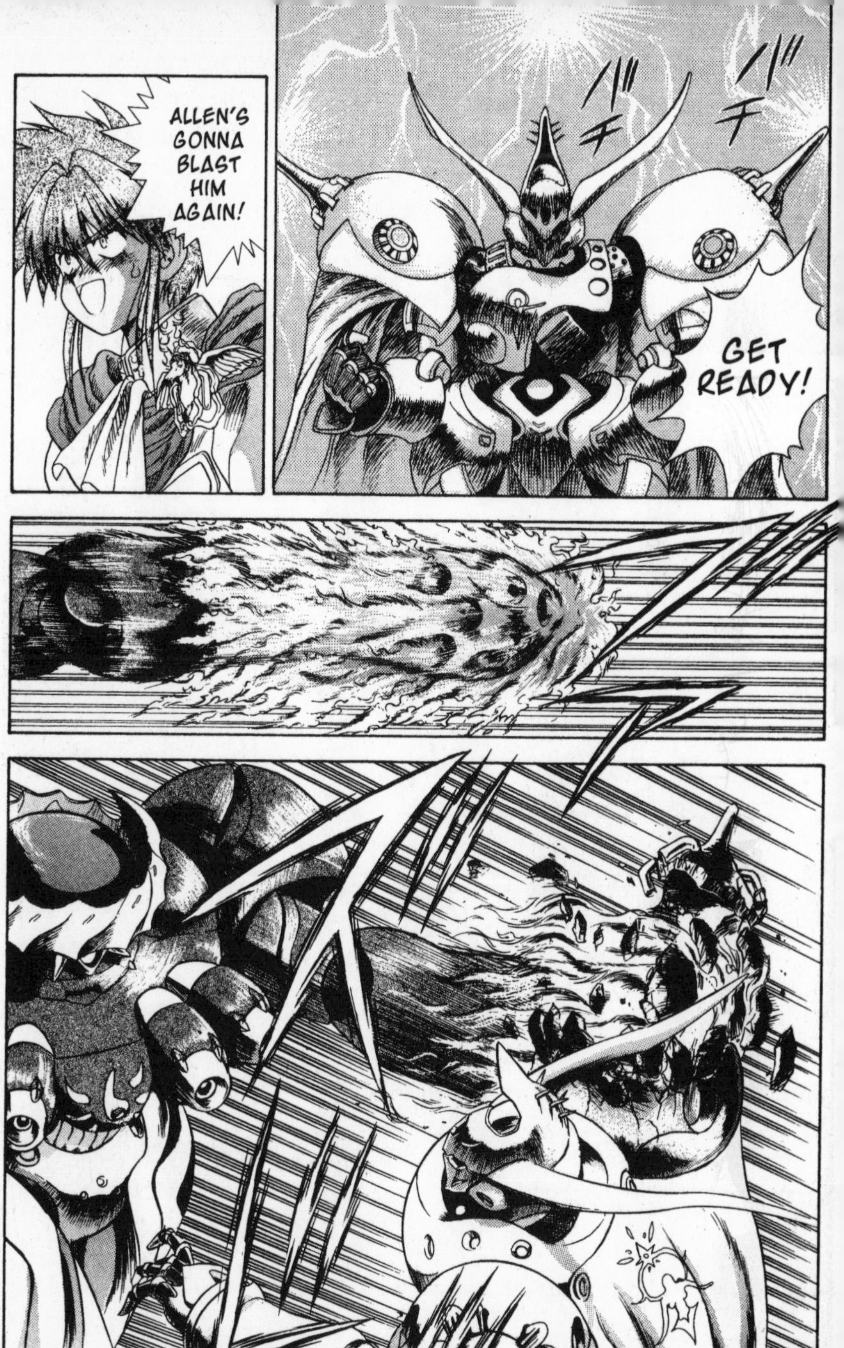
バチ
バチ
GET READY!
ALLEN'S GONNA BLAST HIM AGAIN!

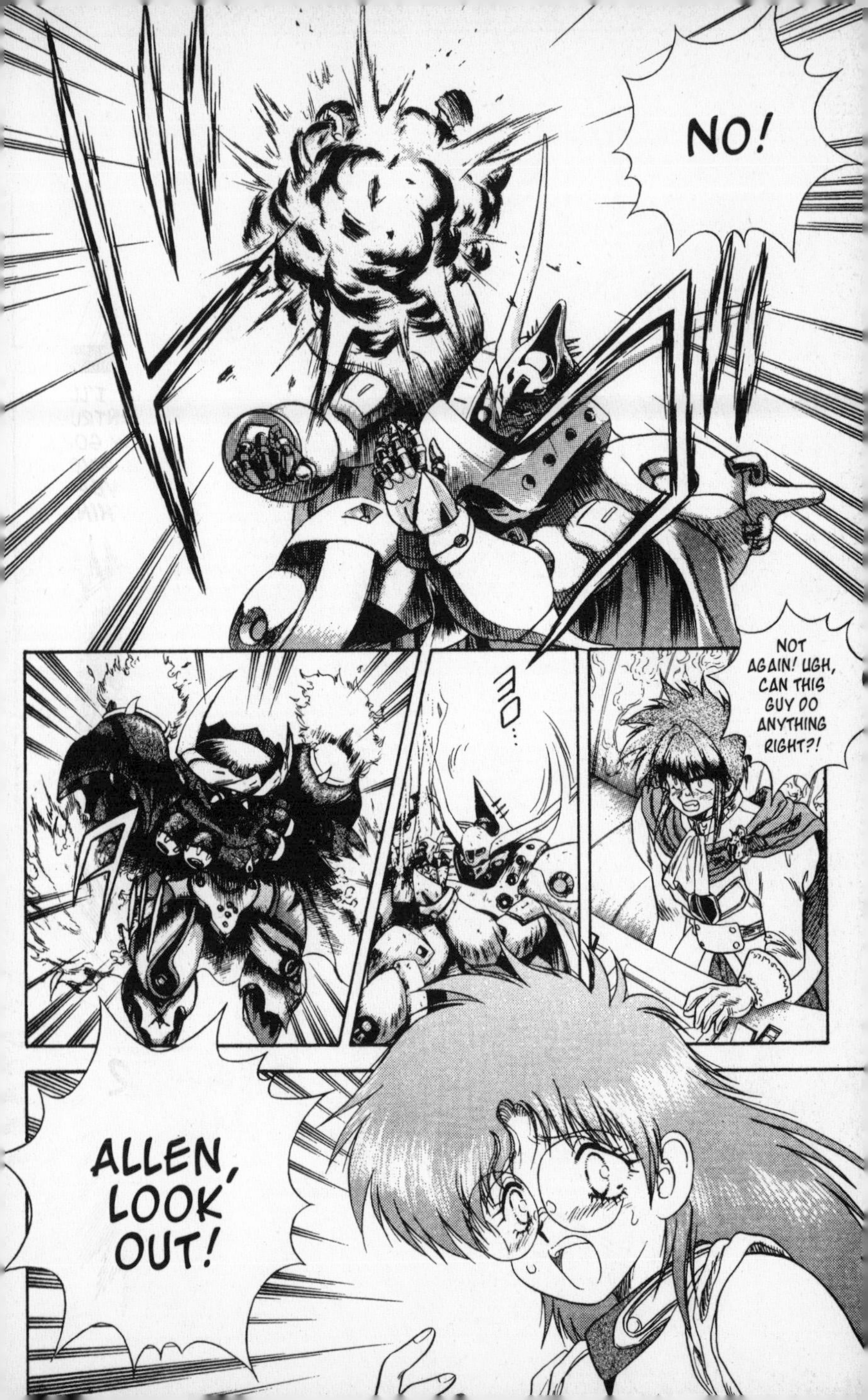
NO!
NOT AGAIN! UGH, CAN THIS GUY DO ANYTHING RIGHT?!
ALLEN, LOOK OUT!

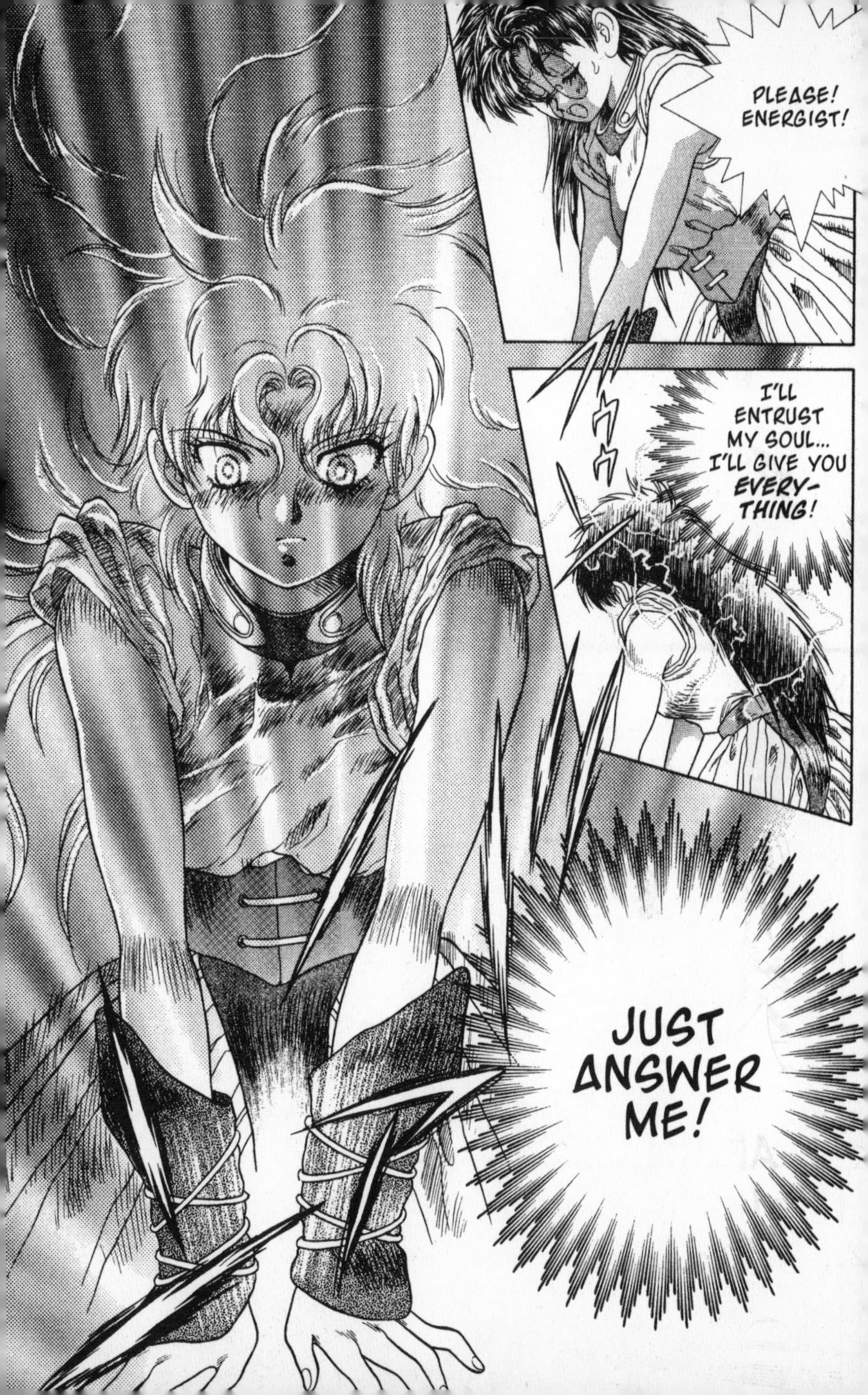
PLEASE! ENERGIST!
I'LL ENTRUST MY SOUL... I'LL GIVE YOU EVERY-THING!
JUST ANSWER ME!

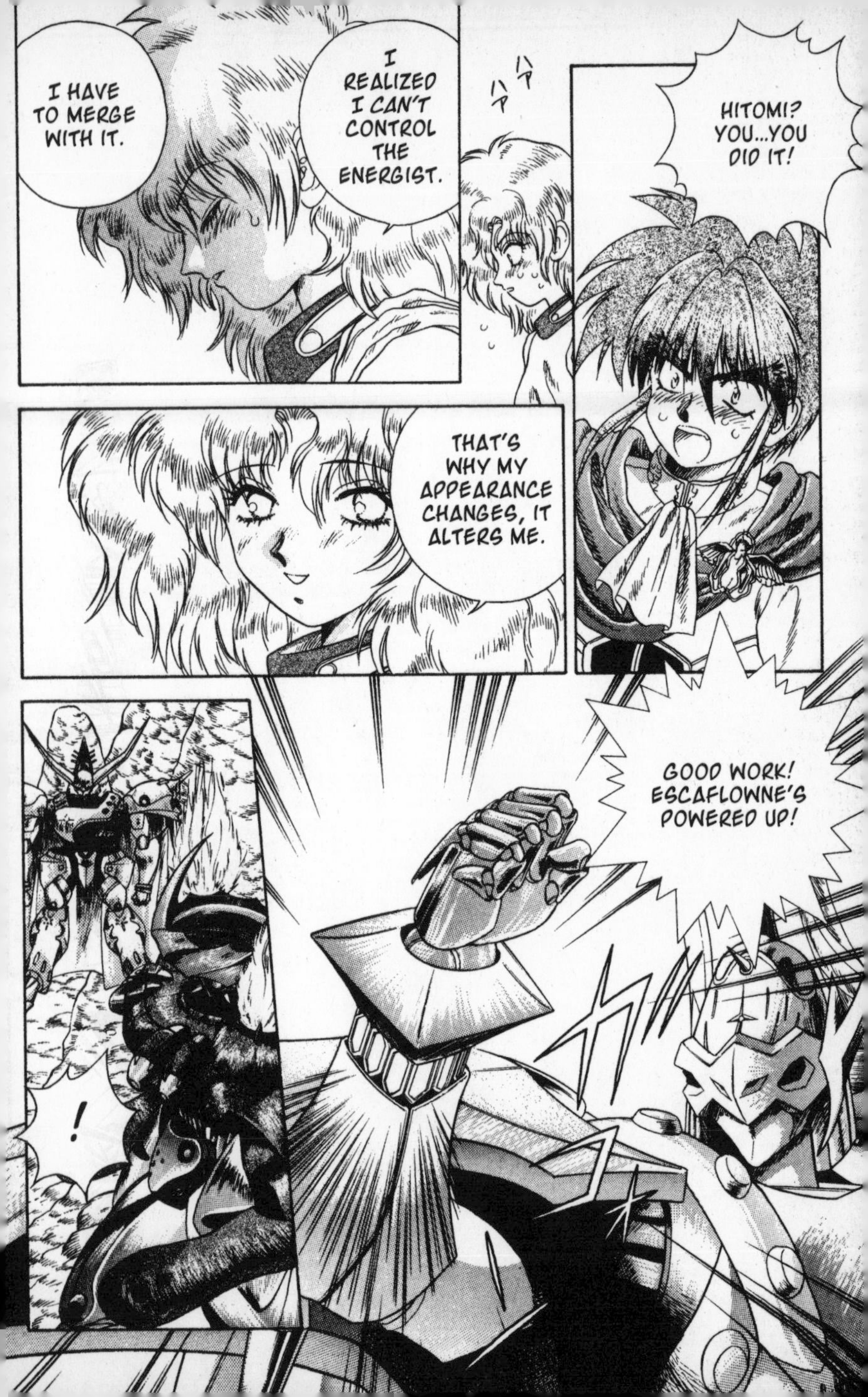
HITOMI? YOU...YOU DID IT!
ハァ ハァ
I REALIZED I CAN'T CONTROL THE ENERGIST.
I HAVE TO MERGE WITH IT.
THAT'S WHY MY APPEARANCE CHANGES, IT ALTERS ME.
GOOD WORK! ESCAFLOWNE'S POWERED UP!
!

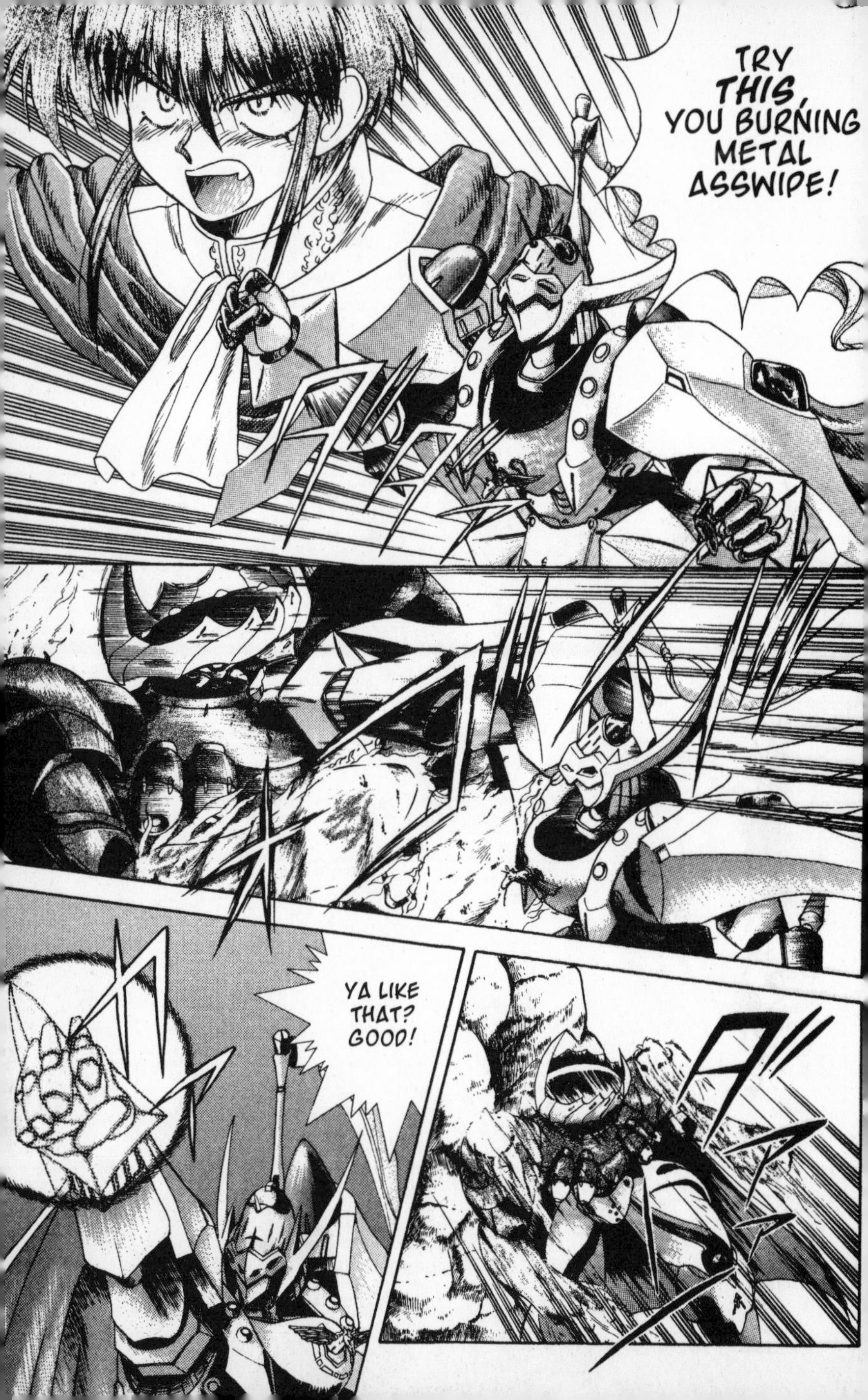
TRY THIS, YOU BURNING METAL ASSWIPE!
YA LIKE THAT? GOOD!

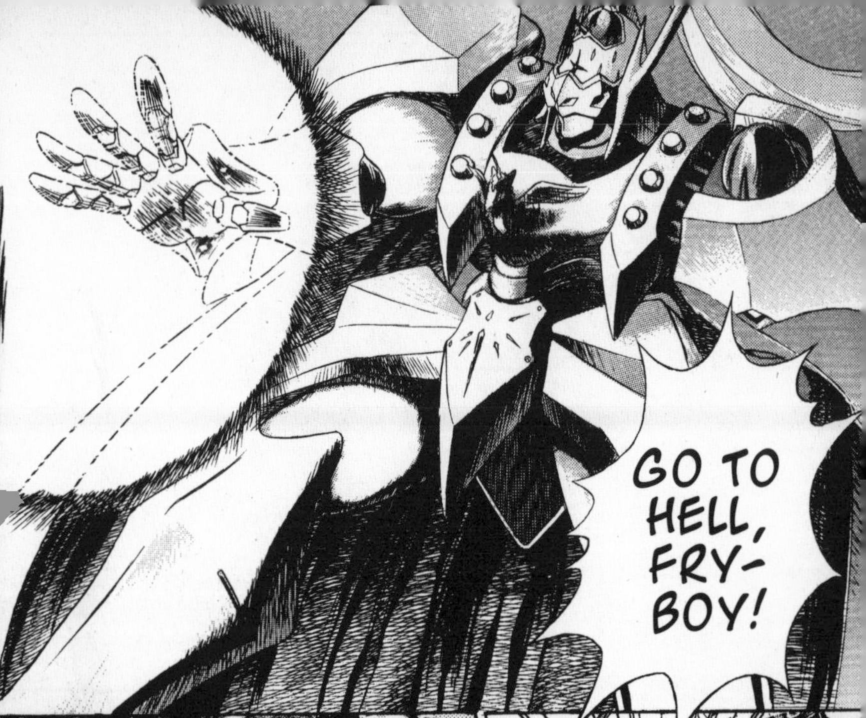
GO TO HELL, FRY-BOY!
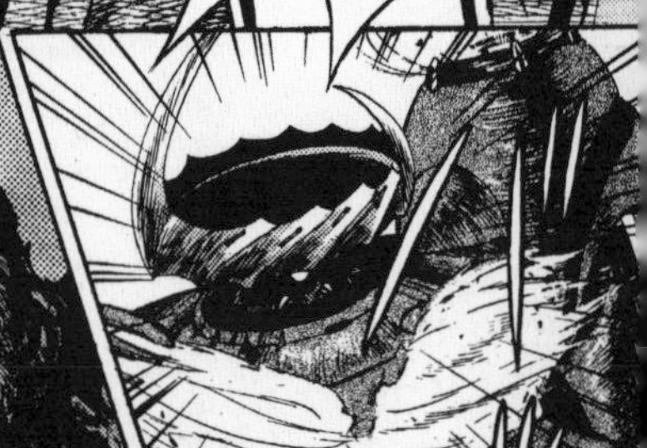
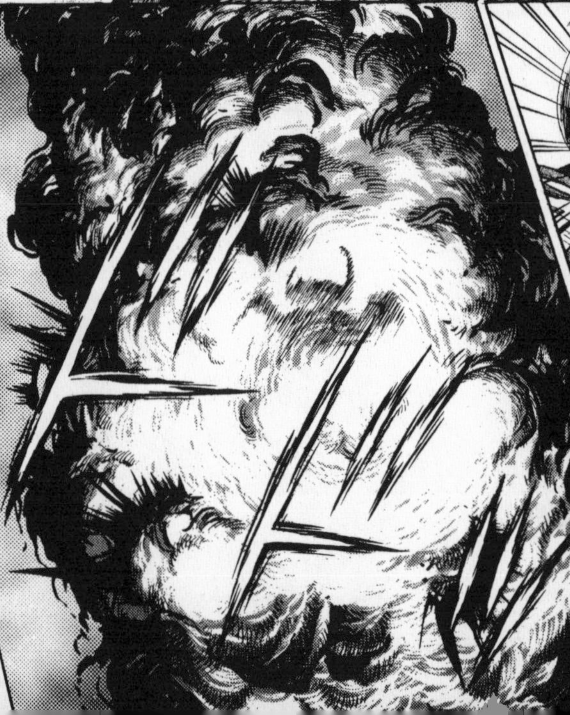

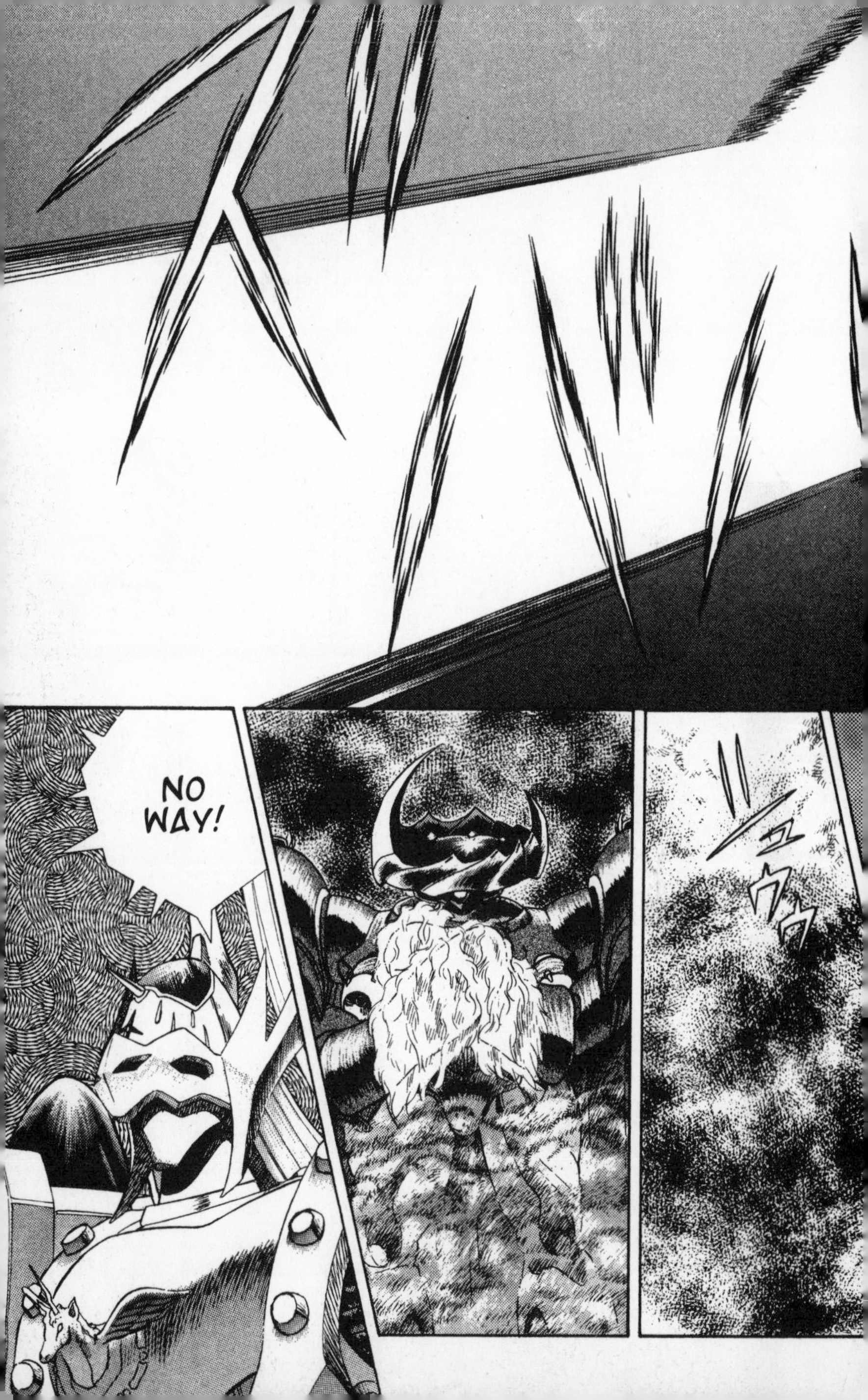
NO WAY!

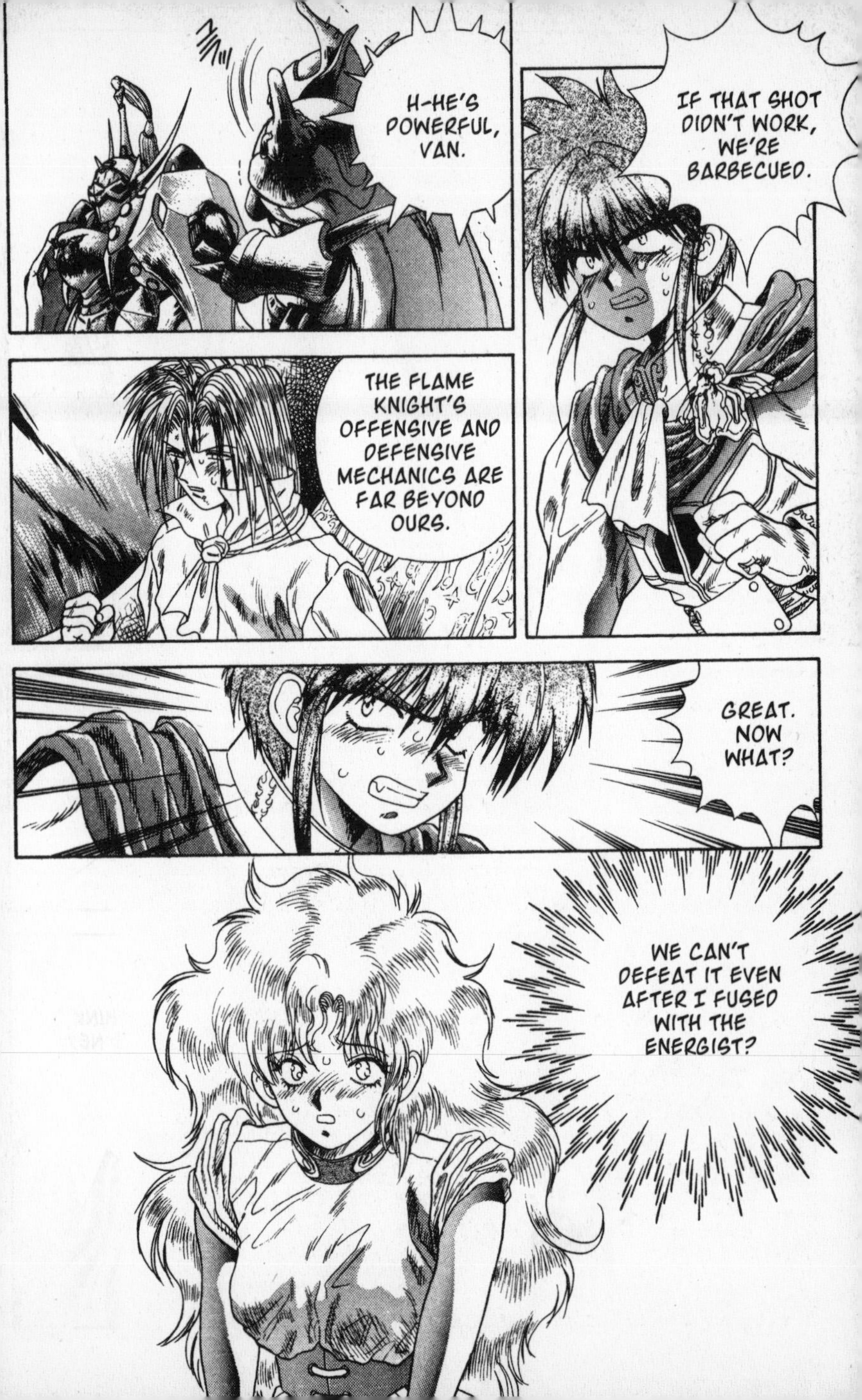
IF THAT SHOT DIDN'T WORK, WE'RE BARBECUED.
H-HE'S POWERFUL, VAN.
THE FLAME KNIGHT'S OFFENSIVE AND DEFENSIVE MECHANICS ARE FAR BEYOND OURS.
GREAT. NOW WHAT?
WE CAN'T DEFEAT IT EVEN AFTER I FUSED WITH THE ENERGIST?

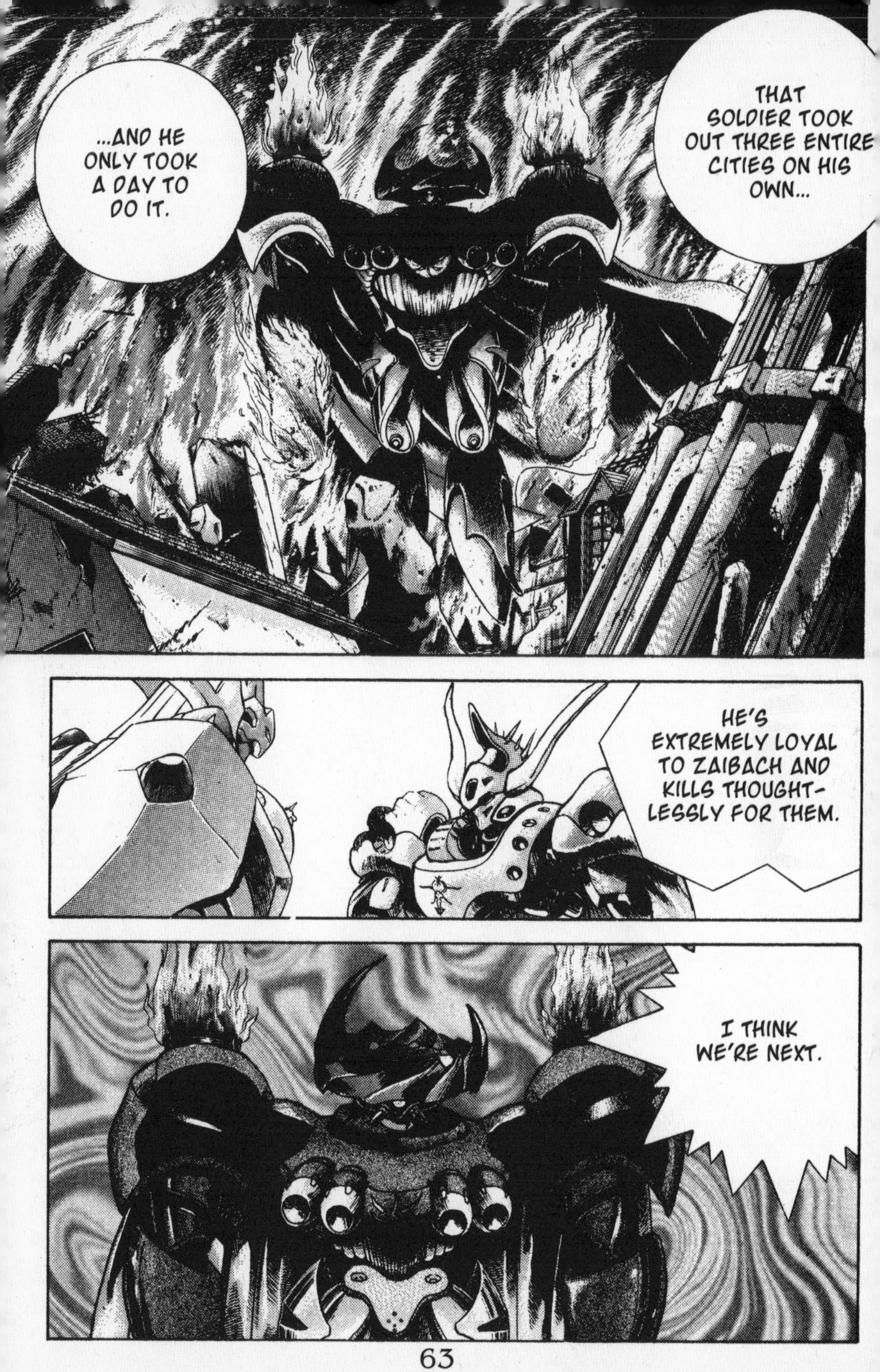
THAT SOLDIER TOOK OUT THREE ENTIRE CITIES ON HIS OWN...
...AND HE ONLY TOOK A DAY TO DO IT.
HE'S EXTREMELY LOYAL TO ZAIBACH AND KILLS THOUGHT-LESSLY FOR THEM.
I THINK WE'RE NEXT.

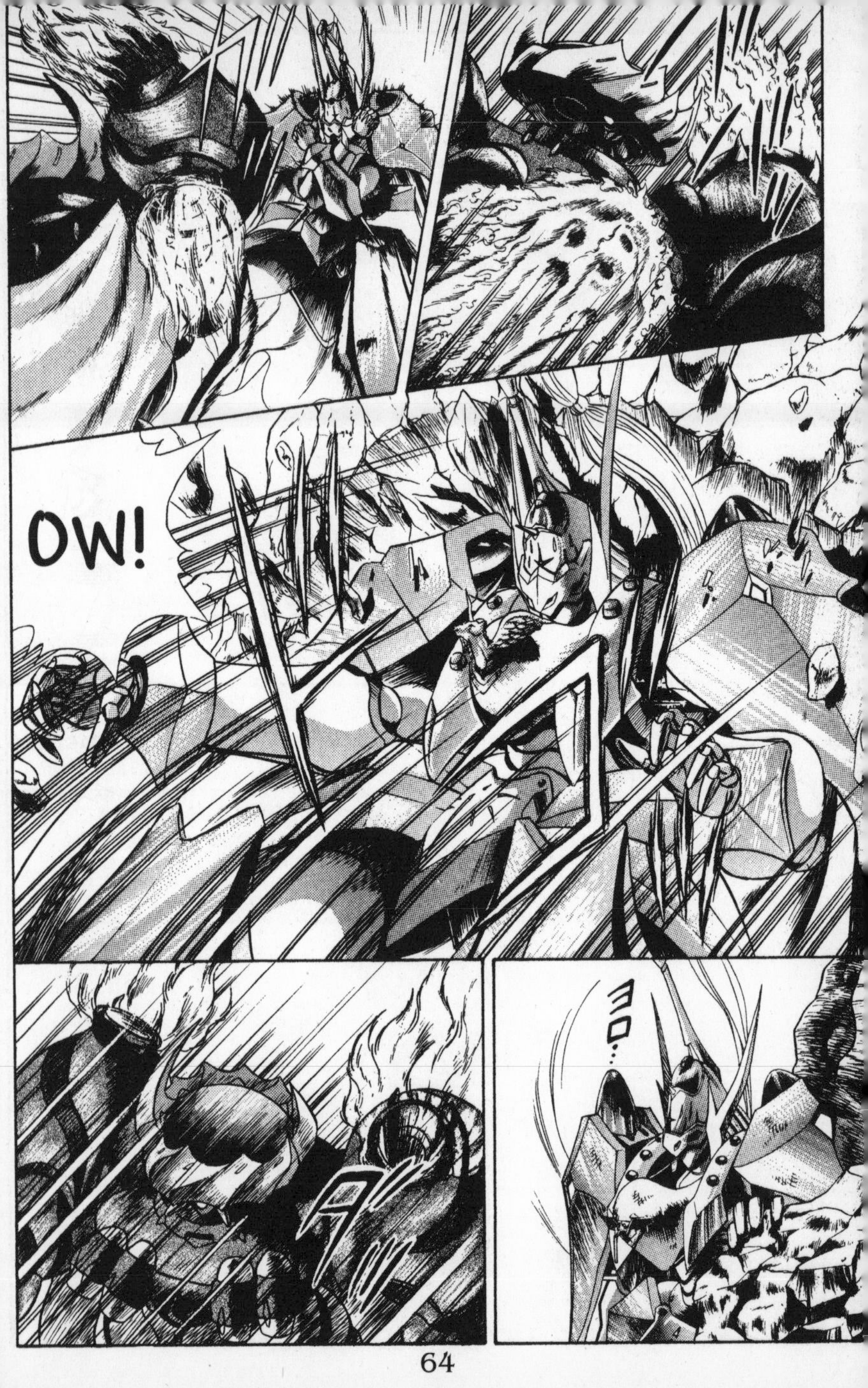
OW!
ヨロ...

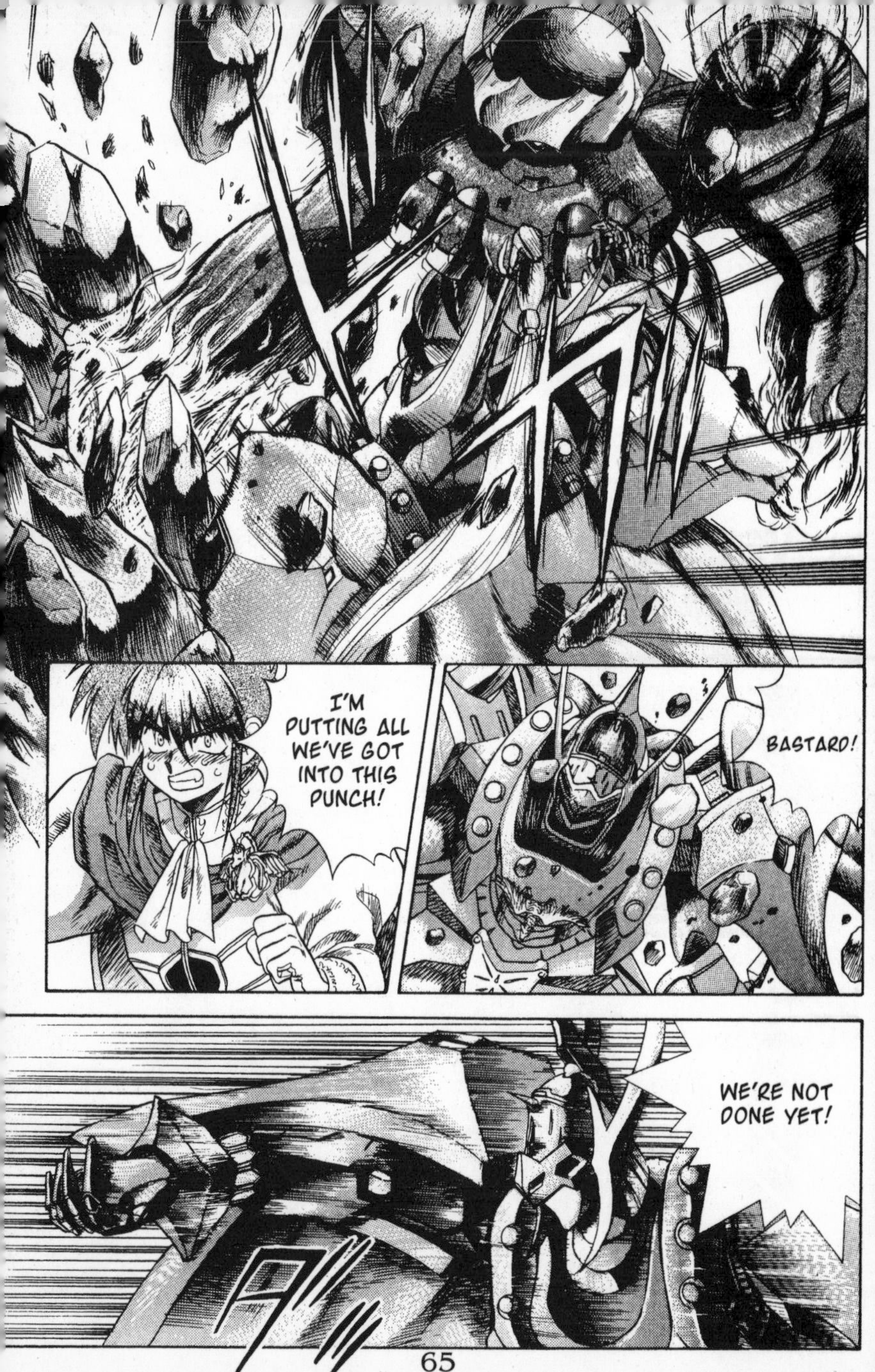
BASTARD!
I'M PUTTING ALL WE'VE GOT INTO THIS PUNCH!
WE'RE NOT DONE YET!

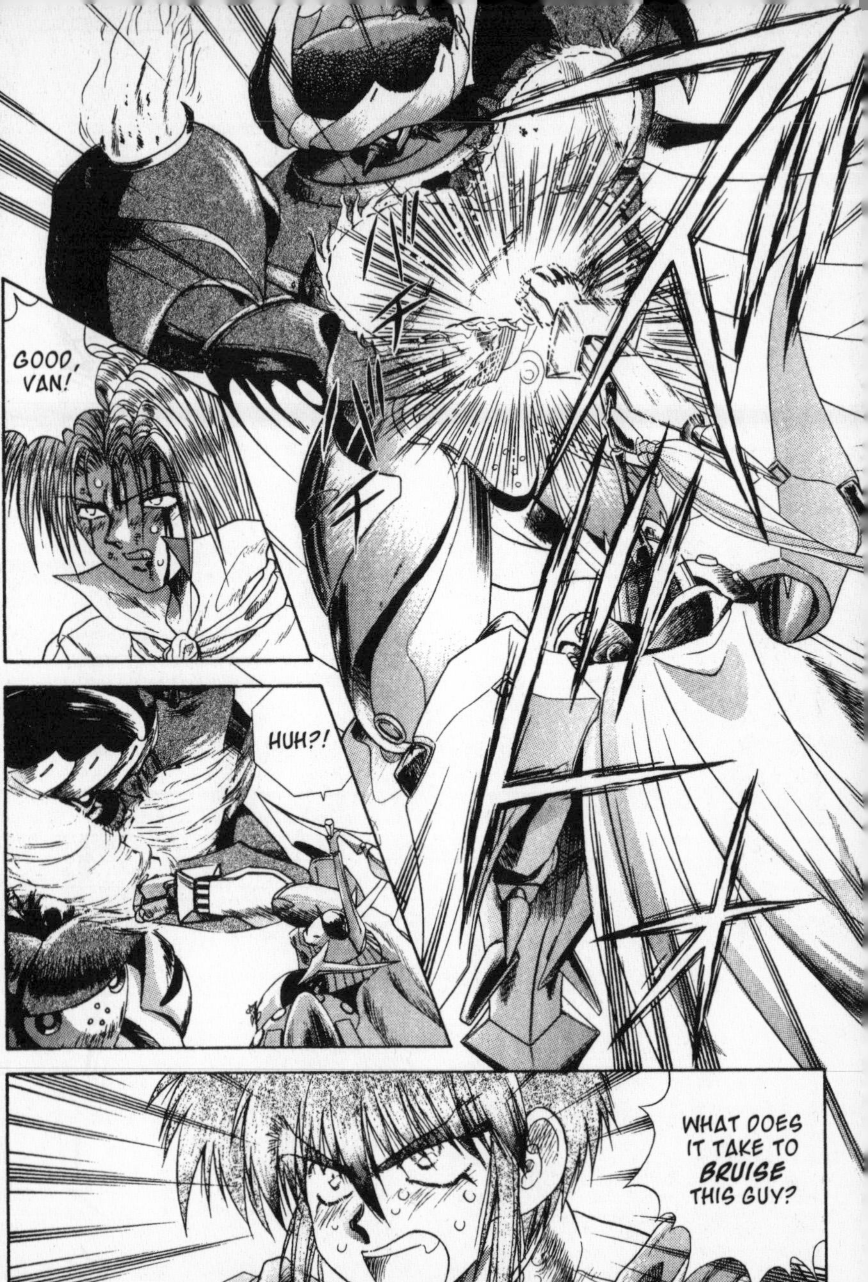
GOOD, VAN!
HUH?!
WHAT DOES IT TAKE TO BRUISE THIS GUY?

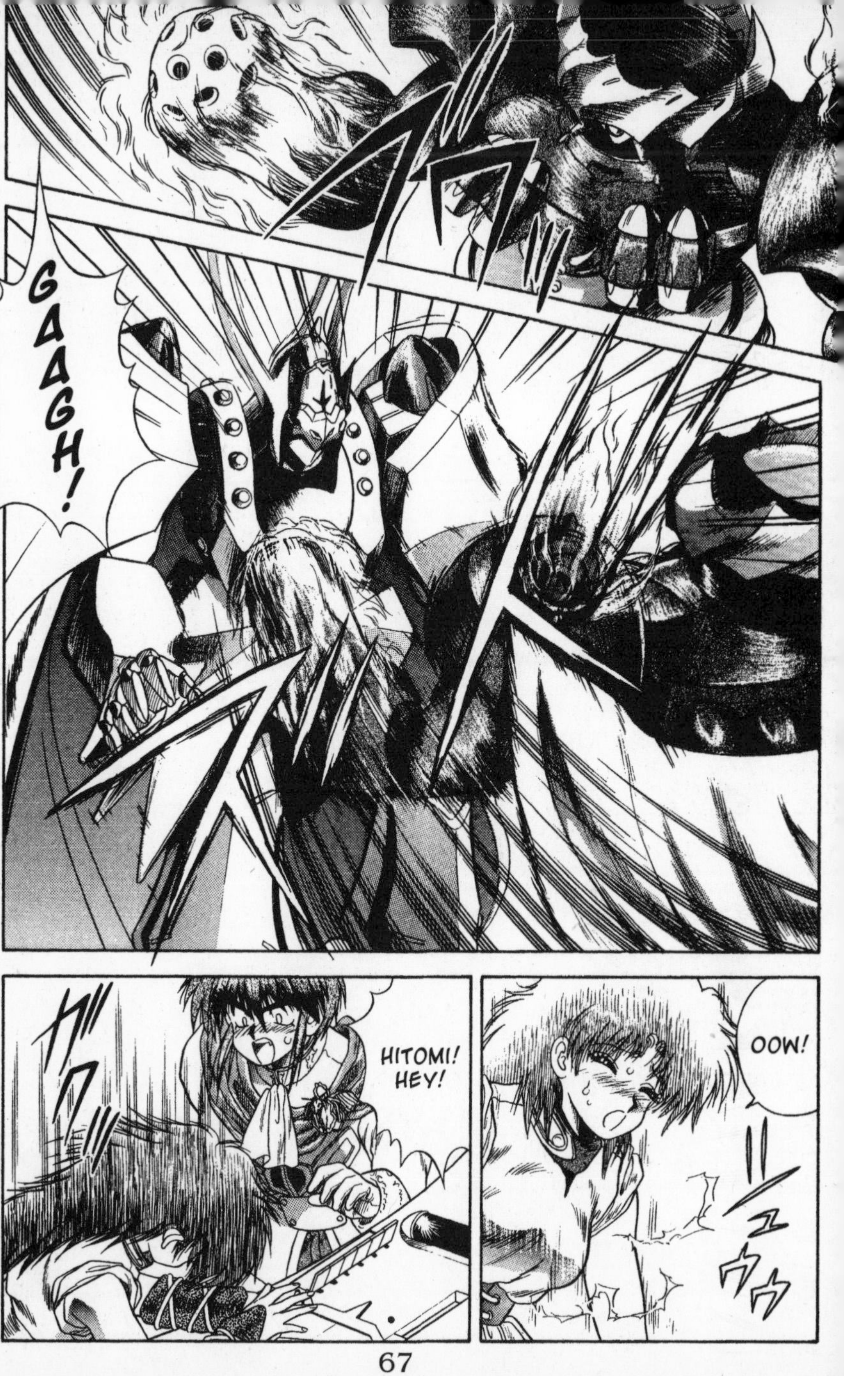
GAAGH!
OOW!
HITOMI! HEY!

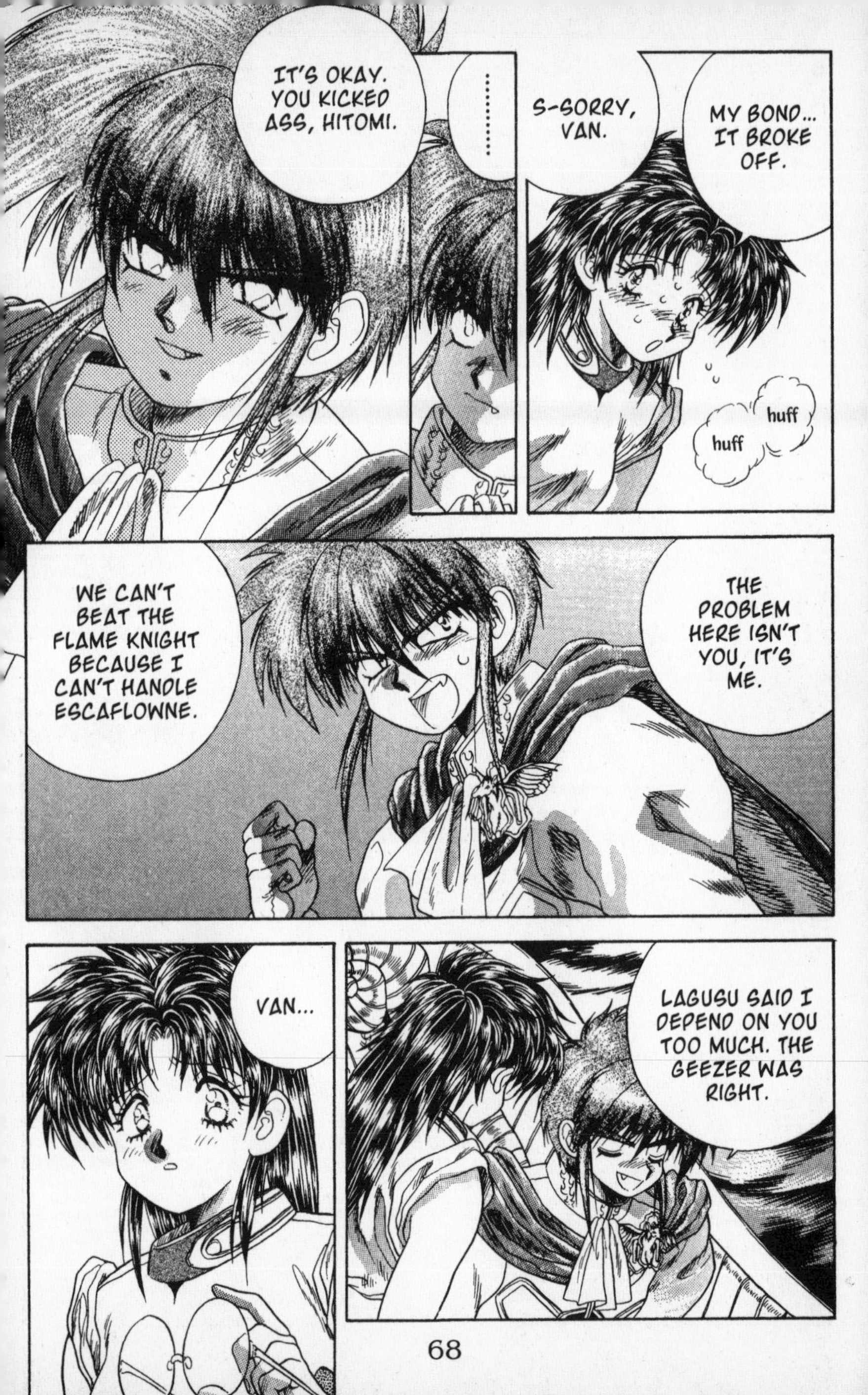
MY BOND... IT BROKE OFF.
S-SORRY, VAN.
huff
huff
......
IT'S OKAY. YOU KICKED ASS, HITOMI.
THE PROBLEM HERE ISN'T YOU, IT'S ME.
WE CAN'T BEAT THE FLAME KNIGHT BECAUSE I CAN'T HANDLE ESCAFLOWNE.
LAGUSU SAID I DEPEND ON YOU TOO MUCH. THE GEEZER WAS RIGHT.
VAN...

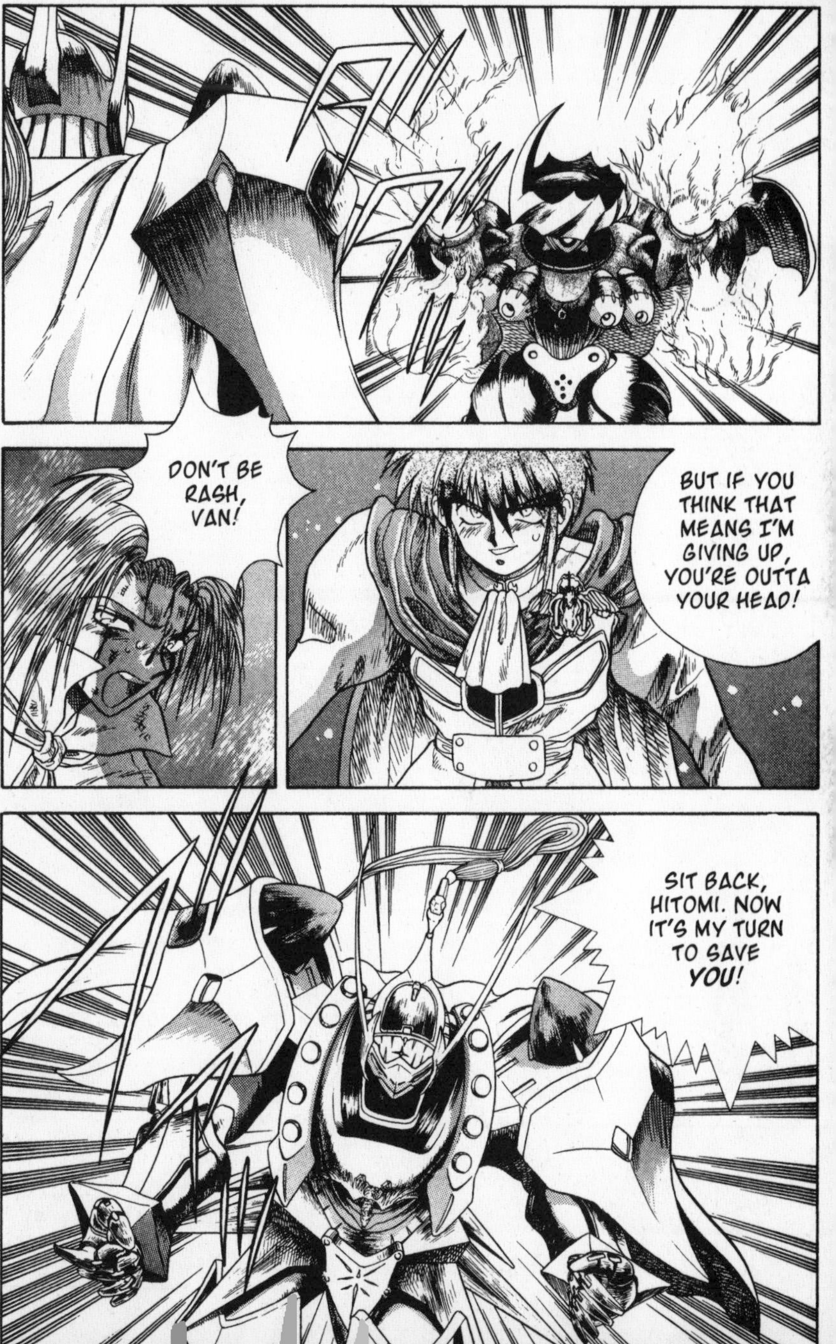
BUT IF YOU THINK THAT MEANS I'M GIVING UP, YOU'RE OUTTA YOUR HEAD!
DON'T BE RASH, VAN!
SIT BACK, HITOMI. NOW IT'S MY TURN TO SAVE *YOU*!

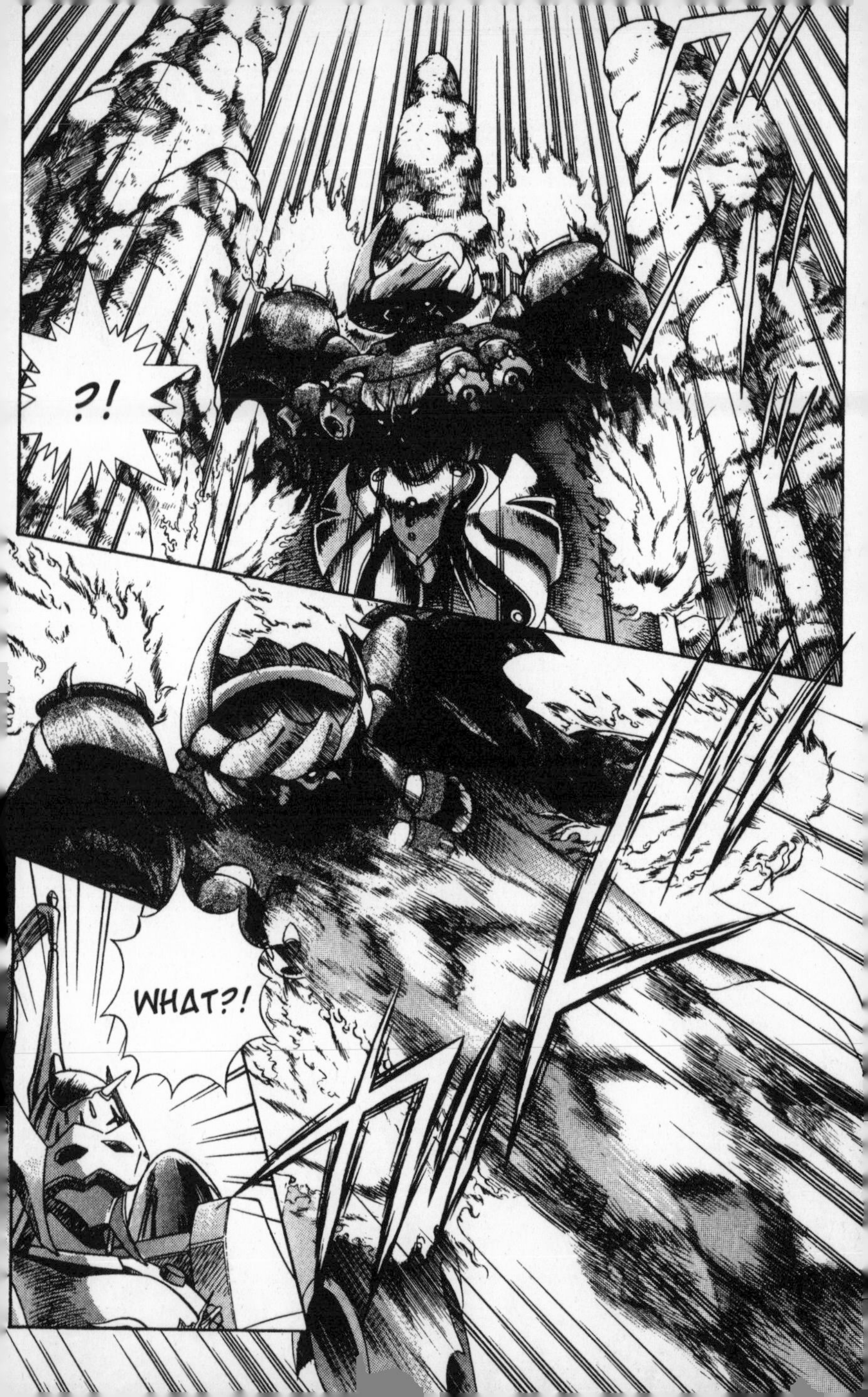
?!
WHAT?!

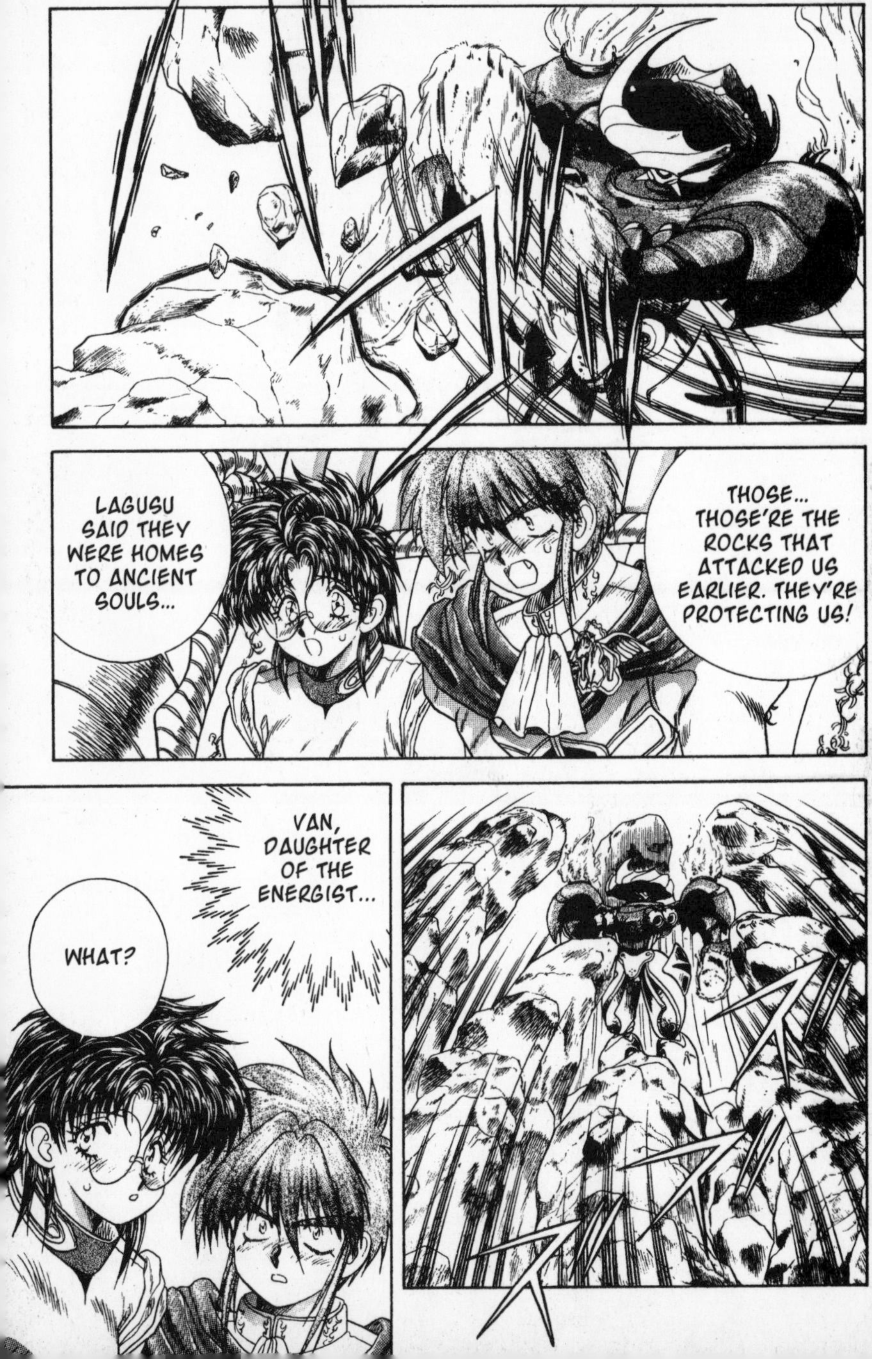
THOSE... THOSE'RE THE ROCKS THAT ATTACKED US EARLIER. THEY'RE PROTECTING US!
LAGUSU SAID THEY WERE HOMES TO ANCIENT SOULS...
VAN, DAUGHTER OF THE ENERGIST...
WHAT?

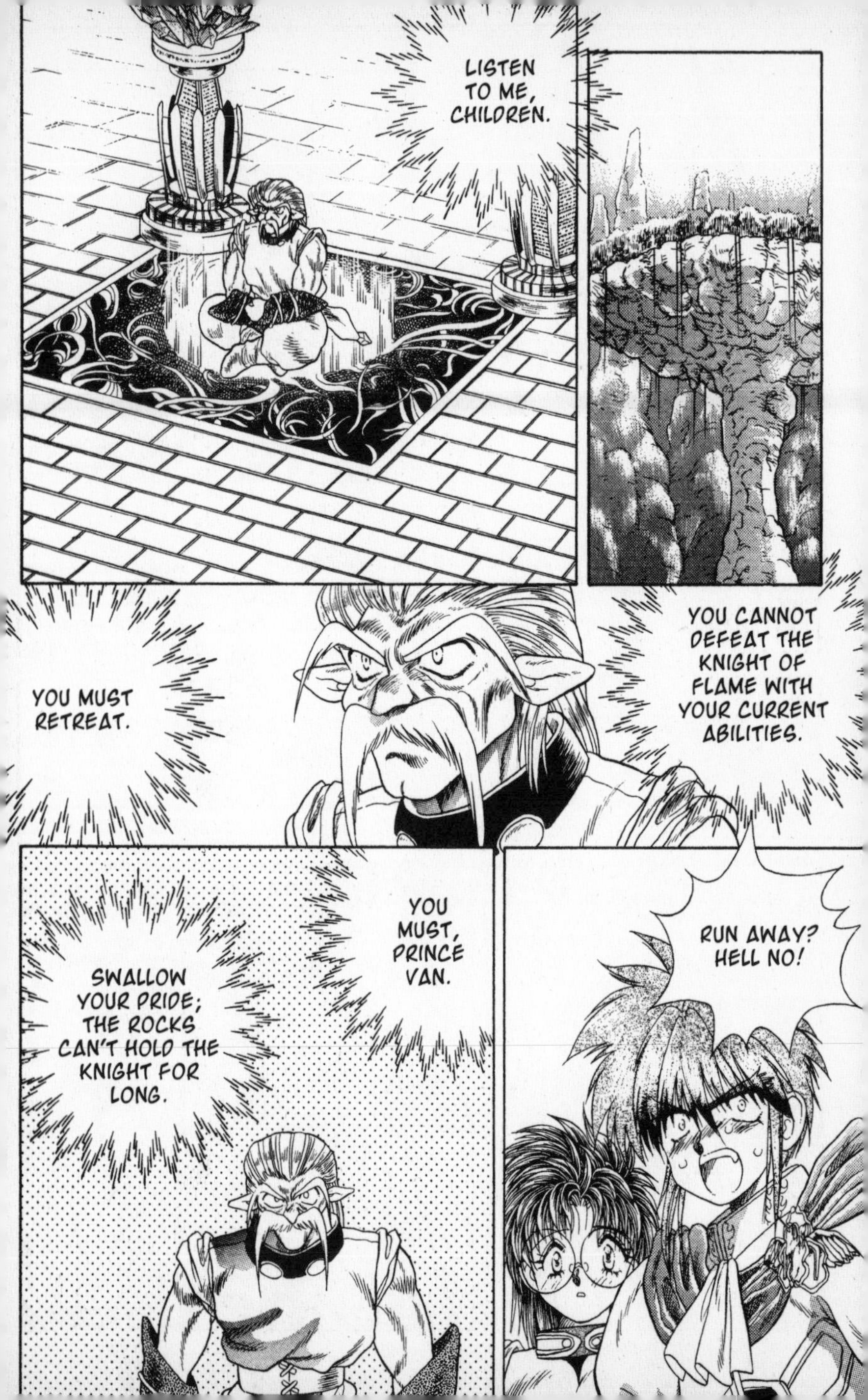
LISTEN TO ME, CHILDREN.
YOU CANNOT DEFEAT THE KNIGHT OF FLAME WITH YOUR CURRENT ABILITIES.
YOU MUST RETREAT.
RUN AWAY? HELL NO!
YOU MUST, PRINCE VAN.
SWALLOW YOUR PRIDE; THE ROCKS CAN'T HOLD THE KNIGHT FOR LONG.

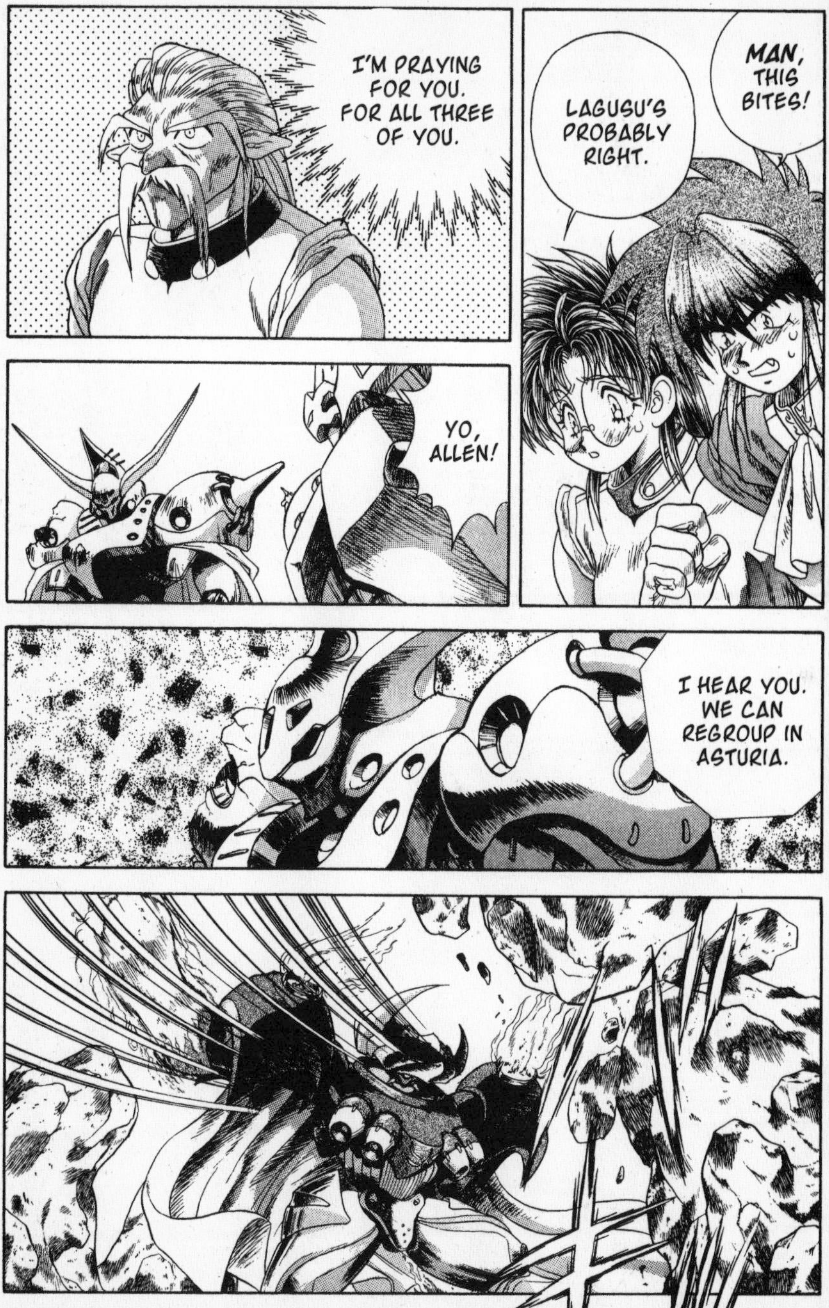
MAN, THIS BITES!
LAGUSU'S PROBABLY RIGHT.
I'M PRAYING FOR YOU. FOR ALL THREE OF YOU.
YO, ALLEN!
I HEAR YOU. WE CAN REGROUP IN ASTURIA.

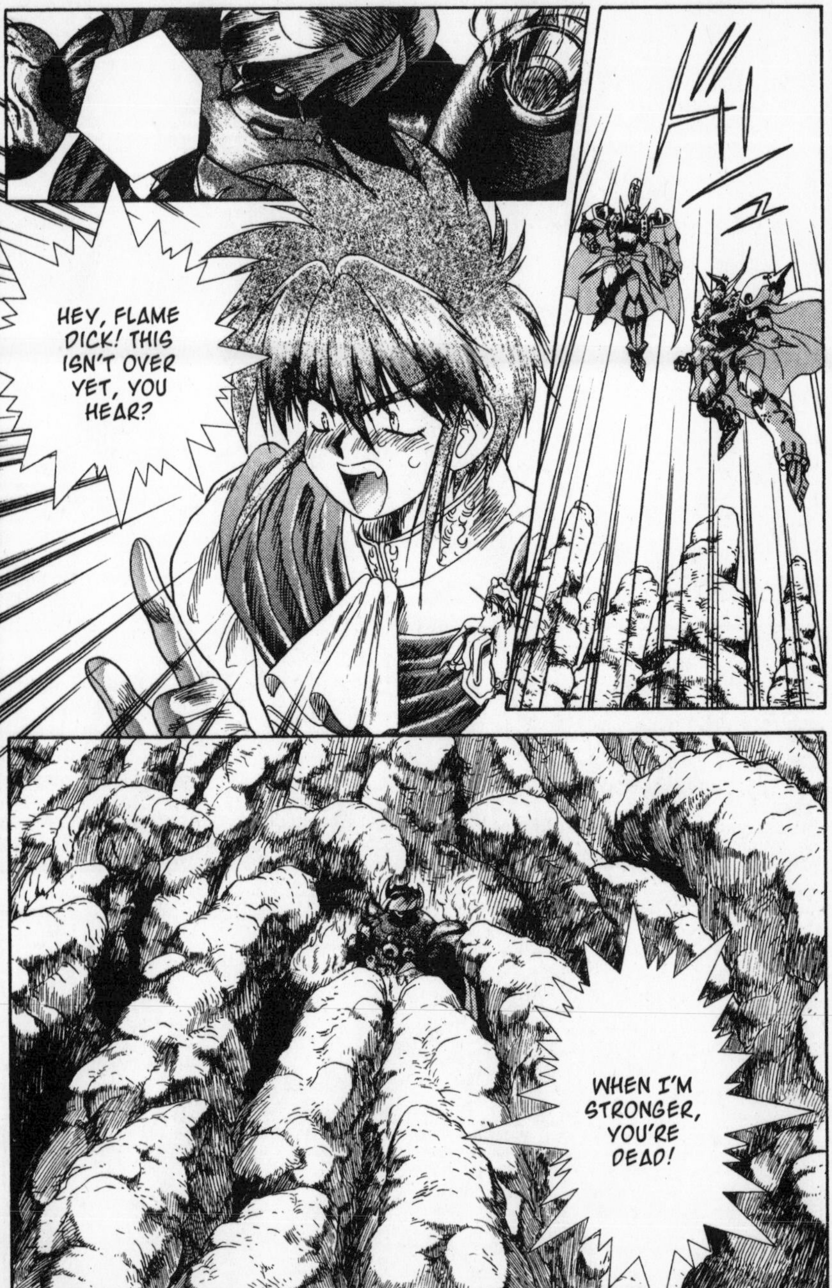
HEY, FLAME DICK! THIS ISN'T OVER YET, YOU HEAR?
WHEN I'M STRONGER, YOU'RE DEAD!

VISION 7:
FAMILIAR FACES

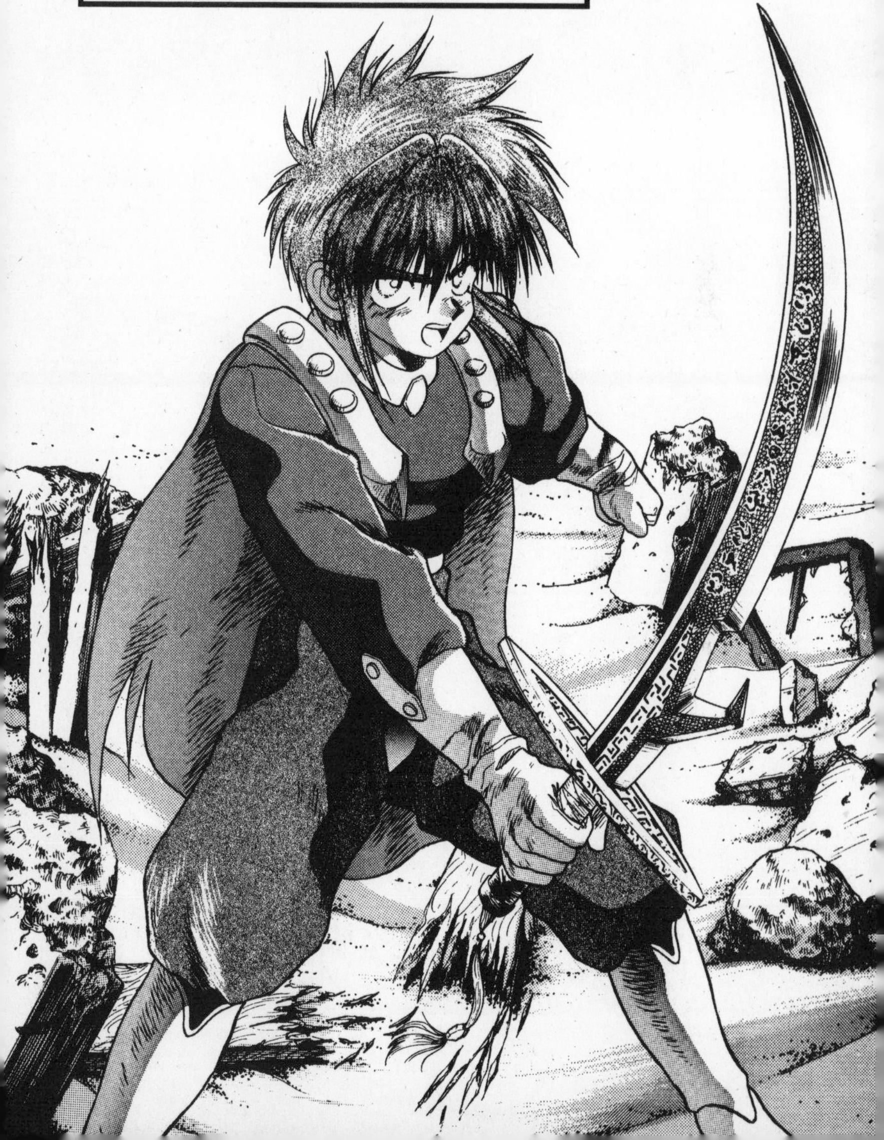

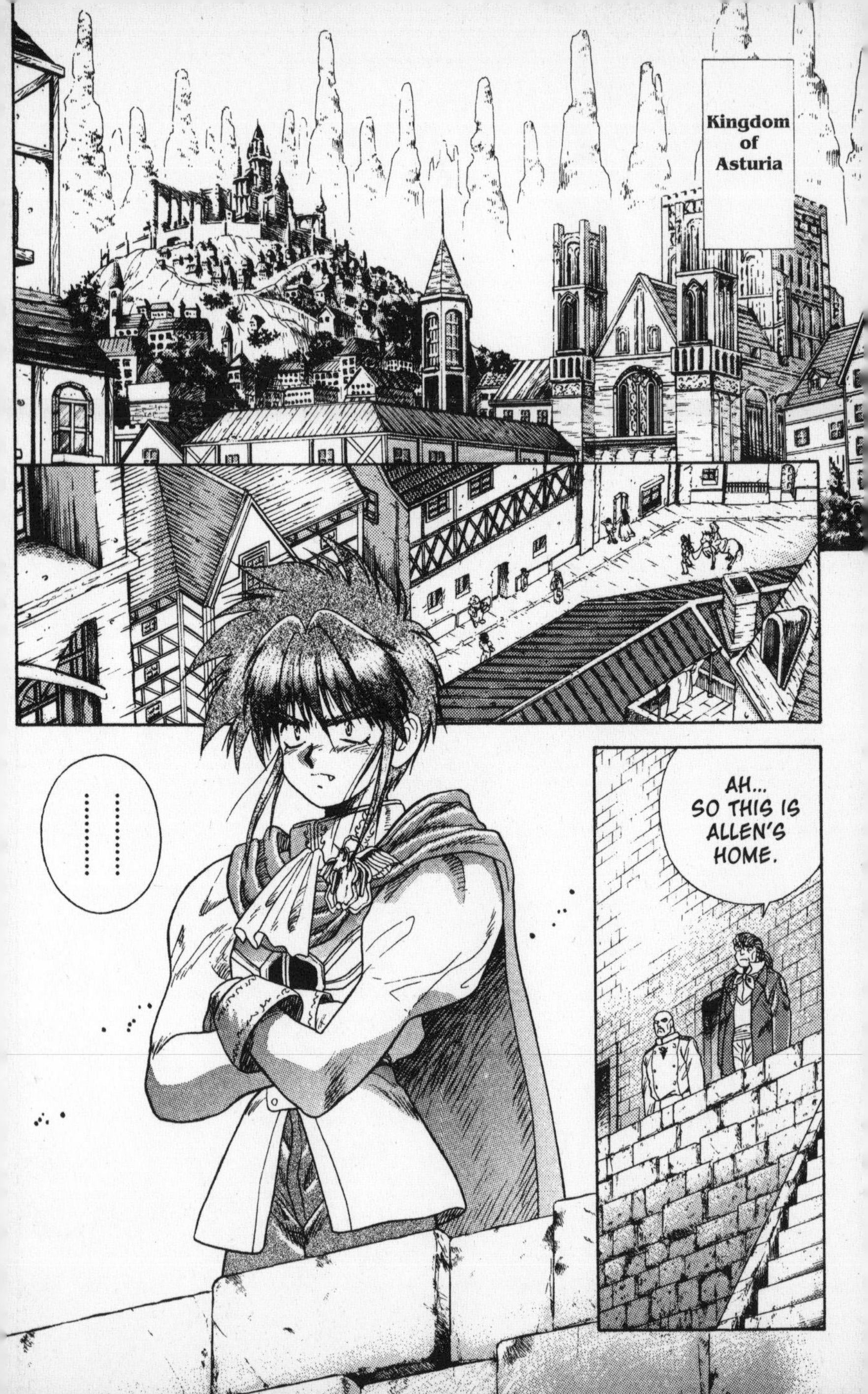
Kingdom of Asturia
AH... SO THIS IS ALLEN'S HOME.
......
......

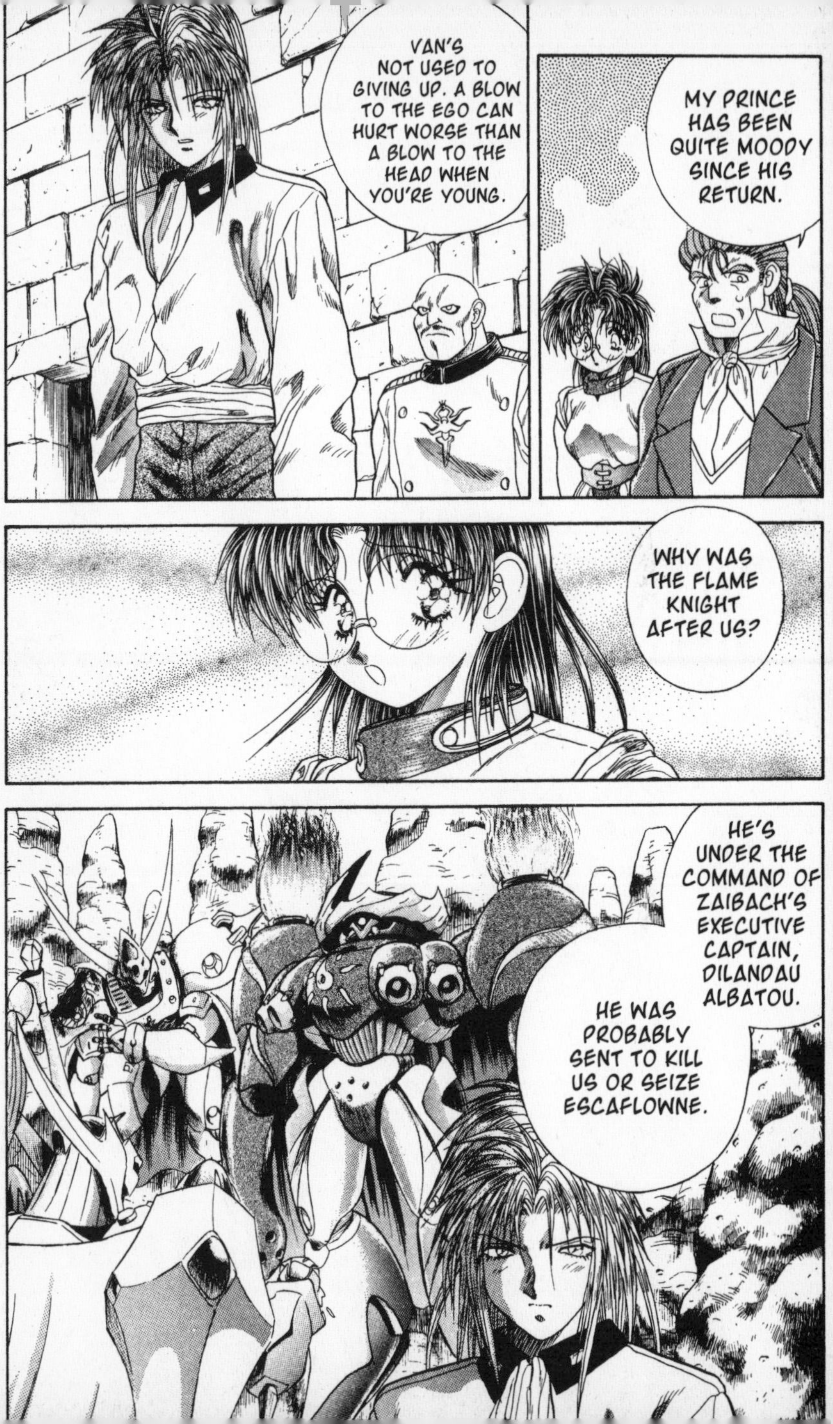
MY PRINCE HAS BEEN QUITE MOODY SINCE HIS RETURN.
VAN'S NOT USED TO GIVING UP. A BLOW TO THE EGO CAN HURT WORSE THAN A BLOW TO THE HEAD WHEN YOU'RE YOUNG.
WHY WAS THE FLAME KNIGHT AFTER US?
HE'S UNDER THE COMMAND OF ZAIBACH'S EXECUTIVE CAPTAIN, DILANDAU ALBATOU.
HE WAS PROBABLY SENT TO KILL US OR SEIZE ESCAFLOWNE.

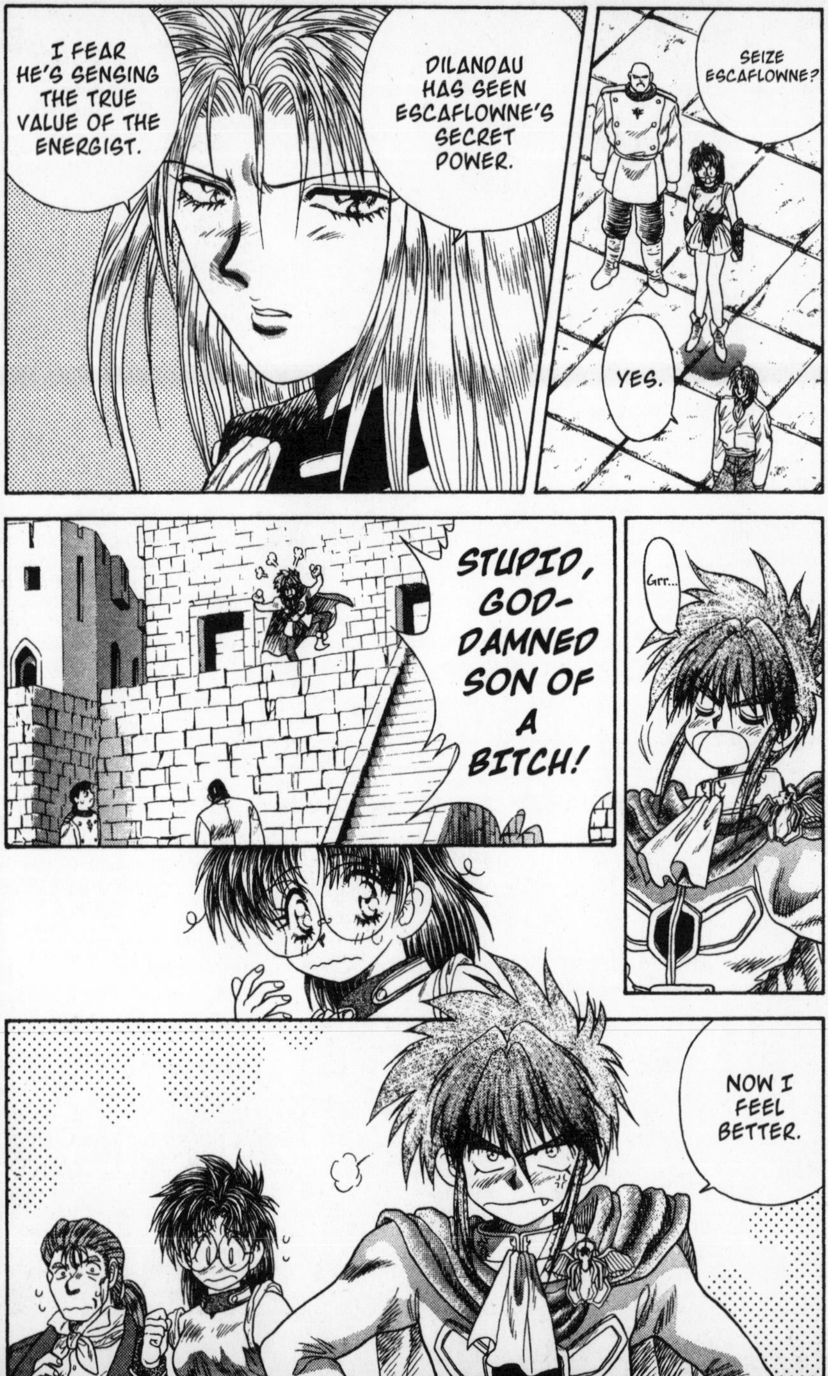
SEIZE ESCAFLOWNE?
YES.
DILANDAU HAS SEEN ESCAFLOWNE'S SECRET POWER.
I FEAR HE'S SENSING THE TRUE VALUE OF THE ENERGIST.
Grr...
STUPID, GOD-DAMNED SON OF A BITCH!
NOW I FEEL BETTER.

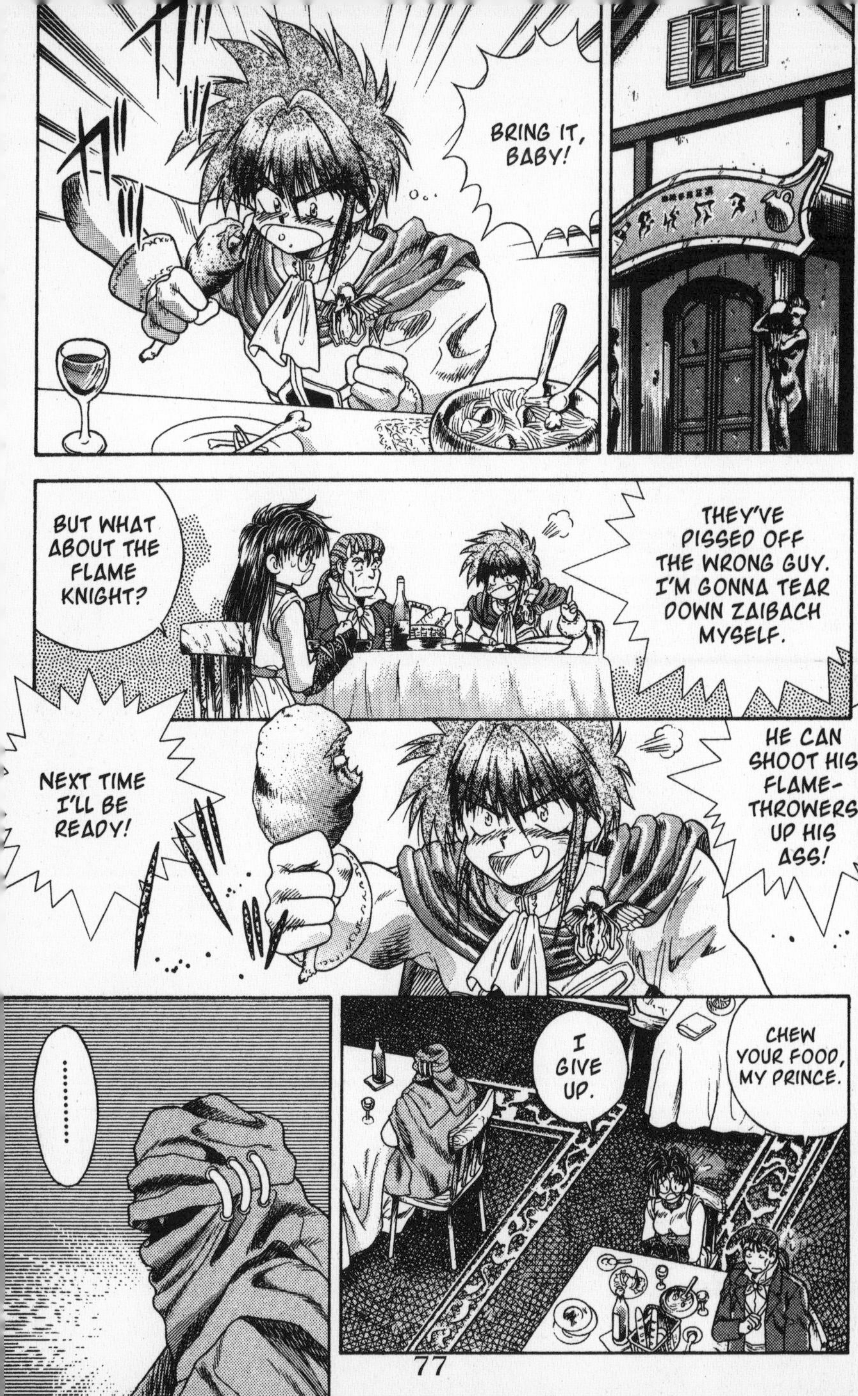
BRING IT, BABY!
THEY'VE PISSED OFF THE WRONG GUY. I'M GONNA TEAR DOWN ZAIBACH MYSELF.
BUT WHAT ABOUT THE FLAME KNIGHT?
HE CAN SHOOT HIS FLAME-THROWERS UP HIS ASS!
NEXT TIME I'LL BE READY!
CHEW YOUR FOOD, MY PRINCE.
I GIVE UP.
....

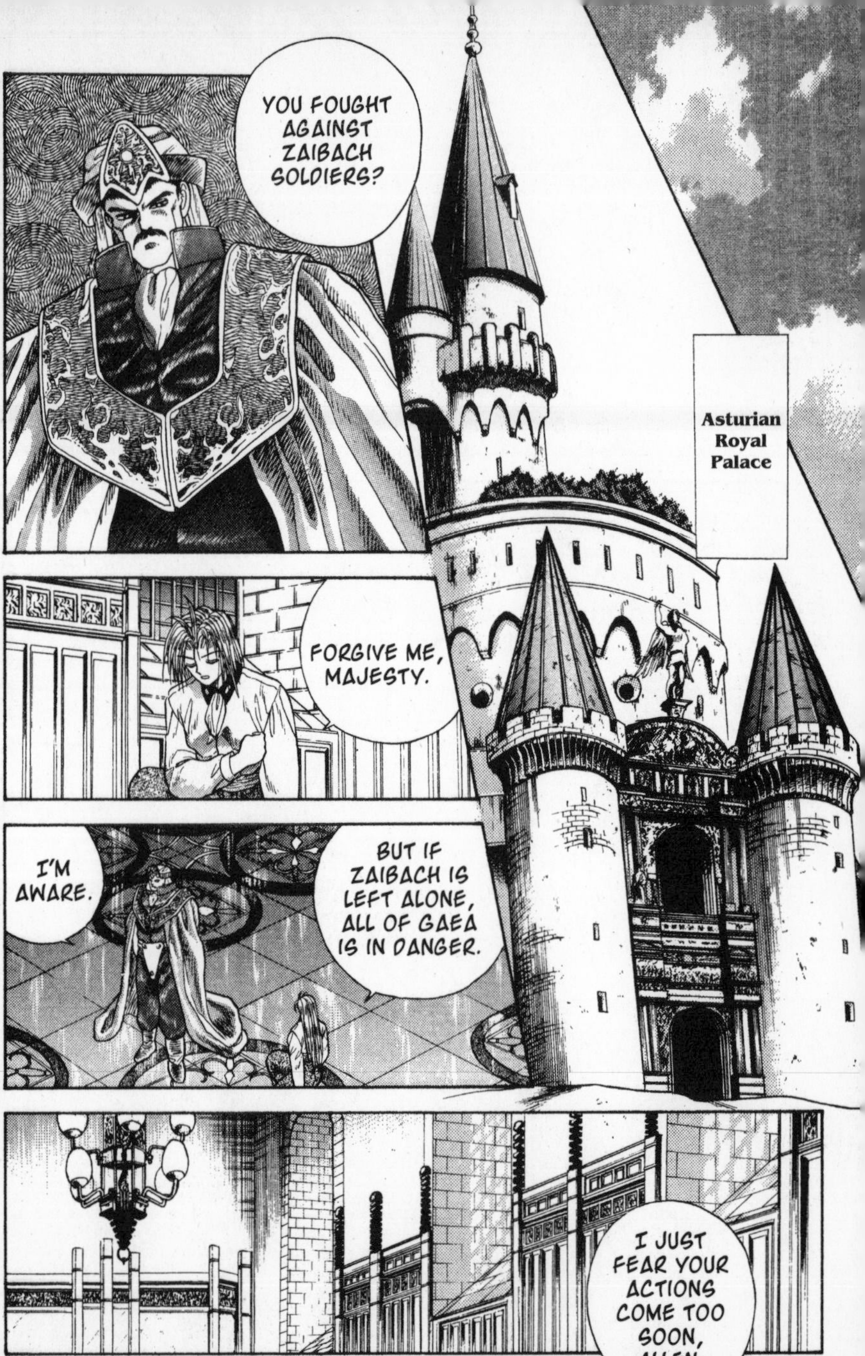
Asturian Royal Palace
YOU FOUGHT AGAINST ZAIBACH SOLDIERS?
FORGIVE ME, MAJESTY.
BUT IF ZAIBACH IS LEFT ALONE, ALL OF GAEA IS IN DANGER.
I'M AWARE.
I JUST FEAR YOUR ACTIONS COME TOO SOON, ALLEN.

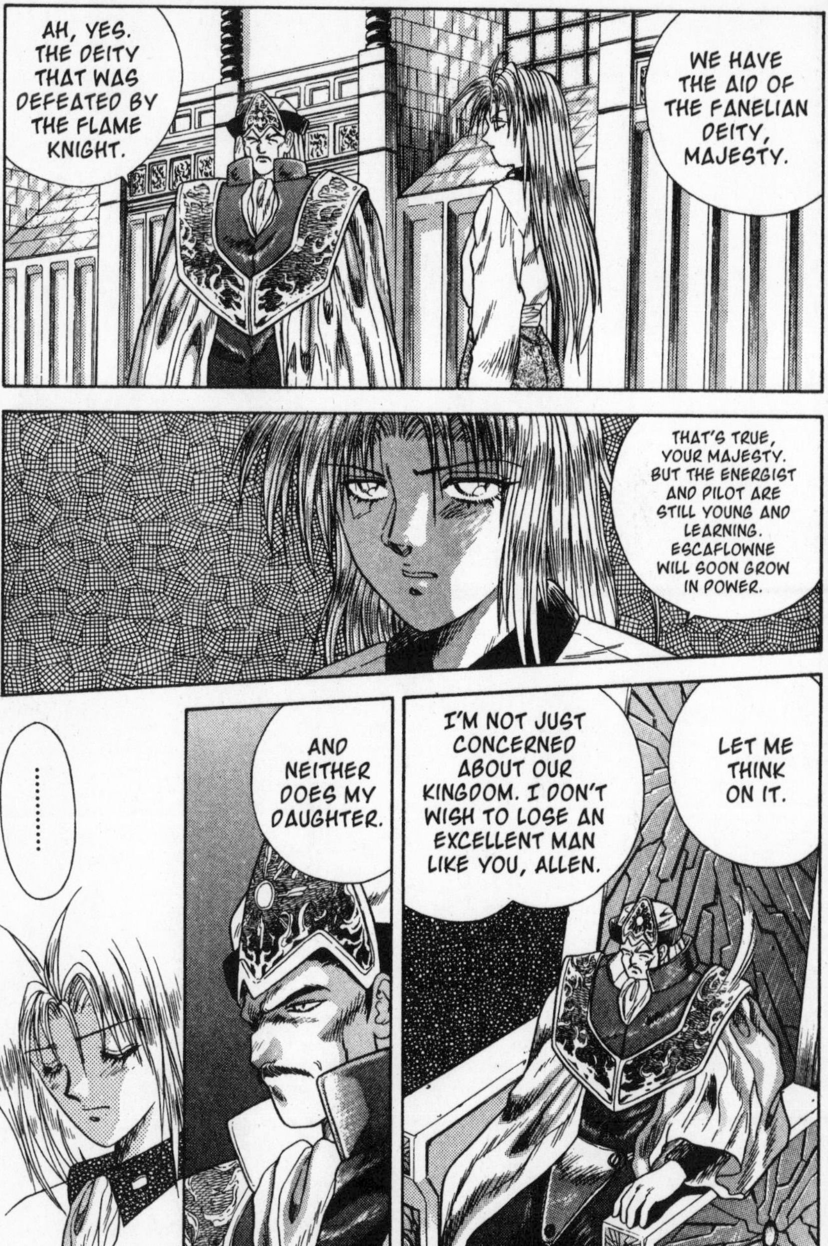
WE HAVE THE AID OF THE FANELIAN DEITY, MAJESTY.
AH, YES. THE DEITY THAT WAS DEFEATED BY THE FLAME KNIGHT.
THAT'S TRUE, YOUR MAJESTY. BUT THE ENERGIST AND PILOT ARE STILL YOUNG AND LEARNING. ESCAFLOWNE WILL SOON GROW IN POWER.
LET ME THINK ON IT.
I'M NOT JUST CONCERNED ABOUT OUR KINGDOM. I DON'T WISH TO LOSE AN EXCELLENT MAN LIKE YOU, ALLEN.
AND NEITHER DOES MY DAUGHTER.
....

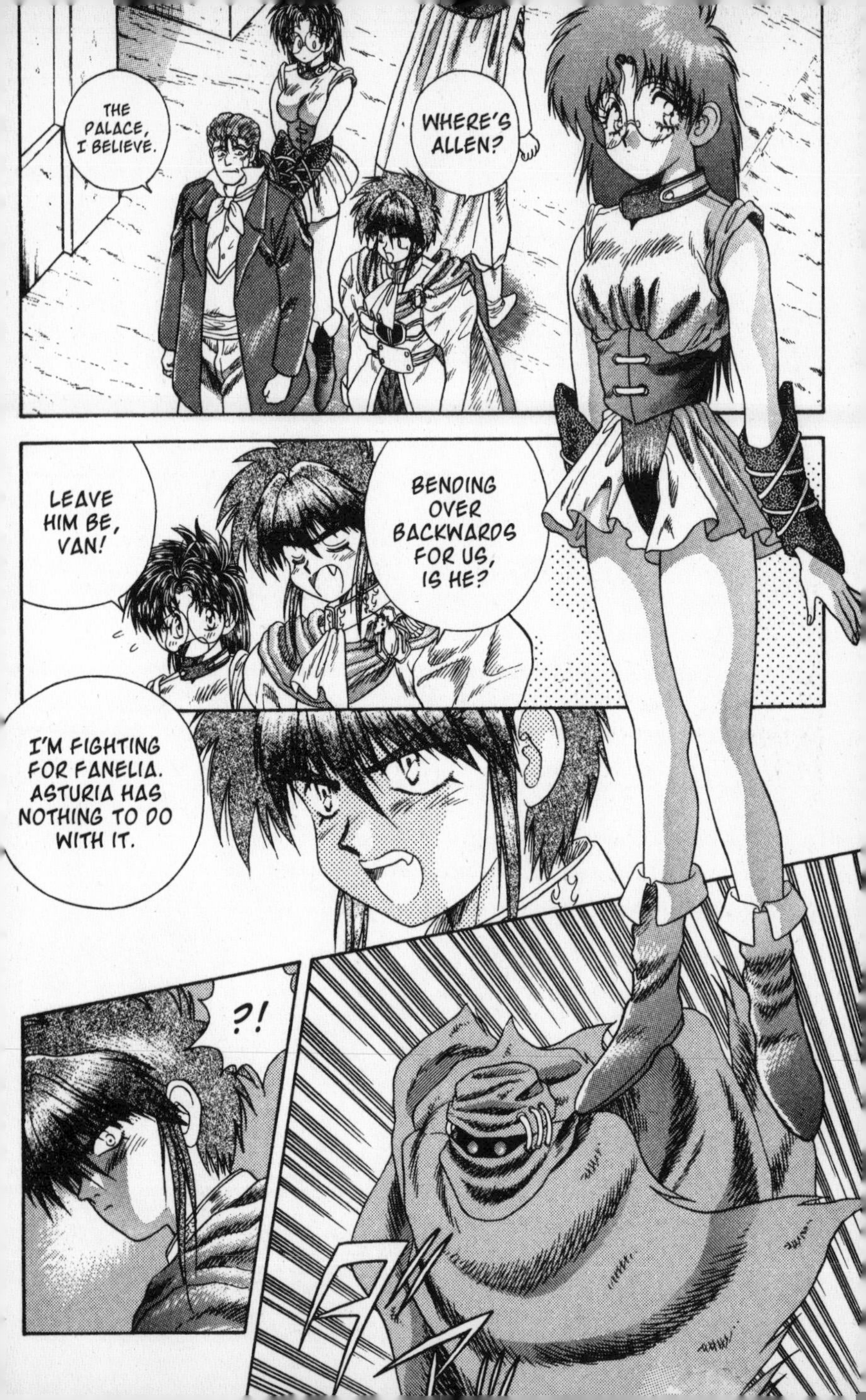
WHERE'S ALLEN?
THE PALACE, I BELIEVE.
BENDING OVER BACKWARDS FOR US, IS HE?
LEAVE HIM BE, VAN!
I'M FIGHTING FOR FANELIA. ASTURIA HAS NOTHING TO DO WITH IT.
?!

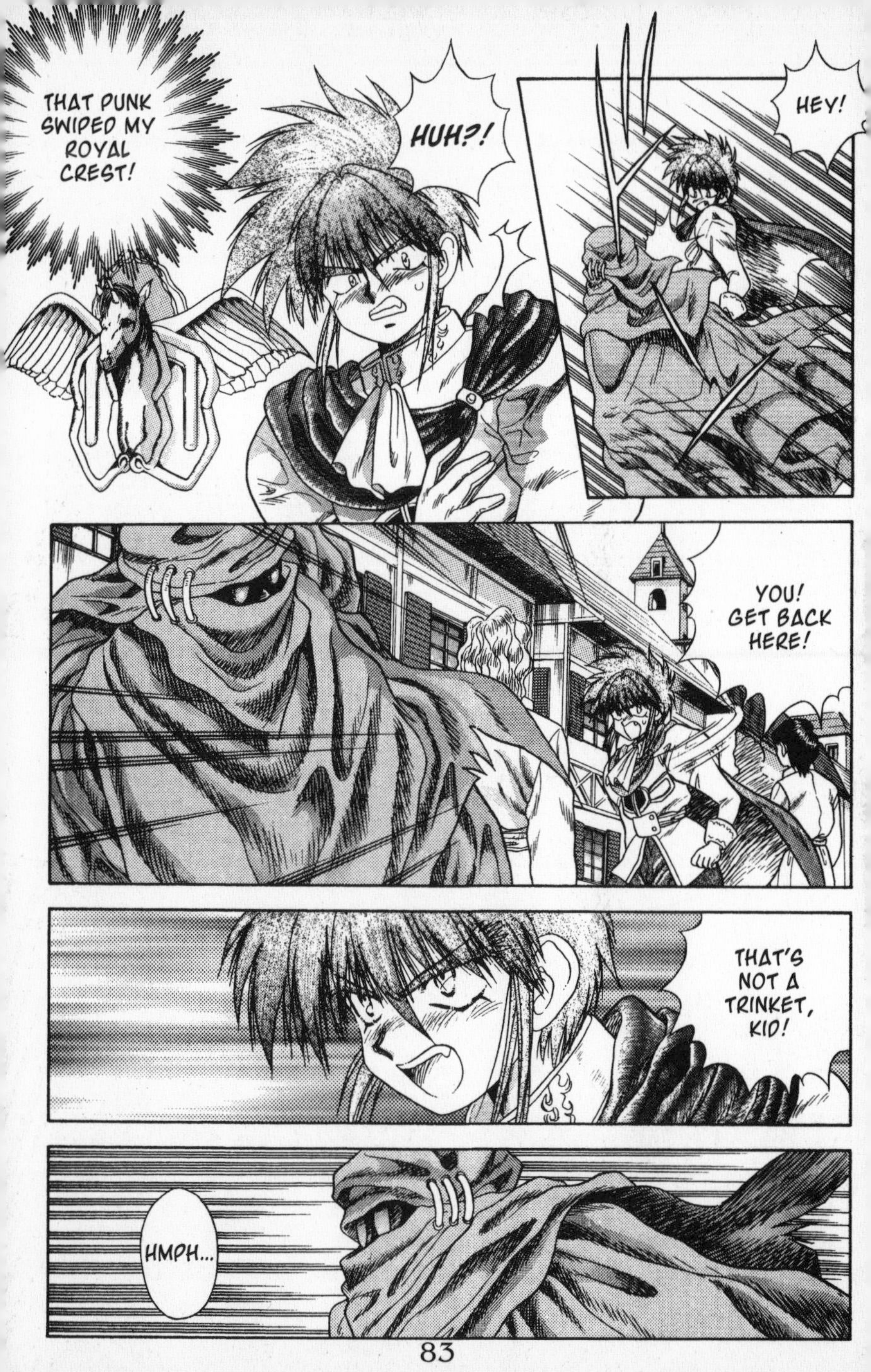
HEY!
HUH?!
THAT PUNK SWIPED MY ROYAL CREST!
YOU! GET BACK HERE!
THAT'S NOT A TRINKET, KID!
HMPH...

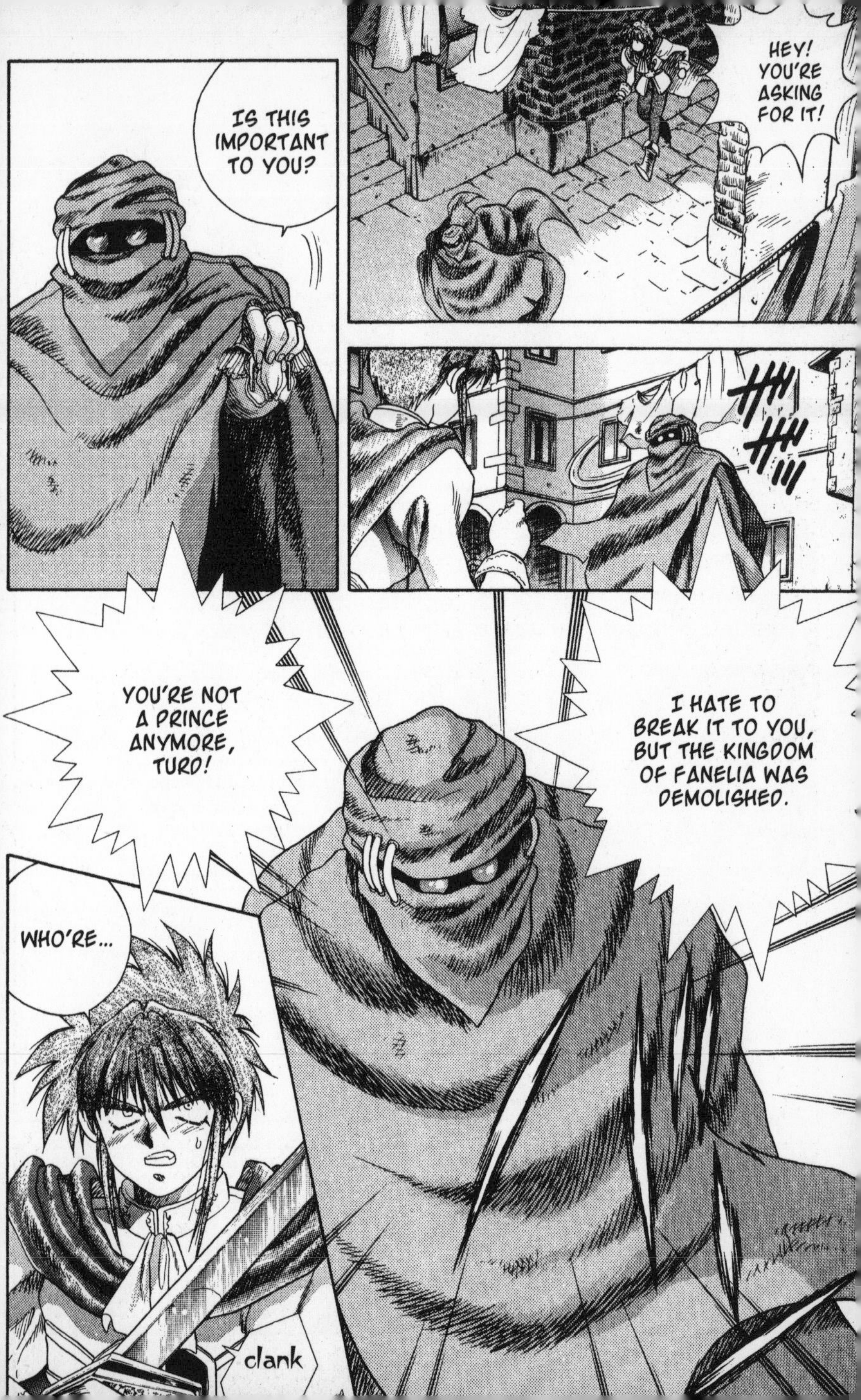
HEY! YOU'RE ASKING FOR IT!
IS THIS IMPORTANT TO YOU?
I HATE TO BREAK IT TO YOU, BUT THE KINGDOM OF FANELIA WAS DEMOLISHED.
YOU'RE NOT A PRINCE ANYMORE, TURD!
WHO'RE...
clank

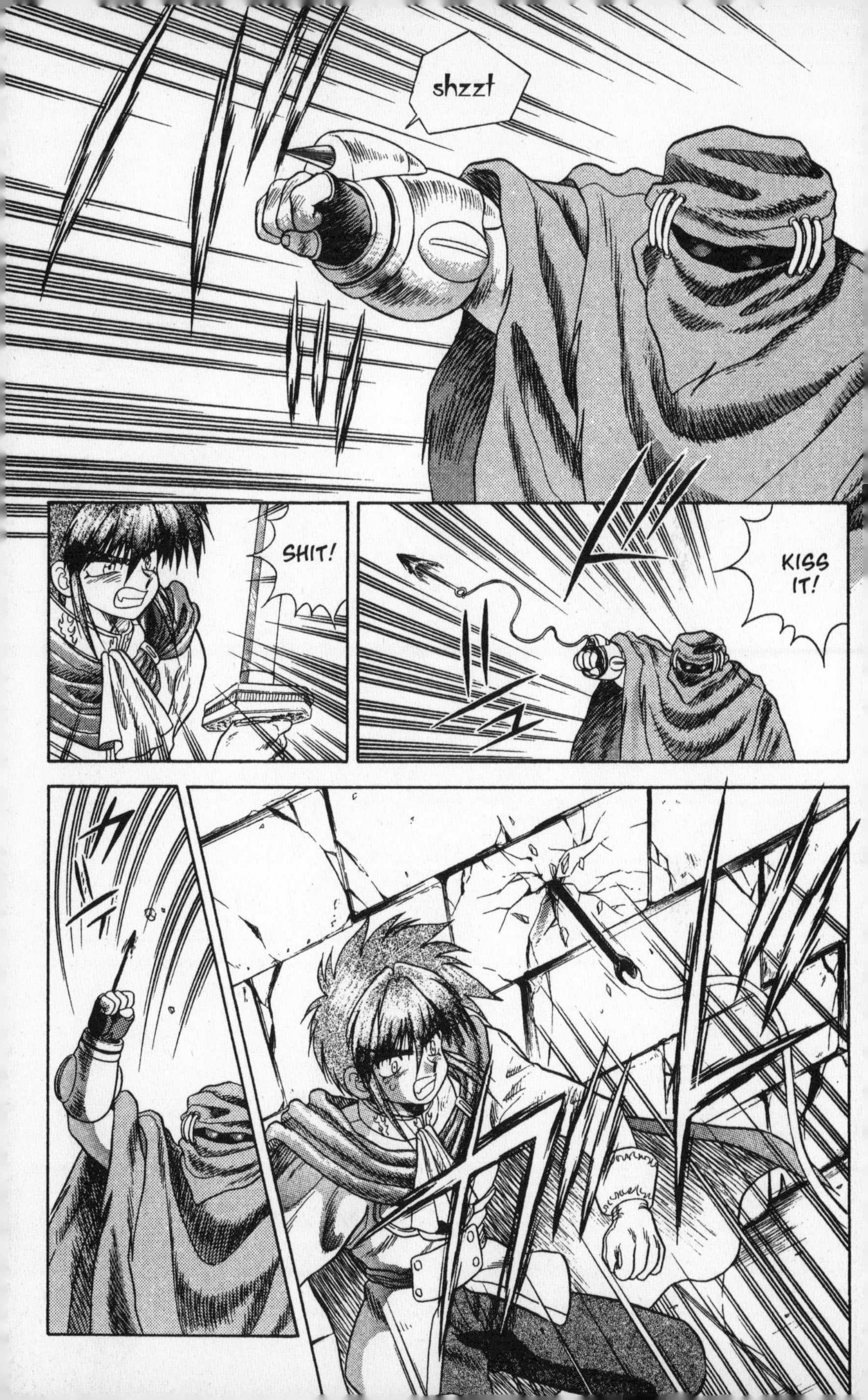
shzzt
KISS IT!
SHIT!

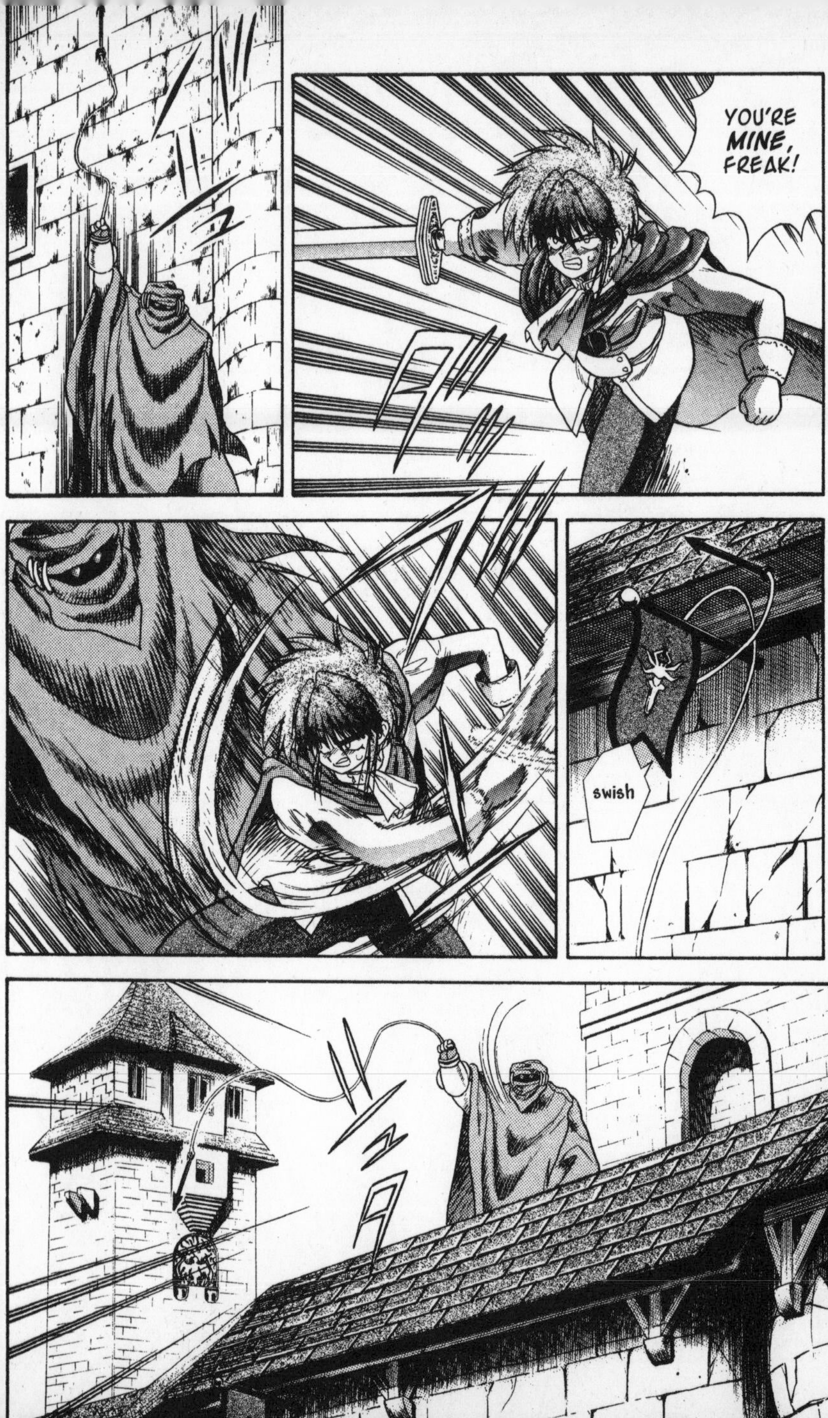
YOU'RE MINE, FREAK!
swish

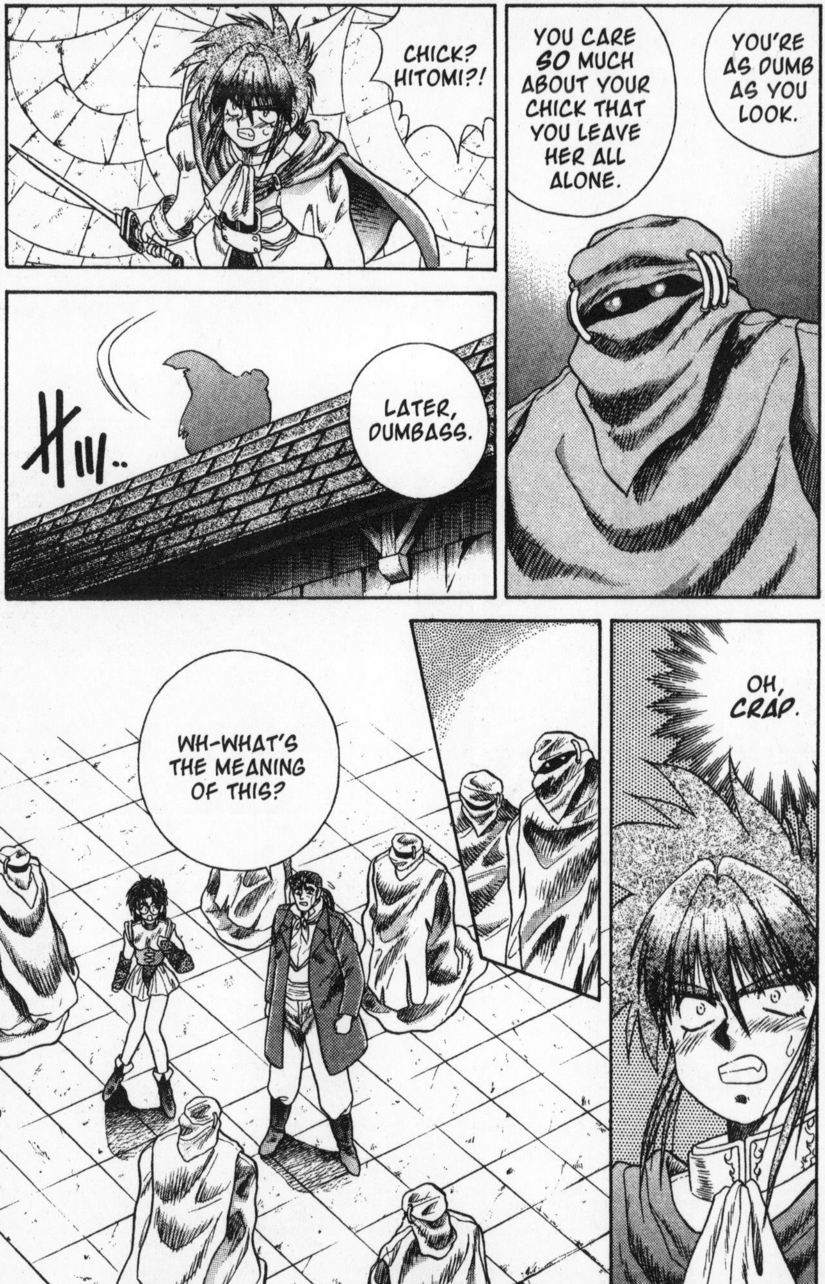
YOU CARE SO MUCH ABOUT YOUR CHICK THAT YOU LEAVE HER ALL ALONE.
YOU'RE AS DUMB AS YOU LOOK.
CHICK? HITOMI?!
LATER, DUMBASS.
OH, CRAP.
WH-WHAT'S THE MEANING OF THIS?

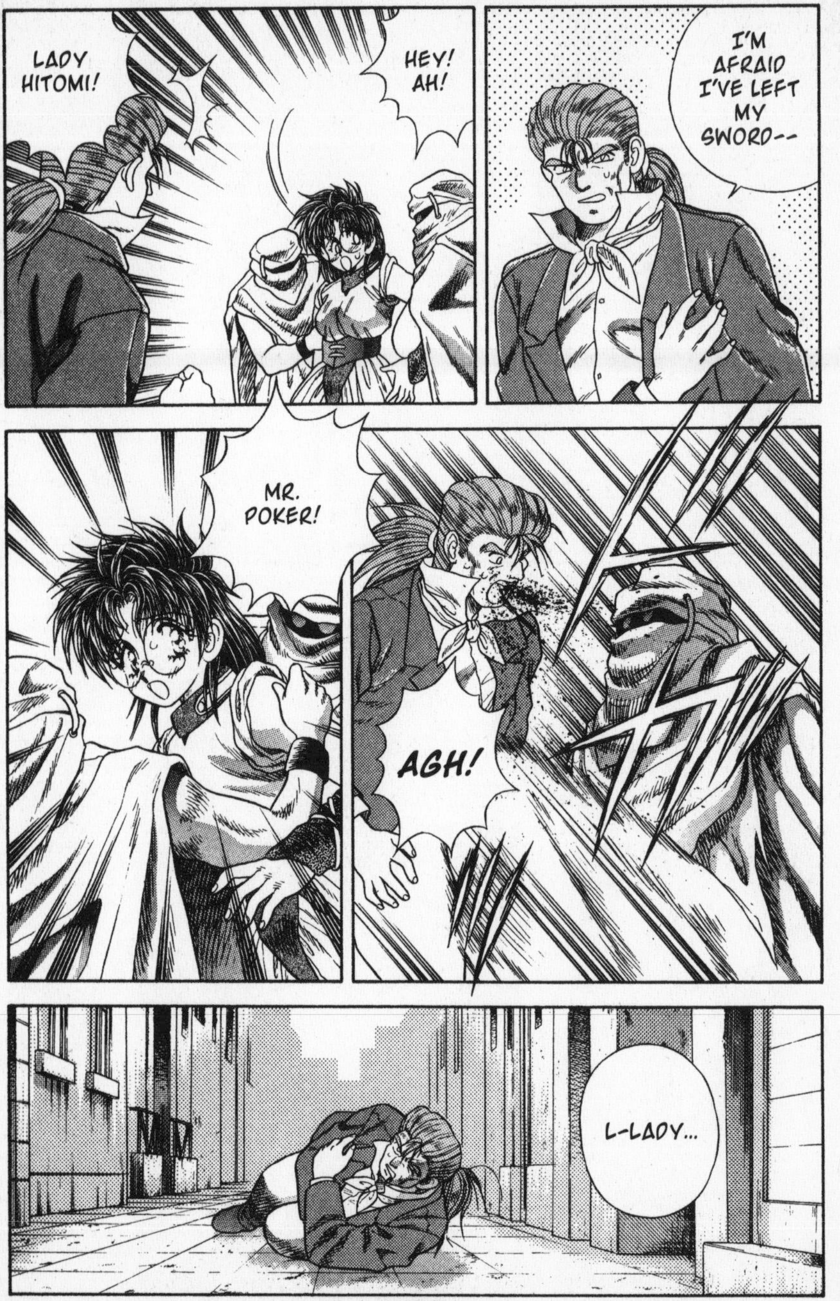
I'M AFRAID I'VE LEFT MY SWORD--
HEY! AH!
LADY HITOMI!
AGH!
MR. POKER!
L-LADY...

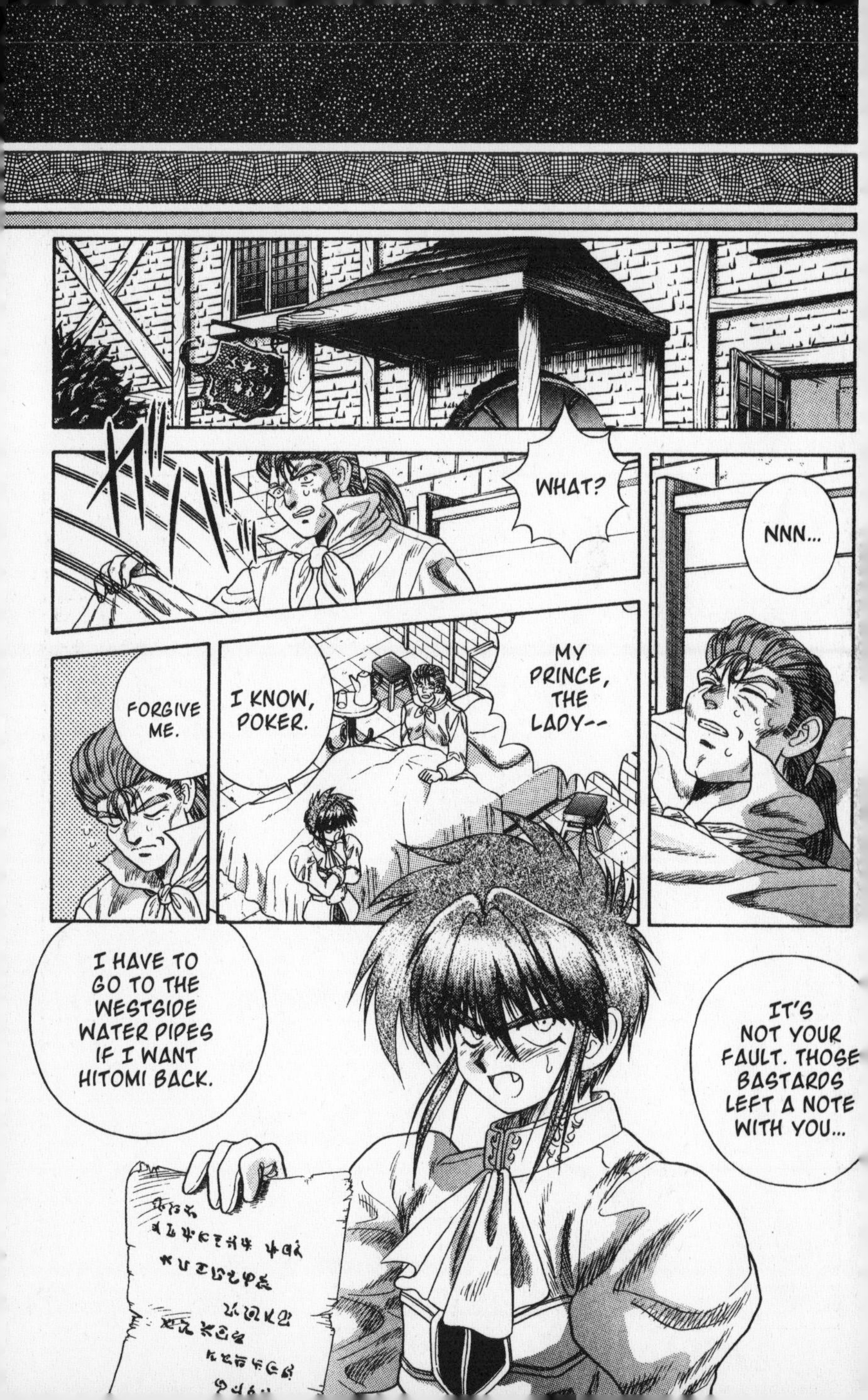
NNN...
WHAT?
MY PRINCE, THE LADY--
I KNOW, POKER.
FORGIVE ME.
IT'S NOT YOUR FAULT. THOSE BASTARDS LEFT A NOTE WITH YOU...
I HAVE TO GO TO THE WESTSIDE WATER PIPES IF I WANT HITOMI BACK.

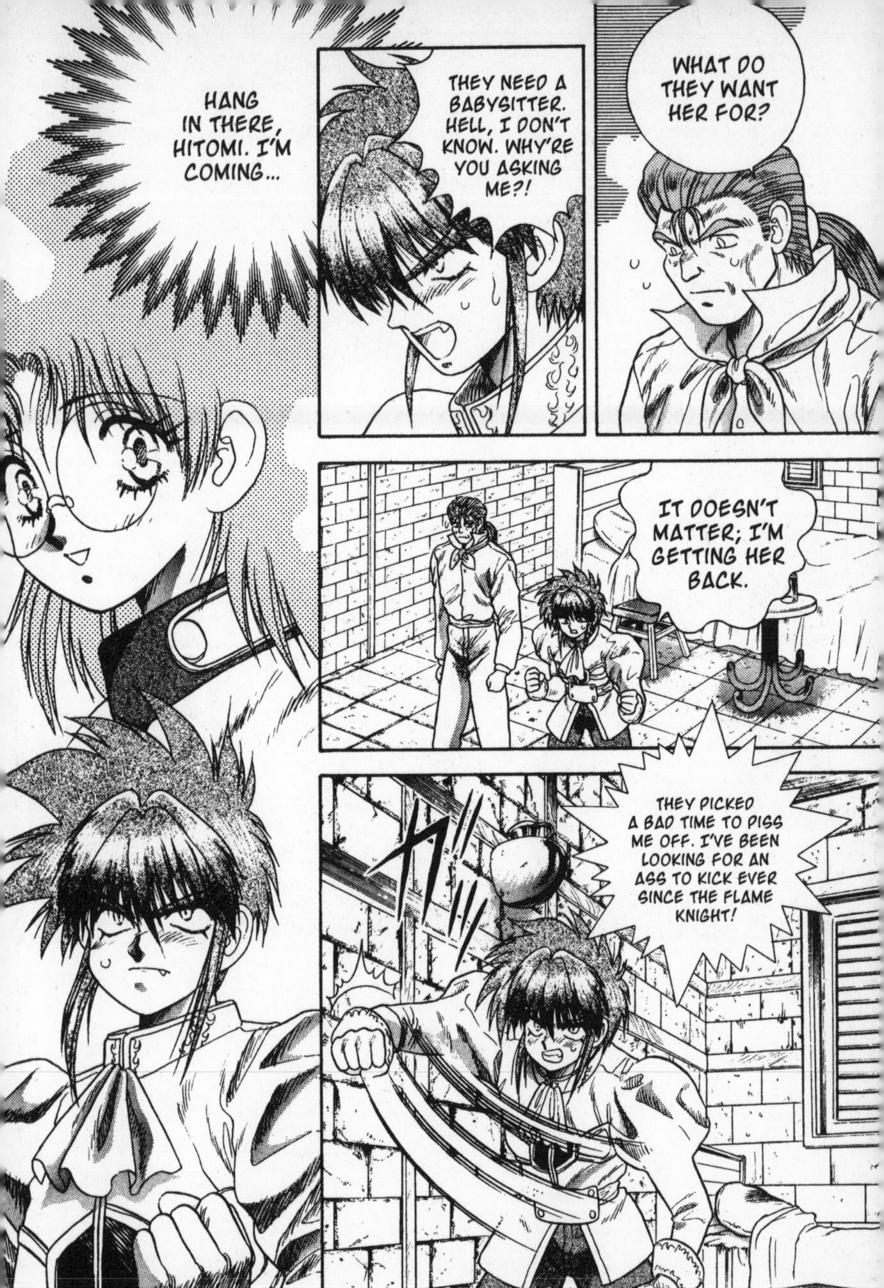
WHAT DO THEY WANT HER FOR?
THEY NEED A BABYSITTER. HELL, I DON'T KNOW. WHY'RE YOU ASKING ME?!
IT DOESN'T MATTER; I'M GETTING HER BACK.
THEY PICKED A BAD TIME TO PISS ME OFF. I'VE BEEN LOOKING FOR AN ASS TO KICK EVER SINCE THE FLAME KNIGHT!
HANG IN THERE, HITOMI. I'M COMING...

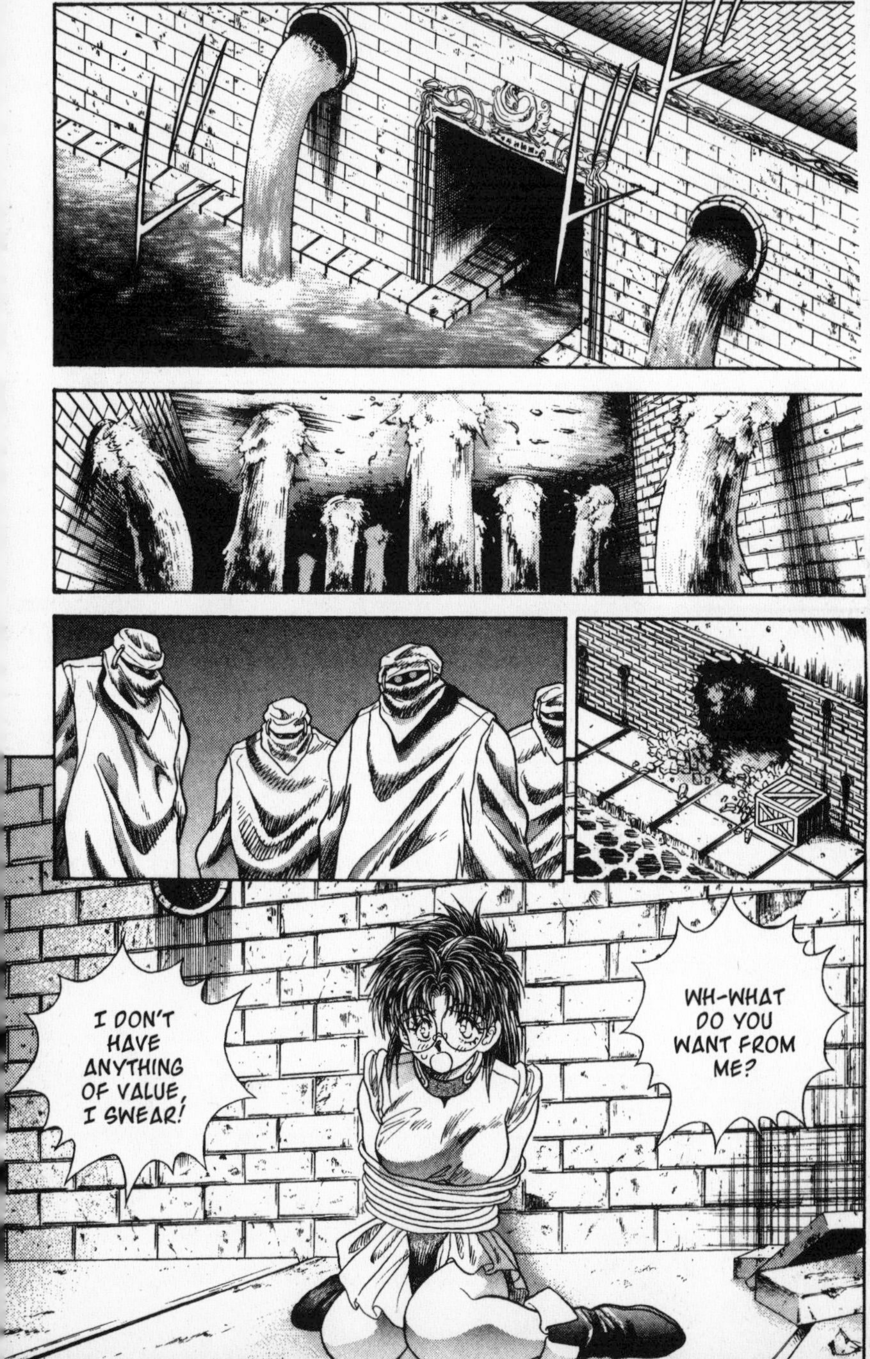
WH-WHAT DO YOU WANT FROM ME?
I DON'T HAVE ANYTHING OF VALUE, I SWEAR!

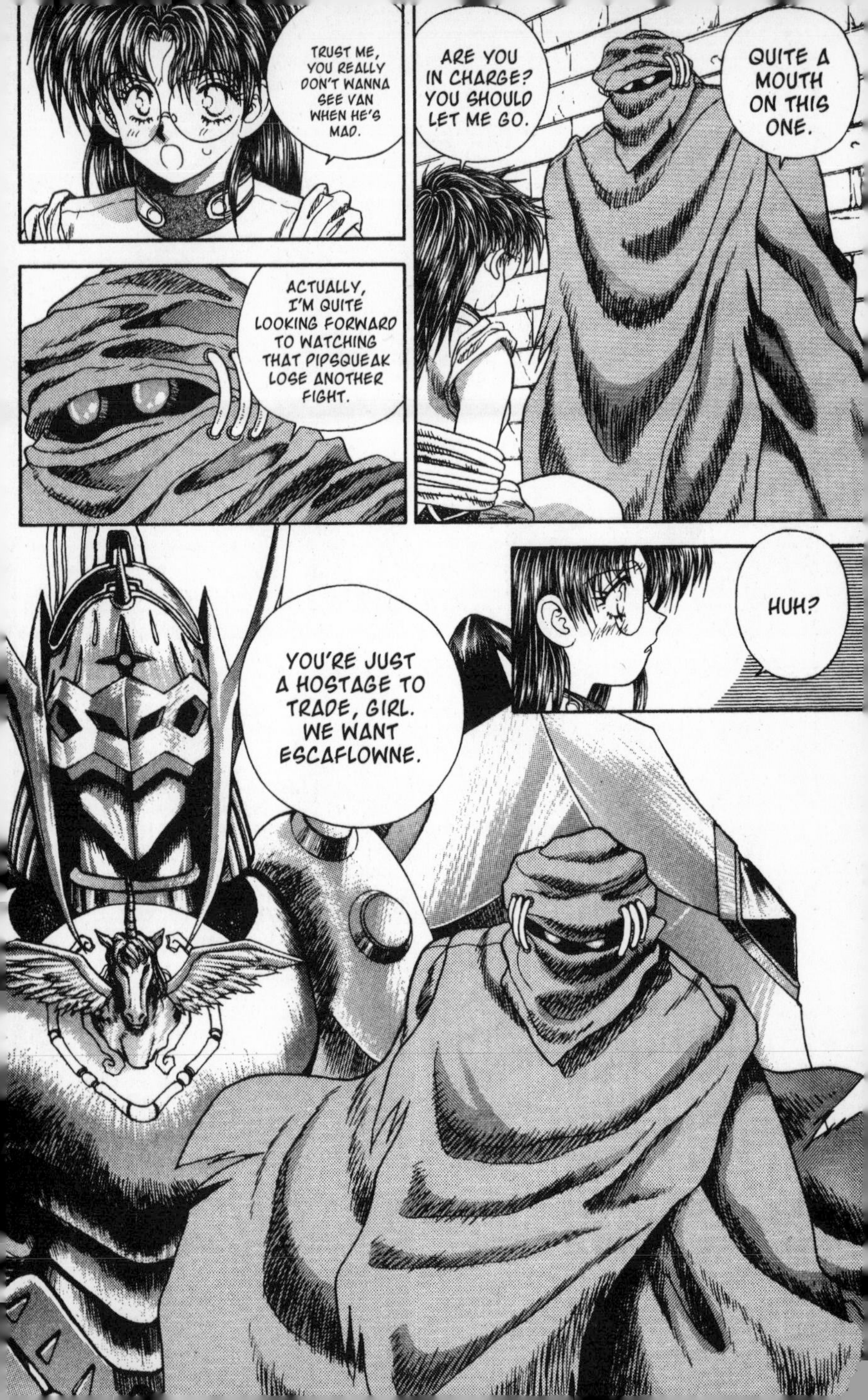
QUITE A MOUTH ON THIS ONE.
ARE YOU IN CHARGE? YOU SHOULD LET ME GO.
TRUST ME, YOU REALLY DON'T WANNA SEE VAN WHEN HE'S MAD.
ACTUALLY, I'M QUITE LOOKING FORWARD TO WATCHING THAT PIPSQUEAK LOSE ANOTHER FIGHT.
HUH?
YOU'RE JUST A HOSTAGE TO TRADE, GIRL. WE WANT ESCAFLOWNE.

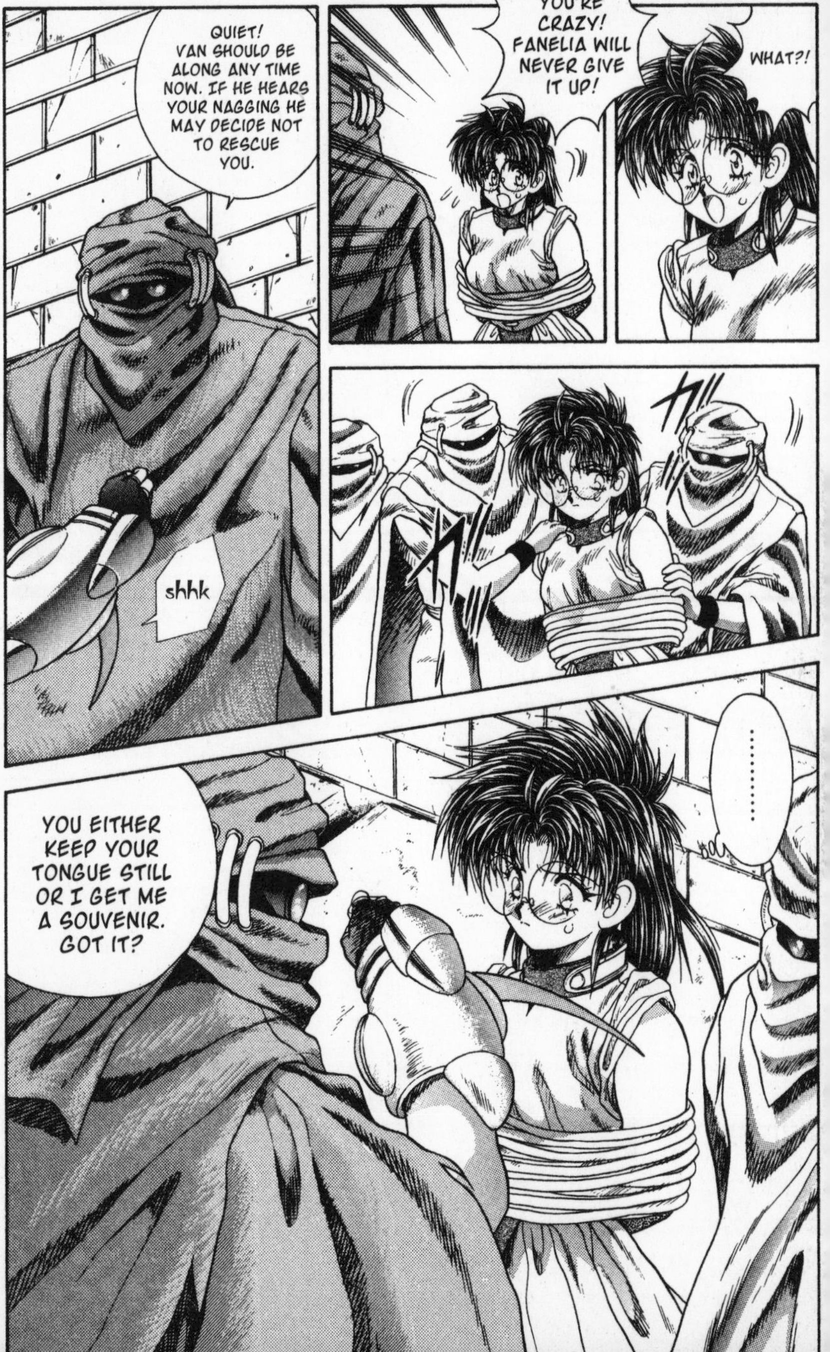
WHAT?!
YOU'RE CRAZY! FANELIA WILL NEVER GIVE IT UP!
QUIET! VAN SHOULD BE ALONG ANY TIME NOW. IF HE HEARS YOUR NAGGING HE MAY DECIDE NOT TO RESCUE YOU.
shhk
......
YOU EITHER KEEP YOUR TONGUE STILL OR I GET ME A SOUVENIR. GOT IT?

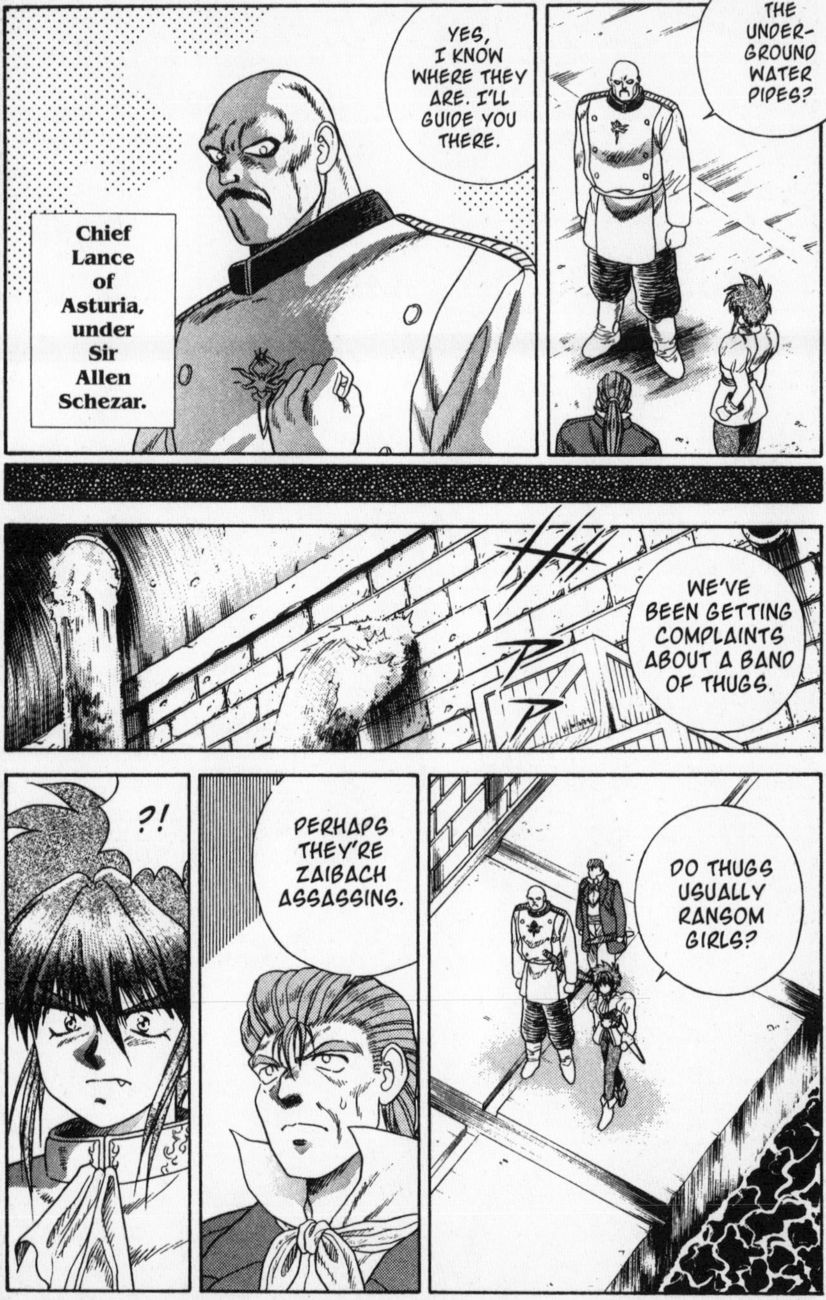
THE UNDER-GROUND WATER PIPES?
YES, I KNOW WHERE THEY ARE. I'LL GUIDE YOU THERE.
Chief Lance of Asturia, under Sir Allen Schezar.
WE'VE BEEN GETTING COMPLAINTS ABOUT A BAND OF THUGS.
DO THUGS USUALLY RANSOM GIRLS?
PERHAPS THEY'RE ZAIBACH ASSASSINS.
?!

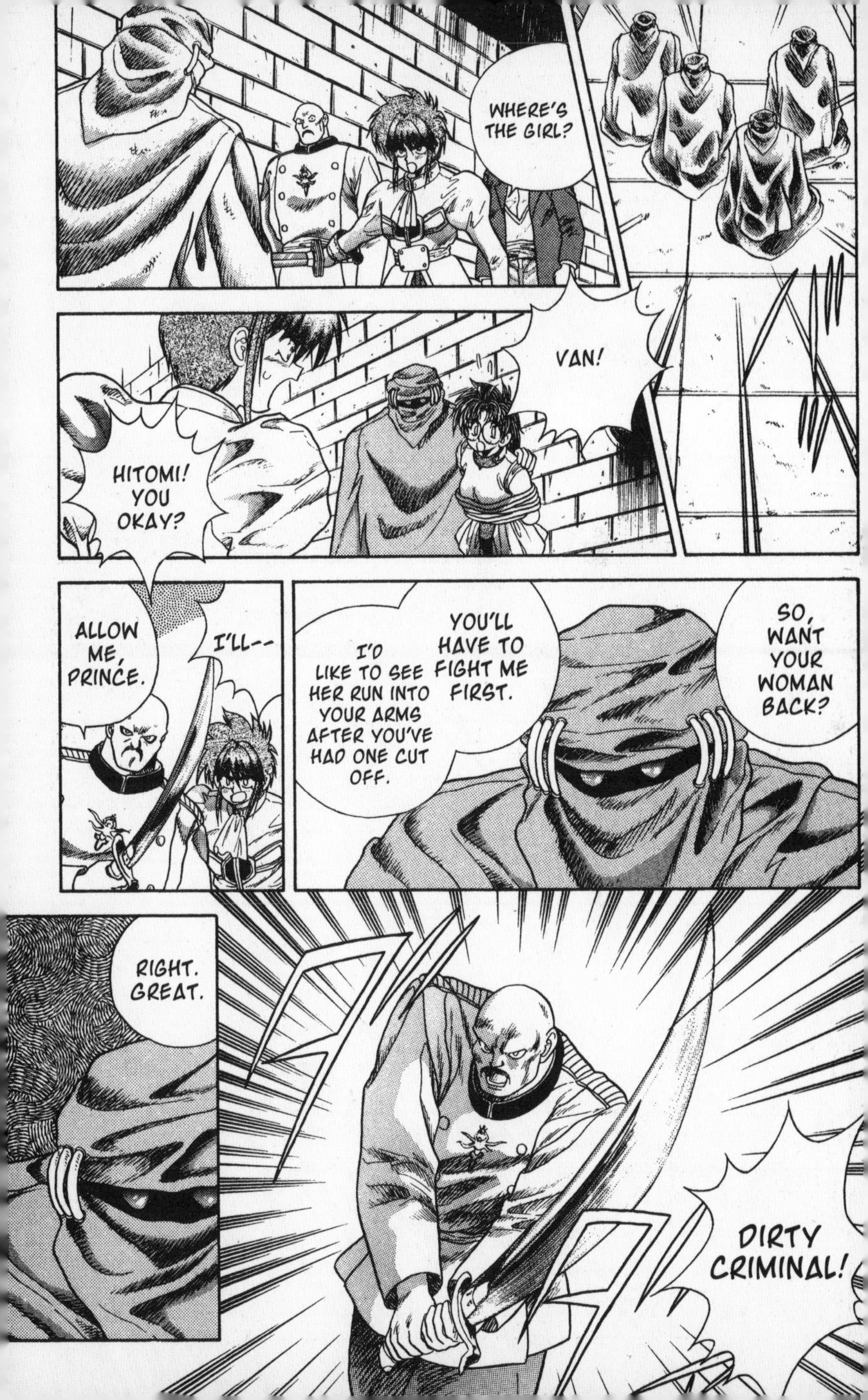
WHERE'S THE GIRL?
VAN!
HITOMI! YOU OKAY?
SO, WANT YOUR WOMAN BACK?
YOU'LL HAVE TO FIGHT ME FIRST.
I'D LIKE TO SEE HER RUN INTO YOUR ARMS AFTER YOU'VE HAD ONE CUT OFF.
I'LL--
ALLOW ME, PRINCE.
DIRTY CRIMINAL!
RIGHT. GREAT.

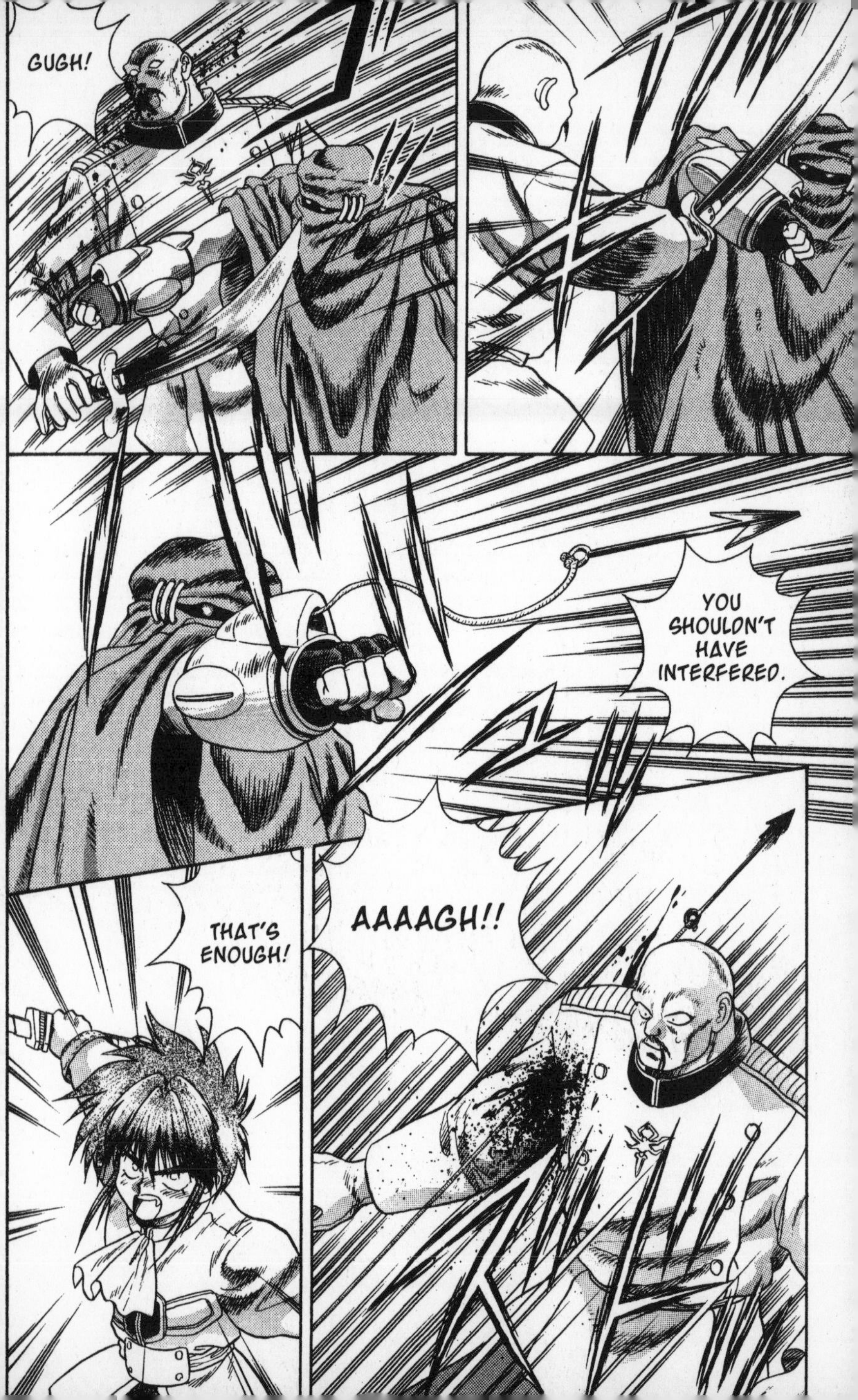
GUGH!
YOU SHOULDN'T HAVE INTERFERED.
AAAAGH!!
THAT'S ENOUGH!

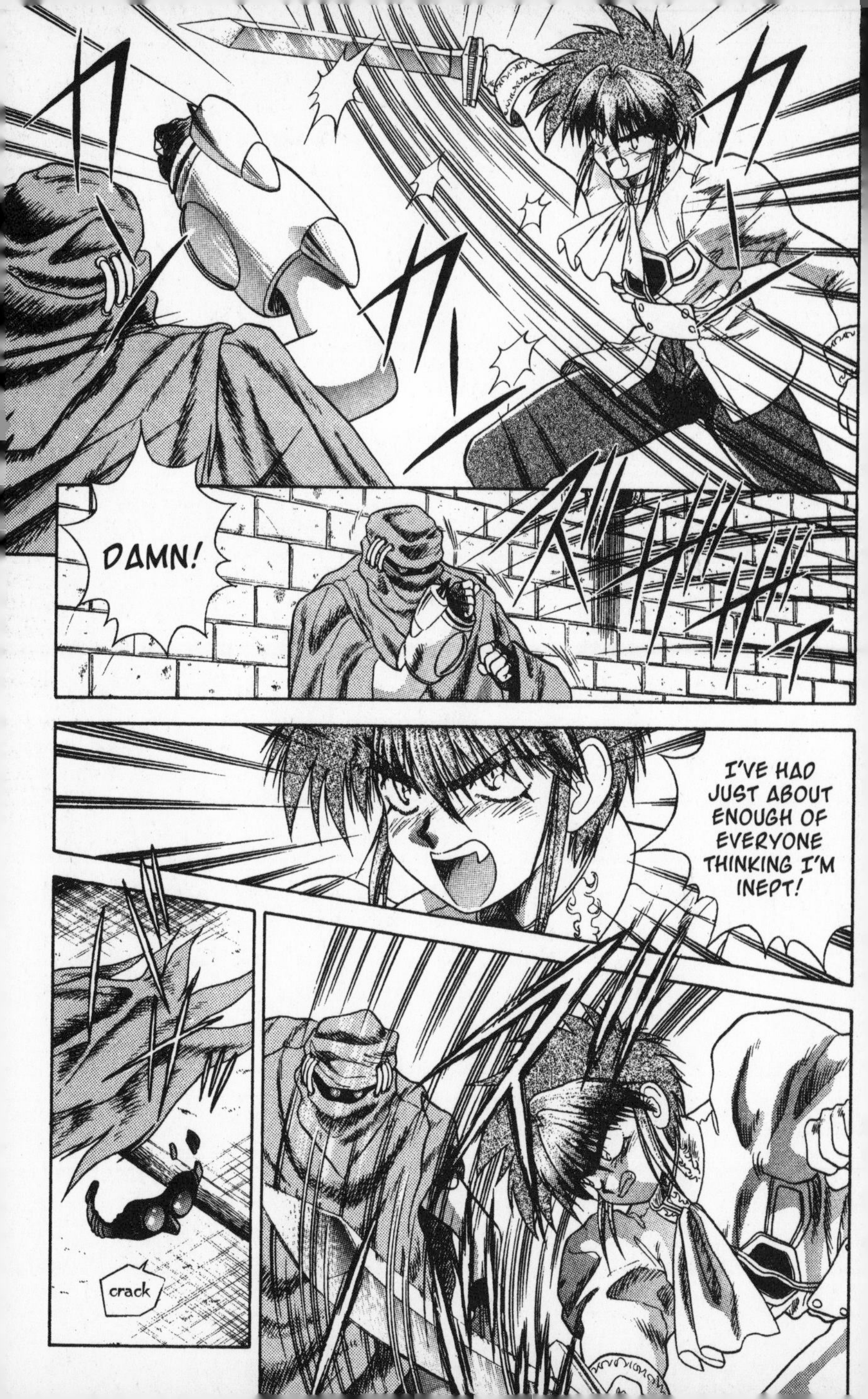
DAMN!
I'VE HAD JUST ABOUT ENOUGH OF EVERYONE THINKING I'M INEPT!
crack

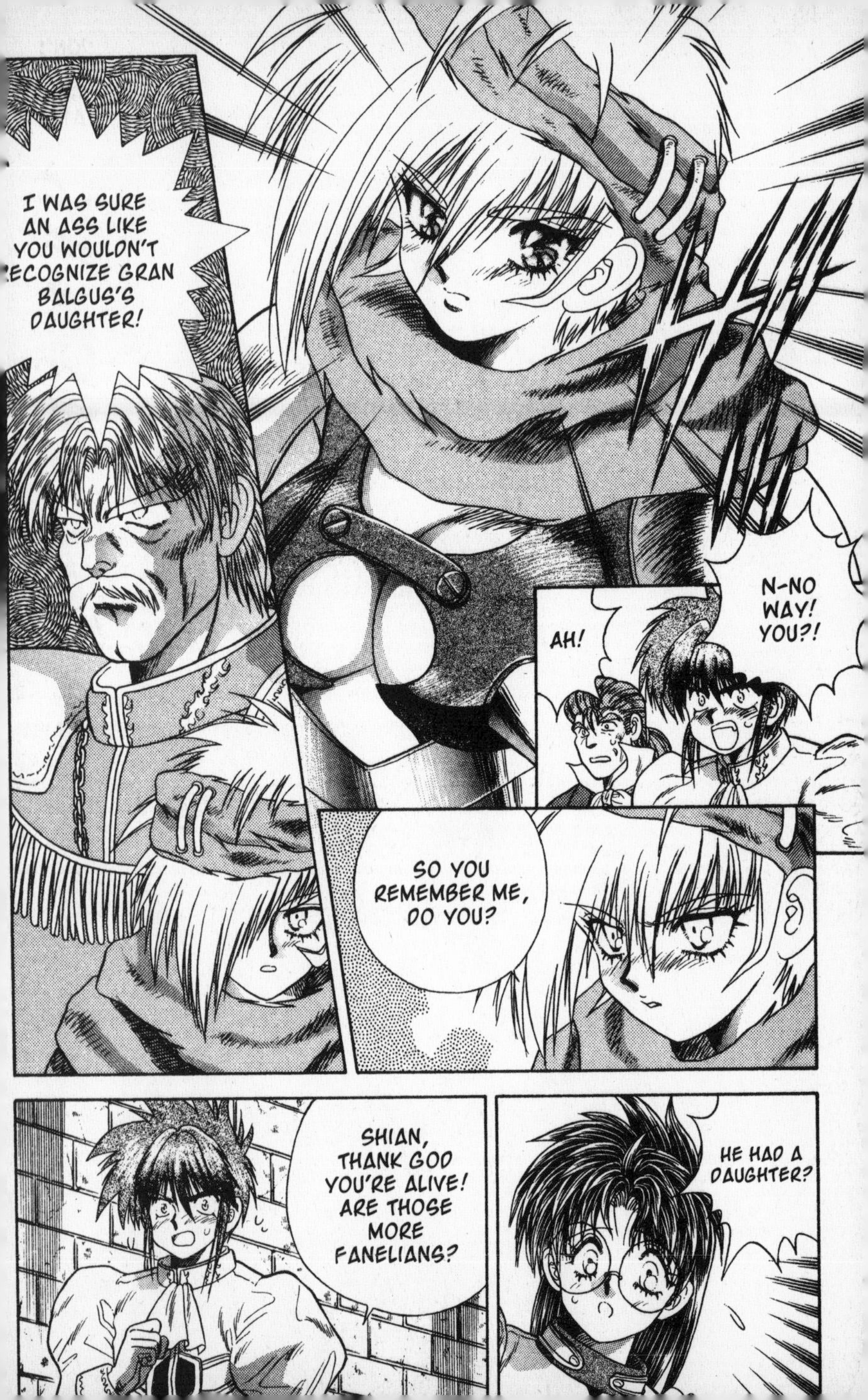
I WAS SURE AN ASS LIKE YOU WOULDN'T ECOGNIZE GRAN BALGUS'S DAUGHTER!
N-NO WAY! YOU?!
AH!
SO YOU REMEMBER ME, DO YOU?
HE HAD A DAUGHTER?
SHIAN, THANK GOD YOU'RE ALIVE! ARE THOSE MORE FANELIANS?

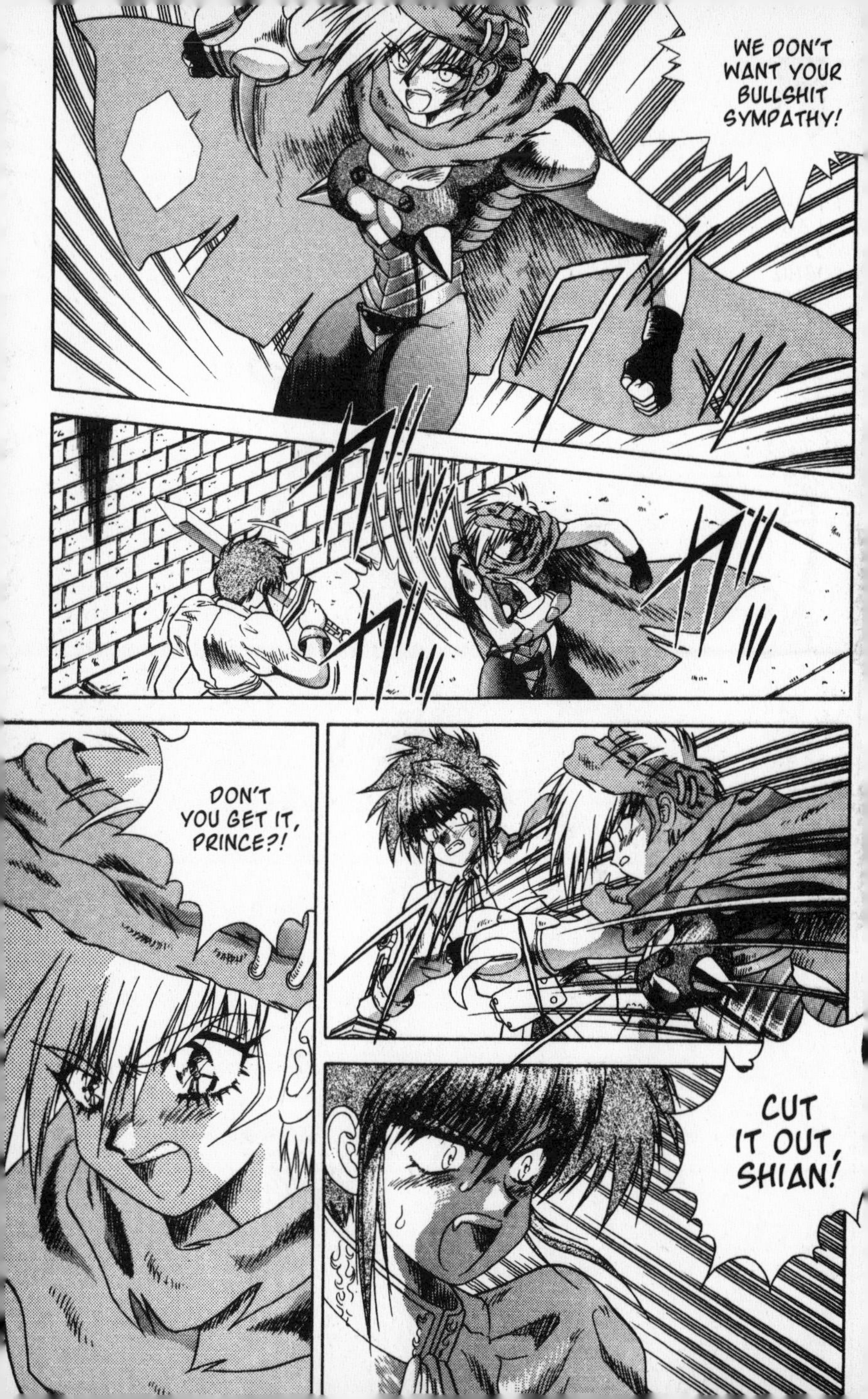
WE DON'T WANT YOUR BULLSHIT SYMPATHY!
CUT IT OUT, SHIAN!
DON'T YOU GET IT, PRINCE?!

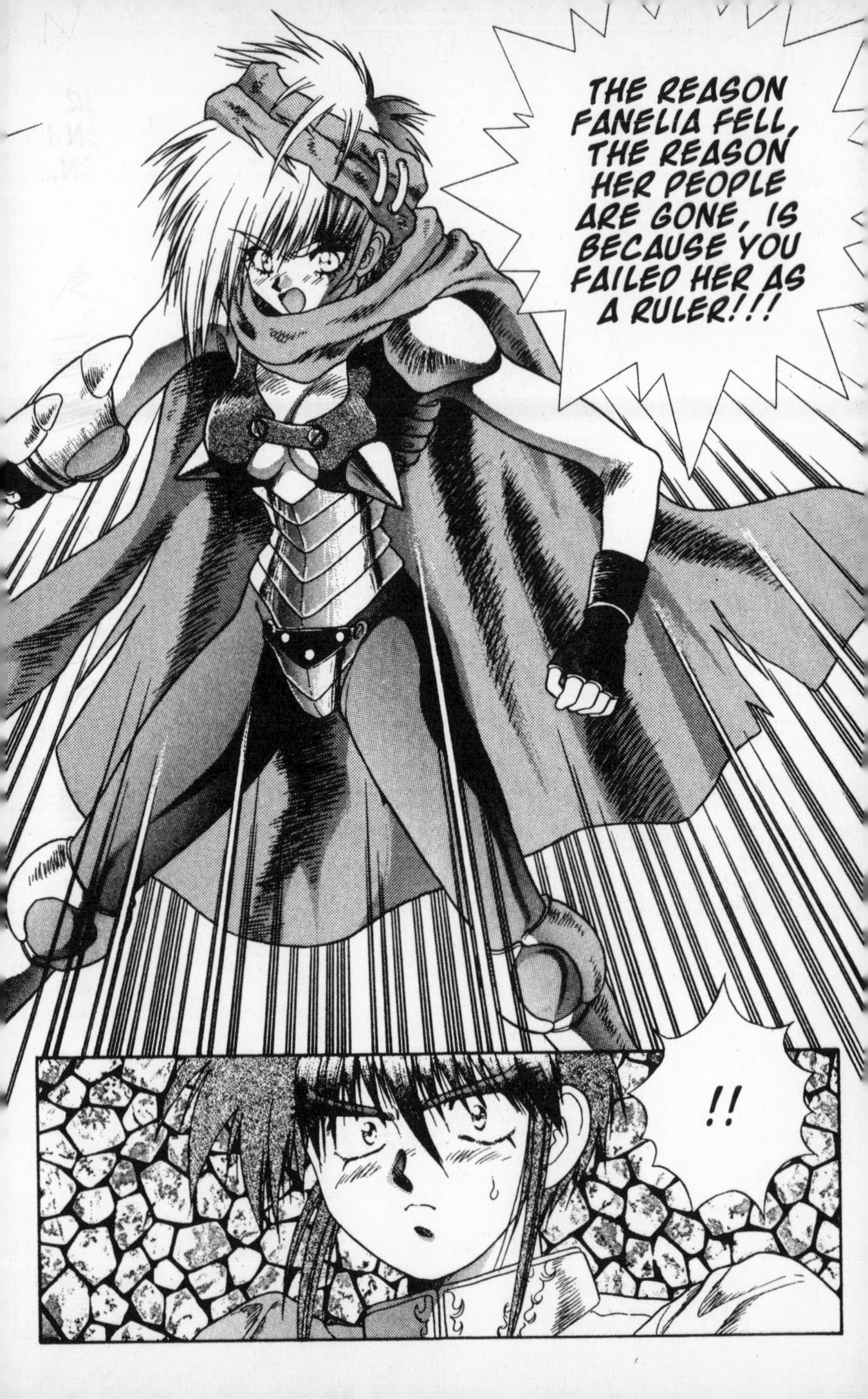
THE REASON FANELIA FELL, THE REASON HER PEOPLE ARE GONE, IS BECAUSE YOU FAILED HER AS A RULER!!!
!!

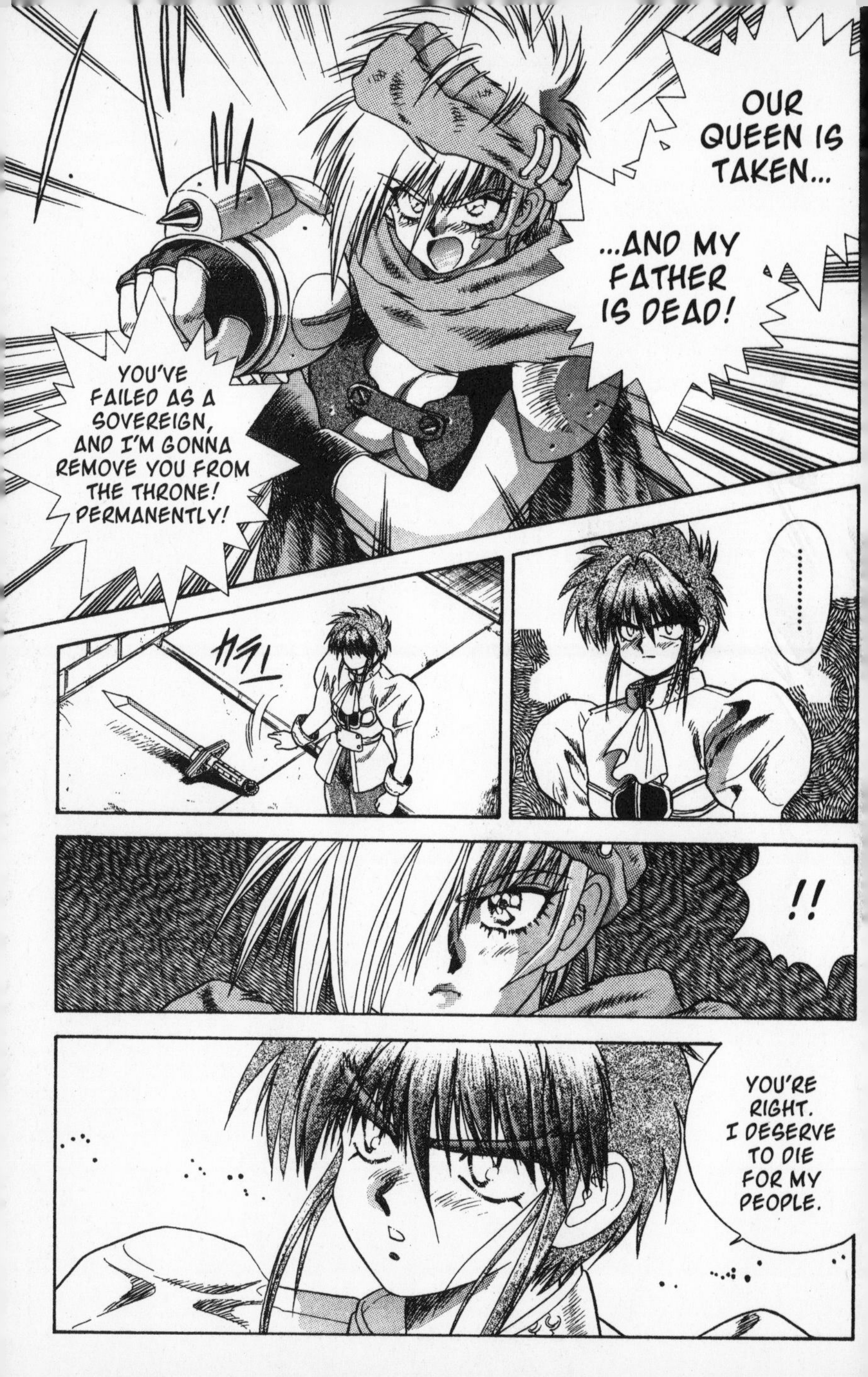
OUR QUEEN IS TAKEN...
...AND MY FATHER IS DEAD!
YOU'VE FAILED AS A SOVEREIGN, AND I'M GONNA REMOVE YOU FROM THE THRONE! PERMANENTLY!
......
カラン
!!
YOU'RE RIGHT. I DESERVE TO DIE FOR MY PEOPLE.

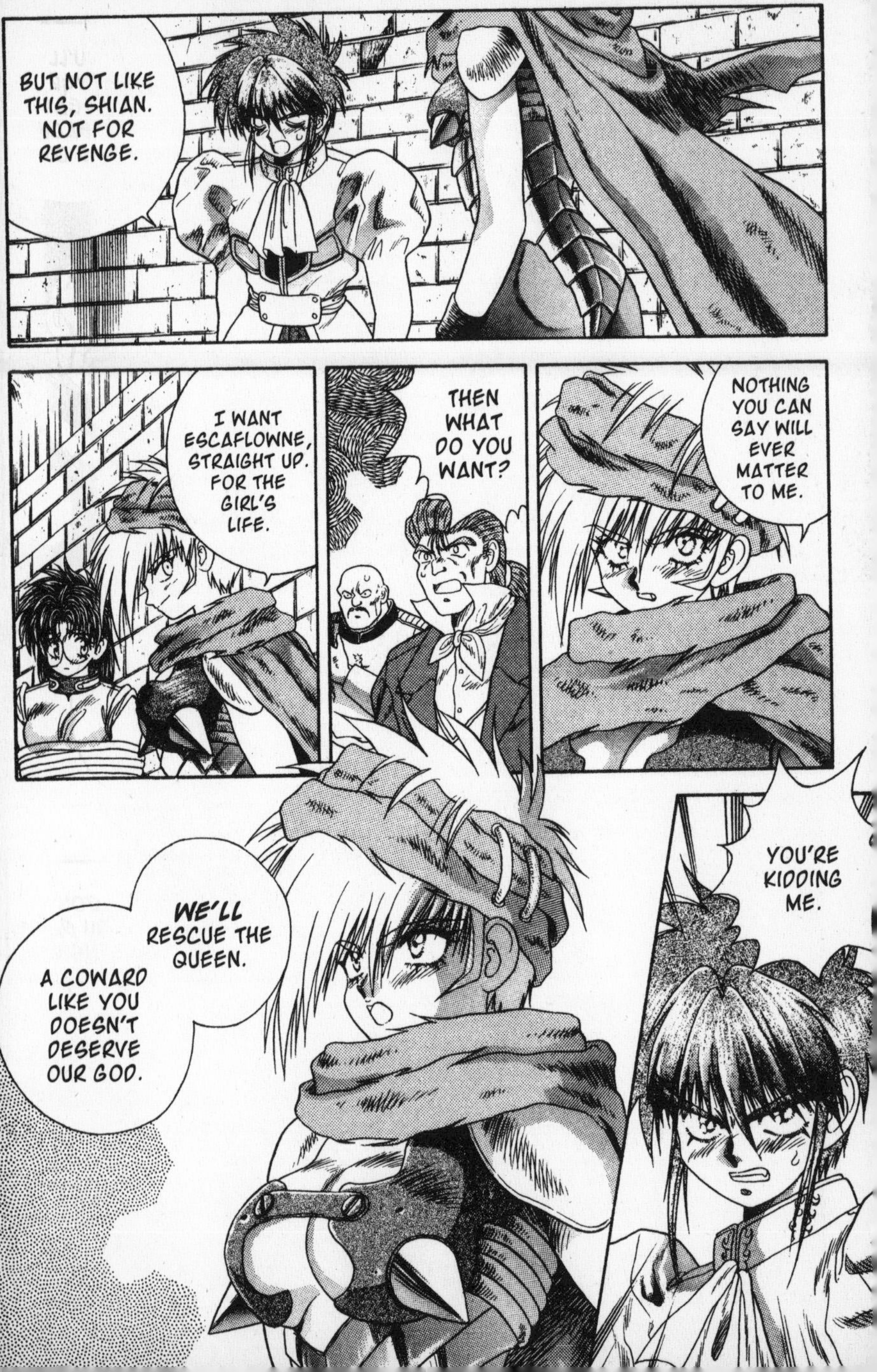
BUT NOT LIKE THIS, SHIAN. NOT FOR REVENGE.
NOTHING YOU CAN SAY WILL EVER MATTER TO ME.
THEN WHAT DO YOU WANT?
I WANT ESCAFLOWNE, STRAIGHT UP. FOR THE GIRL'S LIFE.
YOU'RE KIDDING ME.
WE'LL RESCUE THE QUEEN.
A COWARD LIKE YOU DOESN'T DESERVE OUR GOD.

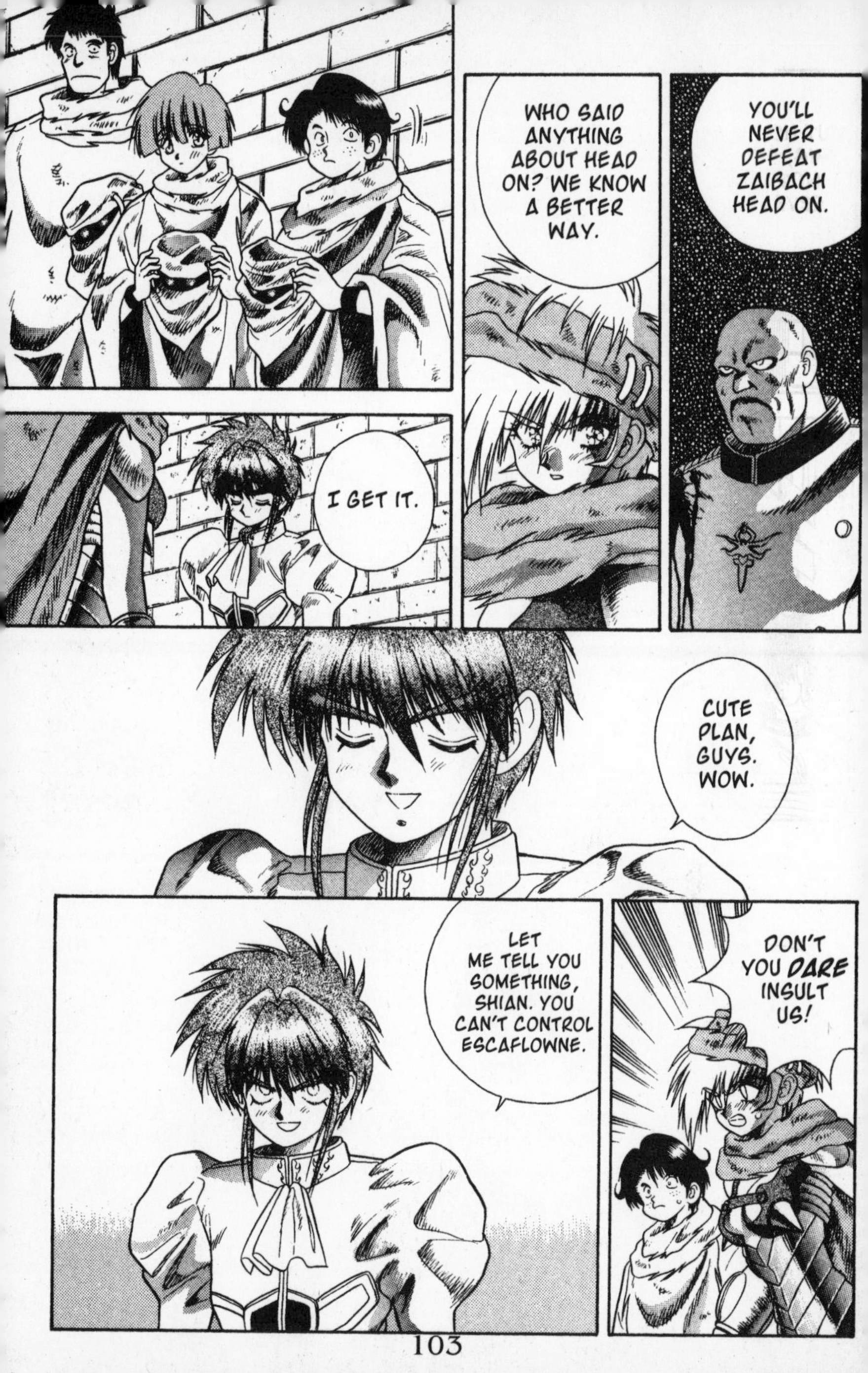
YOU'LL NEVER DEFEAT ZAIBACH HEAD ON.
WHO SAID ANYTHING ABOUT HEAD ON? WE KNOW A BETTER WAY.
I GET IT.
CUTE PLAN, GUYS. WOW.
DON'T YOU *DARE* INSULT US!
LET ME TELL YOU SOMETHING, SHIAN. YOU CAN'T CONTROL ESCAFLOWNE.

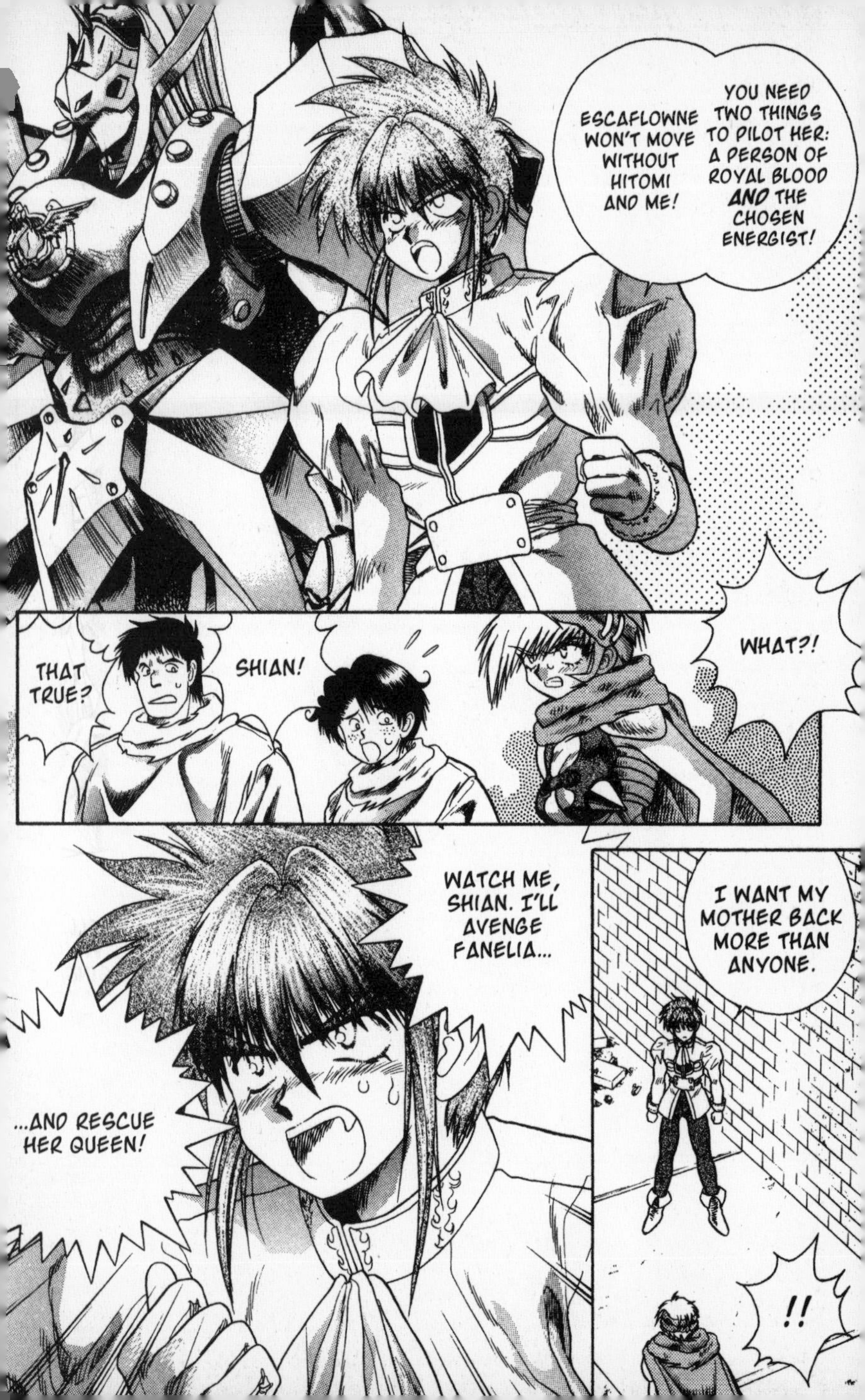
ESCAFLOWNE WON'T MOVE WITHOUT HITOMI AND ME! YOU NEED TWO THINGS TO PILOT HER: A PERSON OF ROYAL BLOOD AND THE CHOSEN ENERGIST!
WHAT?!
SHIAN!
THAT TRUE?
I WANT MY MOTHER BACK MORE THAN ANYONE.
!!
WATCH ME, SHIAN. I'LL AVENGE FANELIA...
...AND RESCUE HER QUEEN!

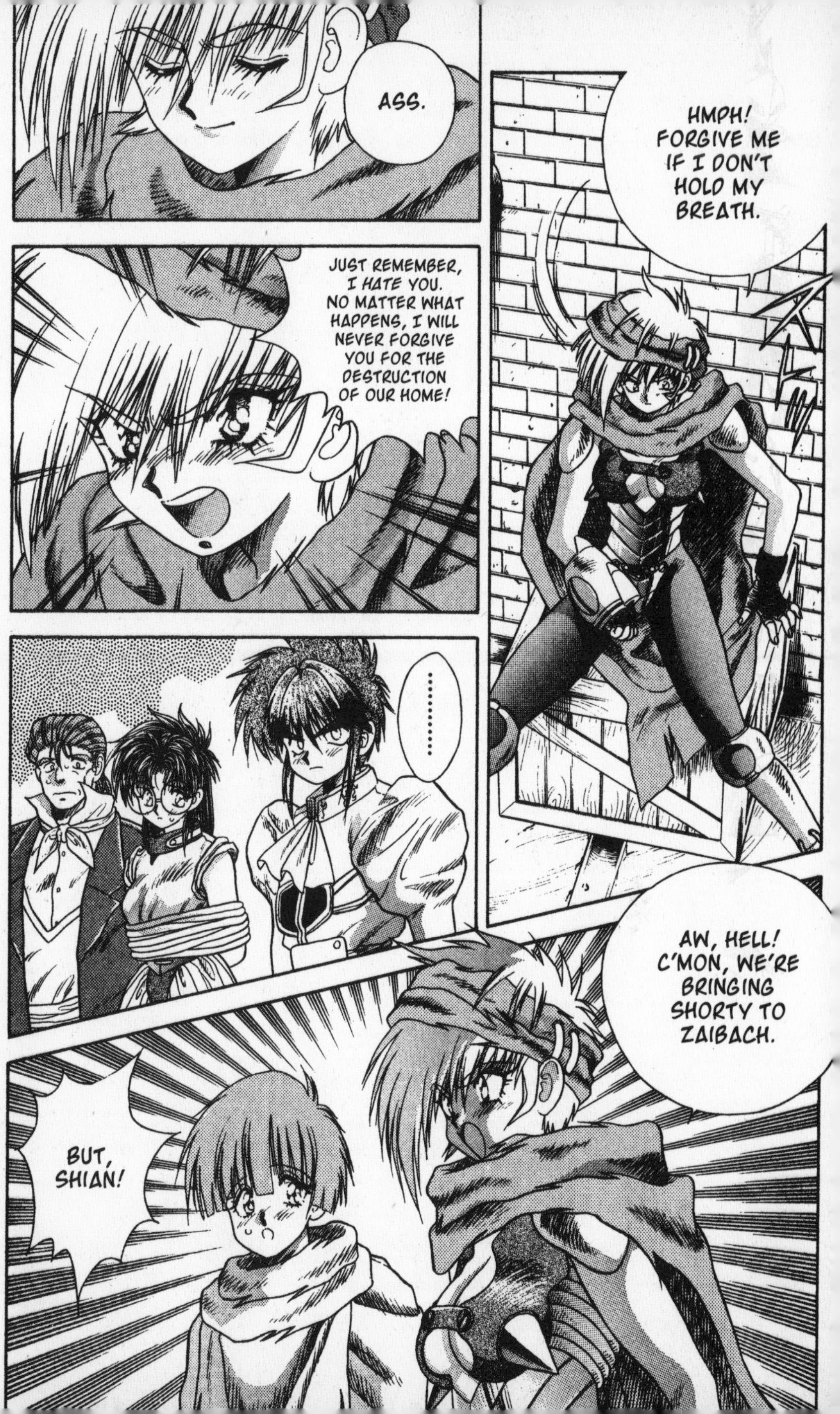
HMPH! FORGIVE ME IF I DON'T HOLD MY BREATH.
ASS.
JUST REMEMBER, I HATE YOU. NO MATTER WHAT HAPPENS, I WILL NEVER FORGIVE YOU FOR THE DESTRUCTION OF OUR HOME!
....
AW, HELL! C'MON, WE'RE BRINGING SHORTY TO ZAIBACH.
BUT, SHIAN!

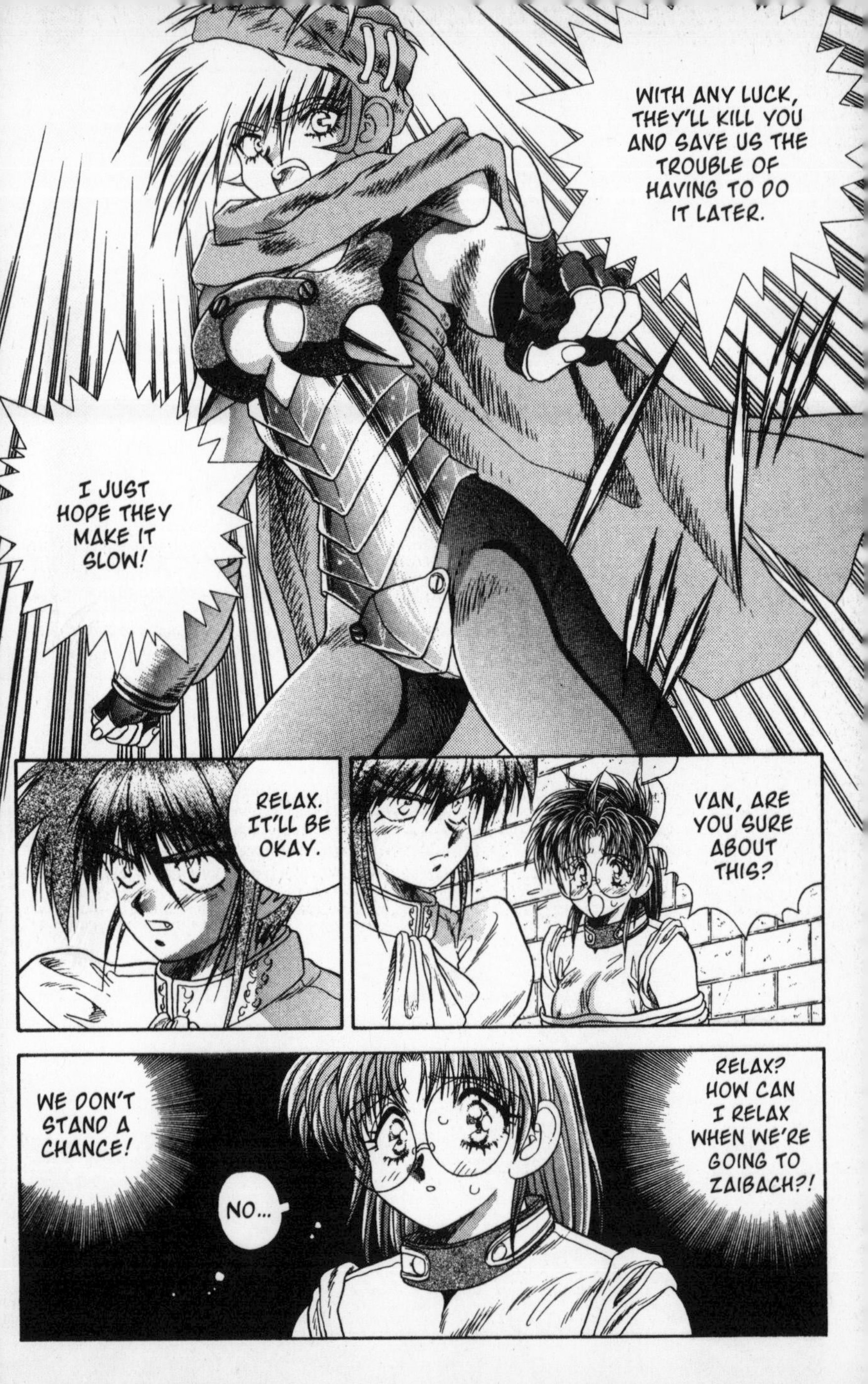
WITH ANY LUCK, THEY'LL KILL YOU AND SAVE US THE TROUBLE OF HAVING TO DO IT LATER.
I JUST HOPE THEY MAKE IT SLOW!
VAN, ARE YOU SURE ABOUT THIS?
RELAX. IT'LL BE OKAY.
RELAX? HOW CAN I RELAX WHEN WE'RE GOING TO ZAIBACH?!
WE DON'T STAND A CHANCE!
NO...

VISION 8: SINGLE PASSAGE

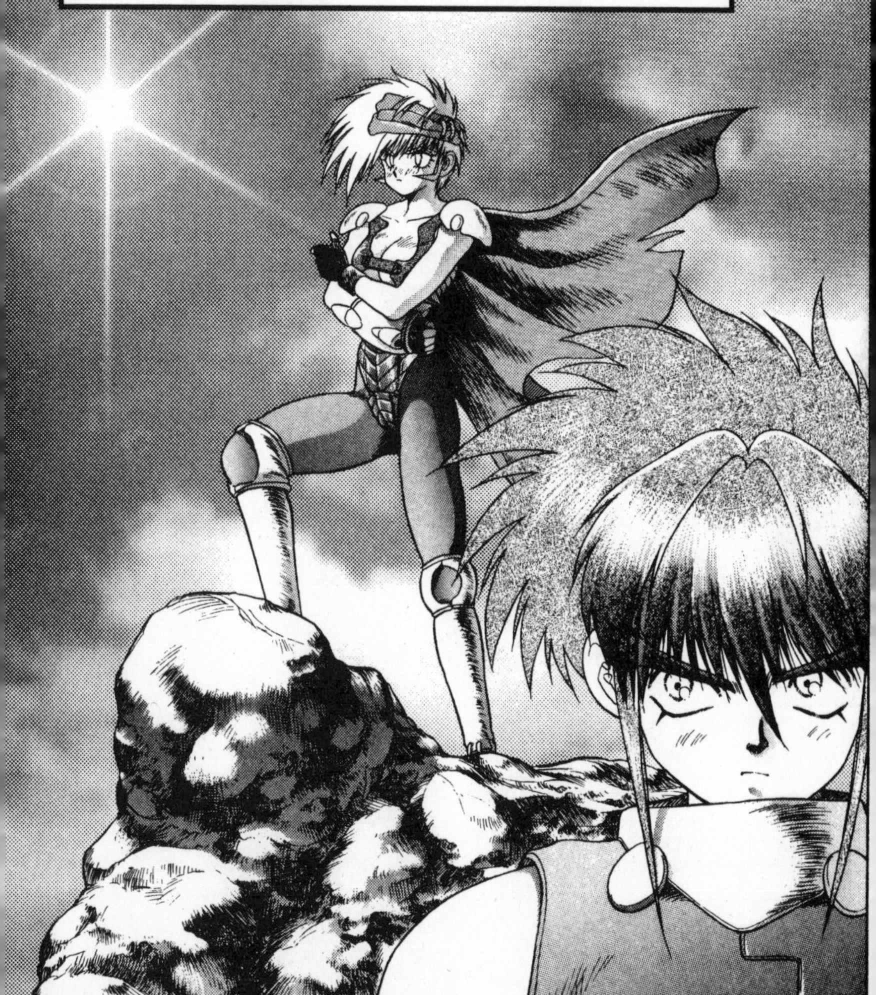

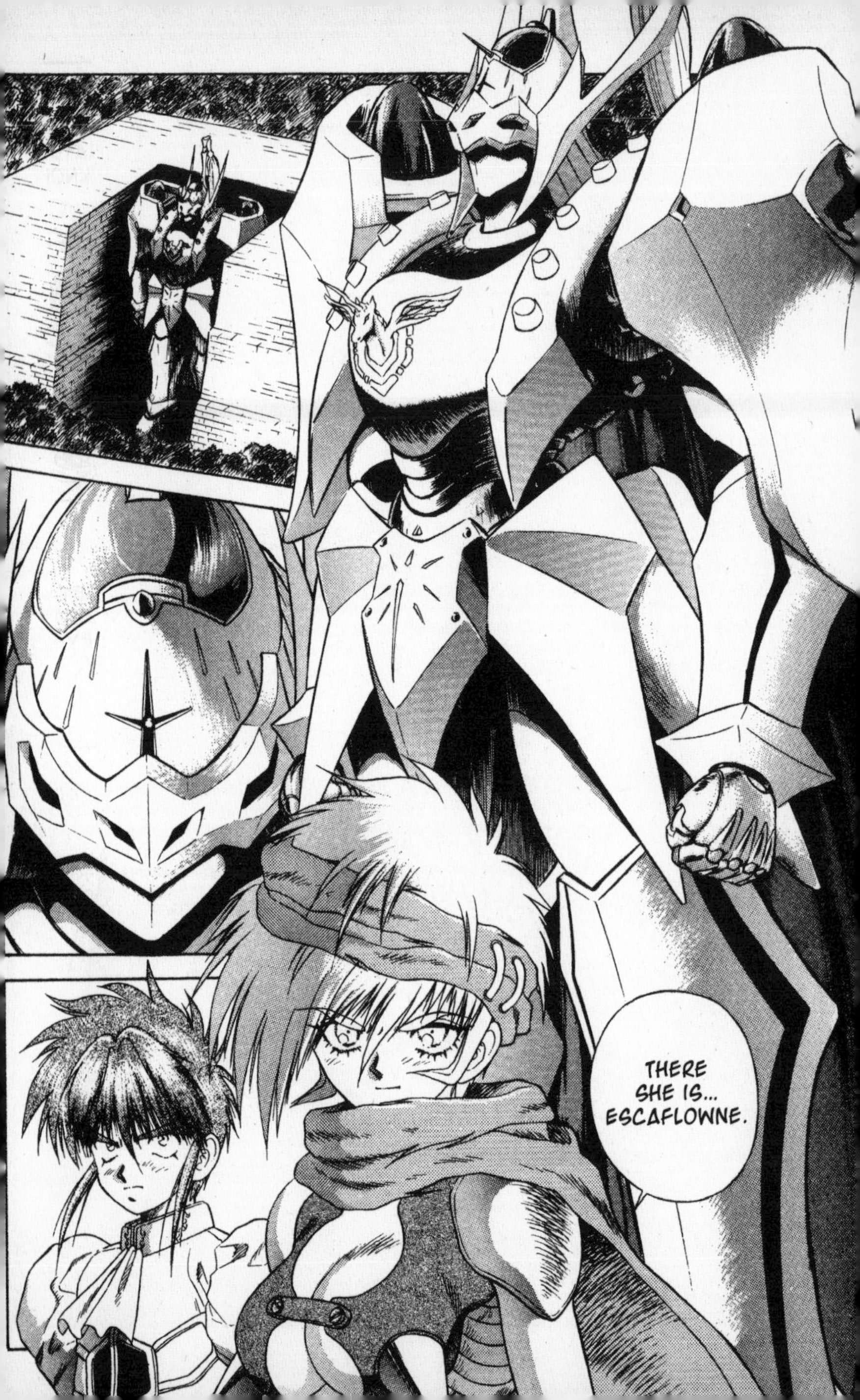
THERE SHE IS... ESCAFLOWNE.

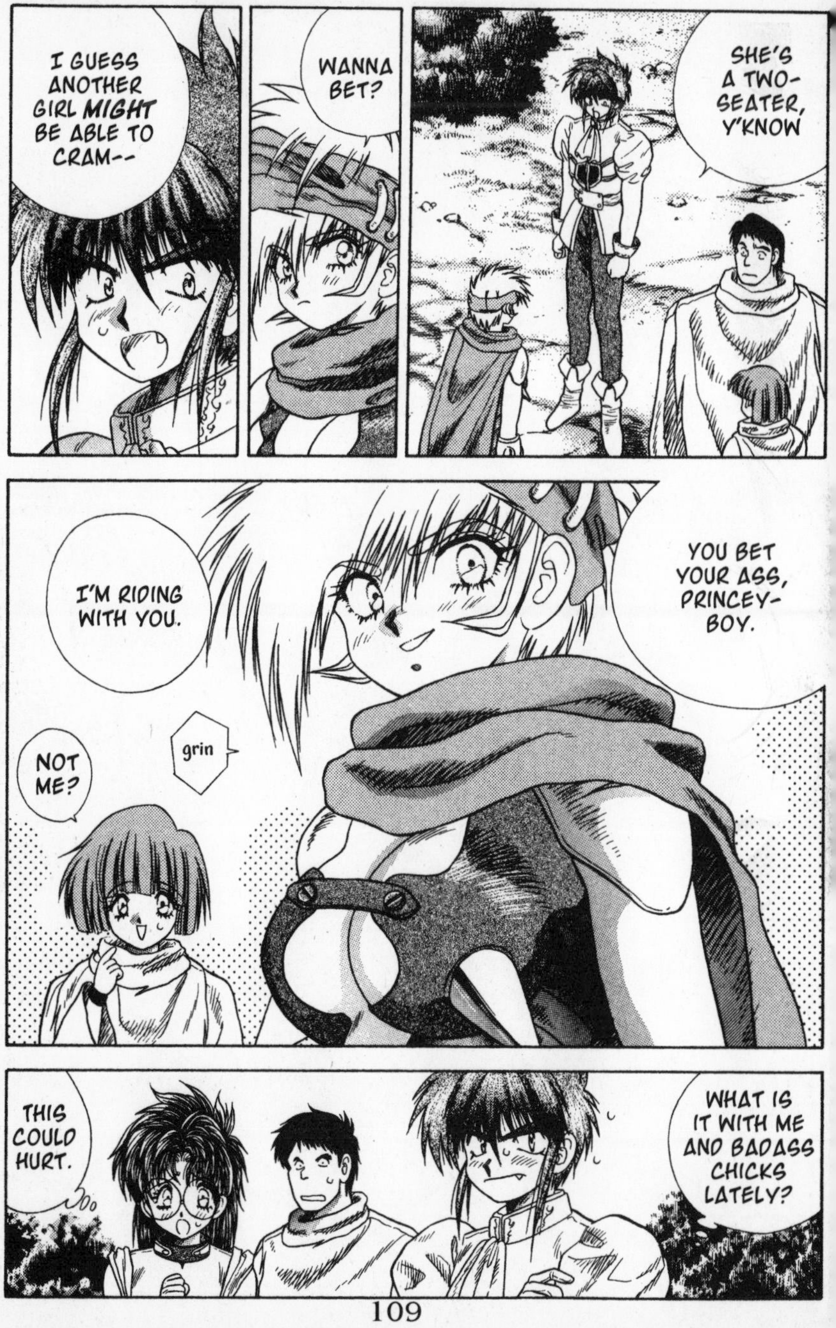
SHE'S A TWO-SEATER, Y'KNOW
WANNA BET?
I GUESS ANOTHER GIRL MIGHT BE ABLE TO CRAM--
YOU BET YOUR ASS, PRINCEY-BOY.
I'M RIDING WITH YOU.
grin
NOT ME?
WHAT IS IT WITH ME AND BADASS CHICKS LATELY?
THIS COULD HURT.

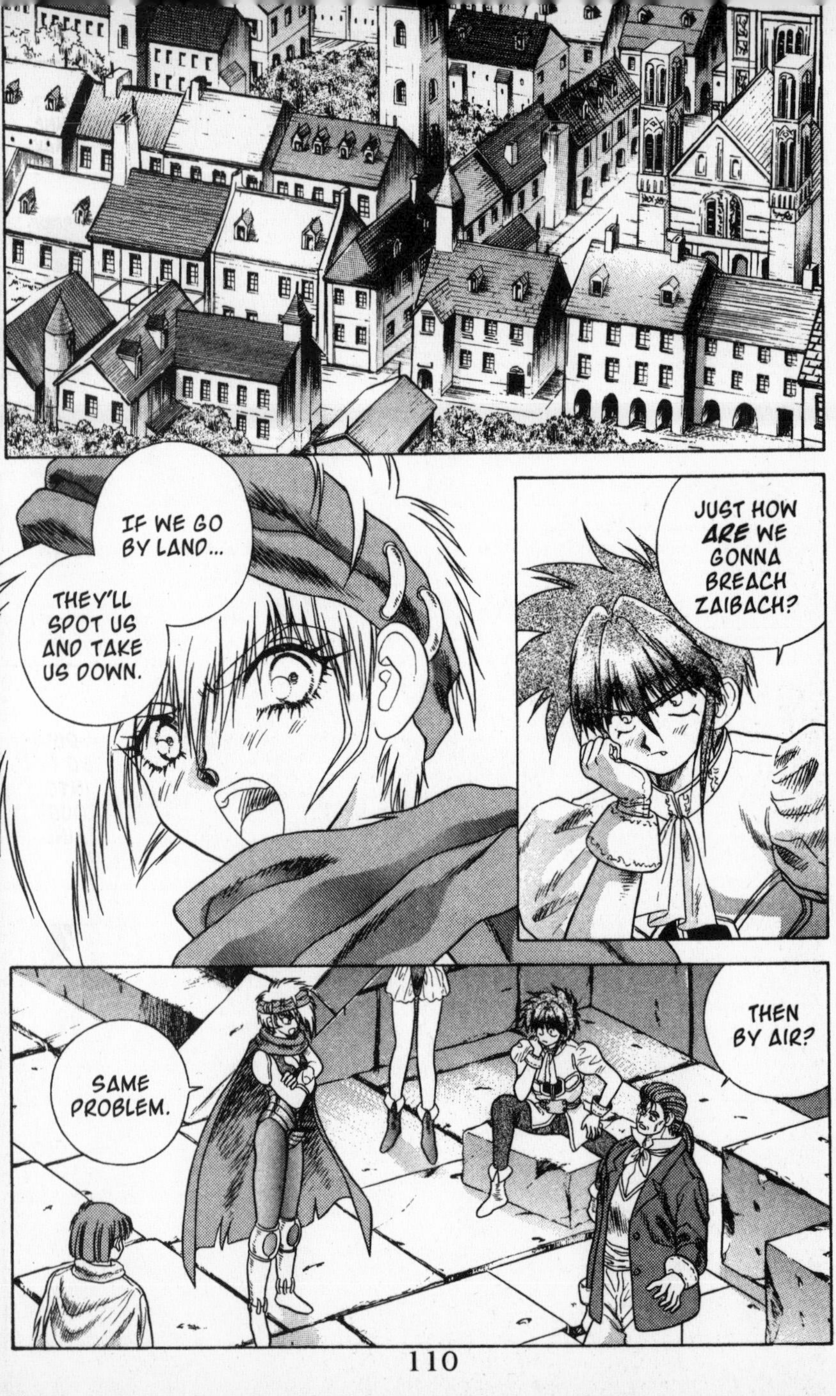
JUST HOW *ARE* WE GONNA BREACH ZAIBACH?
IF WE GO BY LAND...
THEY'LL SPOT US AND TAKE US DOWN.
THEN BY AIR?
SAME PROBLEM.

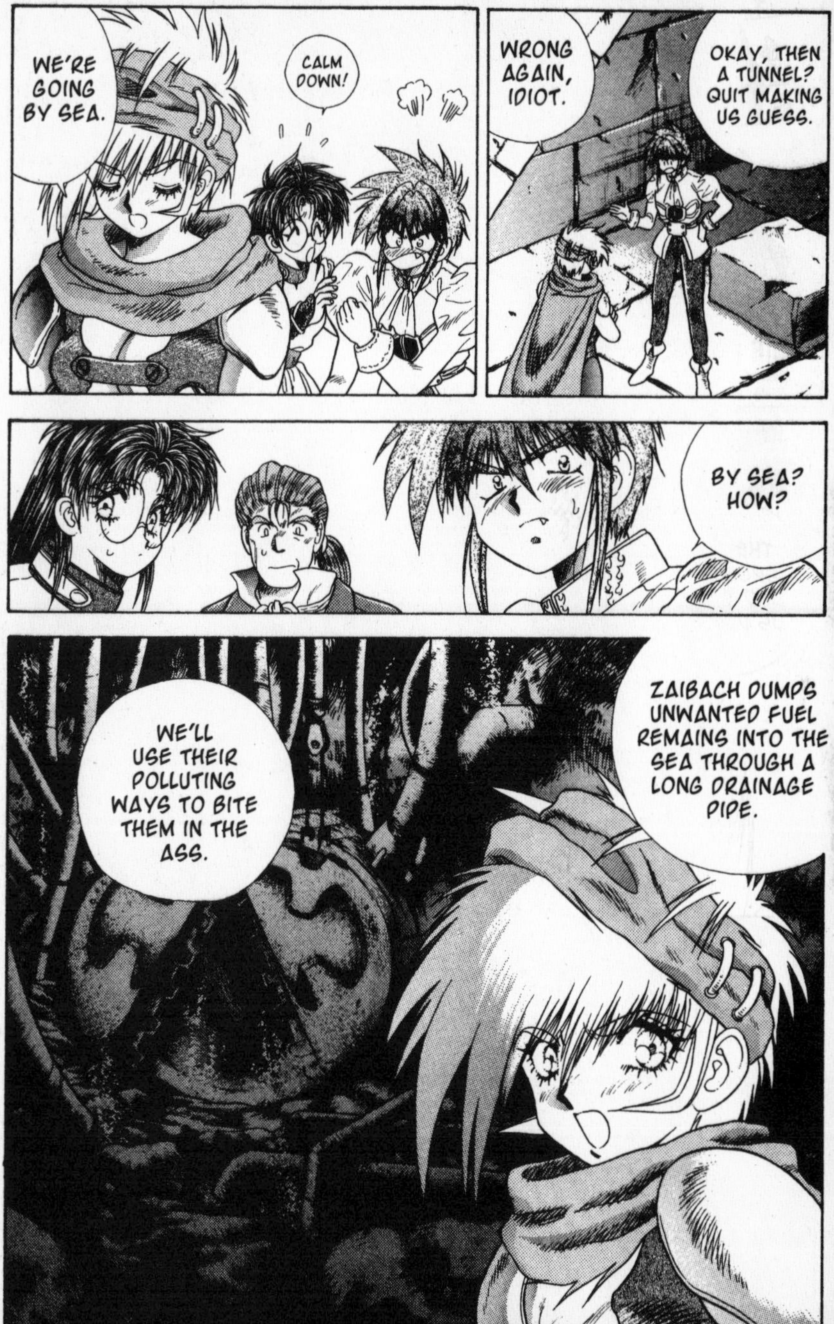
OKAY, THEN A TUNNEL? QUIT MAKING US GUESS.
WRONG AGAIN, IDIOT.
CALM DOWN!
WE'RE GOING BY SEA.
BY SEA? HOW?
ZAIBACH DUMPS UNWANTED FUEL REMAINS INTO THE SEA THROUGH A LONG DRAINAGE PIPE.
WE'LL USE THEIR POLLUTING WAYS TO BITE THEM IN THE ASS.

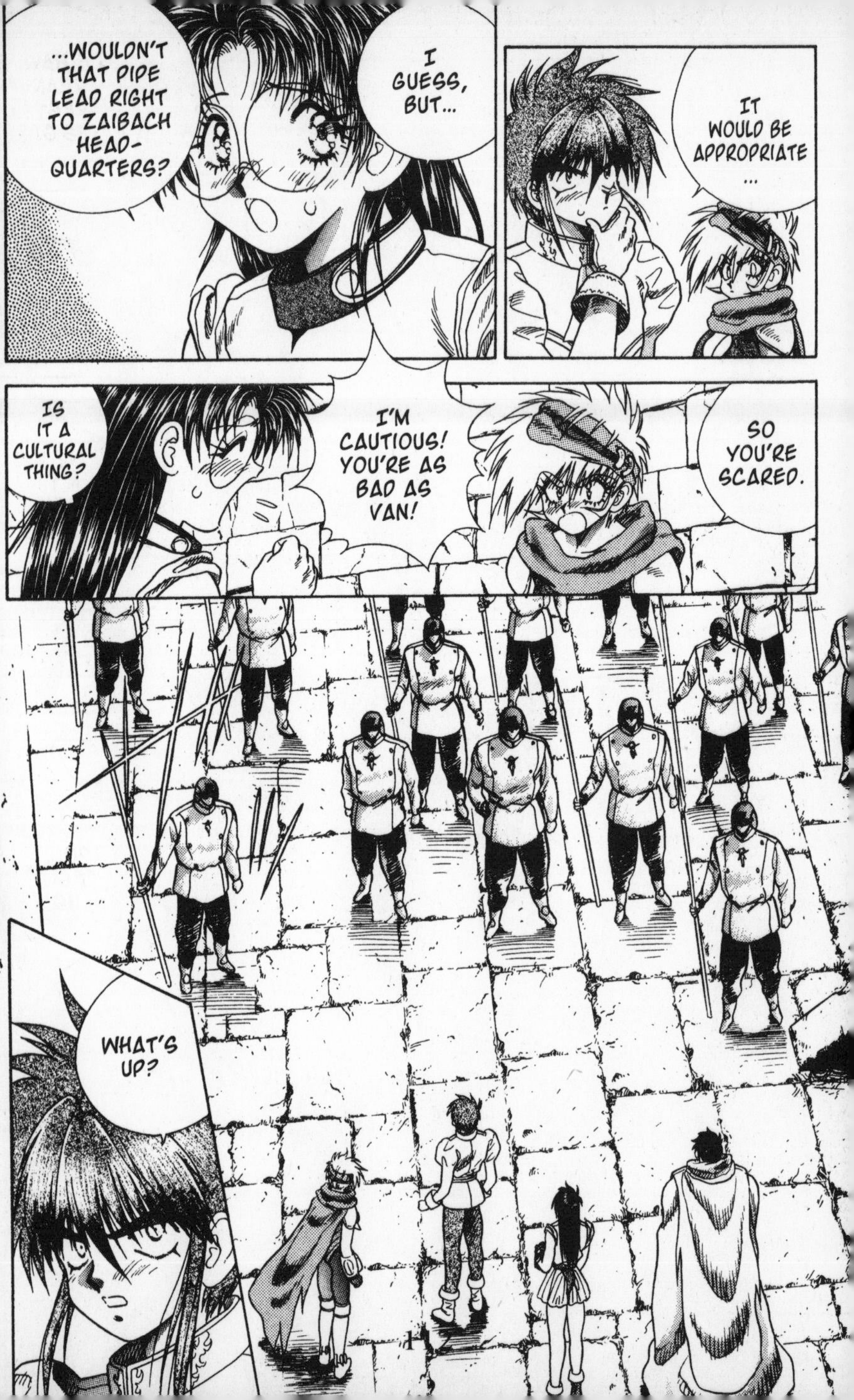
IT WOULD BE APPROPRIATE ...
I GUESS, BUT...
...WOULDN'T THAT PIPE LEAD RIGHT TO ZAIBACH HEAD-QUARTERS?
SO YOU'RE SCARED.
I'M CAUTIOUS! YOU'RE AS BAD AS VAN!
IS IT A CULTURAL THING?
WHAT'S UP?

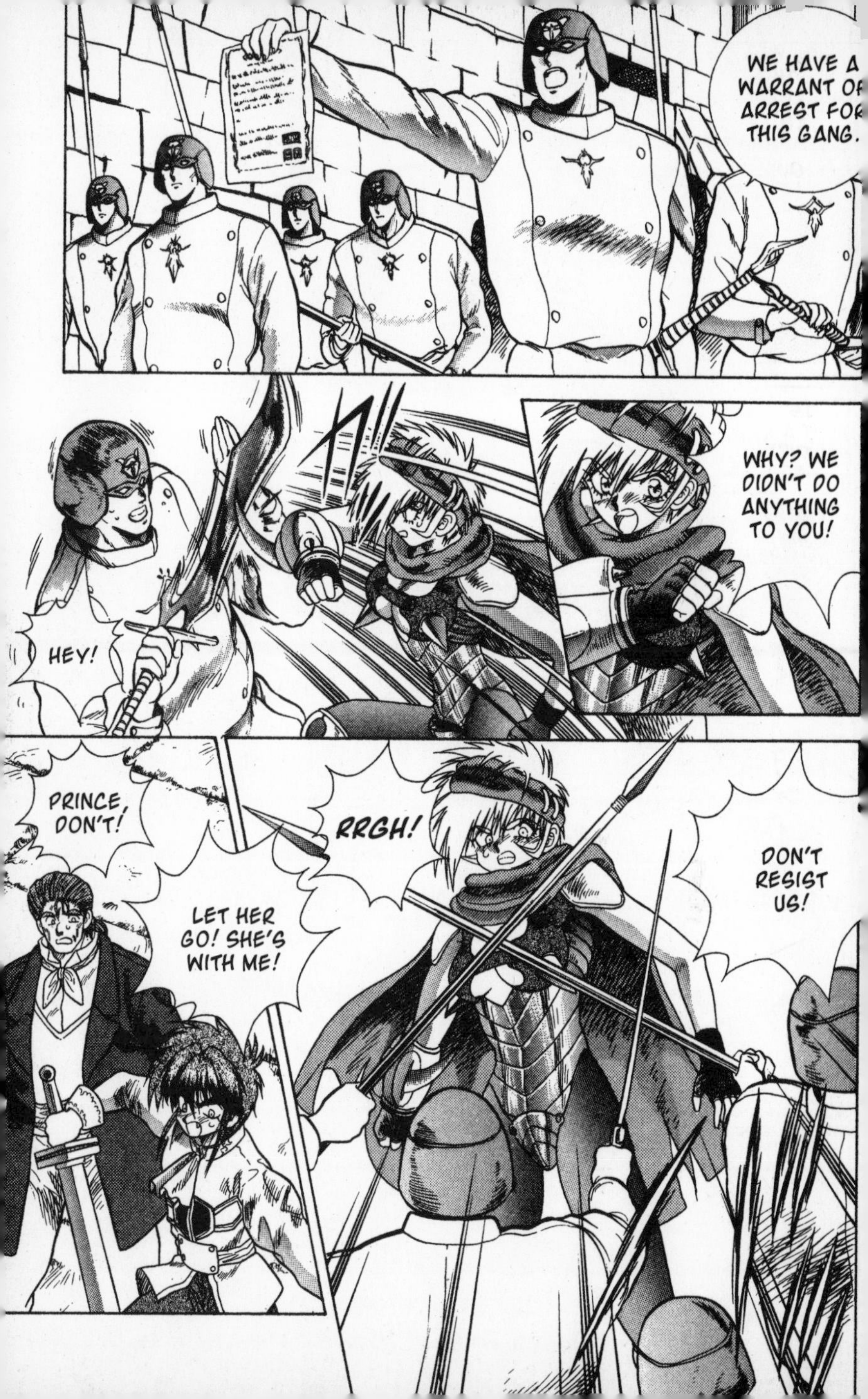
WE HAVE A WARRANT OF ARREST FOR THIS GANG.
WHY? WE DIDN'T DO ANYTHING TO YOU!
HEY!
DON'T RESIST US!
RRGH!
PRINCE DON'T!
LET HER GO! SHE'S WITH ME!

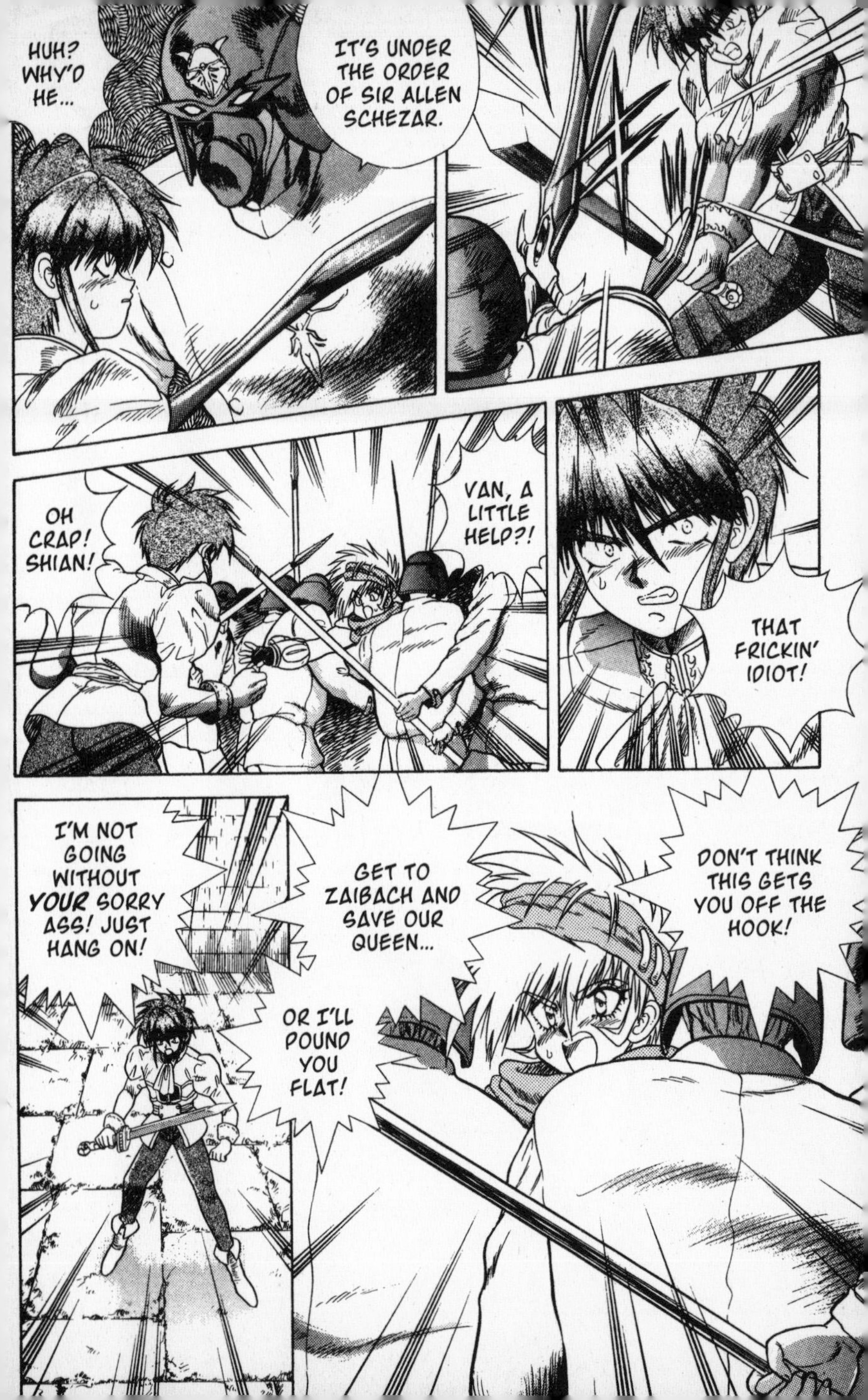
IT'S UNDER THE ORDER OF SIR ALLEN SCHEZAR.
HUH? WHY'D HE...
THAT FRICKIN' IDIOT!
VAN, A LITTLE HELP?!
OH CRAP! SHIAN!
DON'T THINK THIS GETS YOU OFF THE HOOK!
GET TO ZAIBACH AND SAVE OUR QUEEN...
OR I'LL POUND YOU FLAT!
I'M NOT GOING WITHOUT **YOUR** SORRY ASS! JUST HANG ON!

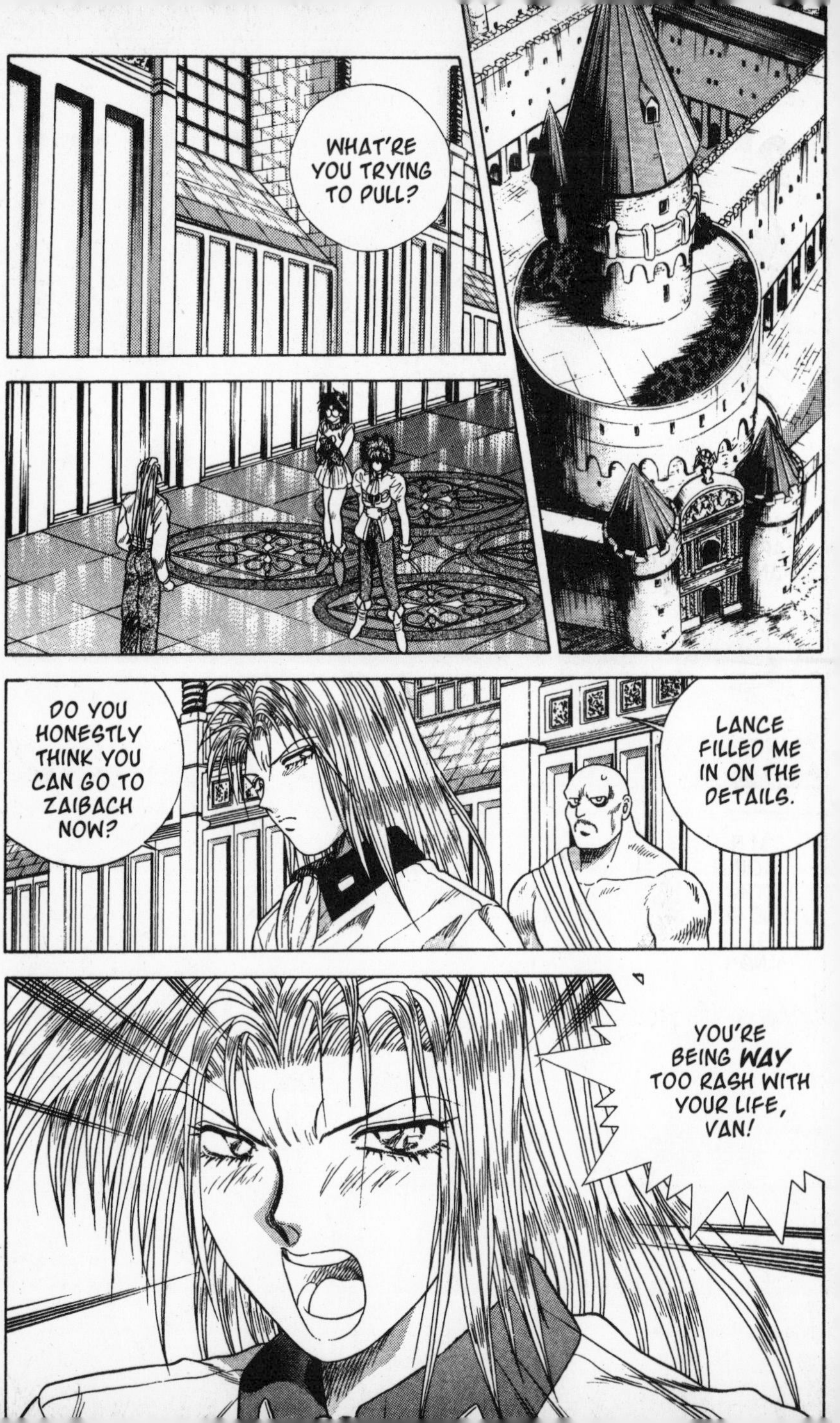
WHAT'RE YOU TRYING TO PULL?
LANCE FILLED ME IN ON THE DETAILS.
DO YOU HONESTLY THINK YOU CAN GO TO ZAIBACH NOW?
YOU'RE BEING **WAY** TOO RASH WITH YOUR LIFE, VAN!

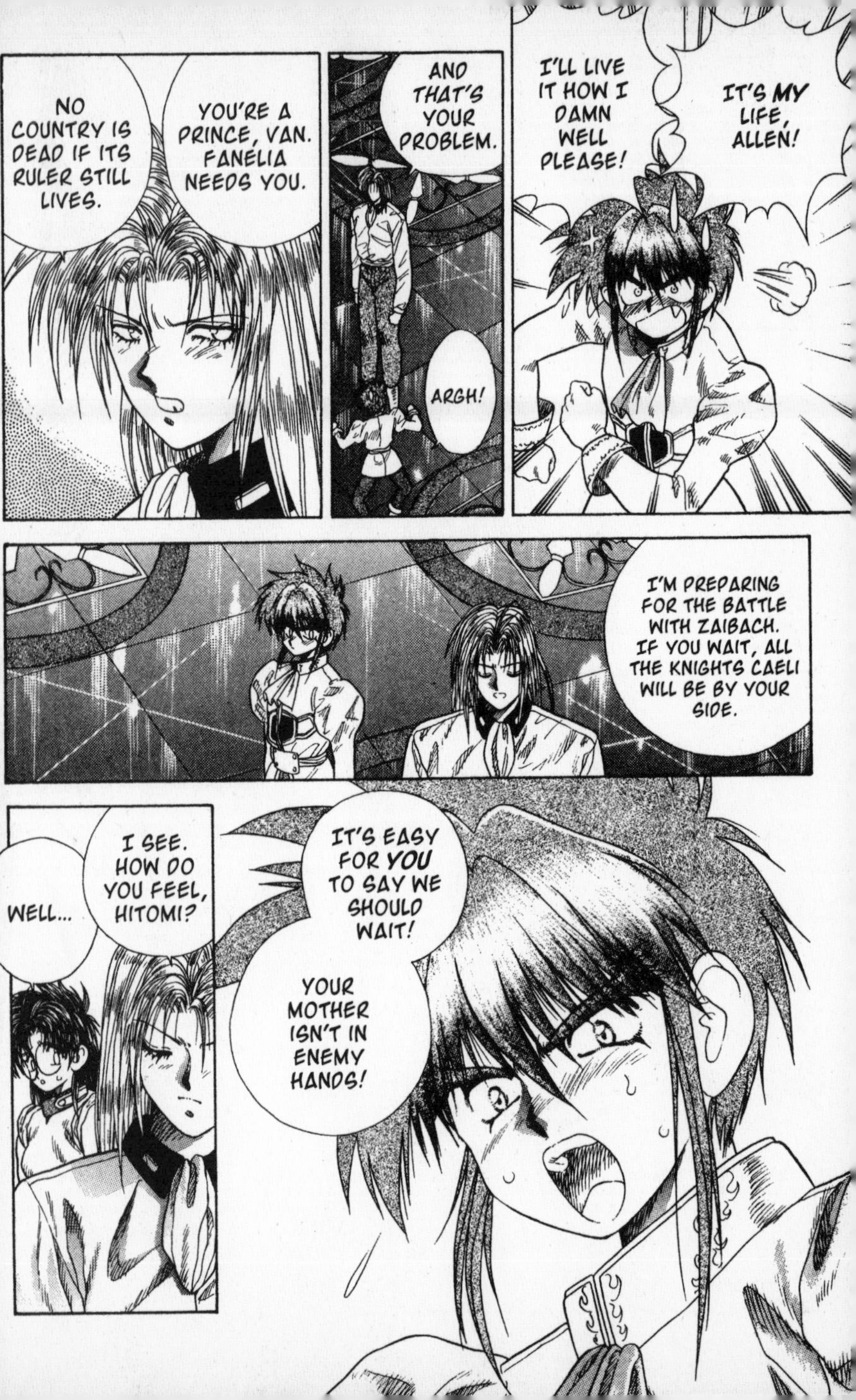
IT'S MY LIFE, ALLEN!
I'LL LIVE IT HOW I DAMN WELL PLEASE!
AND THAT'S YOUR PROBLEM.
ARGH!
YOU'RE A PRINCE, VAN. FANELIA NEEDS YOU.
NO COUNTRY IS DEAD IF ITS RULER STILL LIVES.
I'M PREPARING FOR THE BATTLE WITH ZAIBACH. IF YOU WAIT, ALL THE KNIGHTS CAELI WILL BE BY YOUR SIDE.
IT'S EASY FOR YOU TO SAY WE SHOULD WAIT!
YOUR MOTHER ISN'T IN ENEMY HANDS!
I SEE. HOW DO YOU FEEL, HITOMI?
WELL...

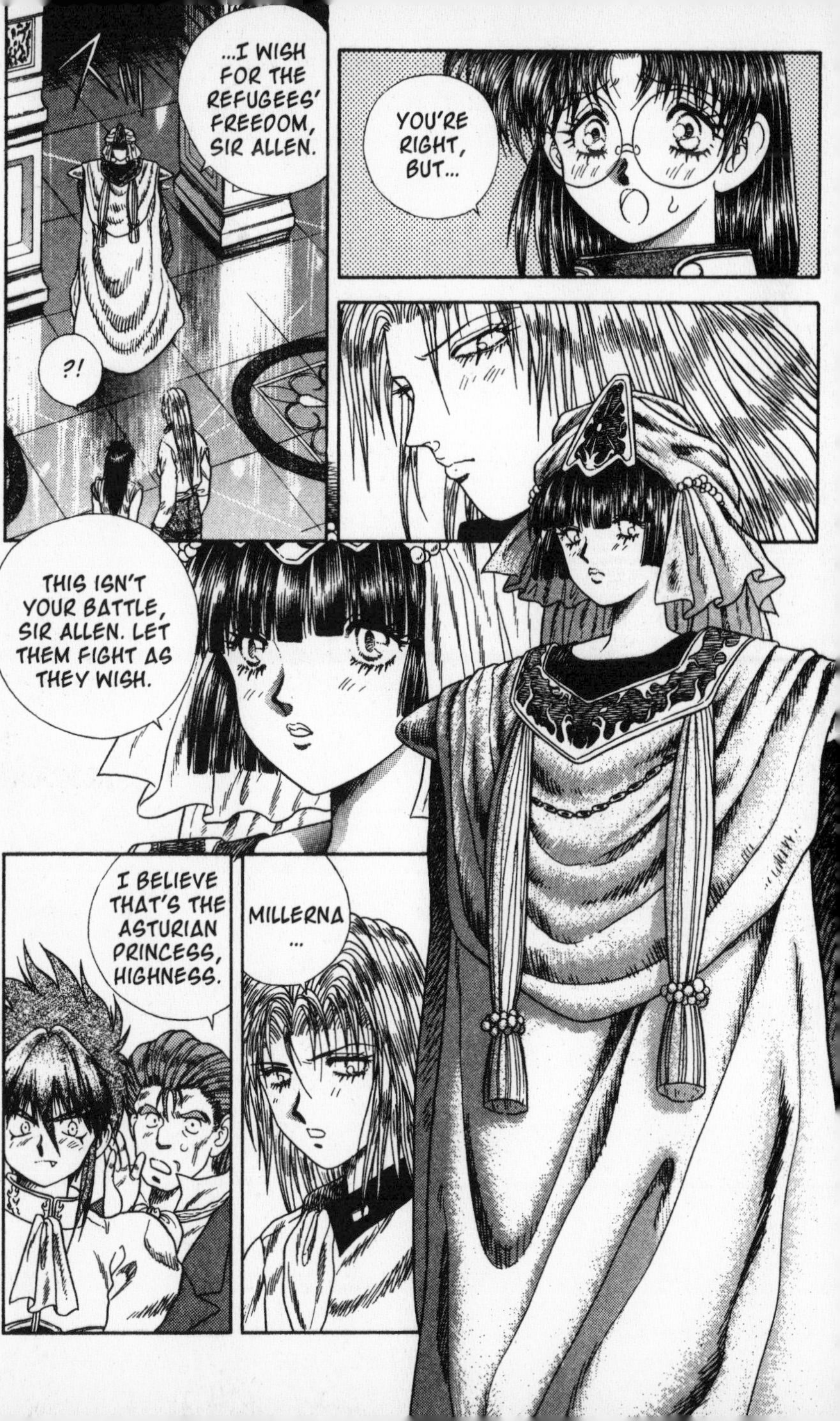
YOU'RE RIGHT, BUT...
...I WISH FOR THE REFUGEES' FREEDOM, SIR ALLEN.
?!
THIS ISN'T YOUR BATTLE, SIR ALLEN. LET THEM FIGHT AS THEY WISH.
MILLERNA ...
I BELIEVE THAT'S THE ASTURIAN PRINCESS, HIGHNESS.

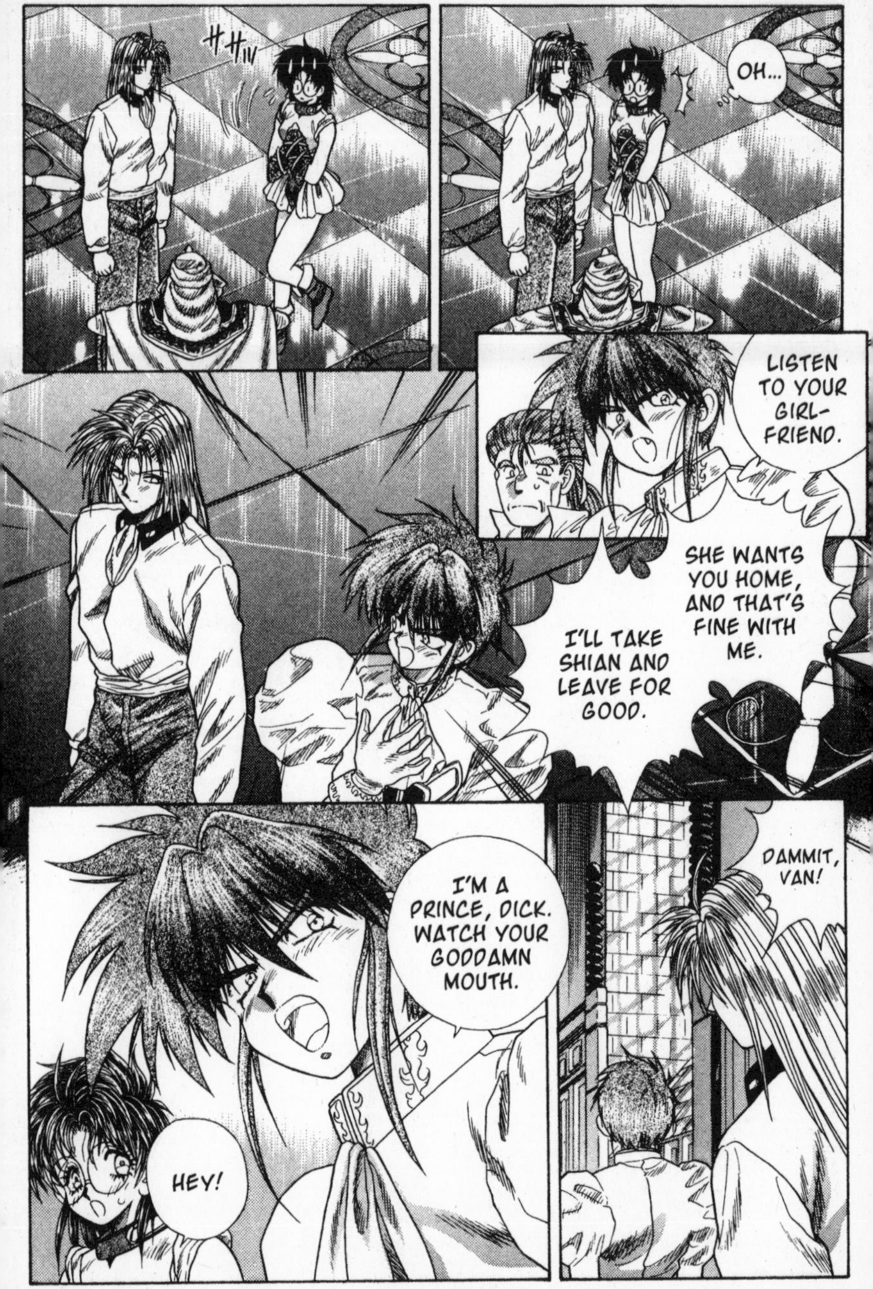
OH...
LISTEN TO YOUR GIRL-FRIEND.
SHE WANTS YOU HOME, AND THAT'S FINE WITH ME.
I'LL TAKE SHIAN AND LEAVE FOR GOOD.
DAMMIT, VAN!
I'M A PRINCE, DICK. WATCH YOUR GODDAMN MOUTH.
HEY!

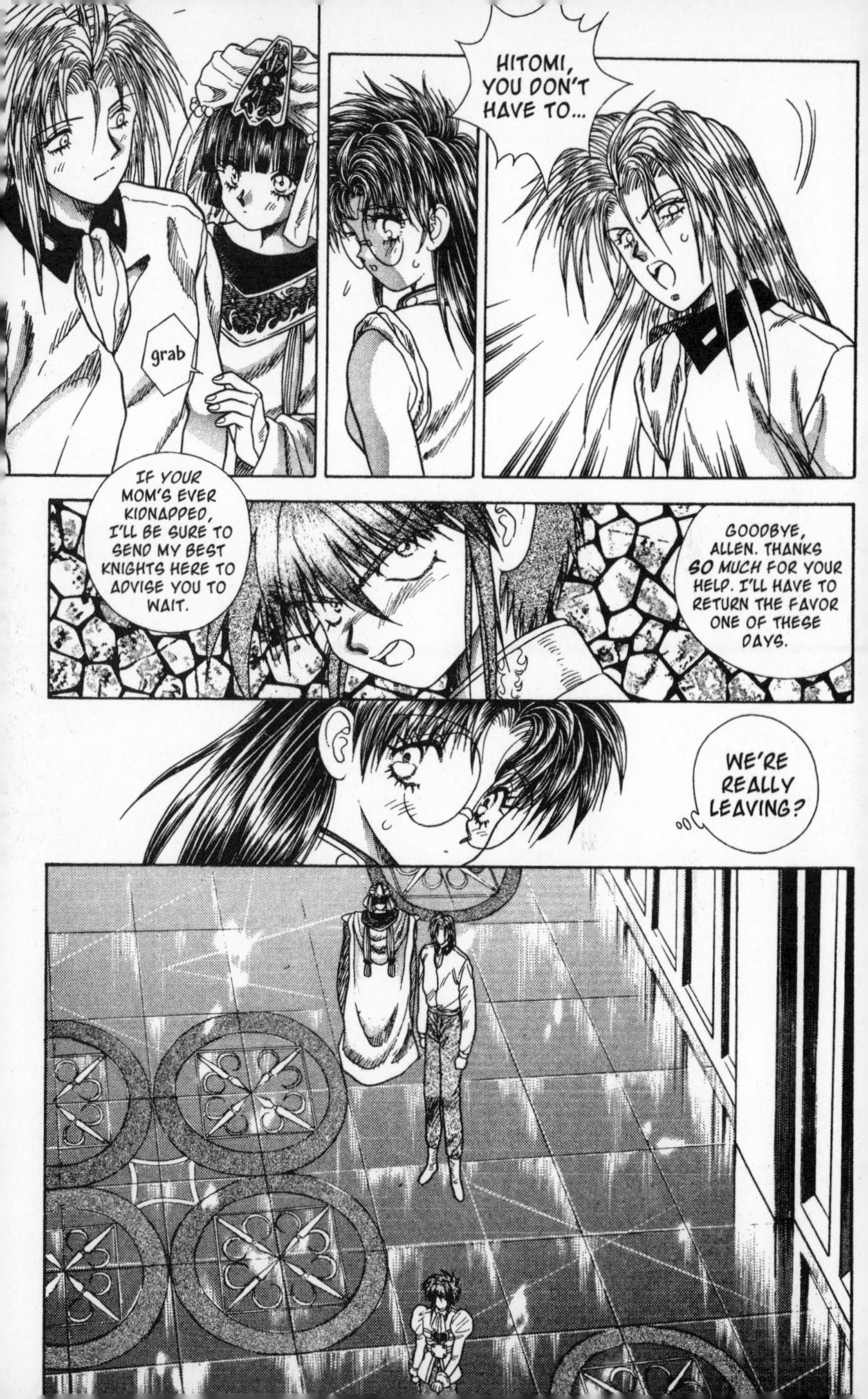
HITOMI, YOU DON'T HAVE TO...
grab
GOODBYE, ALLEN. THANKS SO MUCH FOR YOUR HELP. I'LL HAVE TO RETURN THE FAVOR ONE OF THESE DAYS.
IF YOUR MOM'S EVER KIDNAPPED, I'LL BE SURE TO SEND MY BEST KNIGHTS HERE TO ADVISE YOU TO WAIT.
WE'RE REALLY LEAVING?

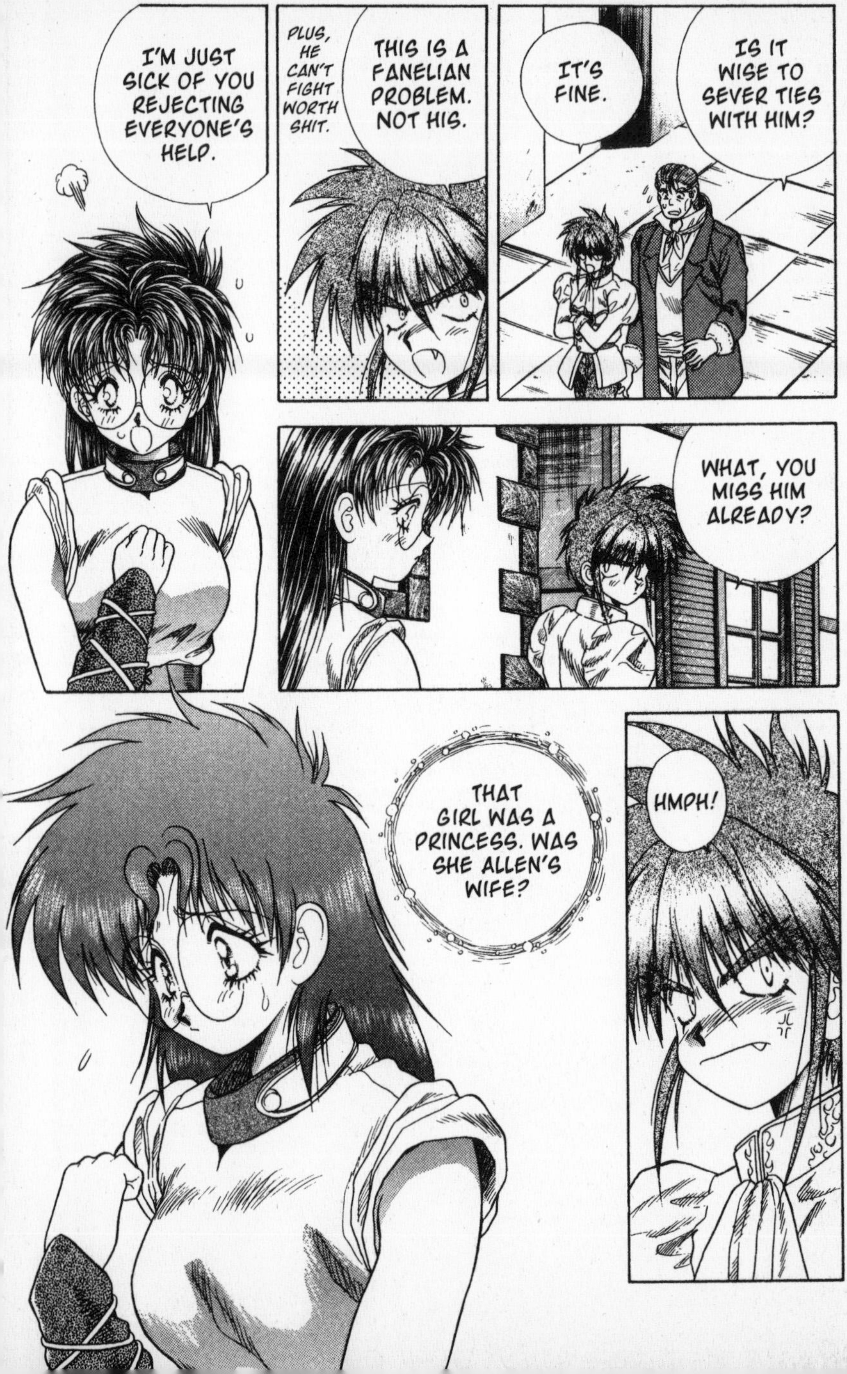
IS IT WISE TO SEVER TIES WITH HIM?
IT'S FINE.
THIS IS A FANELIAN PROBLEM. NOT HIS.
PLUS, HE CAN'T FIGHT WORTH SHIT.
WHAT, YOU MISS HIM ALREADY?
I'M JUST SICK OF YOU REJECTING EVERYONE'S HELP.
HMPH!
THAT GIRL WAS A PRINCESS. WAS SHE ALLEN'S WIFE?

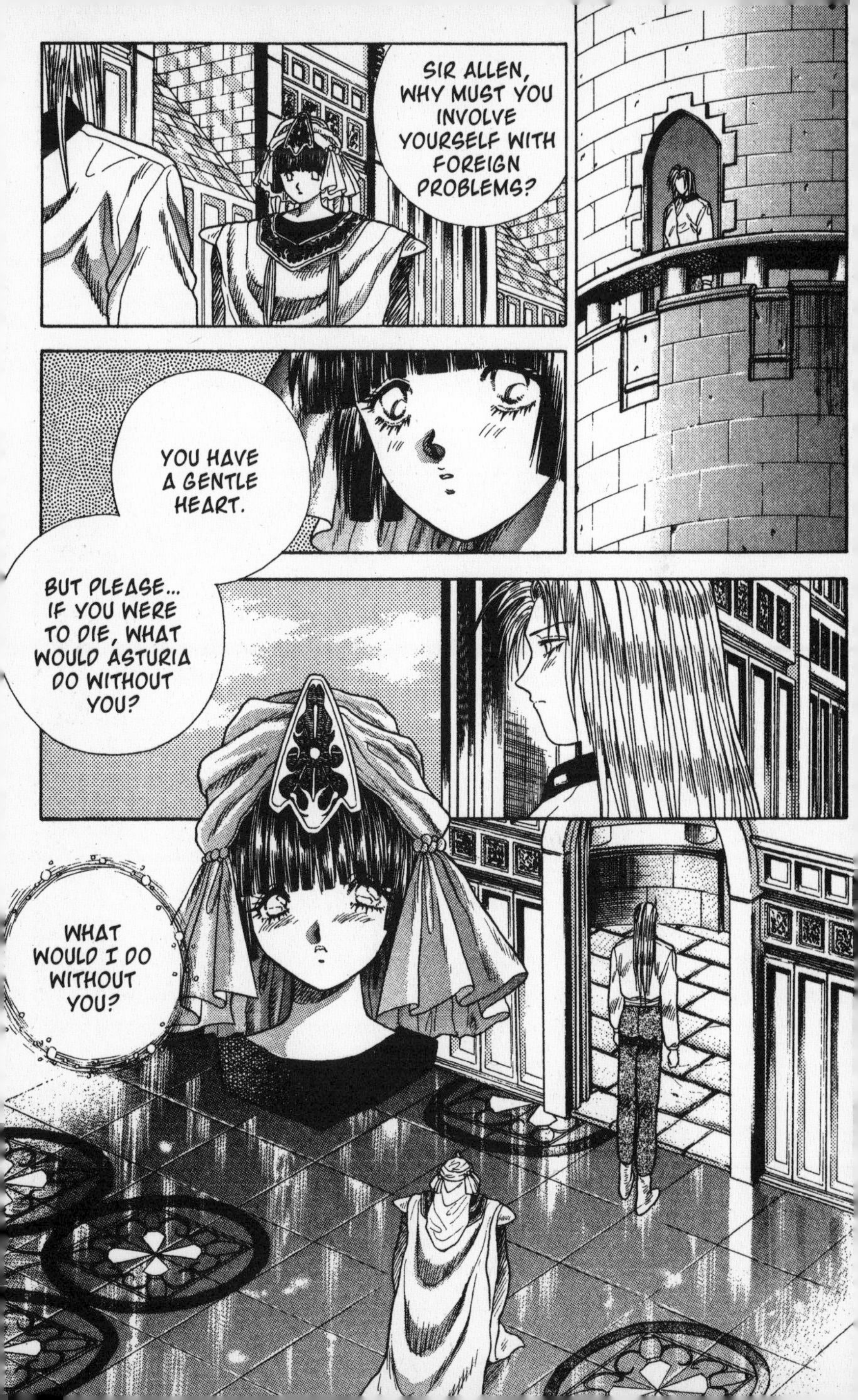
SIR ALLEN, WHY MUST YOU INVOLVE YOURSELF WITH FOREIGN PROBLEMS?
YOU HAVE A GENTLE HEART.
BUT PLEASE... IF YOU WERE TO DIE, WHAT WOULD ASTURIA DO WITHOUT YOU?
WHAT WOULD I DO WITHOUT YOU?

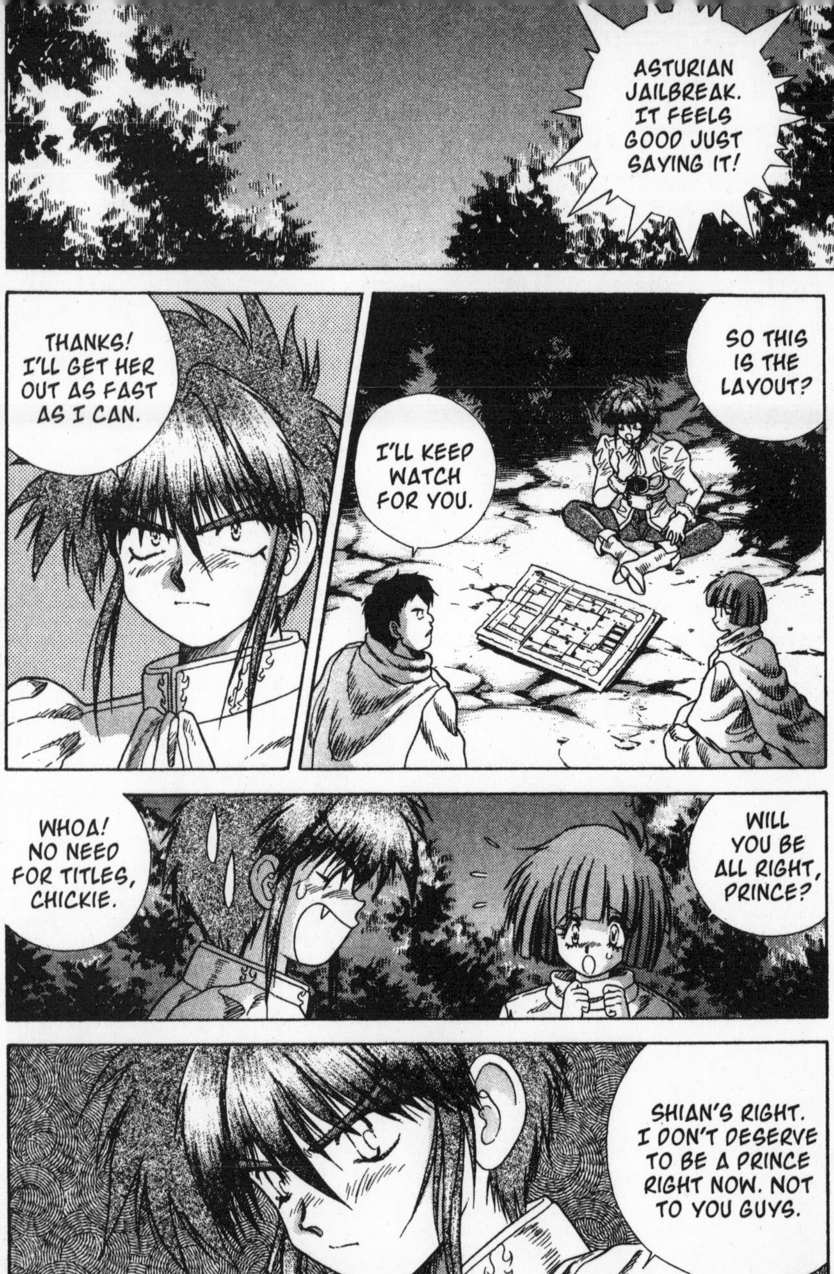
ASTURIAN JAILBREAK. IT FEELS GOOD JUST SAYING IT!
SO THIS IS THE LAYOUT?
I'LL KEEP WATCH FOR YOU.
THANKS! I'LL GET HER OUT AS FAST AS I CAN.
WILL YOU BE ALL RIGHT, PRINCE?
WHOA! NO NEED FOR TITLES, CHICKIE.
SHIAN'S RIGHT. I DON'T DESERVE TO BE A PRINCE RIGHT NOW. NOT TO YOU GUYS.

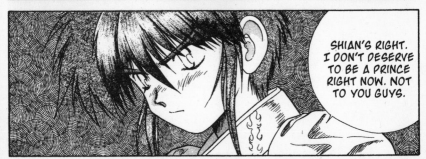

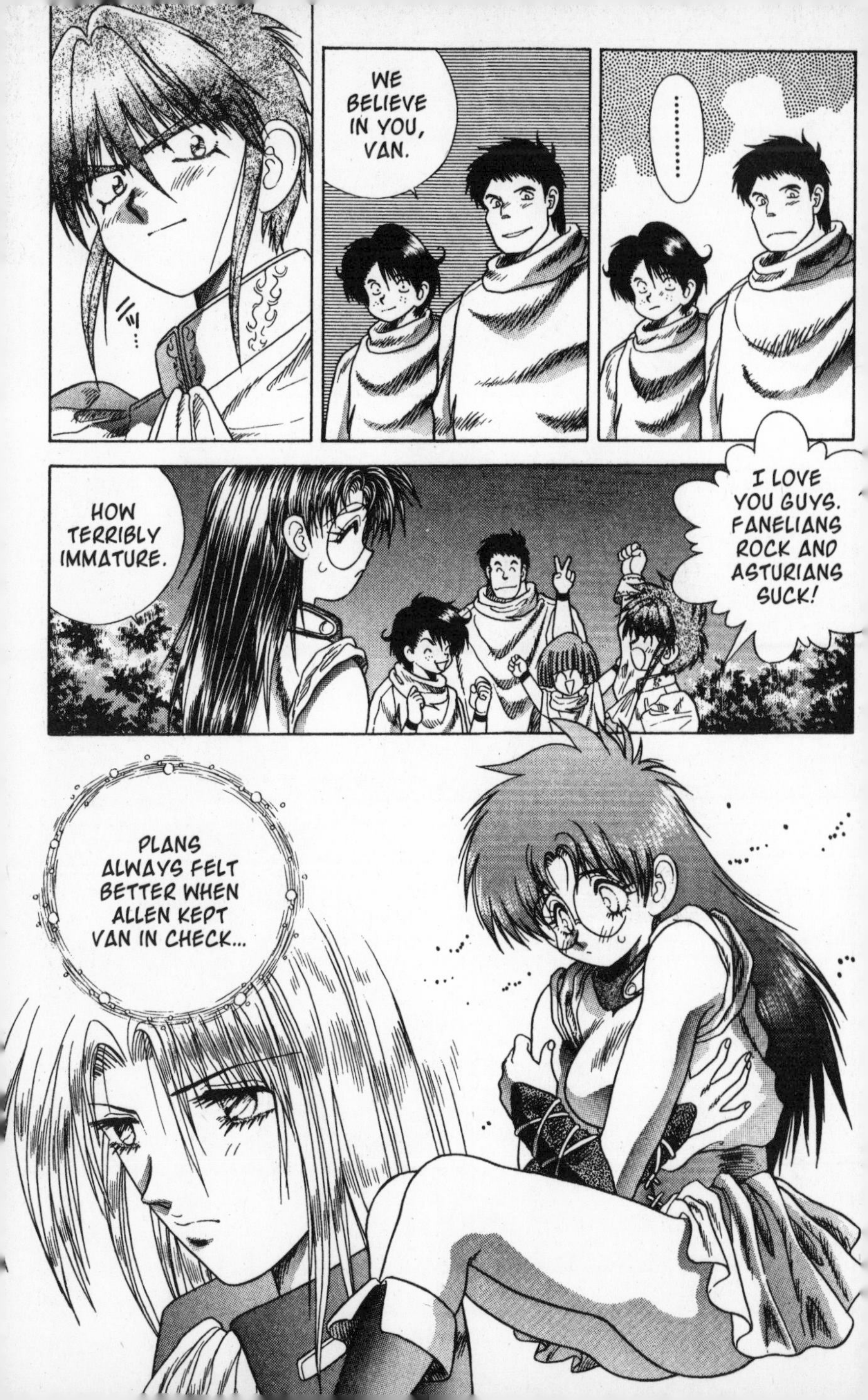
......
WE BELIEVE IN YOU, VAN.
I LOVE YOU GUYS. FANELIANS ROCK AND ASTURIANS SUCK!
HOW TERRIBLY IMMATURE.
PLANS ALWAYS FELT BETTER WHEN ALLEN KEPT VAN IN CHECK...

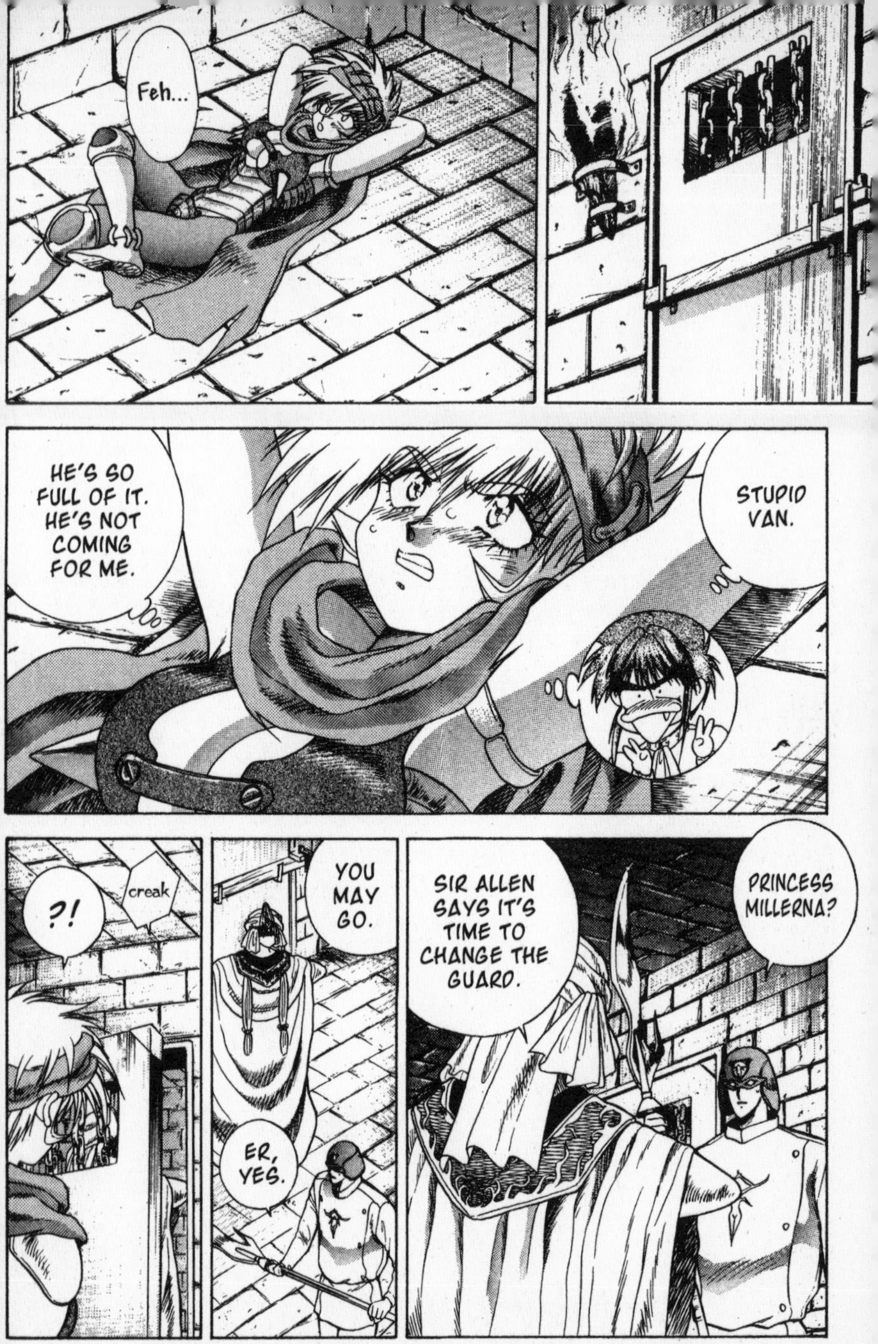
Feh...
STUPID VAN.
HE'S SO FULL OF IT. HE'S NOT COMING FOR ME.
PRINCESS MILLERNA?
SIR ALLEN SAYS IT'S TIME TO CHANGE THE GUARD.
YOU MAY GO.
ER, YES.
creak
?!

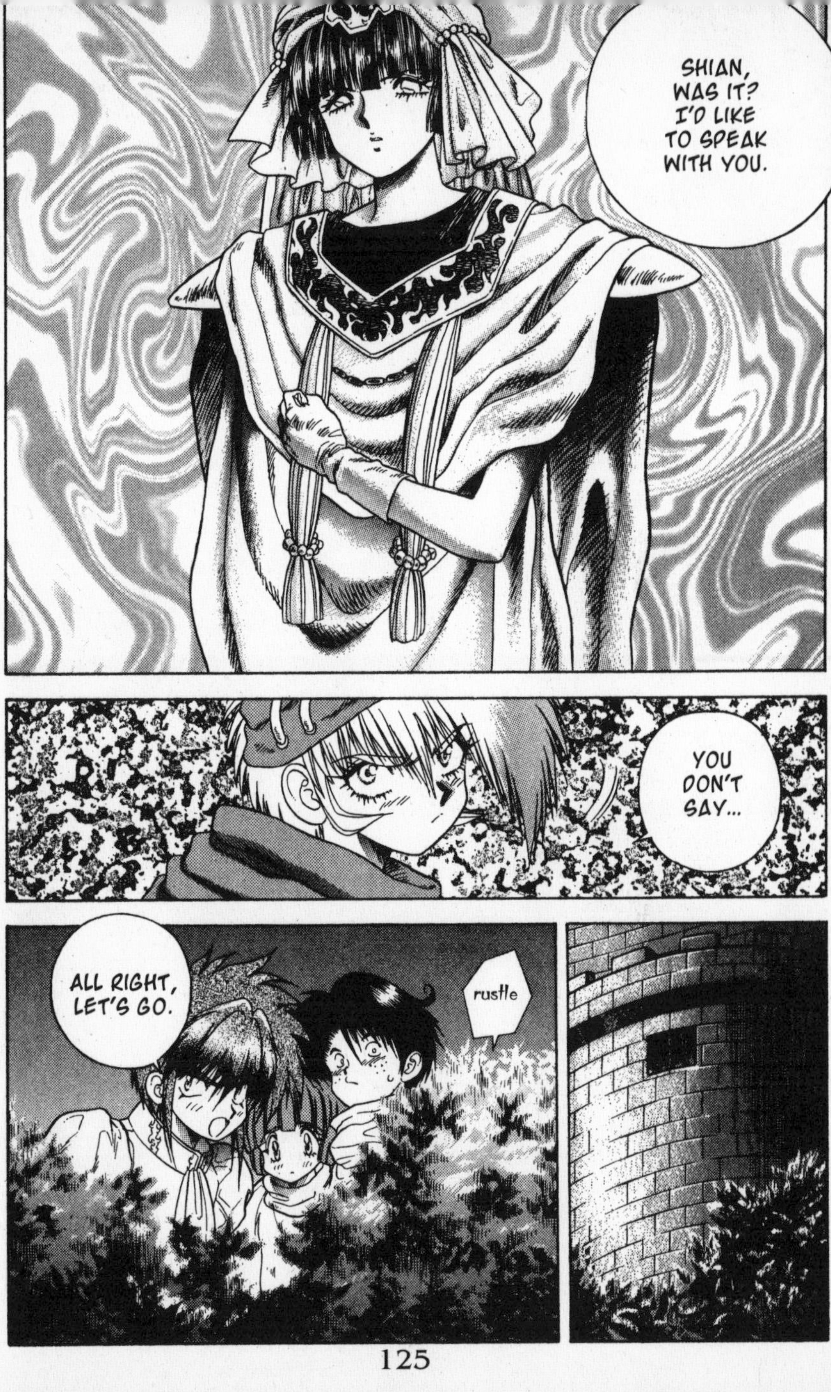
SHIAN, WAS IT? I'D LIKE TO SPEAK WITH YOU.
YOU DON'T SAY...
rustle
ALL RIGHT, LET'S GO.

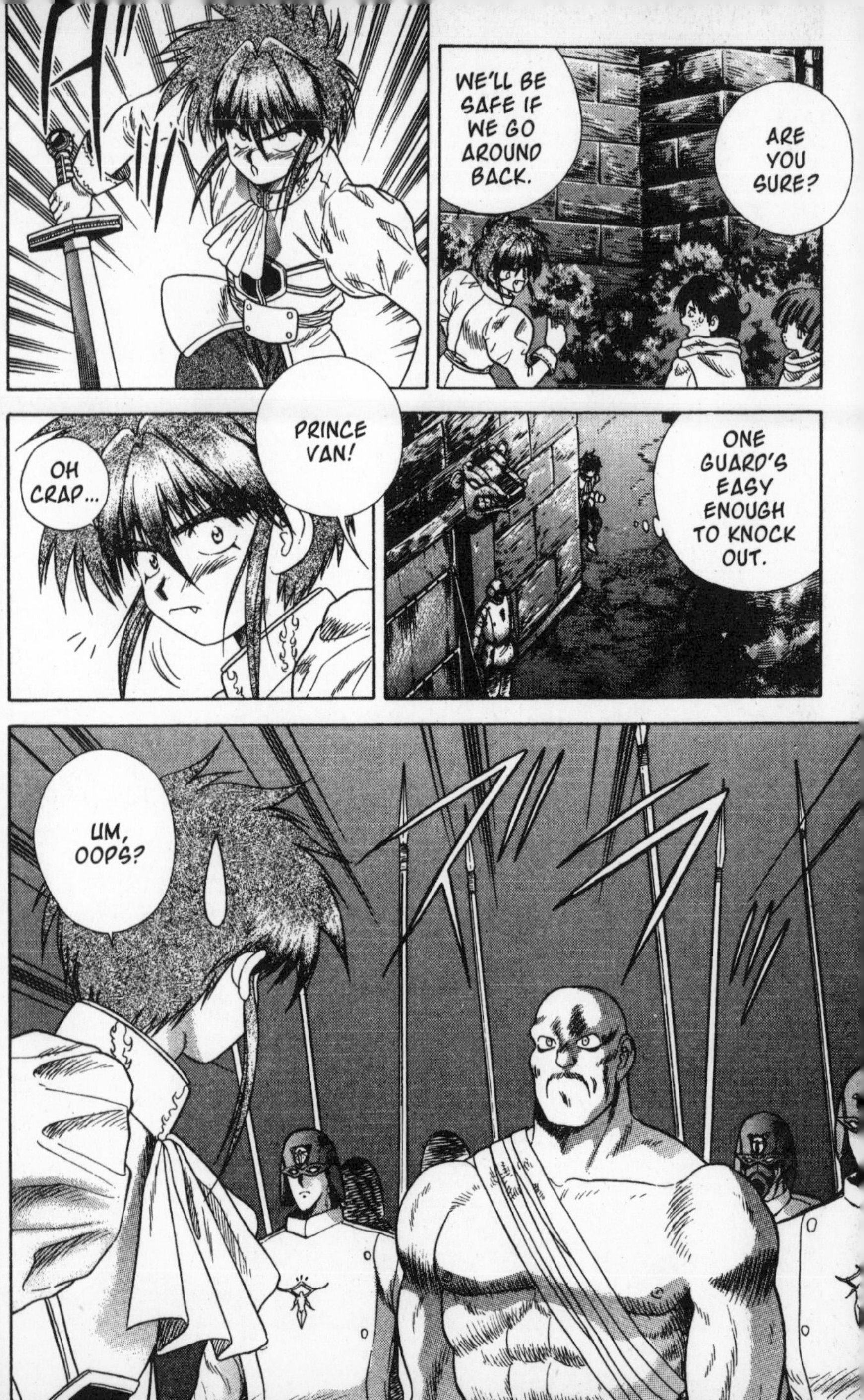
WE'LL BE SAFE IF WE GO AROUND BACK.
ARE YOU SURE?
ONE GUARD'S EASY ENOUGH TO KNOCK OUT.
PRINCE VAN!
OH CRAP...
UM, OOPS?

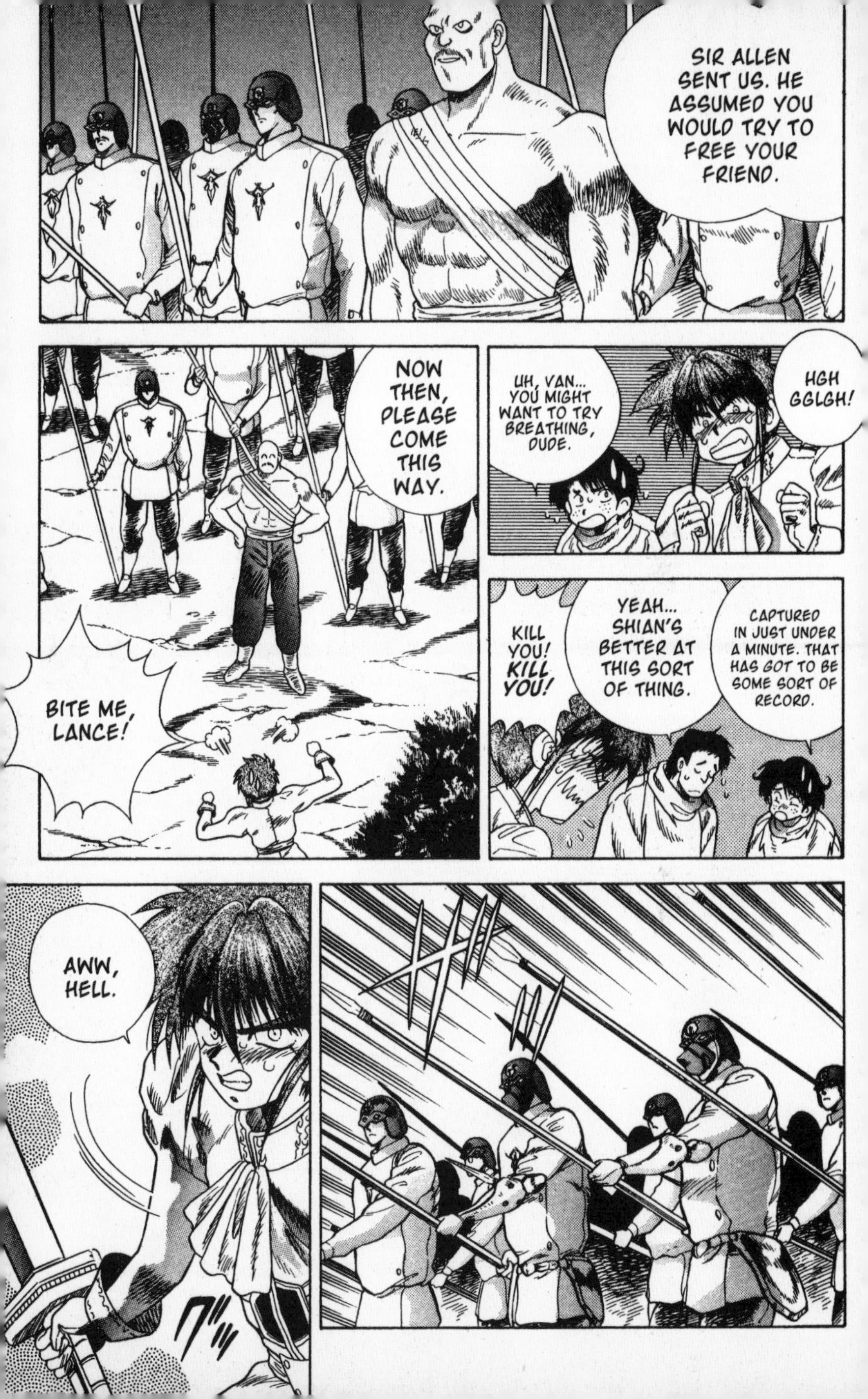
SIR ALLEN SENT US. HE ASSUMED YOU WOULD TRY TO FREE YOUR FRIEND.
HGH GGLGH!
UH, VAN... YOU MIGHT WANT TO TRY BREATHING, DUDE.
CAPTURED IN JUST UNDER A MINUTE. THAT HAS GOT TO BE SOME SORT OF RECORD.
YEAH... SHIAN'S BETTER AT THIS SORT OF THING.
KILL YOU! KILL YOU!
NOW THEN, PLEASE COME THIS WAY.
BITE ME, LANCE!
AWW, HELL.

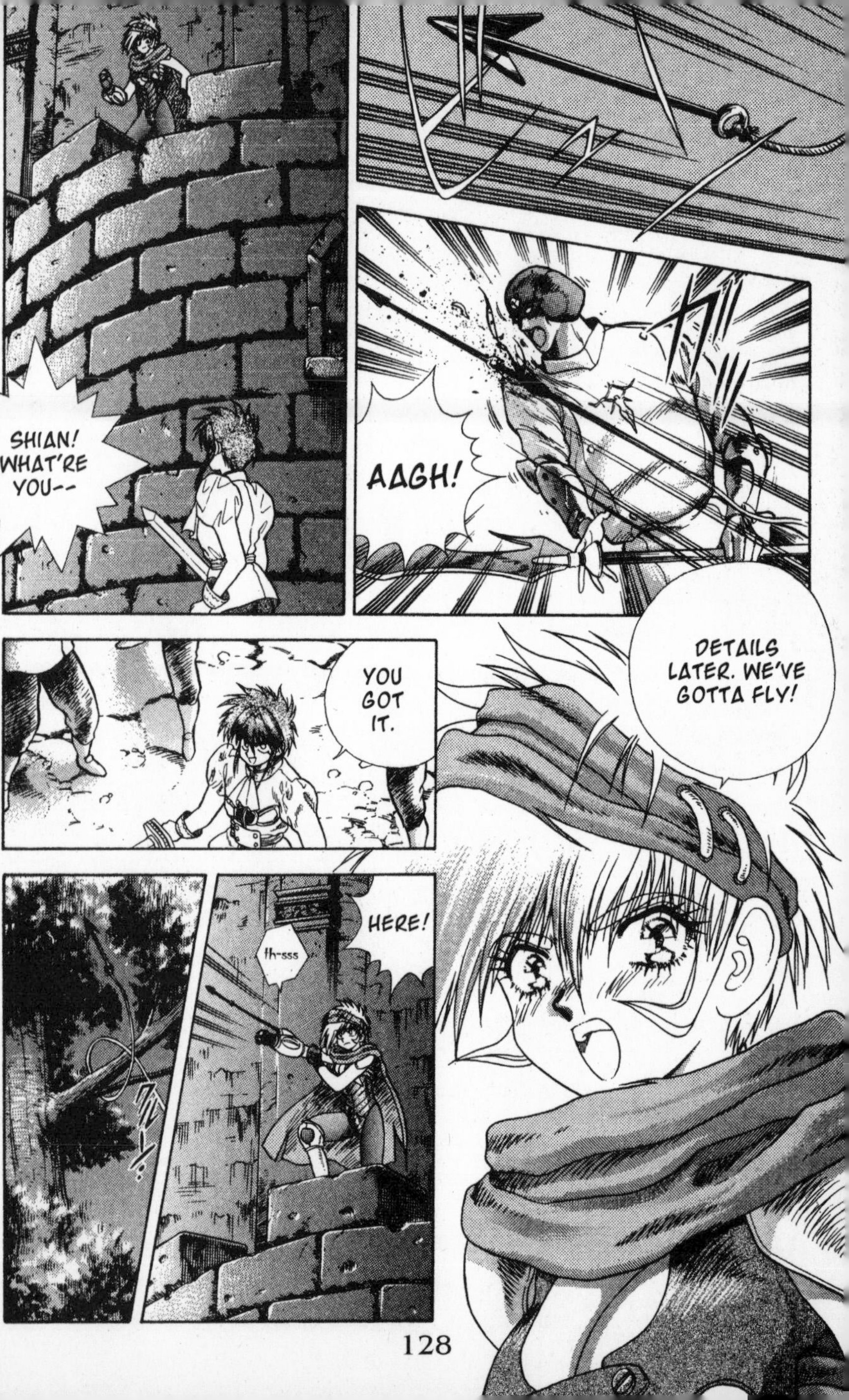
AAGH!
SHIAN! WHAT'RE YOU--
DETAILS LATER. WE'VE GOTTA FLY!
YOU GOT IT.
HERE!
th-sss

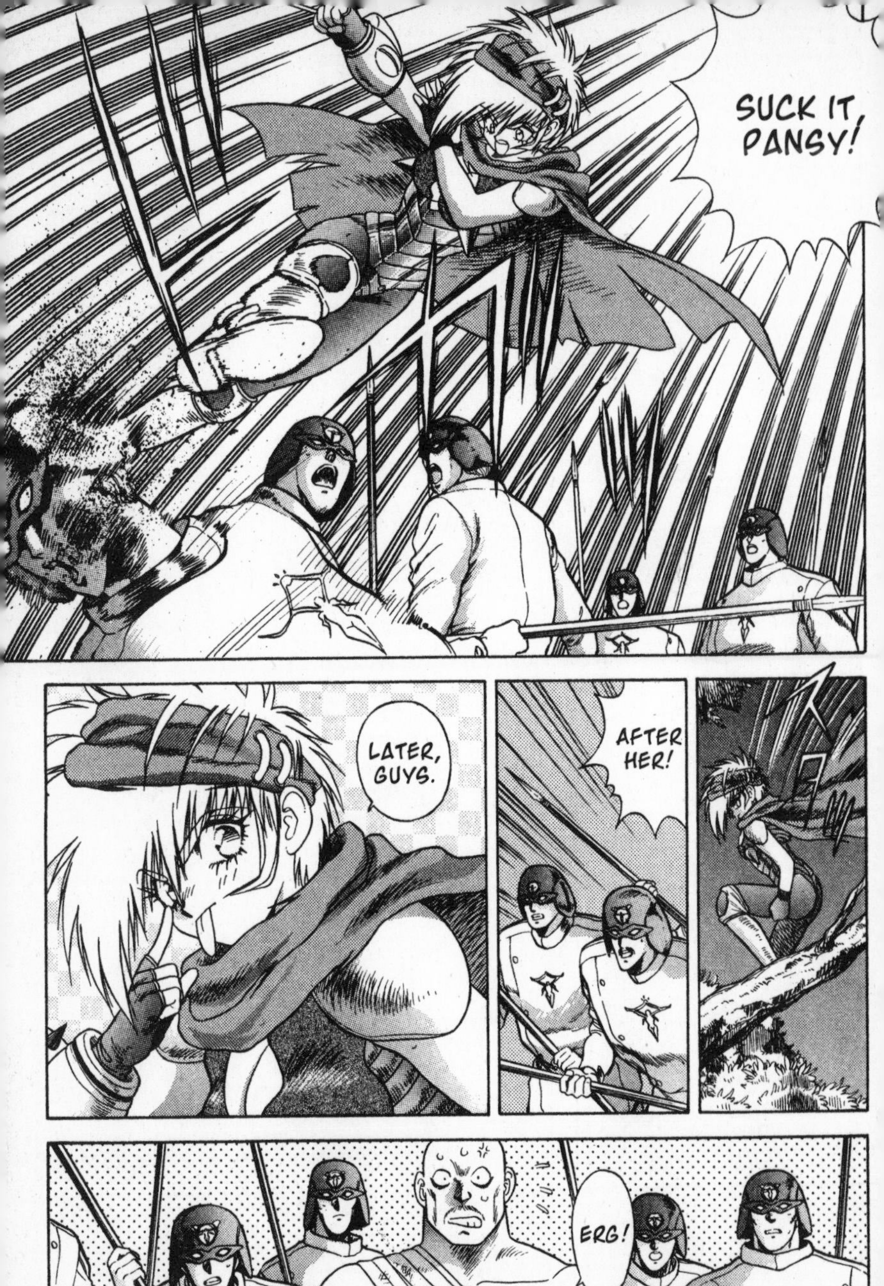
SUCK IT, PANSY!
AFTER HER!
LATER, GUYS.
ERG!

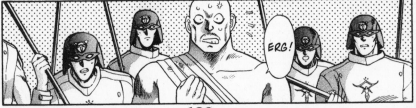

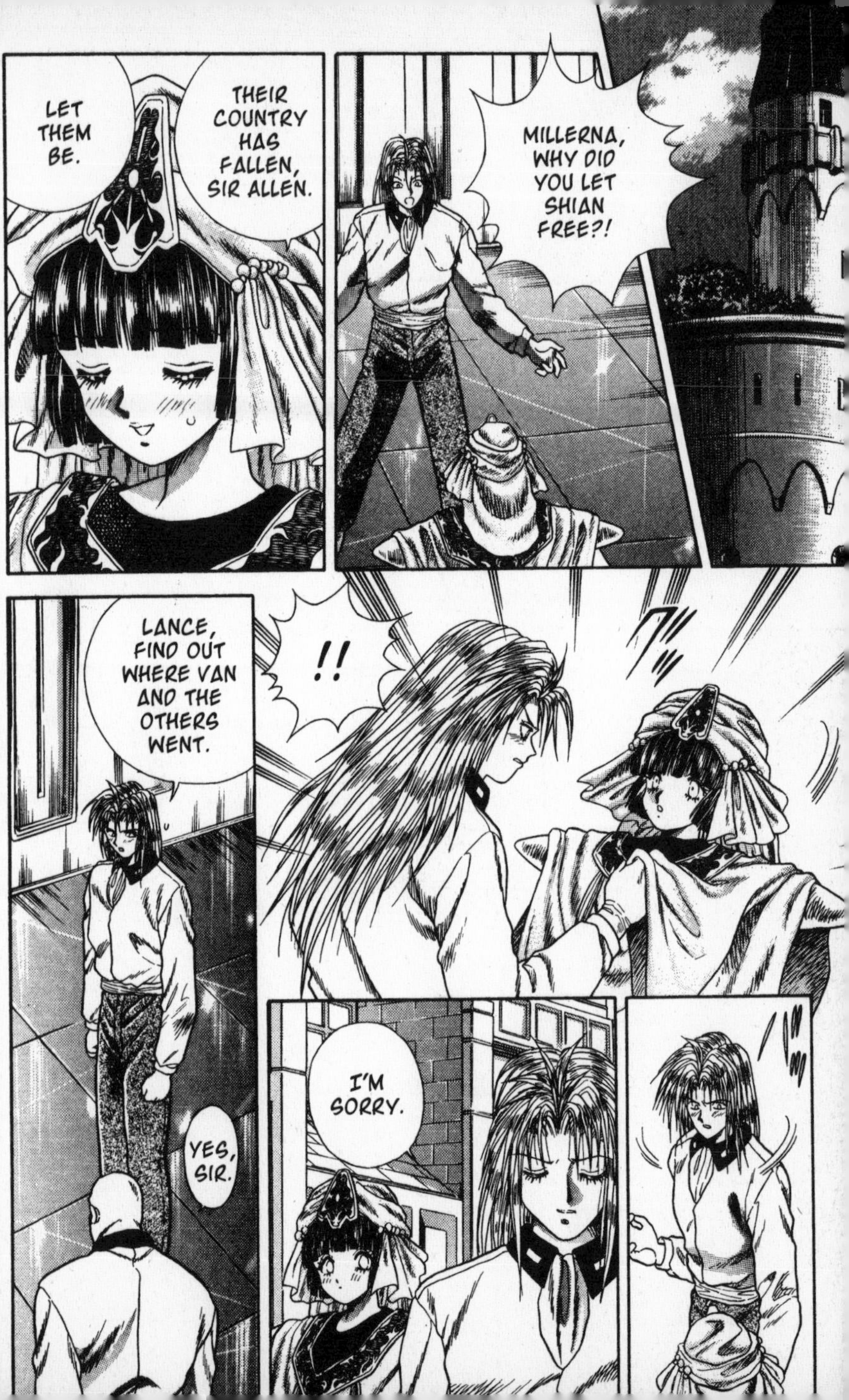
MILLERNA, WHY DID YOU LET SHIAN FREE?!
THEIR COUNTRY HAS FALLEN, SIR ALLEN.
LET THEM BE.
!!
I'M SORRY.
LANCE, FIND OUT WHERE VAN AND THE OTHERS WENT.
YES, SIR.

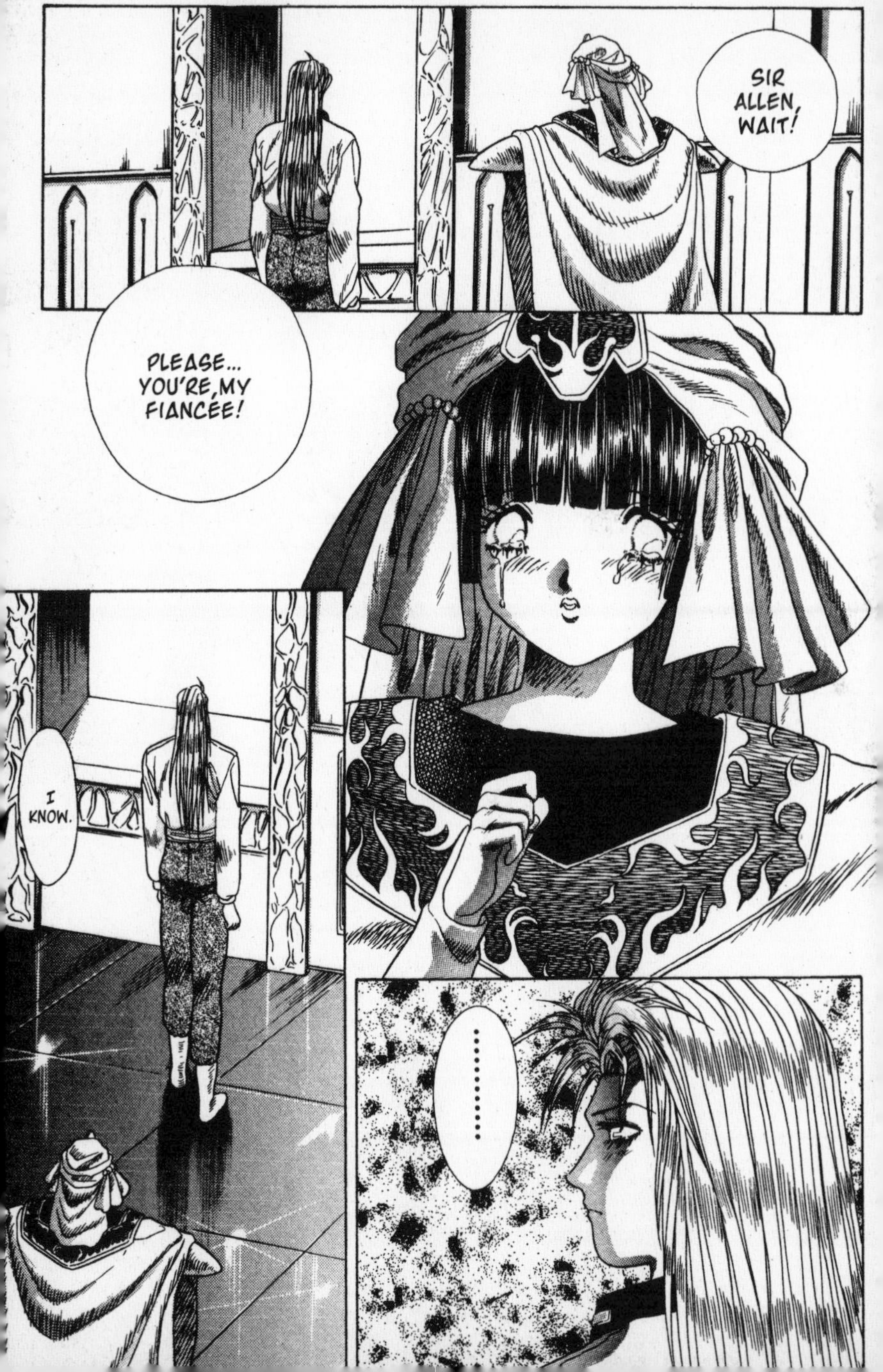
SIR ALLEN, WAIT!
PLEASE... YOU'RE, MY FIANCÉE!
....
I KNOW.

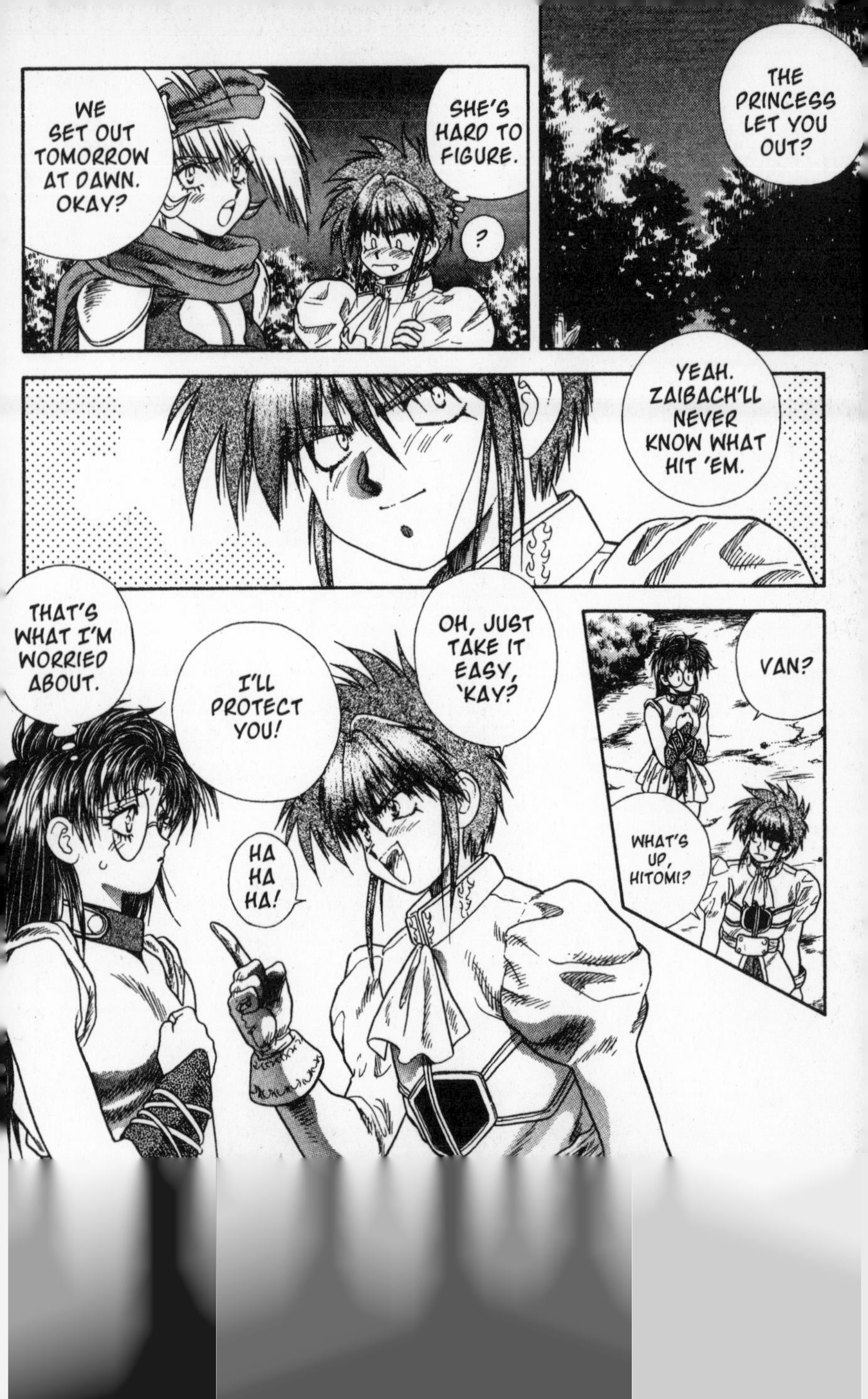

THE PRINCESS LET YOU OUT?
SHE'S HARD TO FIGURE.
WE SET OUT TOMORROW AT DAWN. OKAY?
?
YEAH. ZAIBACH'LL NEVER KNOW WHAT HIT 'EM.
VAN?
WHAT'S UP, HITOMI?
OH, JUST TAKE IT EASY, 'KAY?
I'LL PROTECT YOU!
THAT'S WHAT I'M WORRIED ABOUT.
HA HA HA!

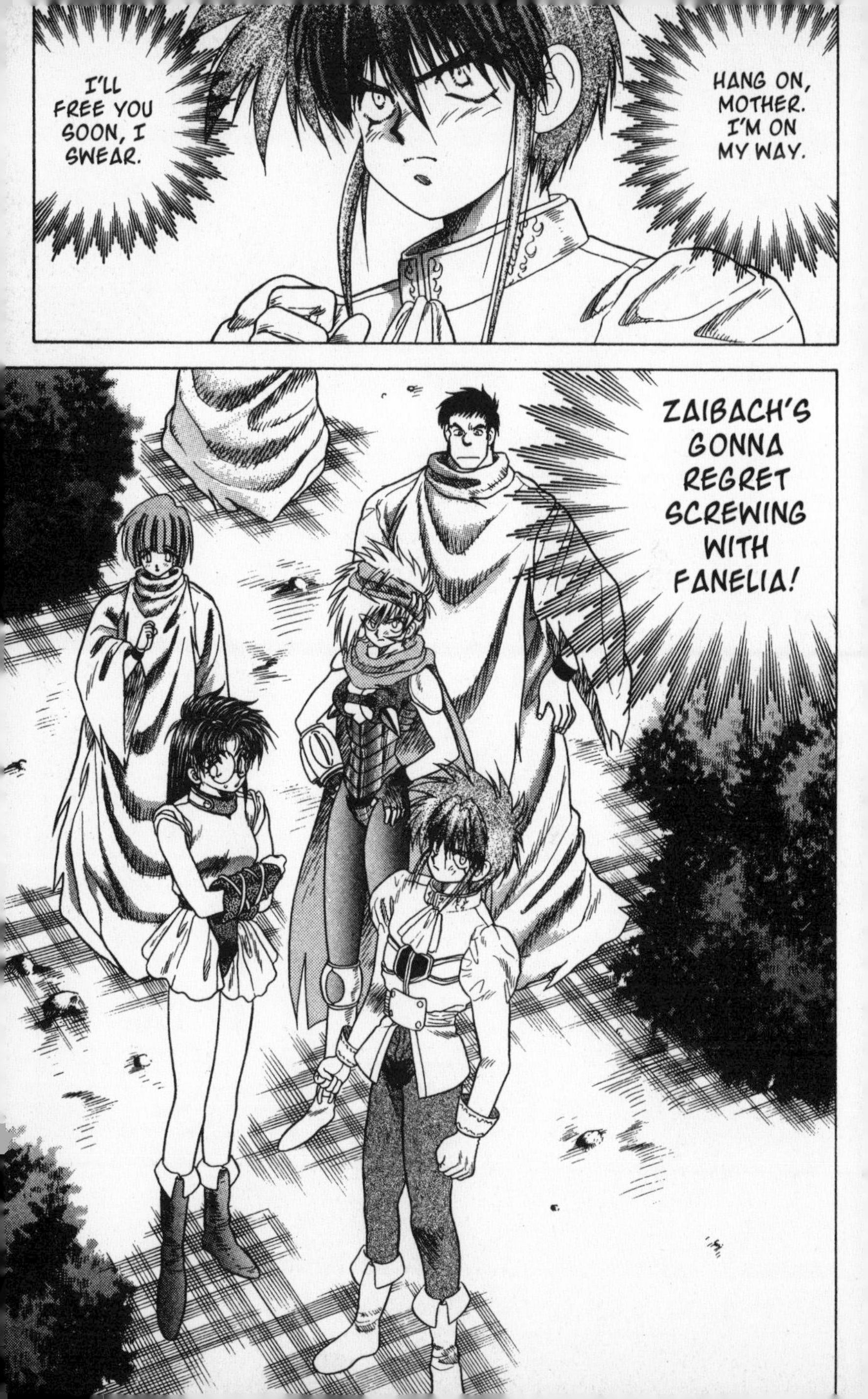
HANG ON, MOTHER. I'M ON MY WAY.
I'LL FREE YOU SOON, I SWEAR.
ZAIBACH'S GONNA REGRET SCREWING WITH FANELIA!

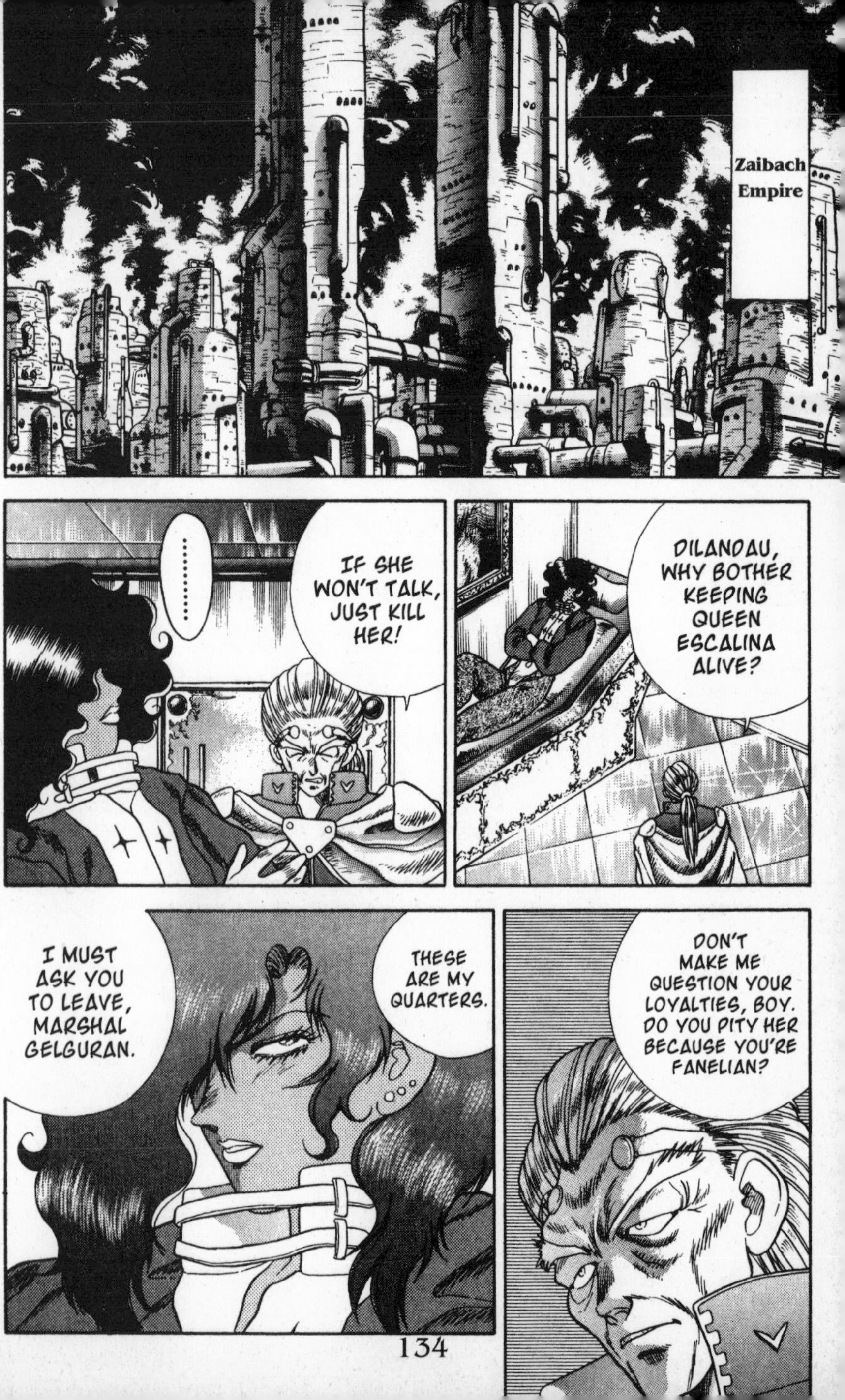

Zaibach Empire
DILANDAU, WHY BOTHER KEEPING QUEEN ESCALINA ALIVE?
IF SHE WON'T TALK, JUST KILL HER!
......
DON'T MAKE ME QUESTION YOUR LOYALTIES, BOY. DO YOU PITY HER BECAUSE YOU'RE FANELIAN?
THESE ARE MY QUARTERS.
I MUST ASK YOU TO LEAVE, MARSHAL GELGURAN.

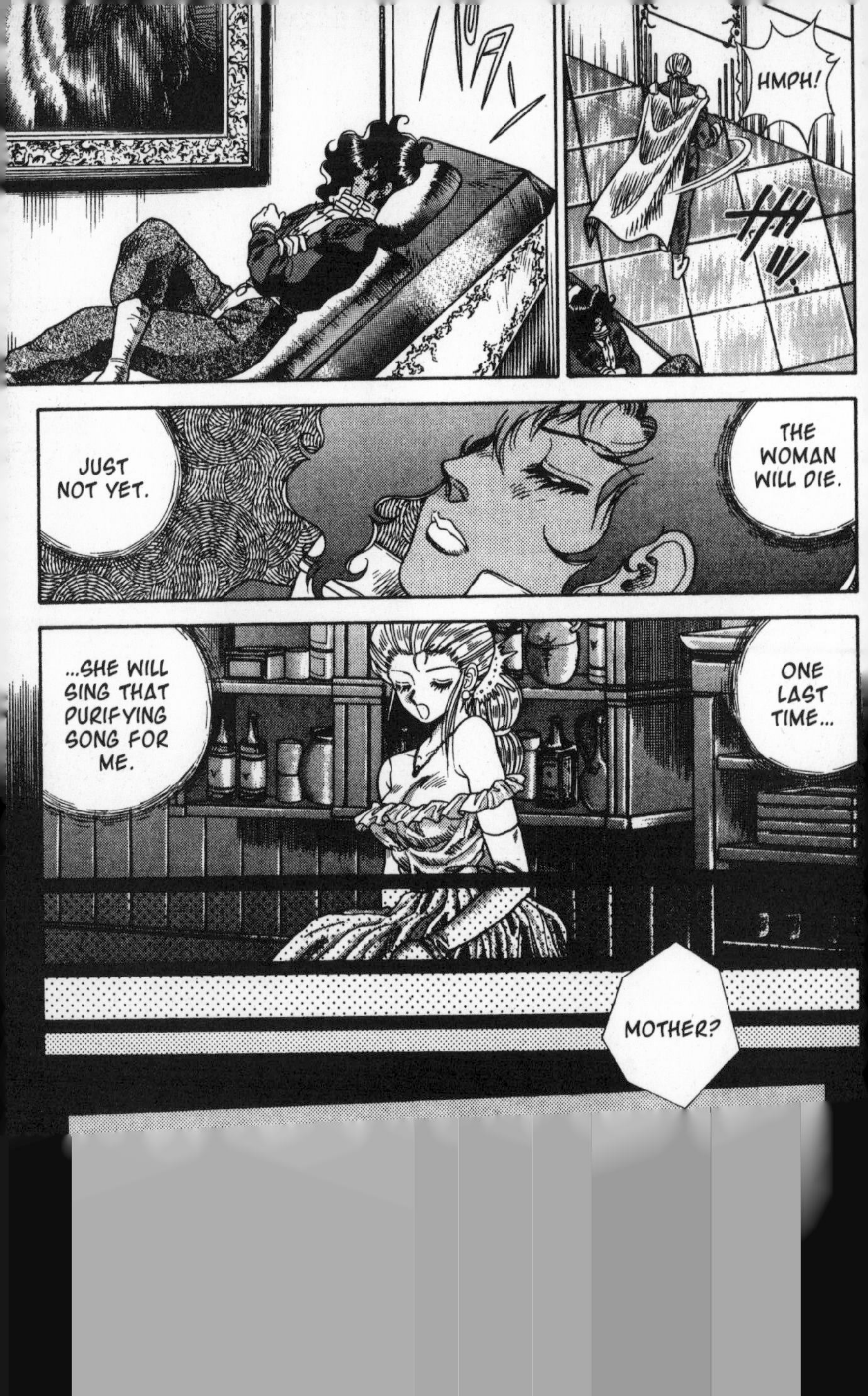
HMPH!
THE WOMAN WILL DIE.
JUST NOT YET.
ONE LAST TIME...
...SHE WILL SING THAT PURIFYING SONG FOR ME.
MOTHER?

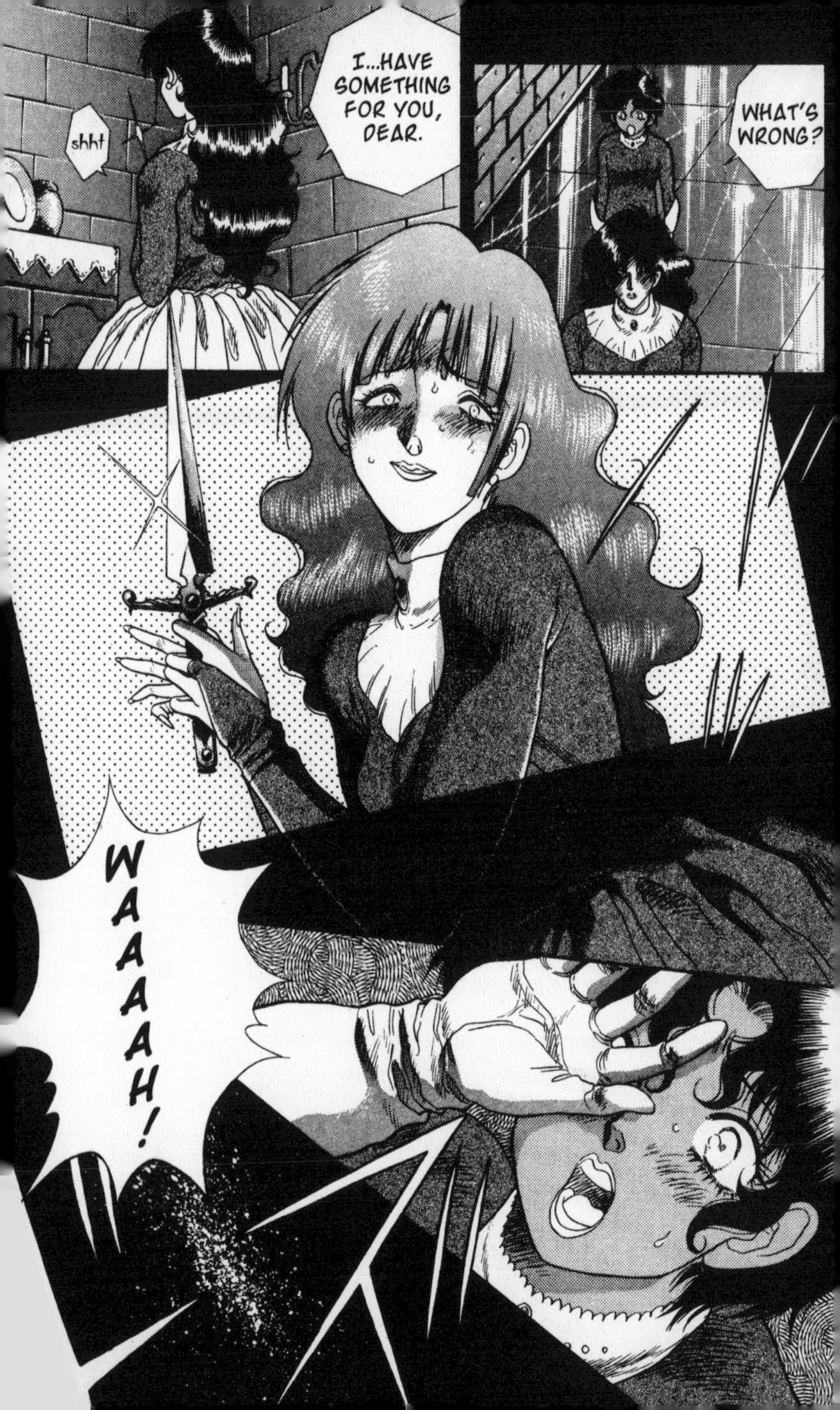
WHAT'S WRONG?
I...HAVE SOMETHING FOR YOU, DEAR.
shht
WAAAAAH!

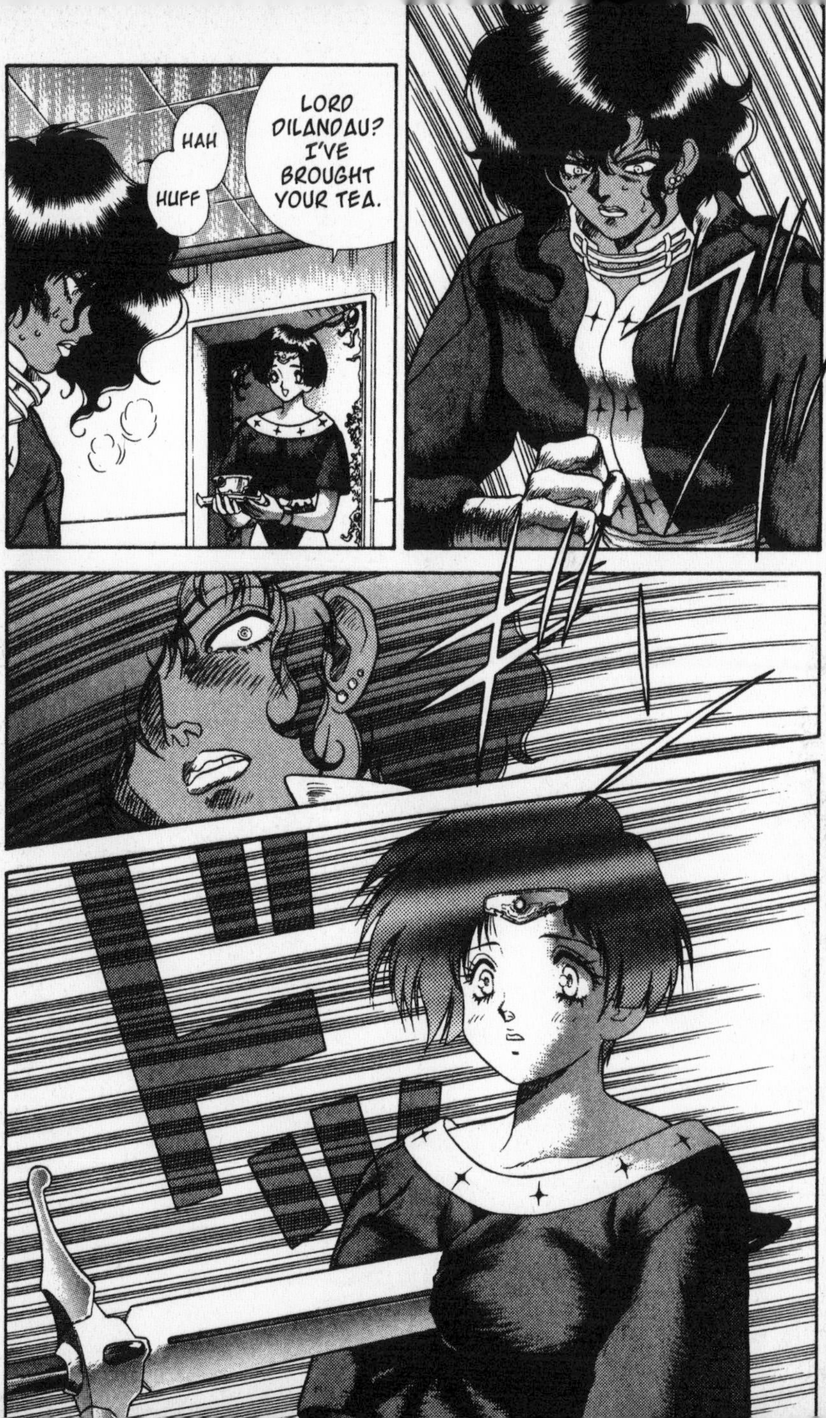
LORD DILANDAU? I'VE BROUGHT YOUR TEA.
HAH
HUFF

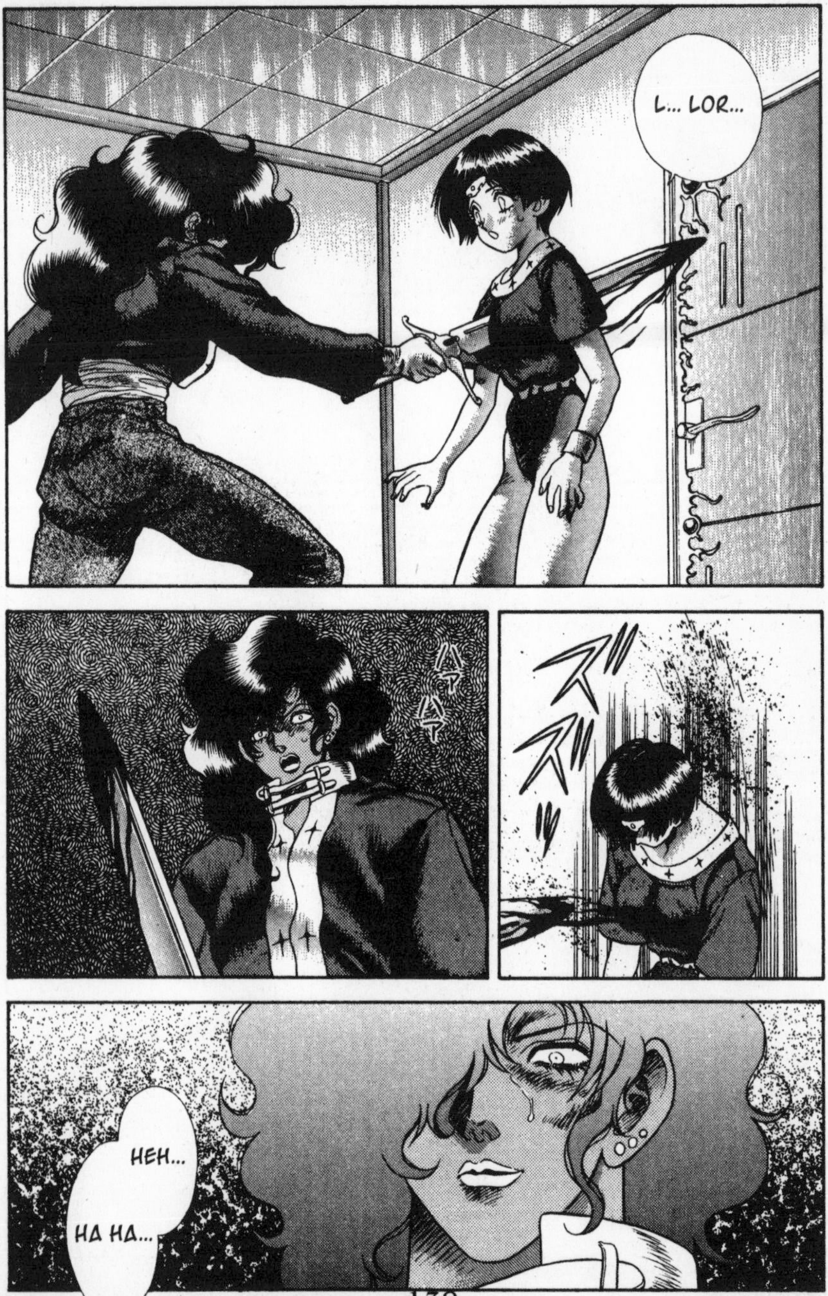
L... LOR...
ズズズ
ハァハァ
HEH...
HA HA...

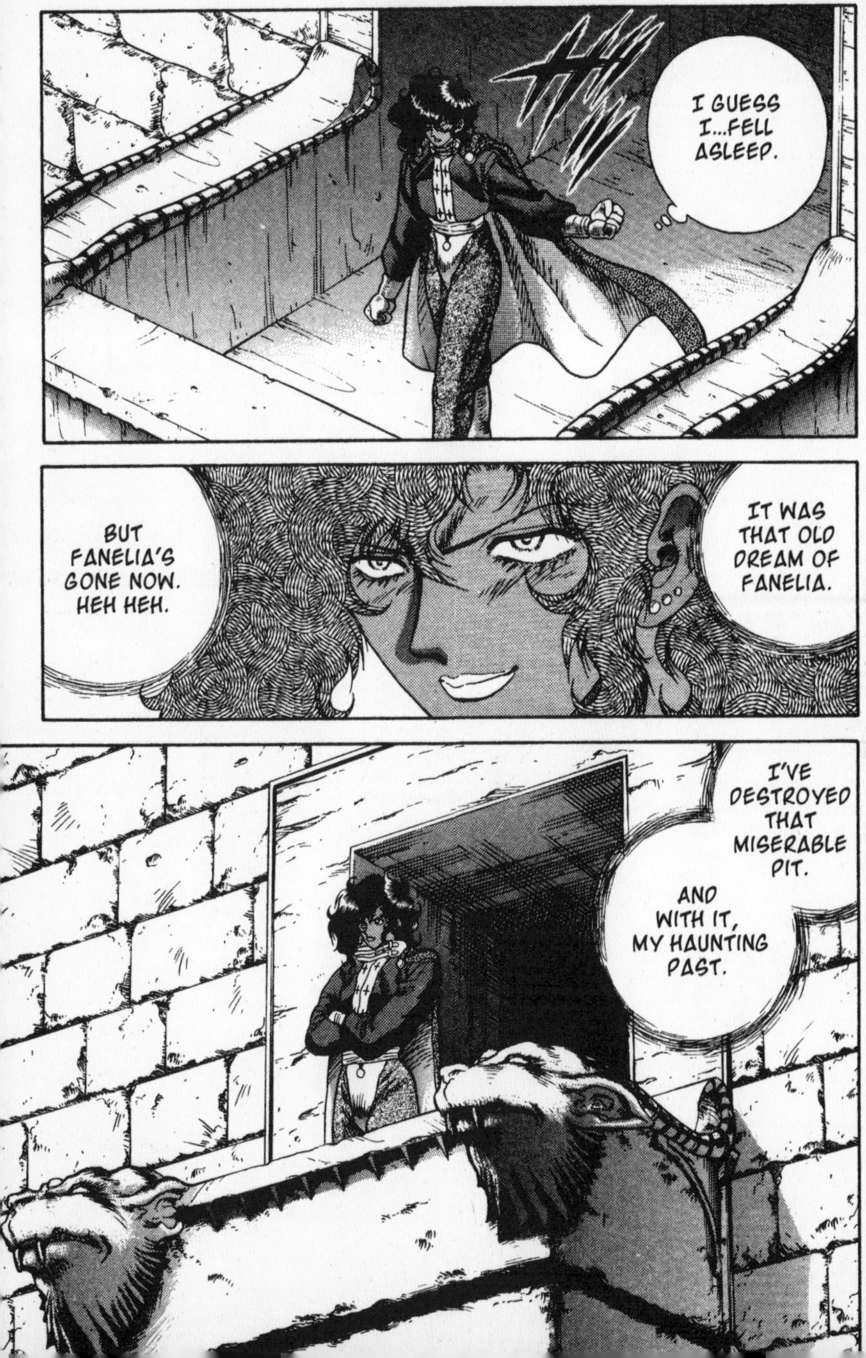
I GUESS I...FELL ASLEEP.
IT WAS THAT OLD DREAM OF FANELIA.
BUT FANELIA'S GONE NOW. HEH HEH.
I'VE DESTROYED THAT MISERABLE PIT.
AND WITH IT, MY HAUNTING PAST.

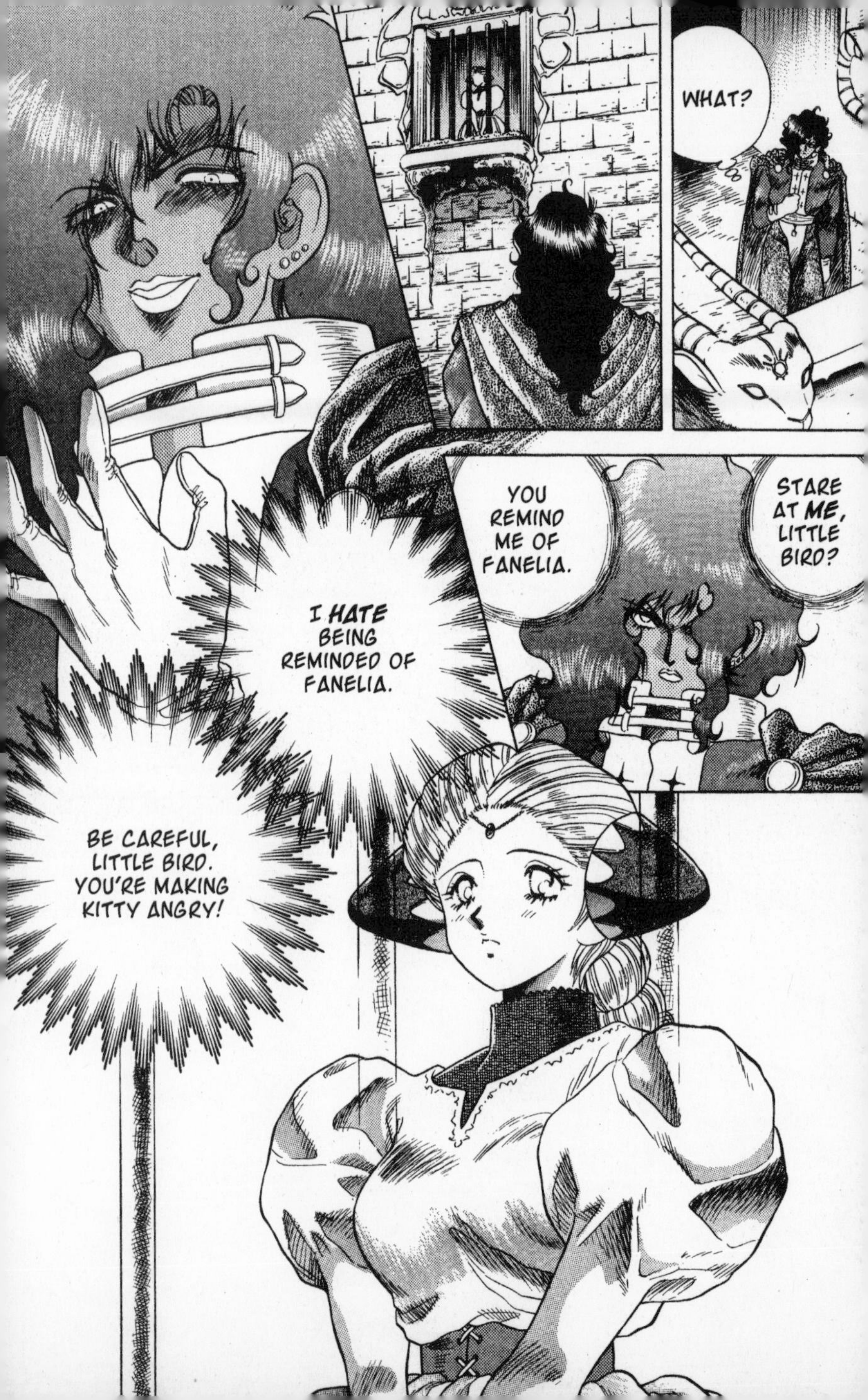
WHAT?
STARE AT ME, LITTLE BIRD?
YOU REMIND ME OF FANELIA.
I HATE BEING REMINDED OF FANELIA.
BE CAREFUL, LITTLE BIRD. YOU'RE MAKING KITTY ANGRY!

VISION 9: ZAIBACH INFILTRATION

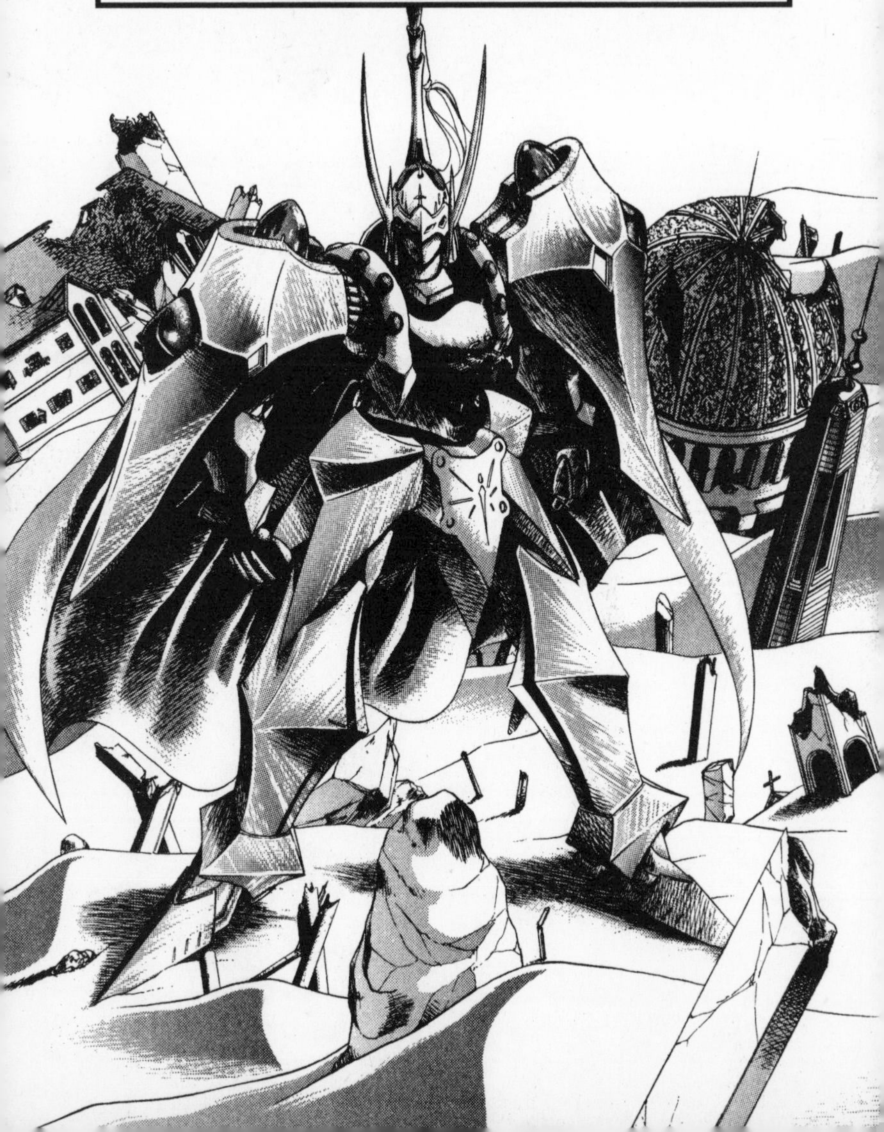

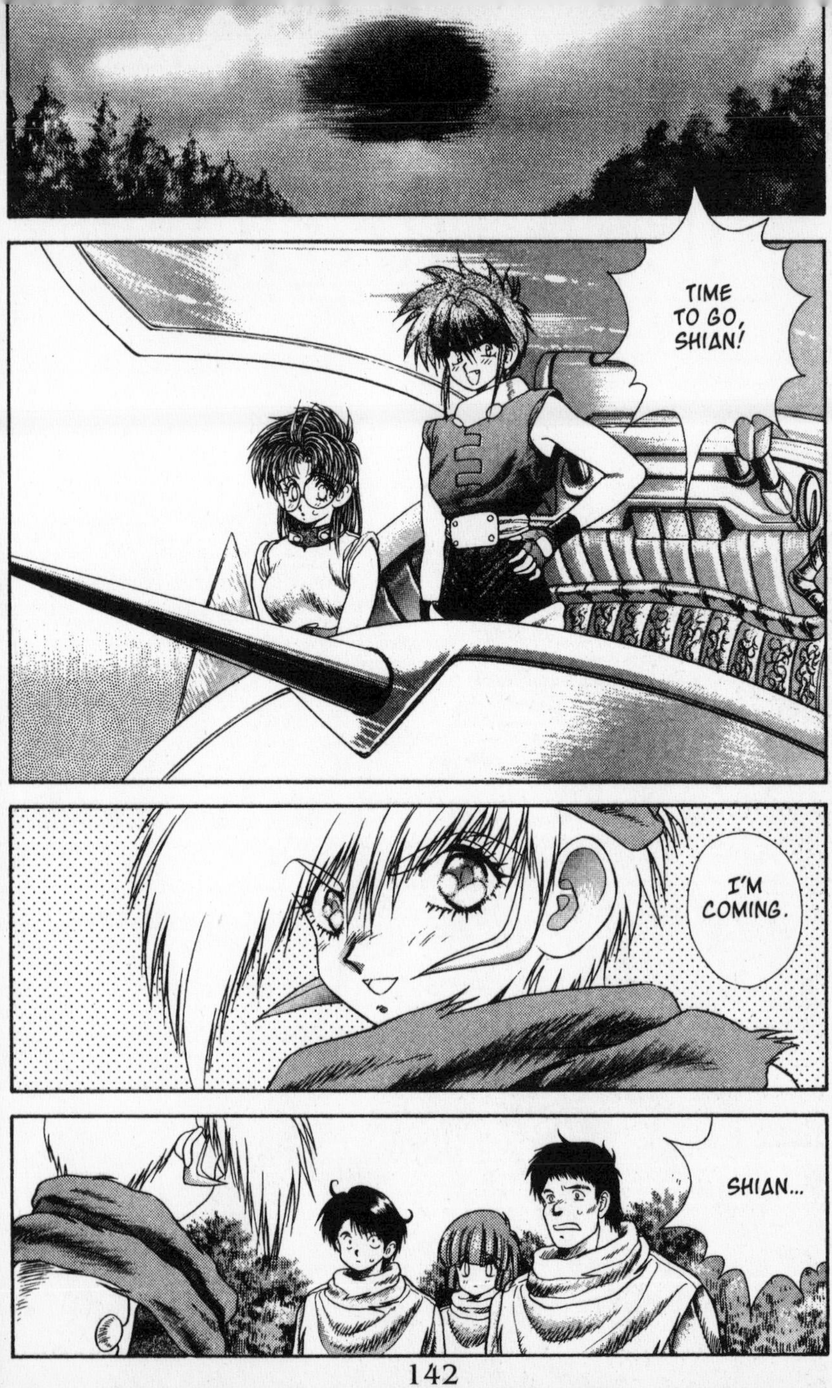
TIME TO GO, SHIAN!
I'M COMING.
SHIAN...

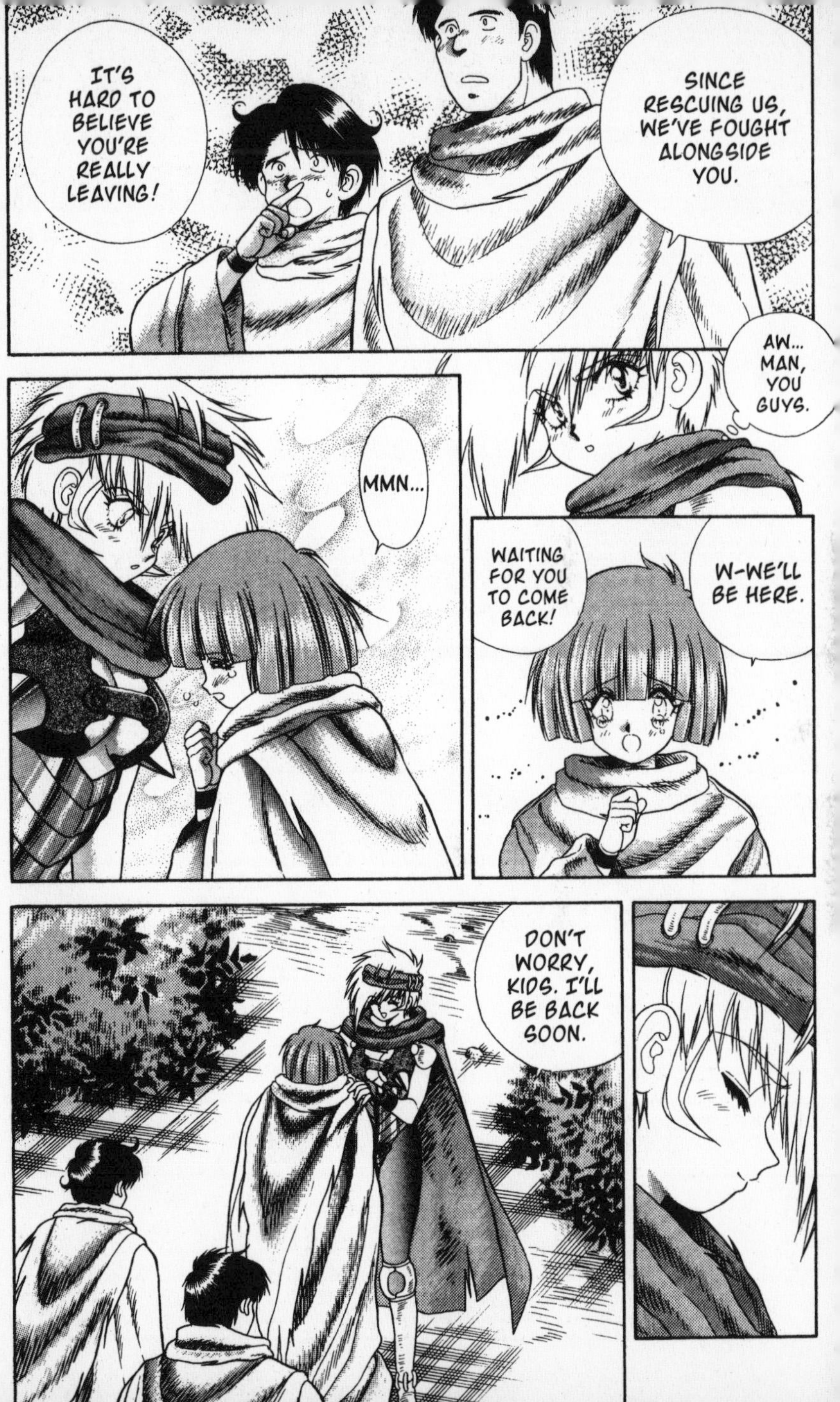
SINCE RESCUING US, WE'VE FOUGHT ALONGSIDE YOU.
IT'S HARD TO BELIEVE YOU'RE REALLY LEAVING!
AW... MAN, YOU GUYS.
W-WE'LL BE HERE.
WAITING FOR YOU TO COME BACK!
MMN...
DON'T WORRY, KIDS. I'LL BE BACK SOON.

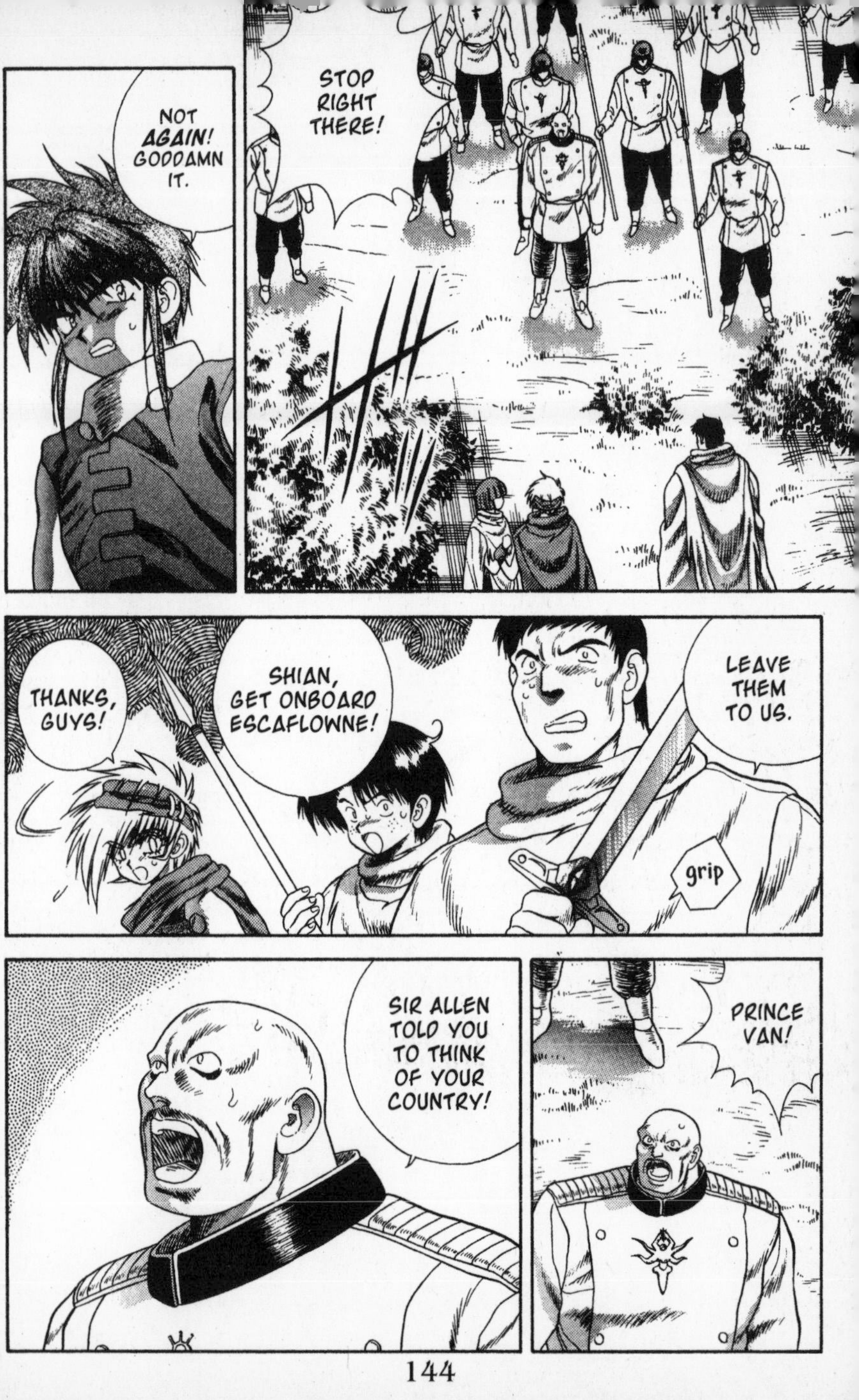
STOP RIGHT THERE!
NOT AGAIN! GODDAMN IT.
LEAVE THEM TO US.
grip
SHIAN, GET ONBOARD ESCAFLOWNE!
THANKS, GUYS!
PRINCE VAN!
SIR ALLEN TOLD YOU TO THINK OF YOUR COUNTRY!

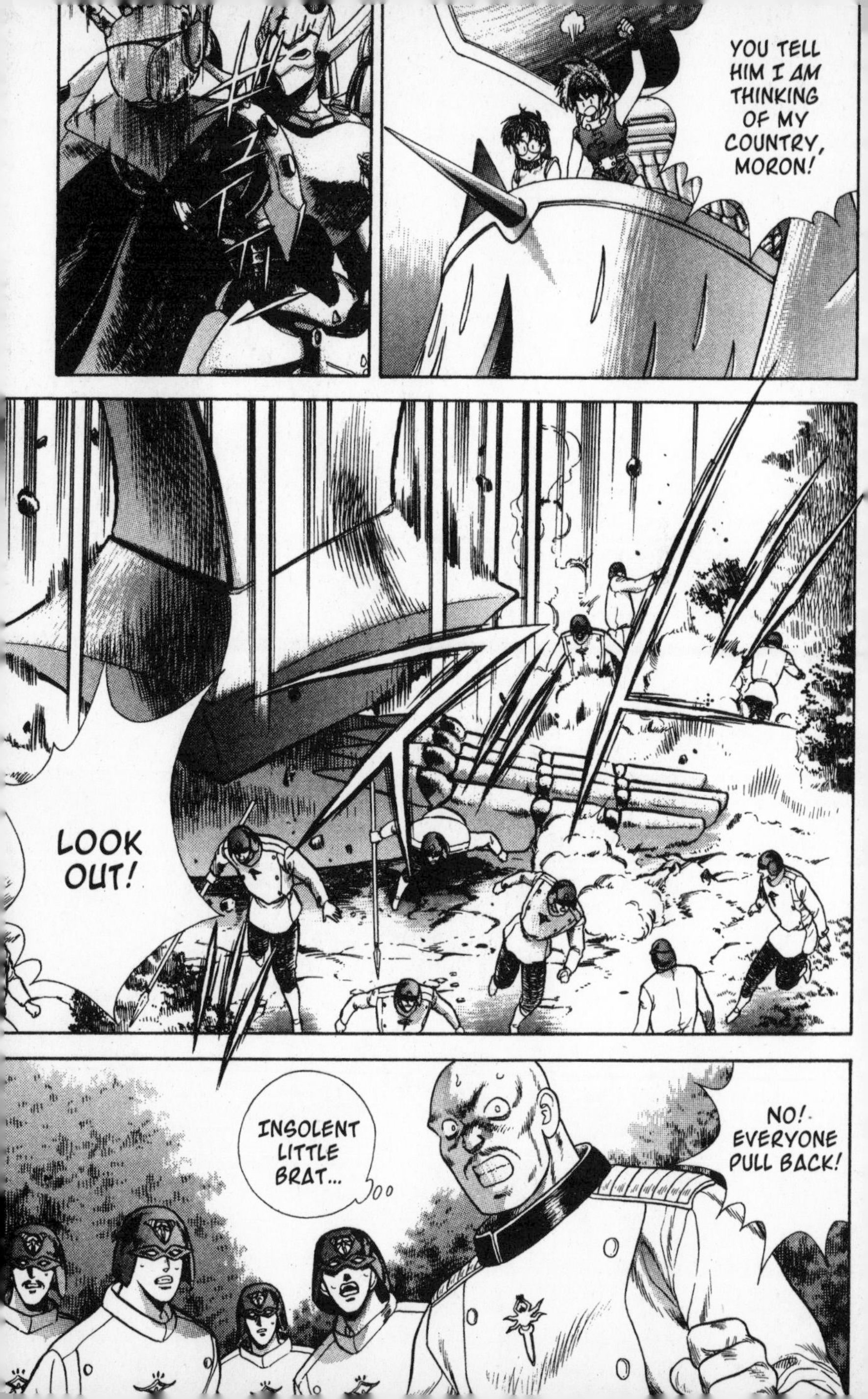
YOU TELL HIM I AM THINKING OF MY COUNTRY, MORON!
LOOK OUT!
NO! EVERYONE PULL BACK!
INSOLENT LITTLE BRAT...

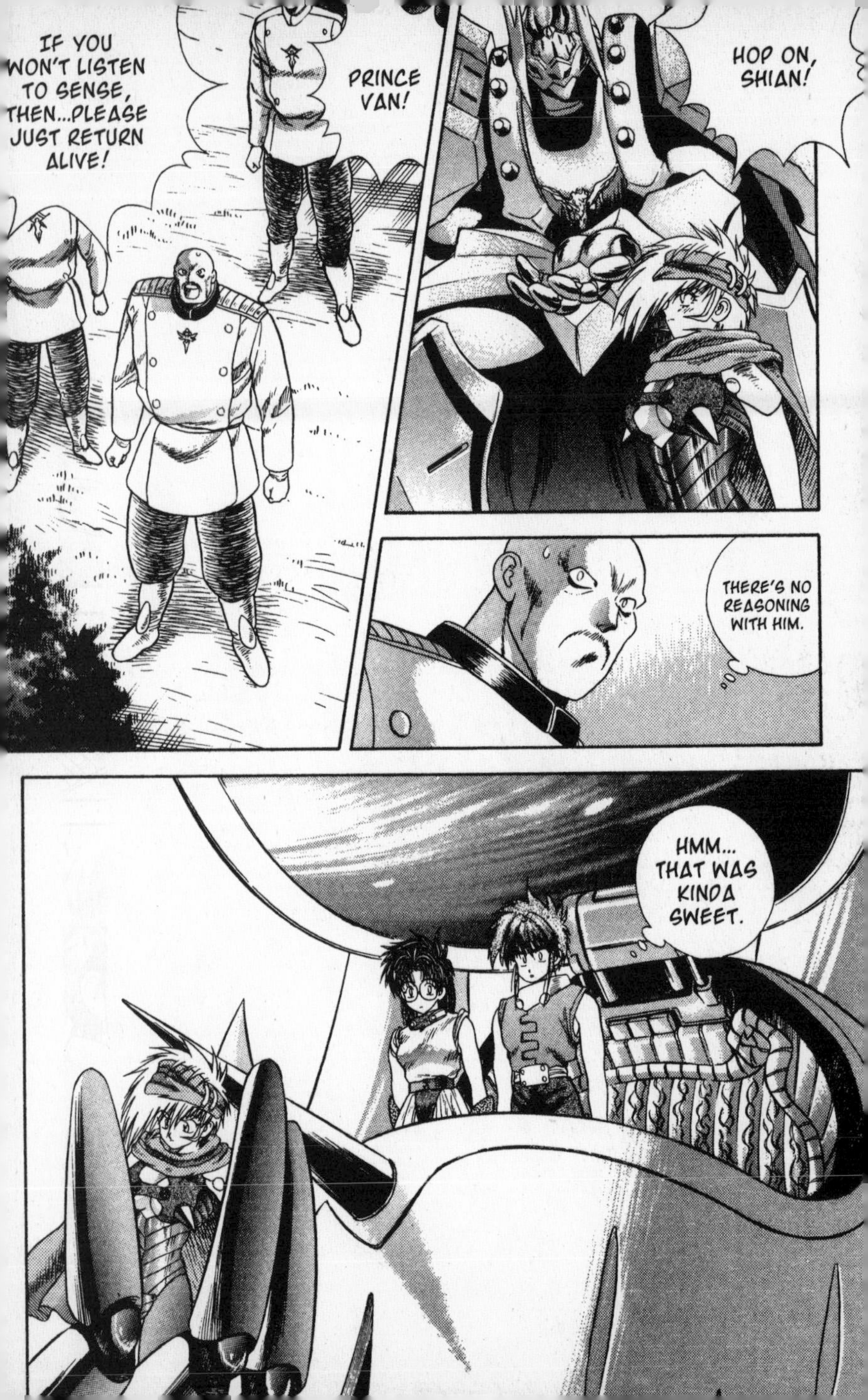
HOP ON, SHIAN!
THERE'S NO REASONING WITH HIM.
PRINCE VAN!
IF YOU WON'T LISTEN TO SENSE, THEN...PLEASE JUST RETURN ALIVE!
HMM... THAT WAS KINDA SWEET.

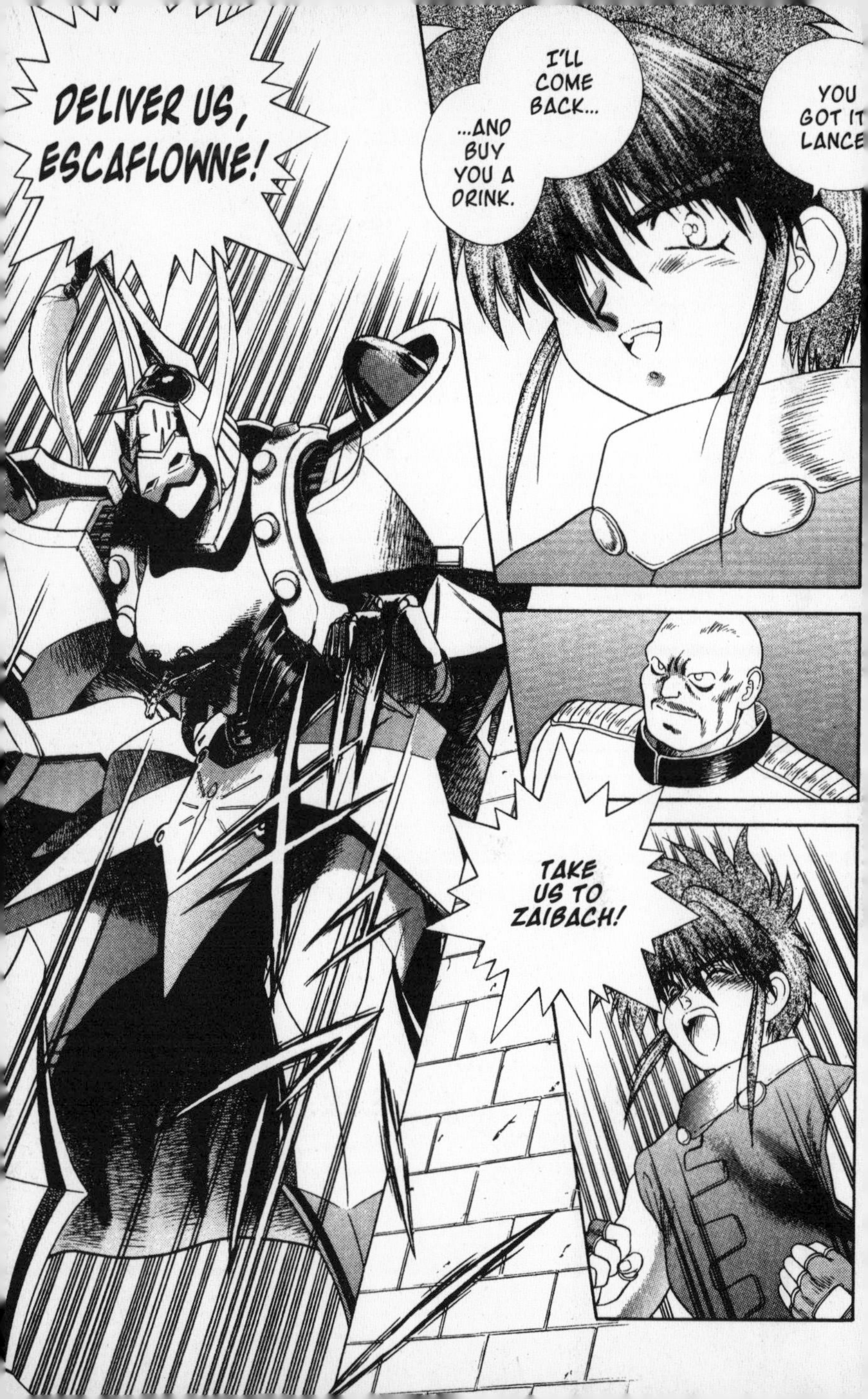

YOU GOT IT LANCE
I'LL COME BACK...
...AND BUY YOU A DRINK.
TAKE US TO ZAIBACH!
DELIVER US, ESCAFLOWNE!

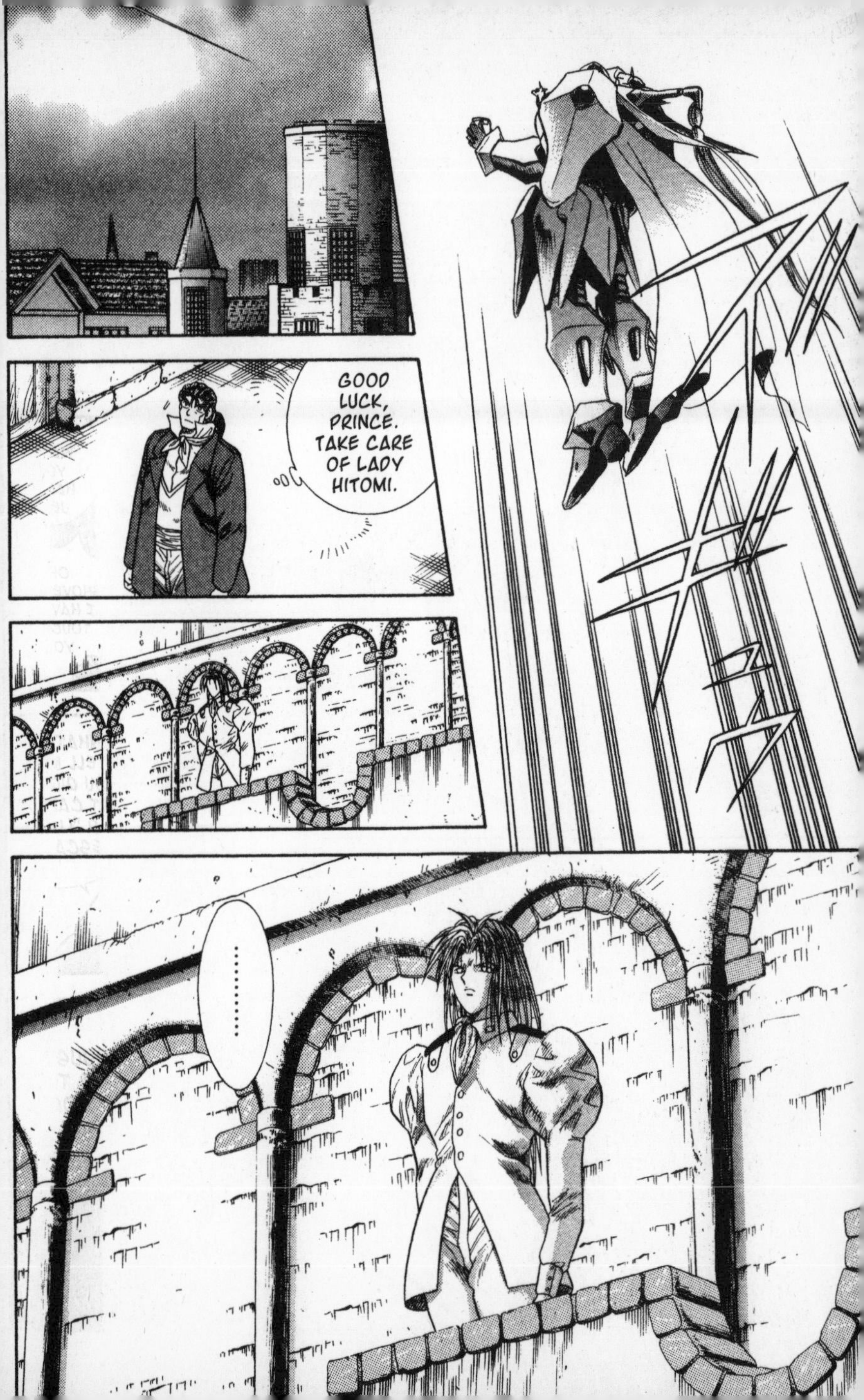
GOOD LUCK, PRINCE. TAKE CARE OF LADY HITOMI.
......

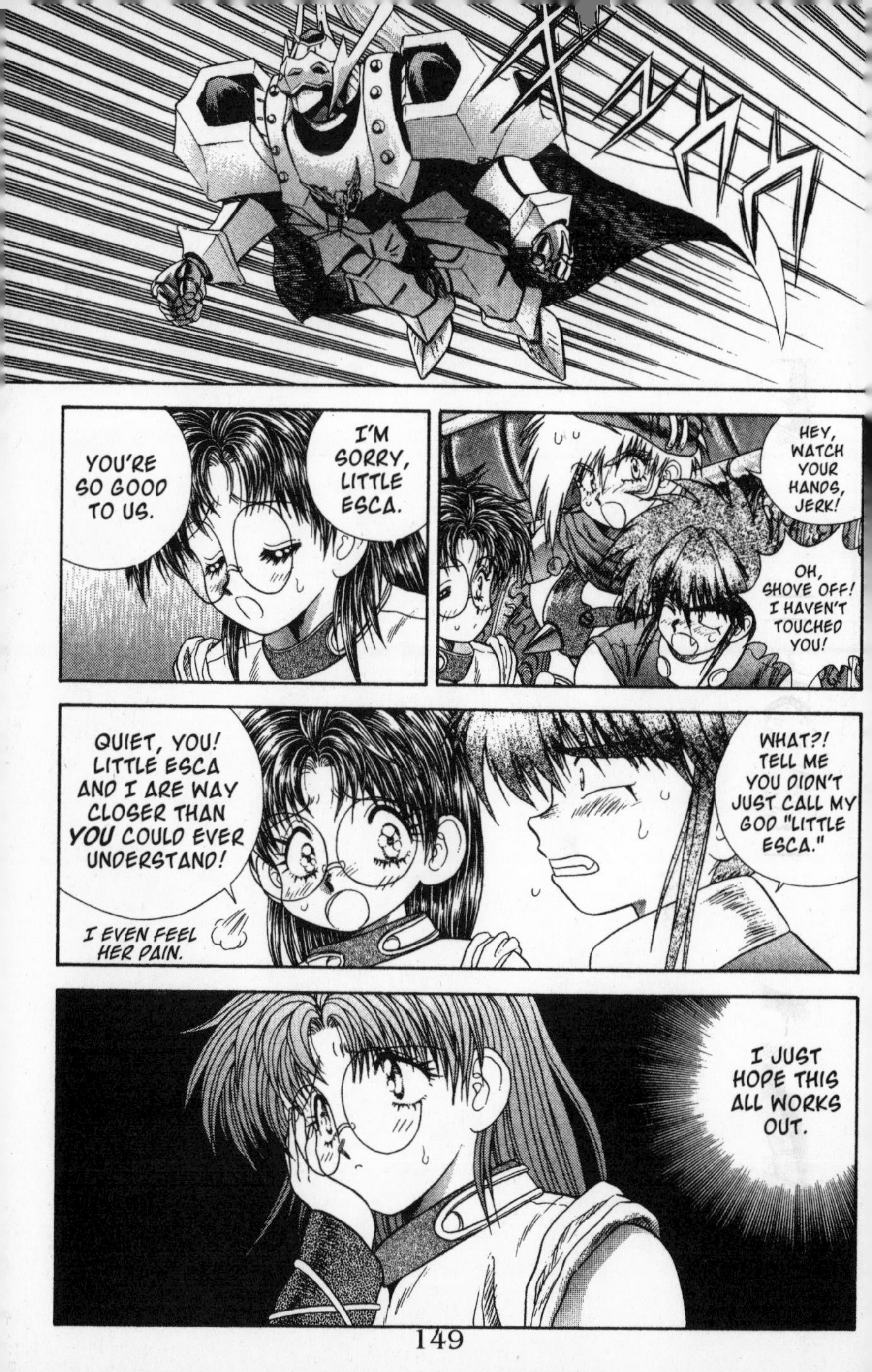
HEY, WATCH YOUR HANDS, JERK!
OH, SHOVE OFF! I HAVEN'T TOUCHED YOU!
I'M SORRY, LITTLE ESCA.
YOU'RE SO GOOD TO US.
WHAT?! TELL ME YOU DIDN'T JUST CALL MY GOD "LITTLE ESCA."
QUIET, YOU! LITTLE ESCA AND I ARE WAY CLOSER THAN YOU COULD EVER UNDERSTAND!
I EVEN FEEL HER PAIN.
I JUST HOPE THIS ALL WORKS OUT.

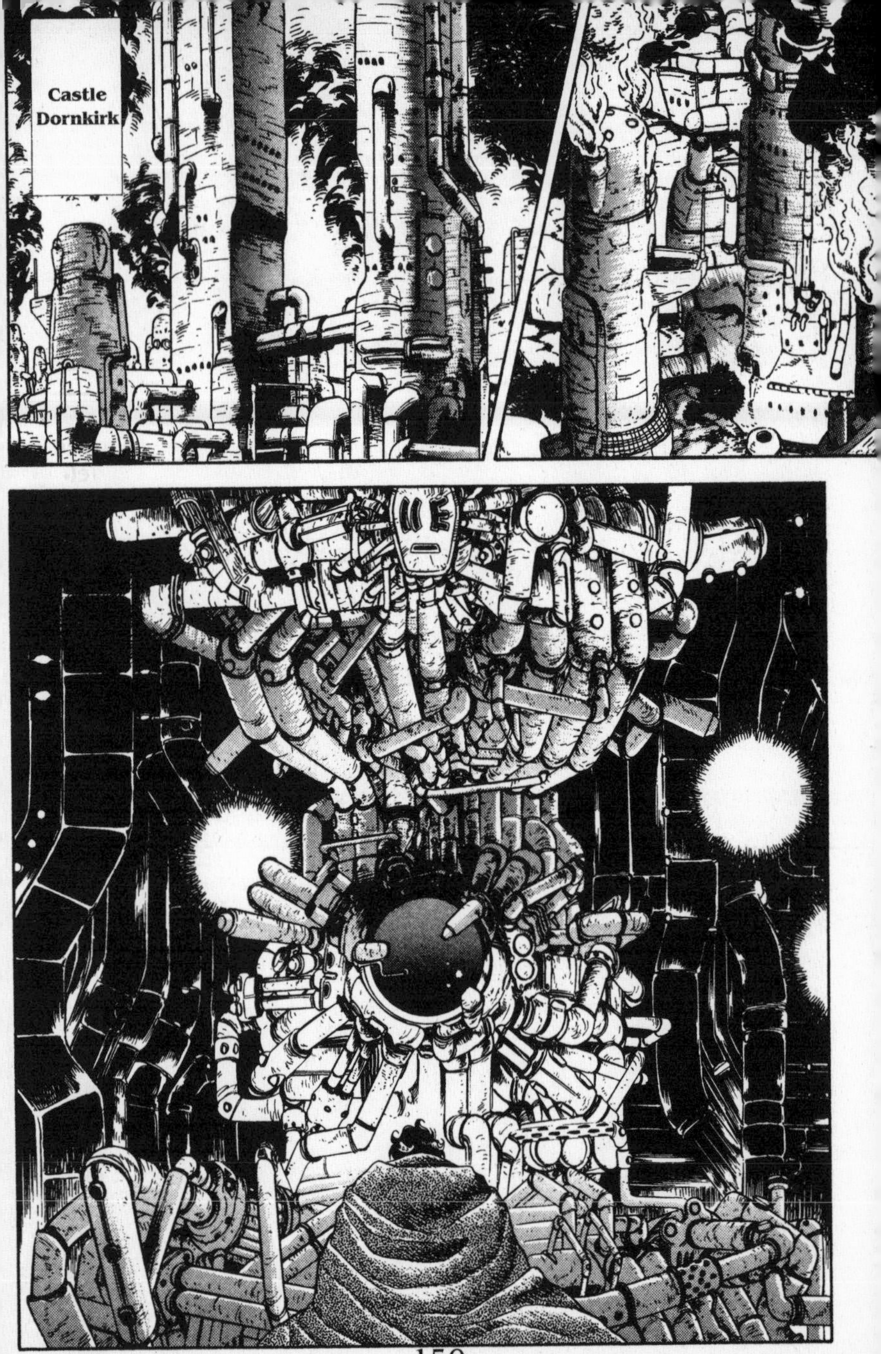
Castle Dornkirk

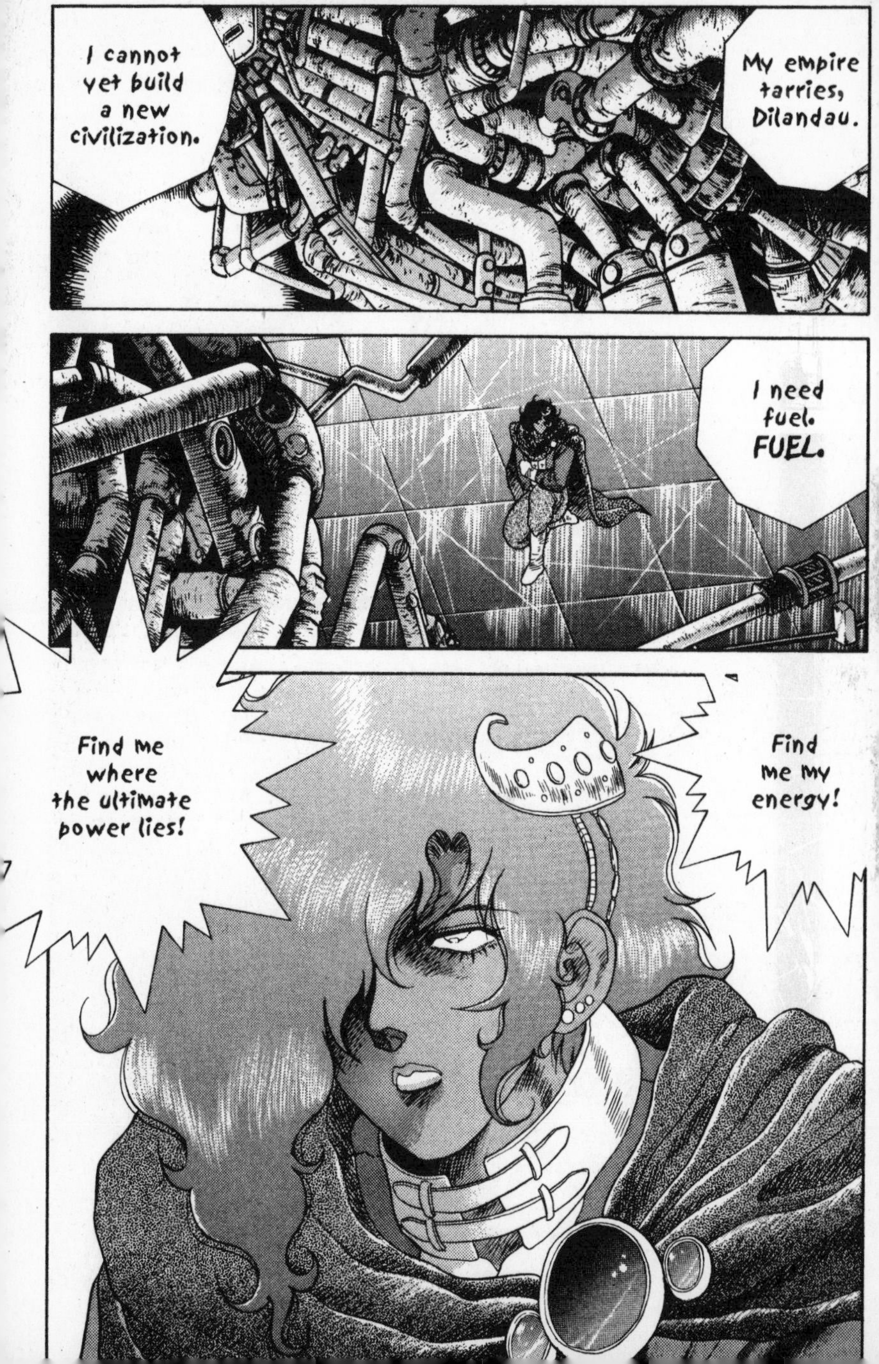
My empire tarries, Dilandau.
I cannot yet build a new civilization.
I need fuel. FUEL.
Find me my energy!
Find me where the ultimate power lies!

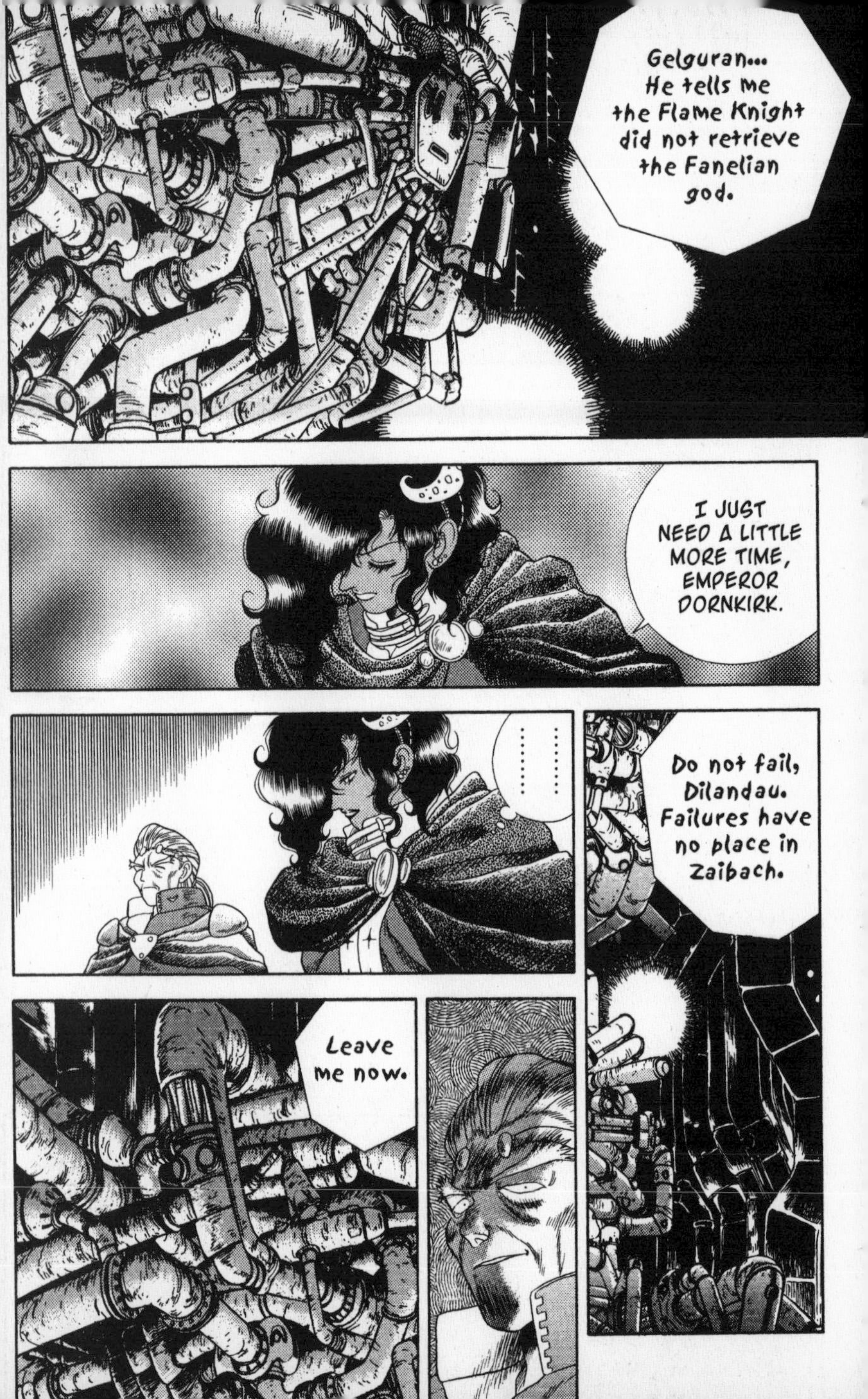
Gelguran... He tells me the Flame Knight did not retrieve the Fanelian god.
I JUST NEED A LITTLE MORE TIME, EMPEROR DORNKIRK.
Do not fail, Dilandau. Failures have no place in Zaibach.
......
Leave me now.

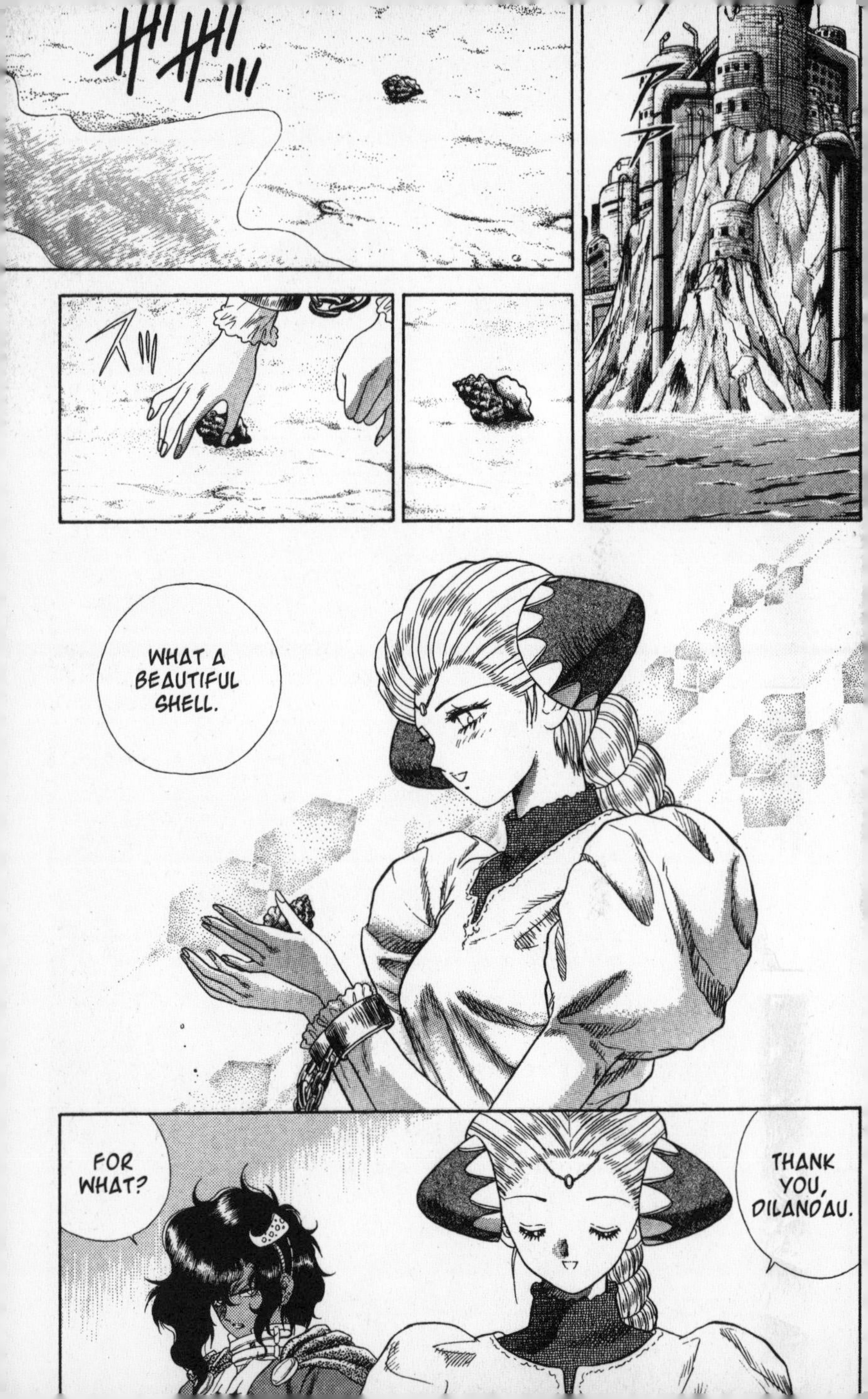
ザザザ
ス
WHAT A BEAUTIFUL SHELL.
THANK YOU, DILANDAU.
FOR WHAT?

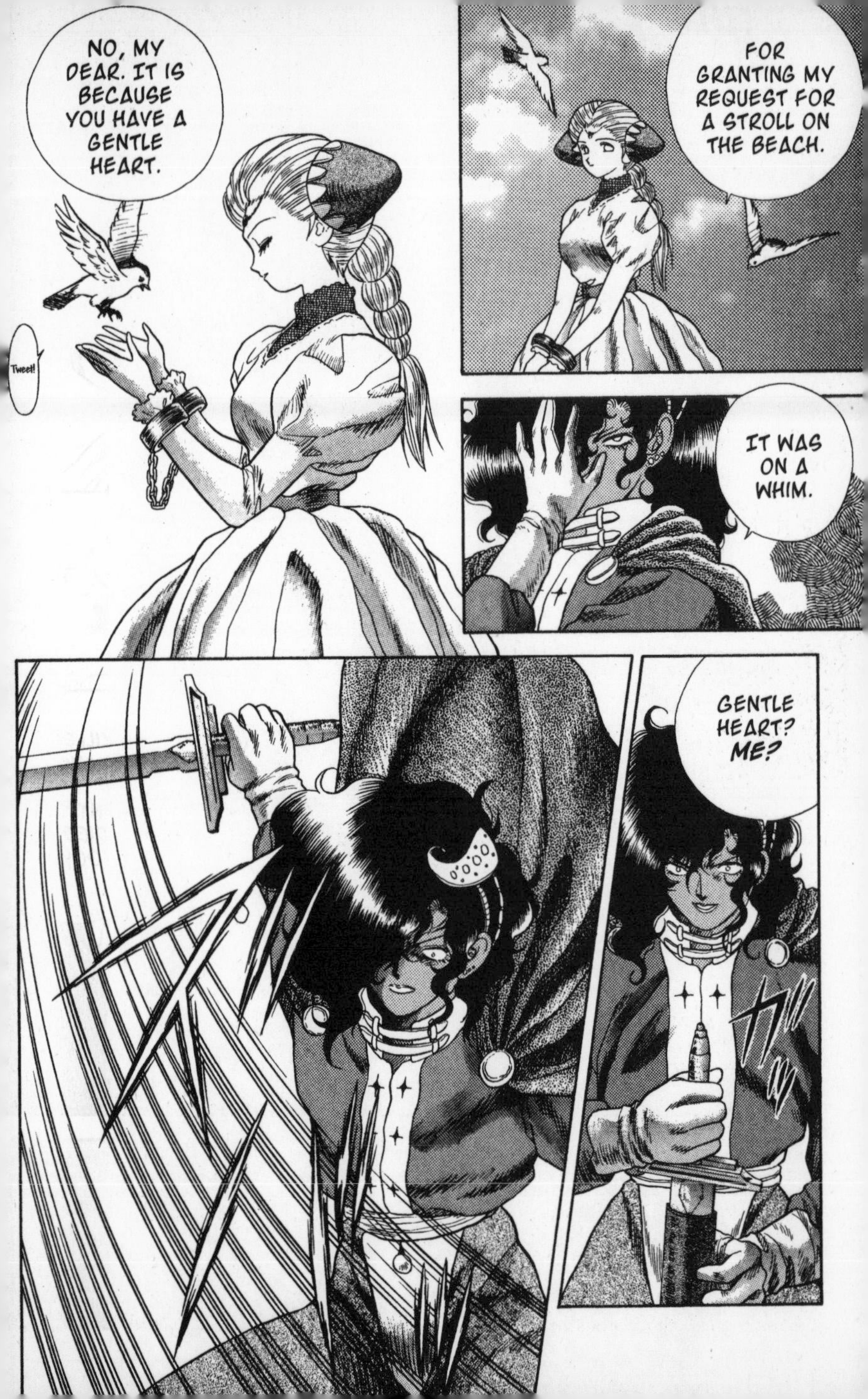
FOR GRANTING MY REQUEST FOR A STROLL ON THE BEACH.
IT WAS ON A WHIM.
NO, MY DEAR. IT IS BECAUSE YOU HAVE A GENTLE HEART.
Tweet!
GENTLE HEART? *ME?*

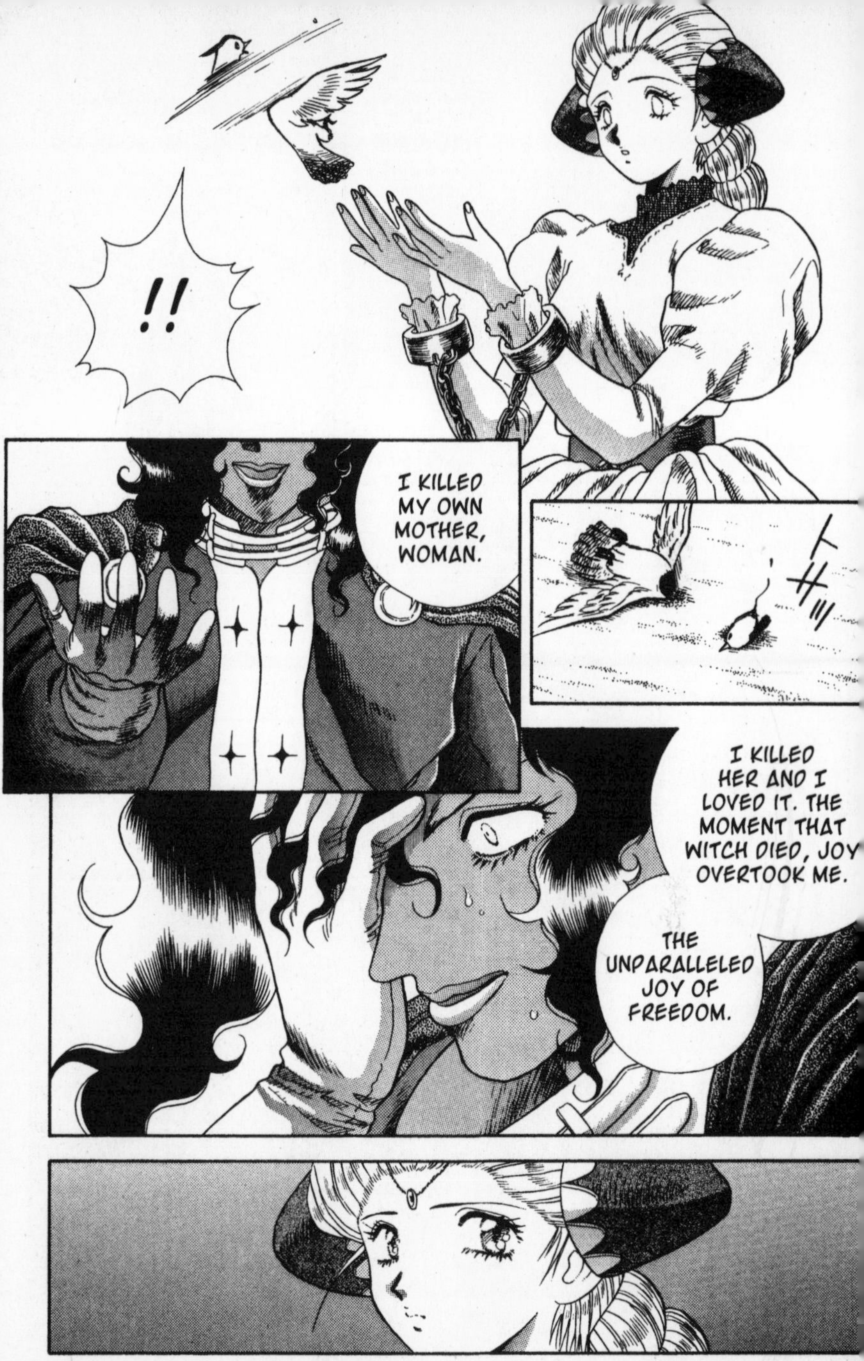
!!
I KILLED MY OWN MOTHER, WOMAN.
I KILLED HER AND I LOVED IT. THE MOMENT THAT WITCH DIED, JOY OVERTOOK ME.
THE UNPARALLELED JOY OF FREEDOM.

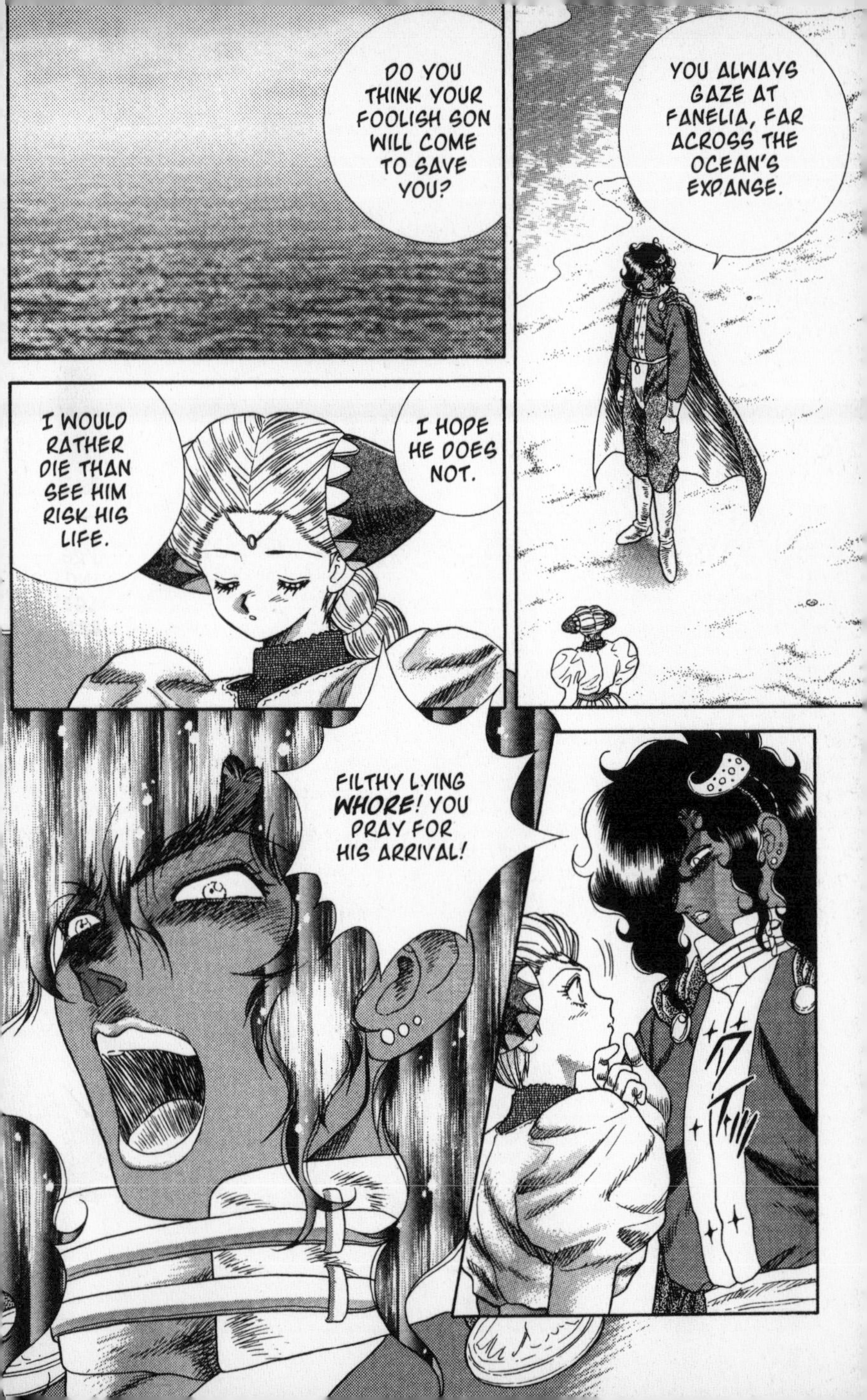
YOU ALWAYS GAZE AT FANELIA, FAR ACROSS THE OCEAN'S EXPANSE.
DO YOU THINK YOUR FOOLISH SON WILL COME TO SAVE YOU?
I HOPE HE DOES NOT.
I WOULD RATHER DIE THAN SEE HIM RISK HIS LIFE.
FILTHY LYING **WHORE**! YOU PRAY FOR HIS ARRIVAL!

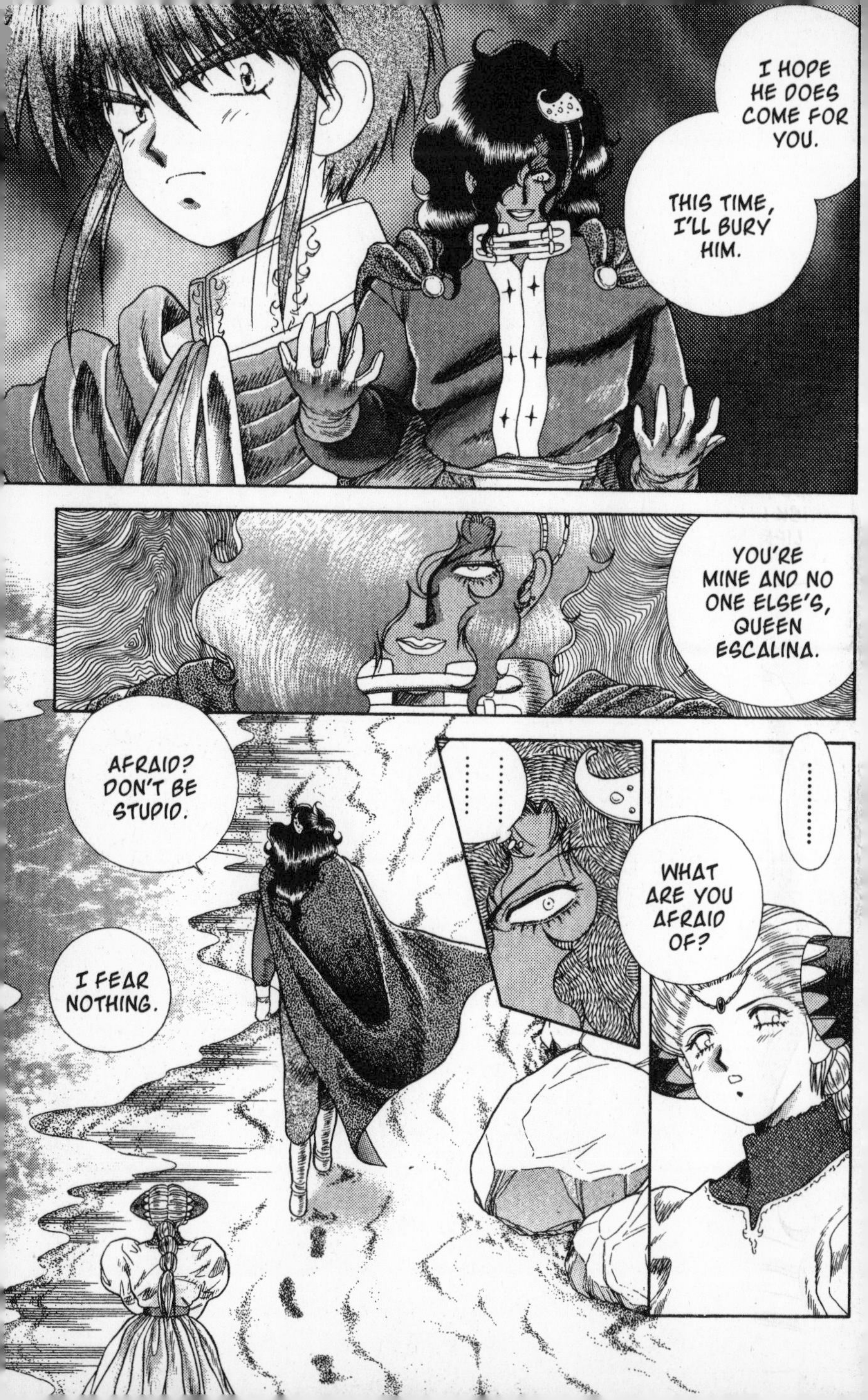
I HOPE HE DOES COME FOR YOU.
THIS TIME, I'LL BURY HIM.
YOU'RE MINE AND NO ONE ELSE'S, QUEEN ESCALINA.
......
WHAT ARE YOU AFRAID OF?
......
AFRAID? DON'T BE STUPID.
I FEAR NOTHING.

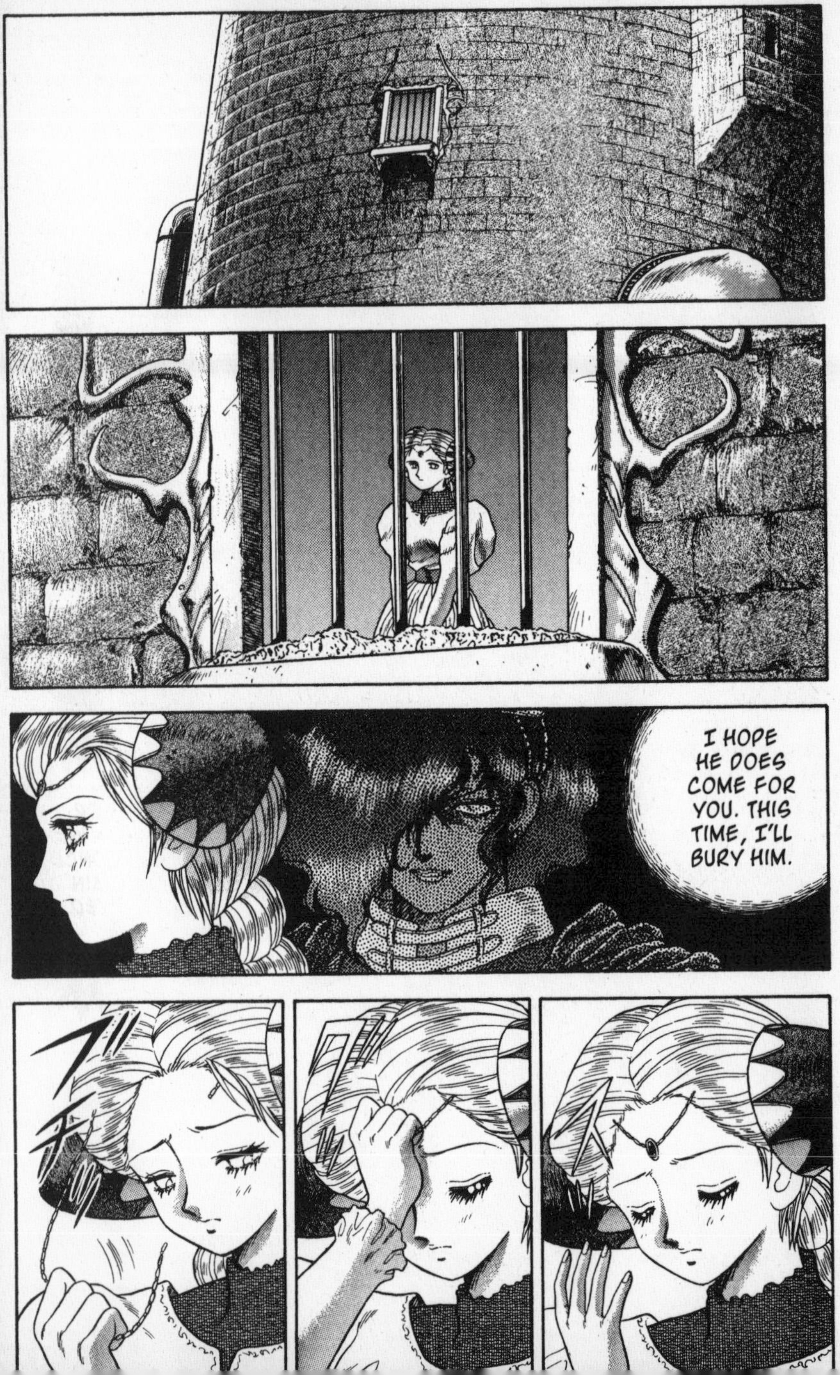
I HOPE HE DOES COME FOR YOU. THIS TIME, I'LL BURY HIM.

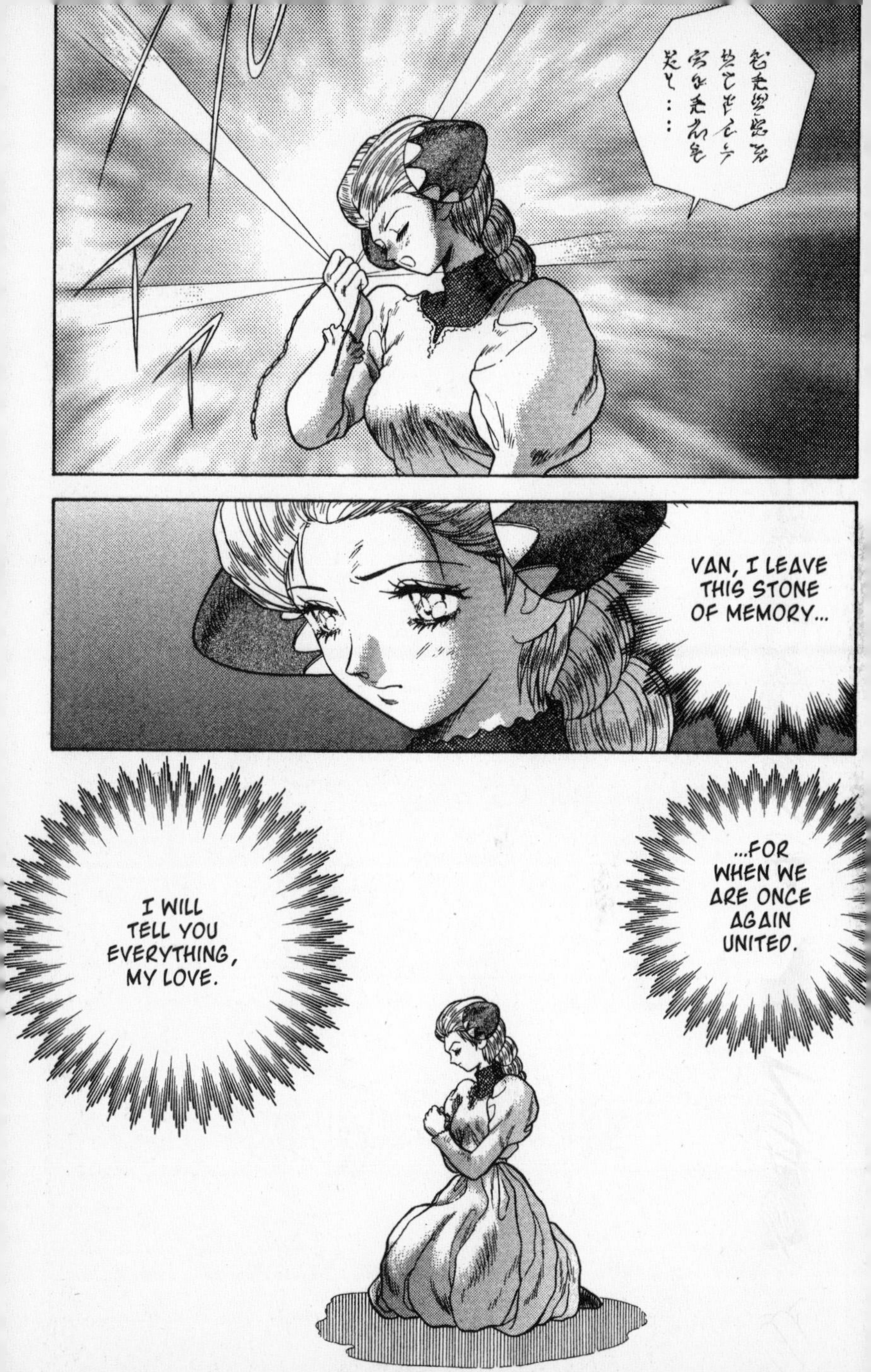
VAN, I LEAVE THIS STONE OF MEMORY...
...FOR WHEN WE ARE ONCE AGAIN UNITED.
I WILL TELL YOU EVERYTHING, MY LOVE.

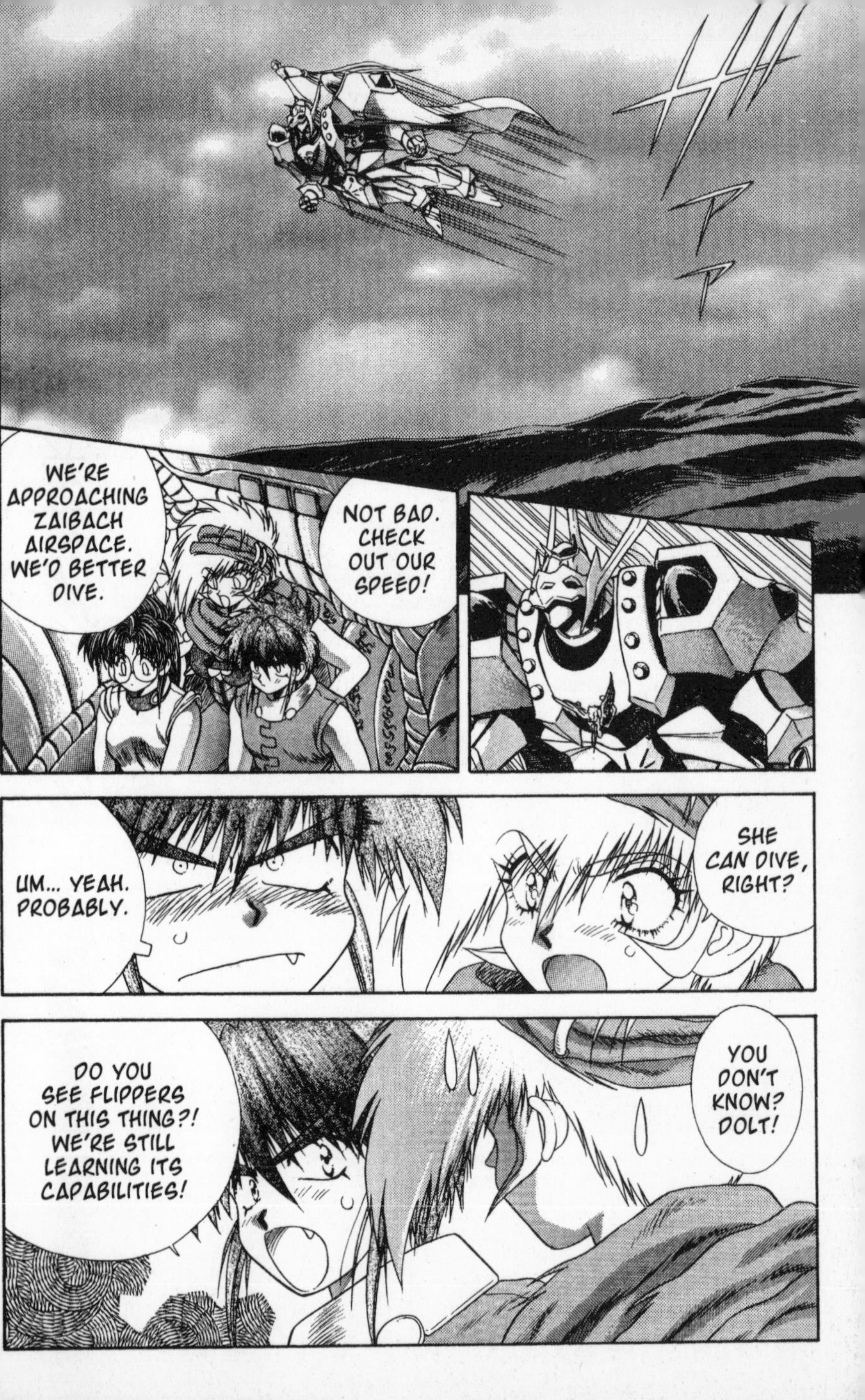
NOT BAD. CHECK OUT OUR SPEED!
WE'RE APPROACHING ZAIBACH AIRSPACE. WE'D BETTER DIVE.
SHE CAN DIVE, RIGHT?
UM... YEAH. PROBABLY.
YOU DON'T KNOW? DOLT!
DO YOU SEE FLIPPERS ON THIS THING?! WE'RE STILL LEARNING ITS CAPABILITIES!

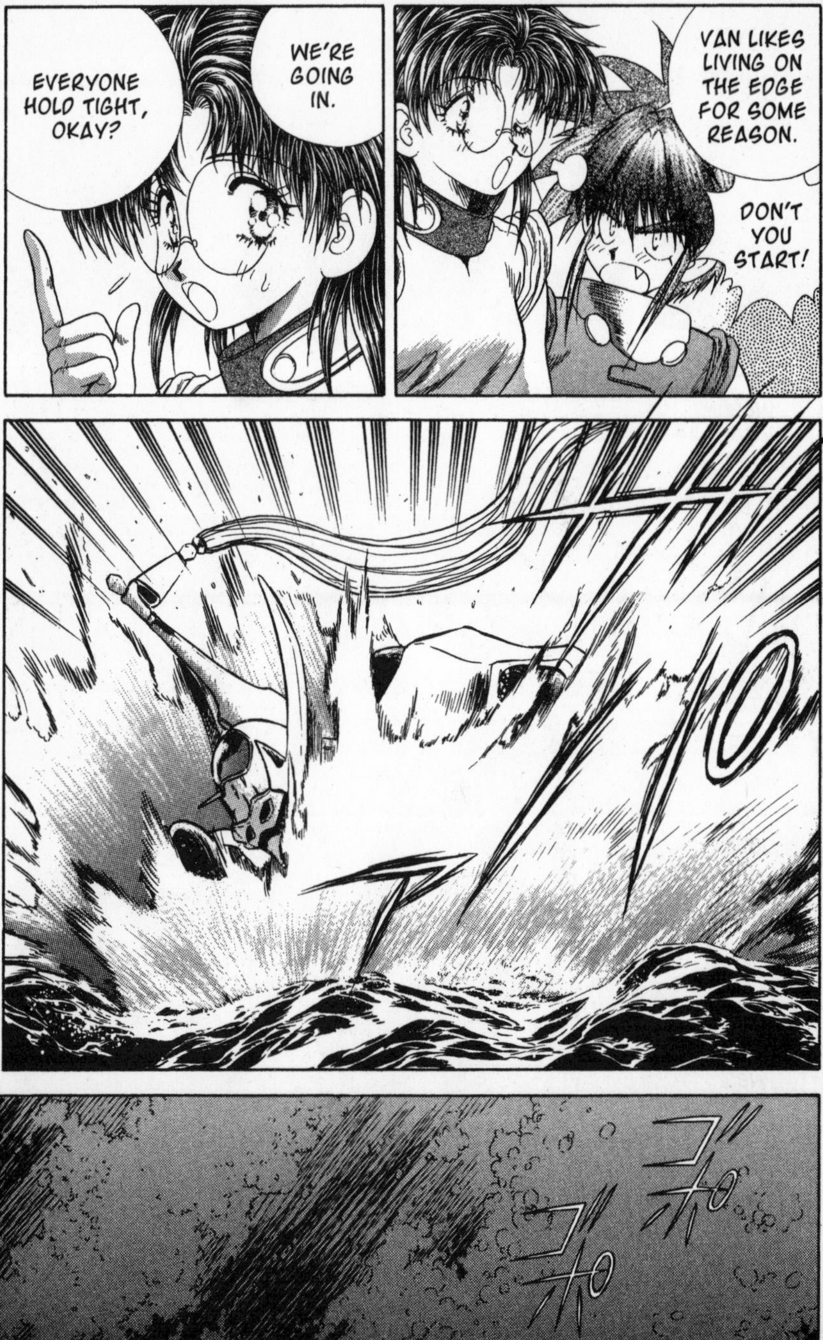
VAN LIKES LIVING ON THE EDGE FOR SOME REASON.
DON'T YOU START!
WE'RE GOING IN.
EVERYONE HOLD TIGHT, OKAY?
ゴポ
ゴポ

NOT DEAD. GOOD SIGN.

TAKE US IN, ESCAFLOWNE!

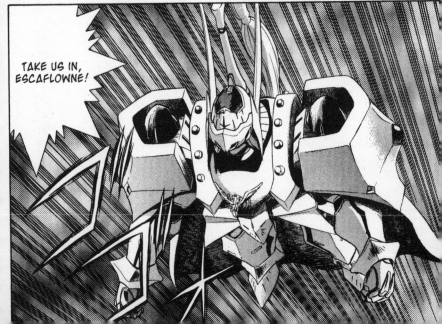

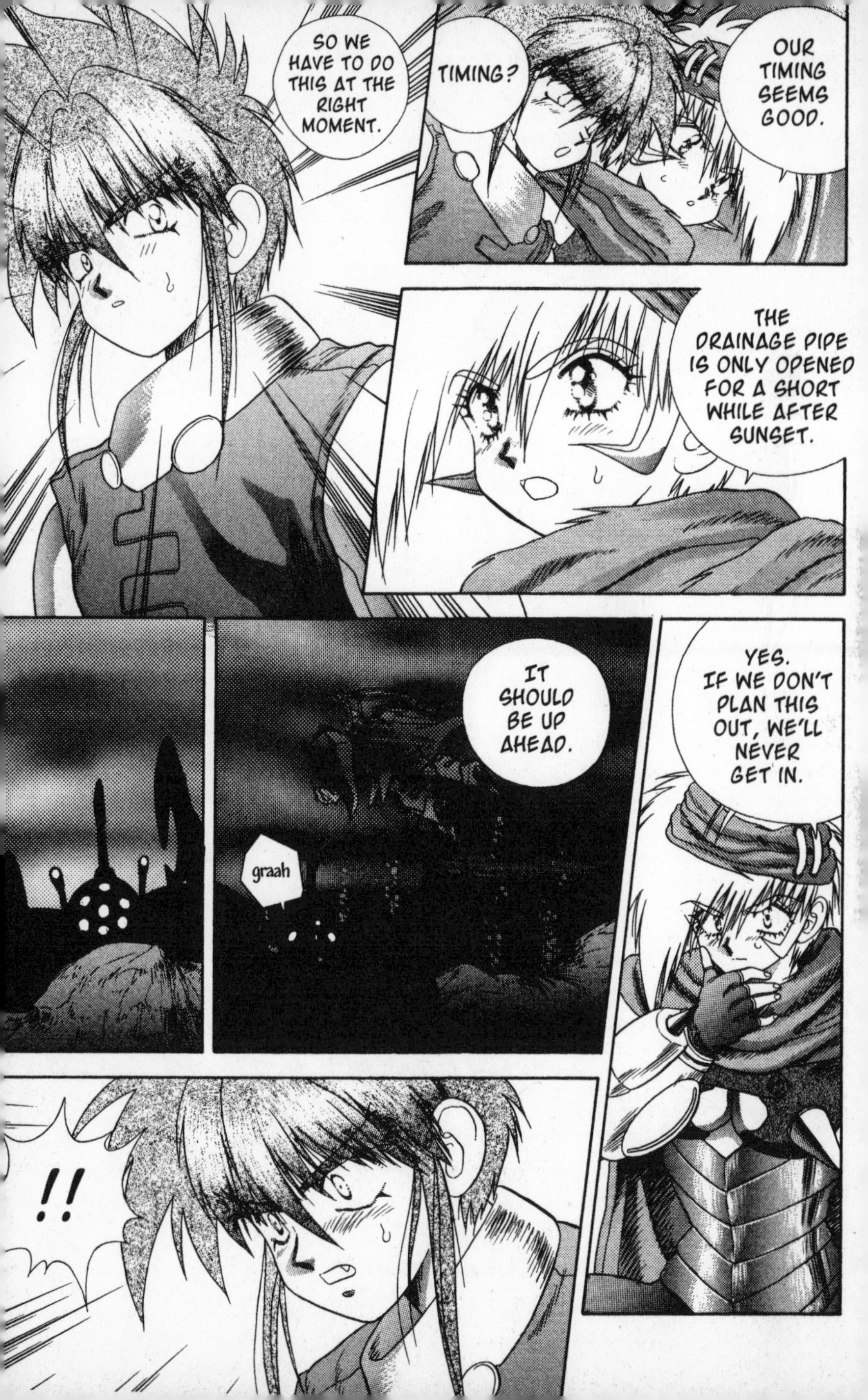
OUR TIMING SEEMS GOOD.
TIMING?
THE DRAINAGE PIPE IS ONLY OPENED FOR A SHORT WHILE AFTER SUNSET.
SO WE HAVE TO DO THIS AT THE RIGHT MOMENT.
YES. IF WE DON'T PLAN THIS OUT, WE'LL NEVER GET IN.
IT SHOULD BE UP AHEAD.
graah
!!

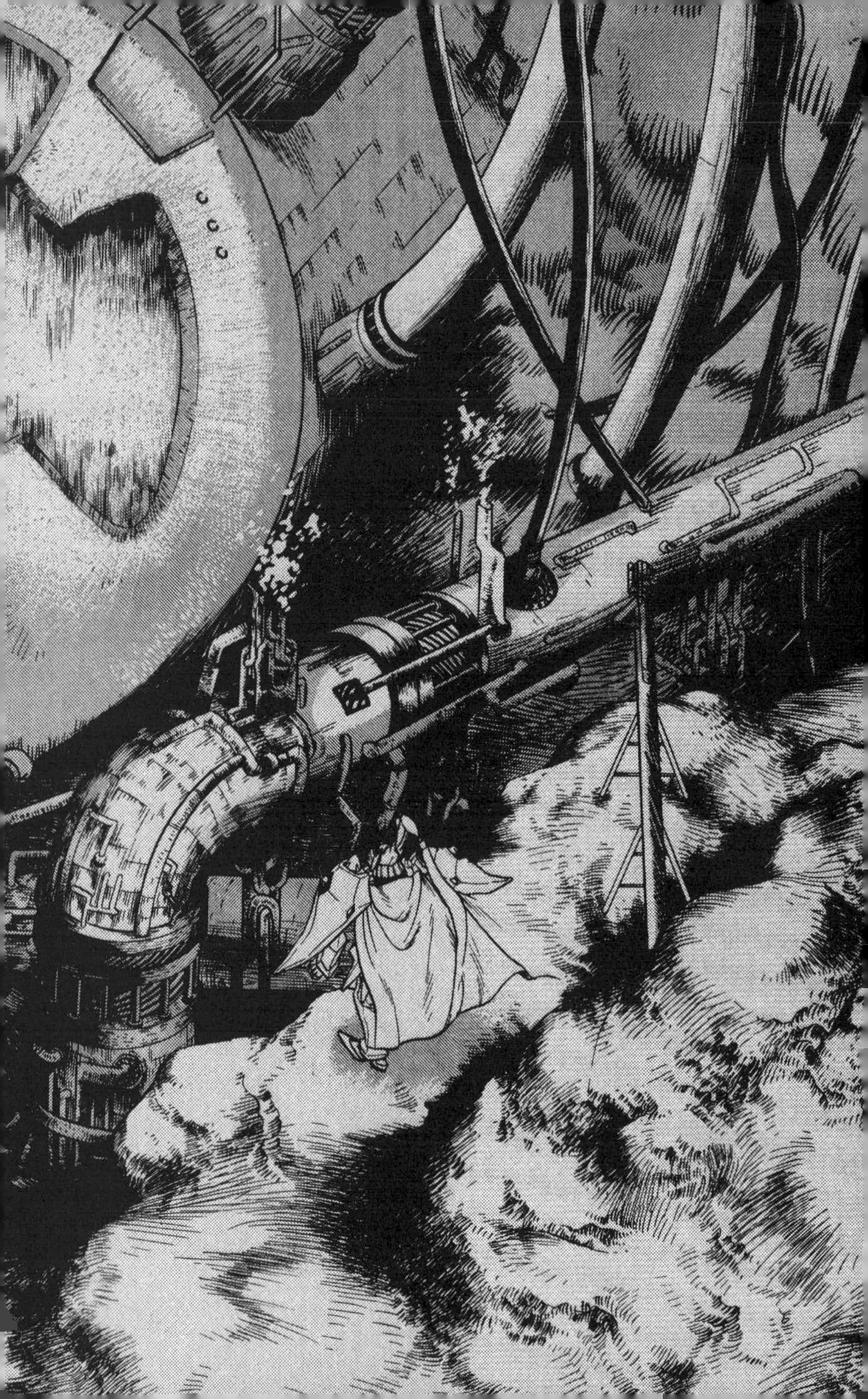

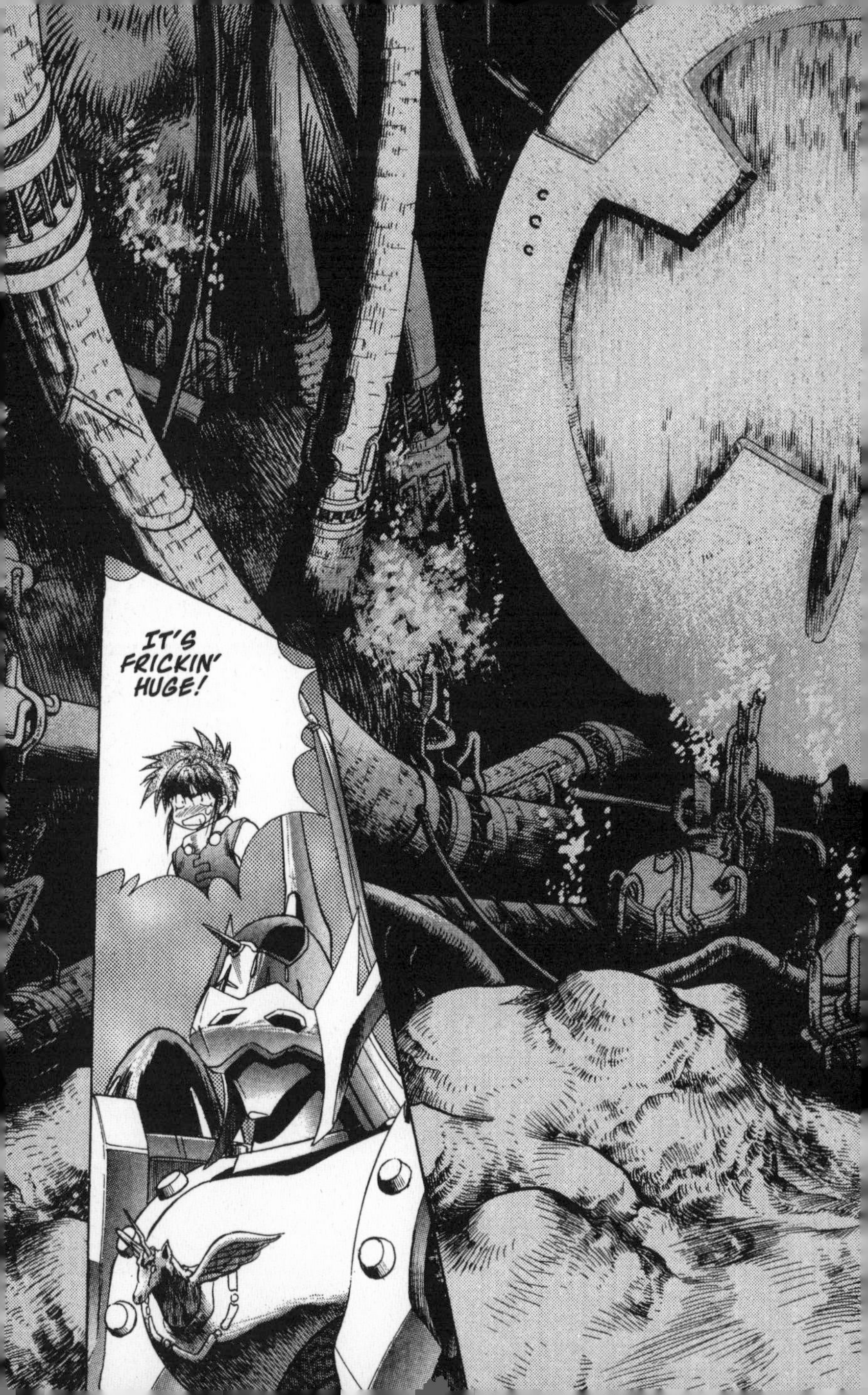
IT'S FRICKIN' HUGE!

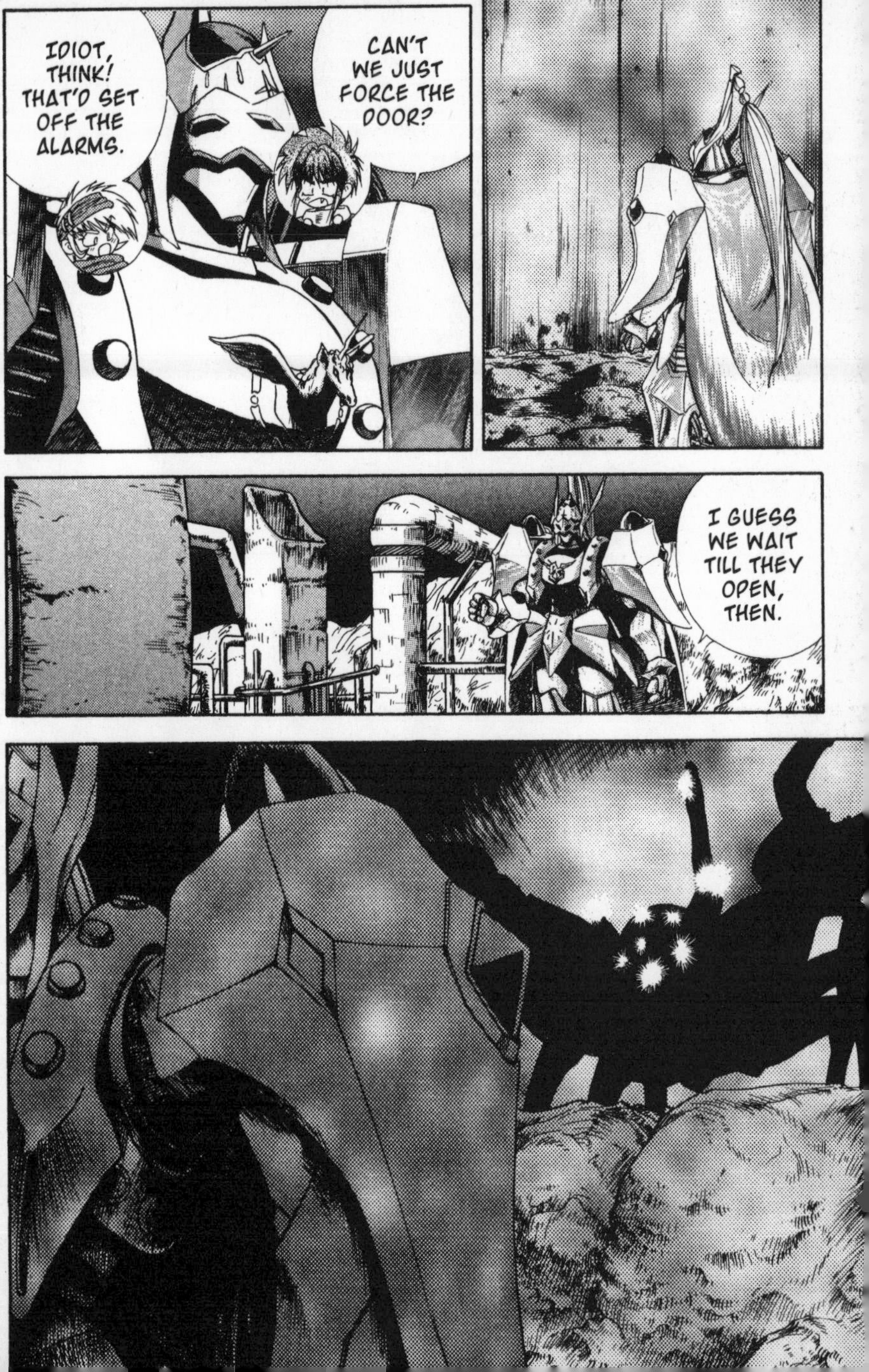
CAN'T WE JUST FORCE THE DOOR?
IDIOT, THINK! THAT'D SET OFF THE ALARMS.
I GUESS WE WAIT TILL THEY OPEN, THEN.

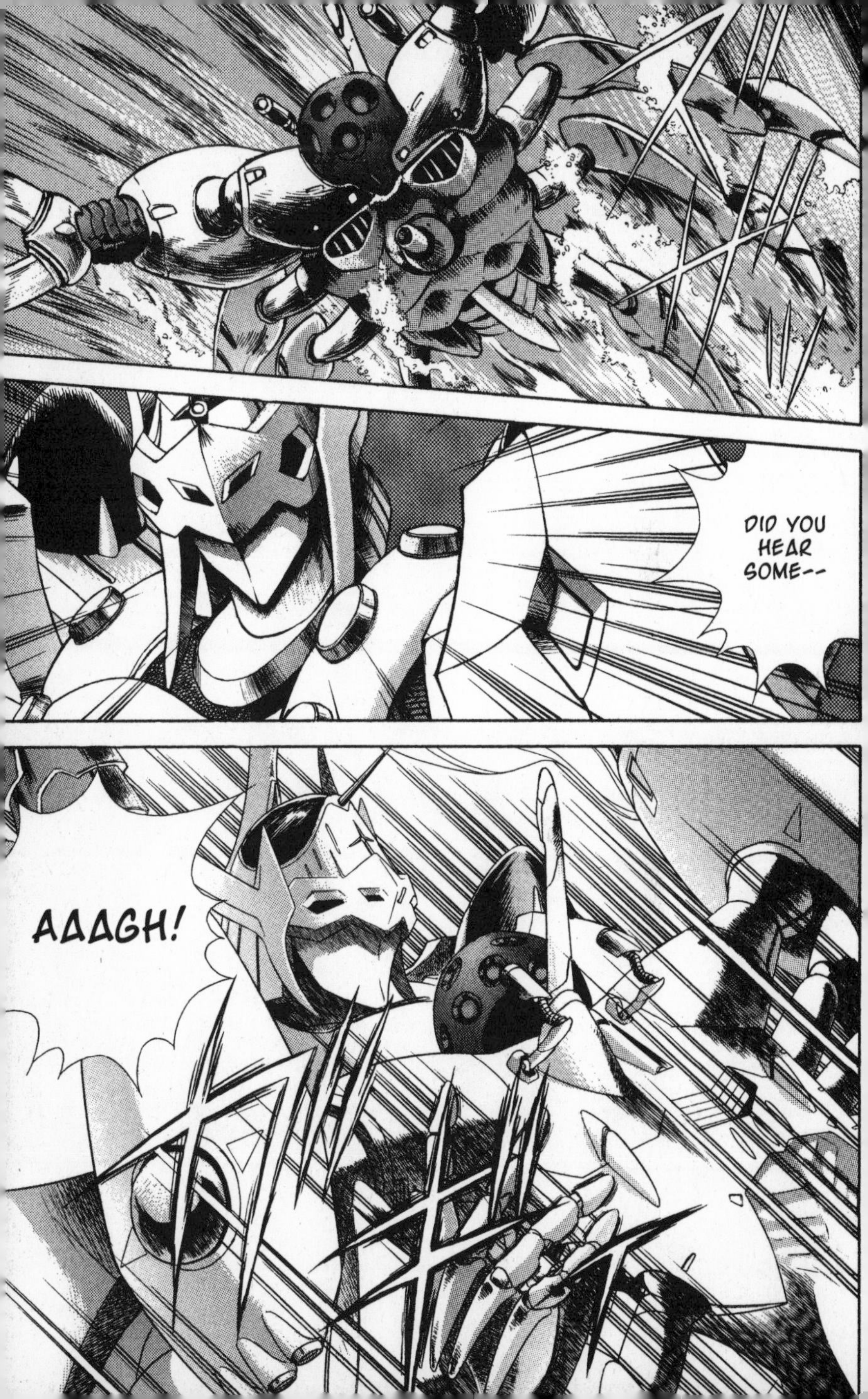
DID YOU HEAR SOME--
AAAGH!

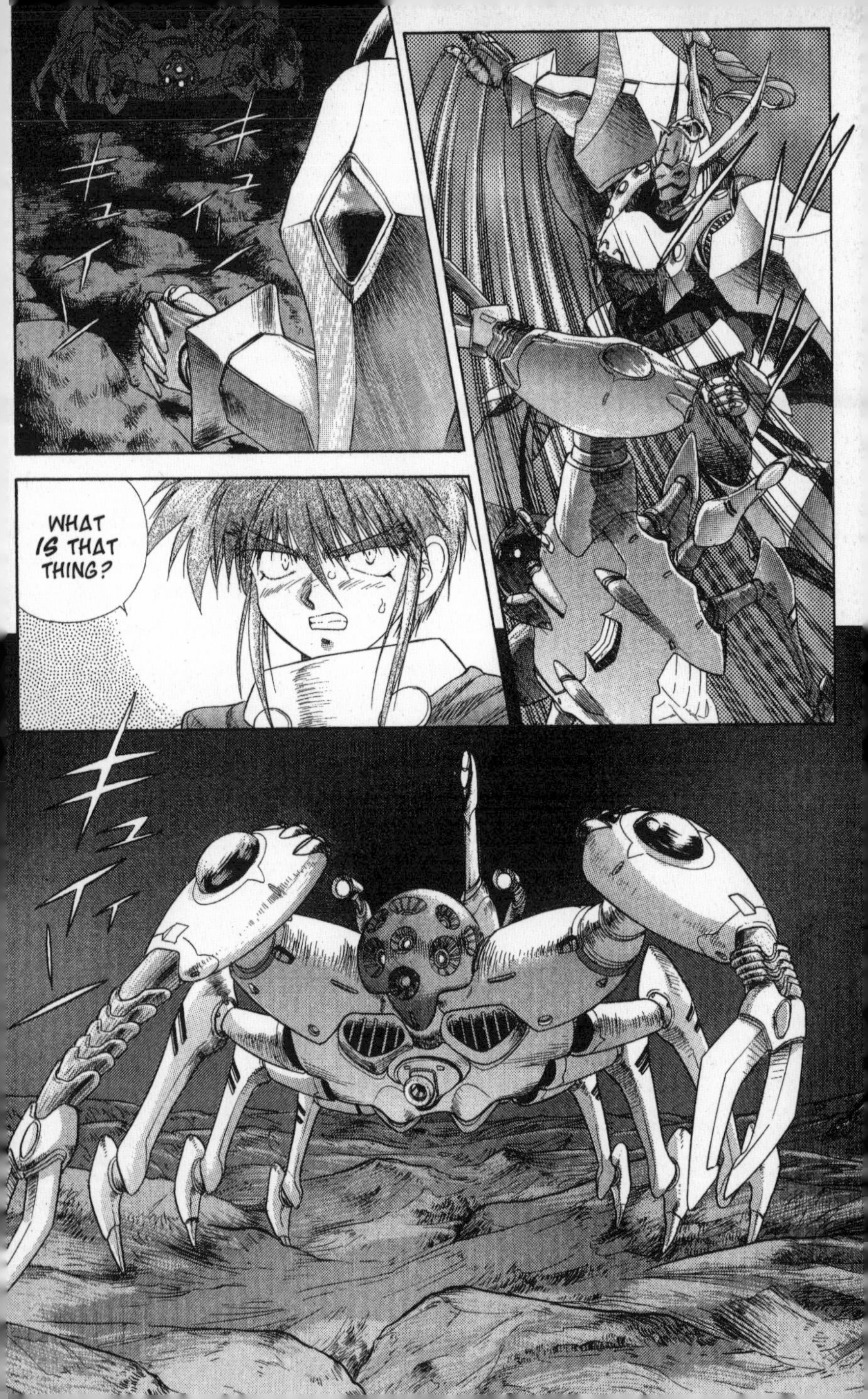
キュイイイー
WHAT IS THAT THING?
キュイイー

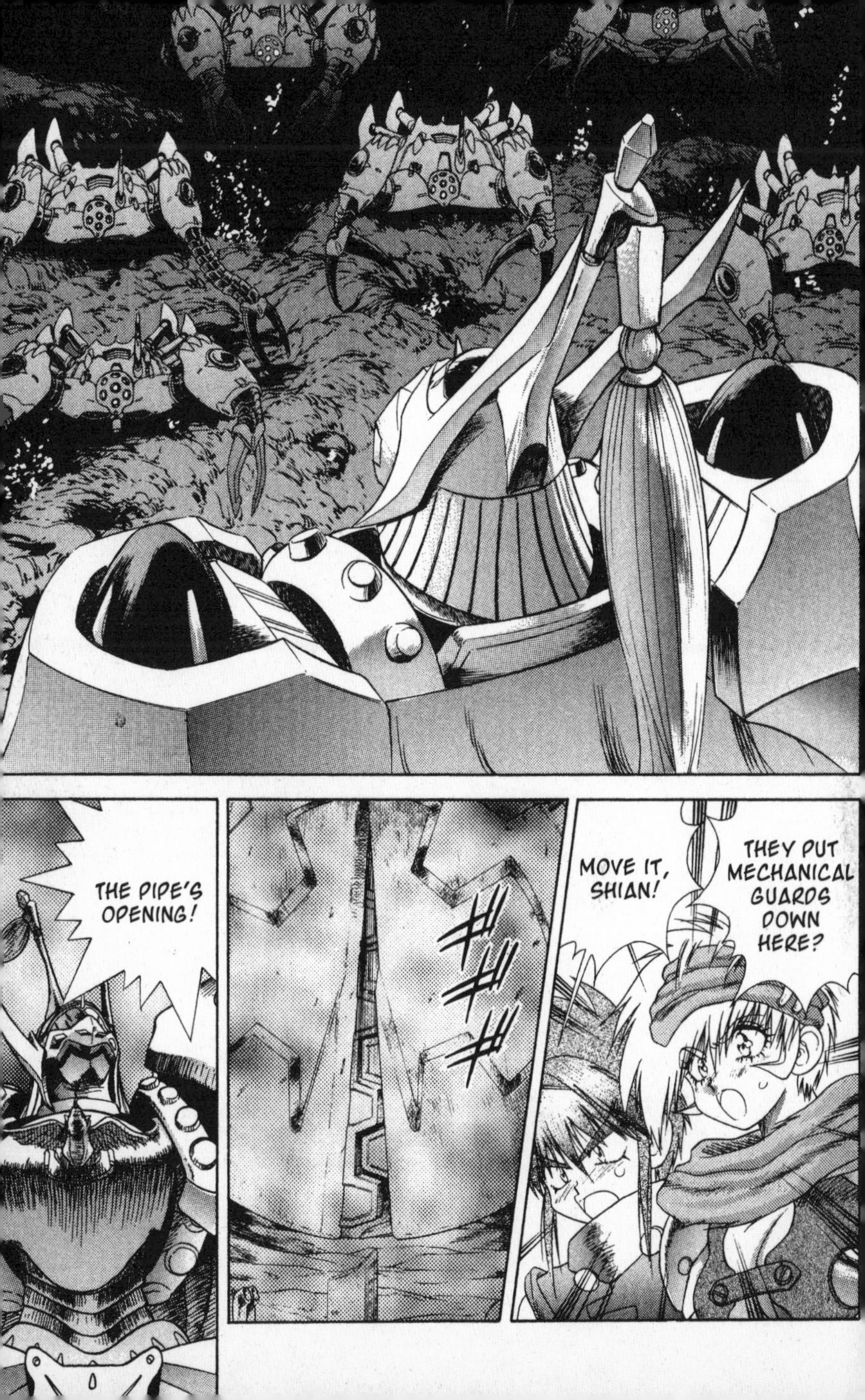
THEY PUT MECHANICAL GUARDS DOWN HERE?
MOVE IT, SHIAN!
THE PIPE'S OPENING!

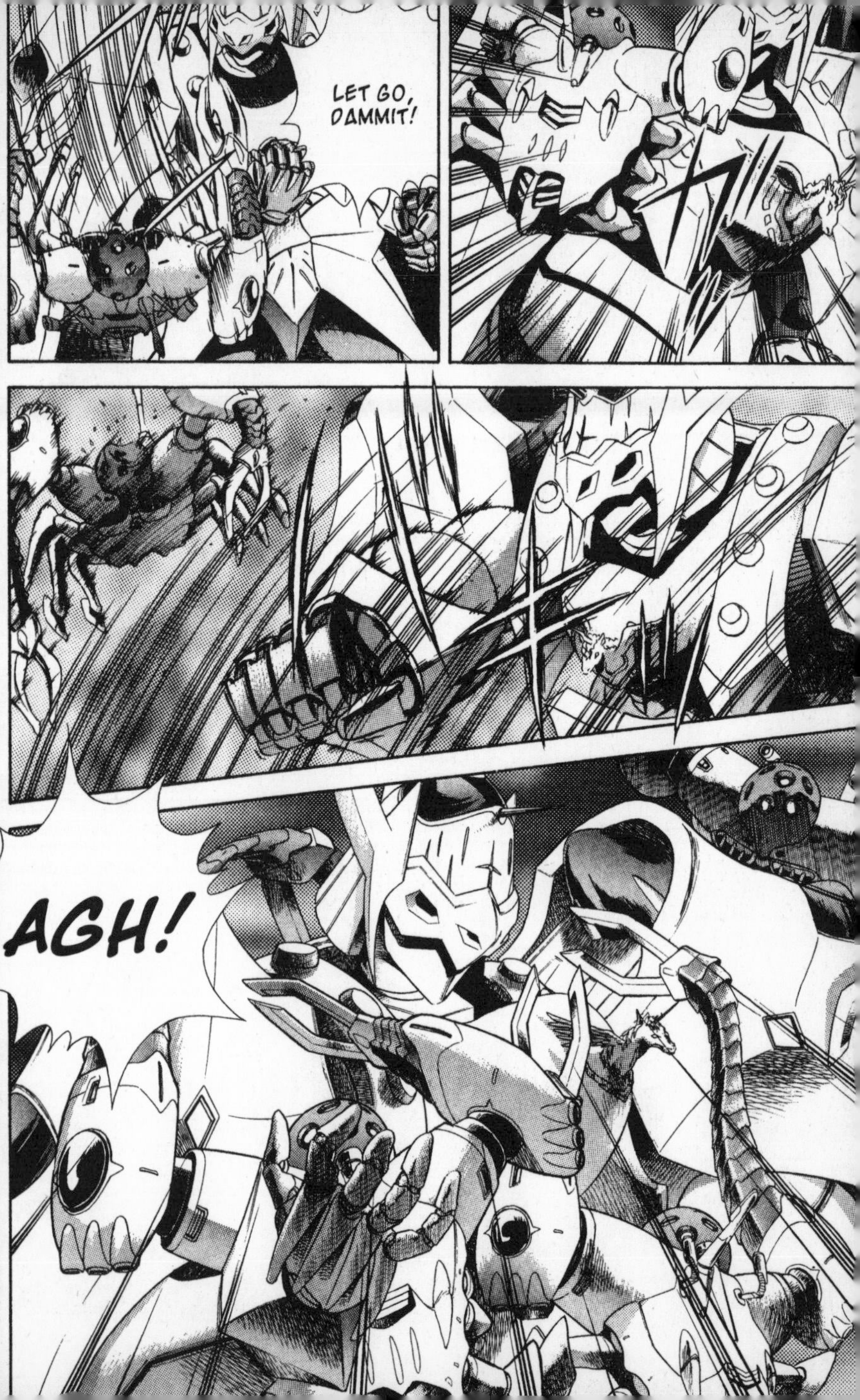
LET GO, DAMMIT!
AGH!

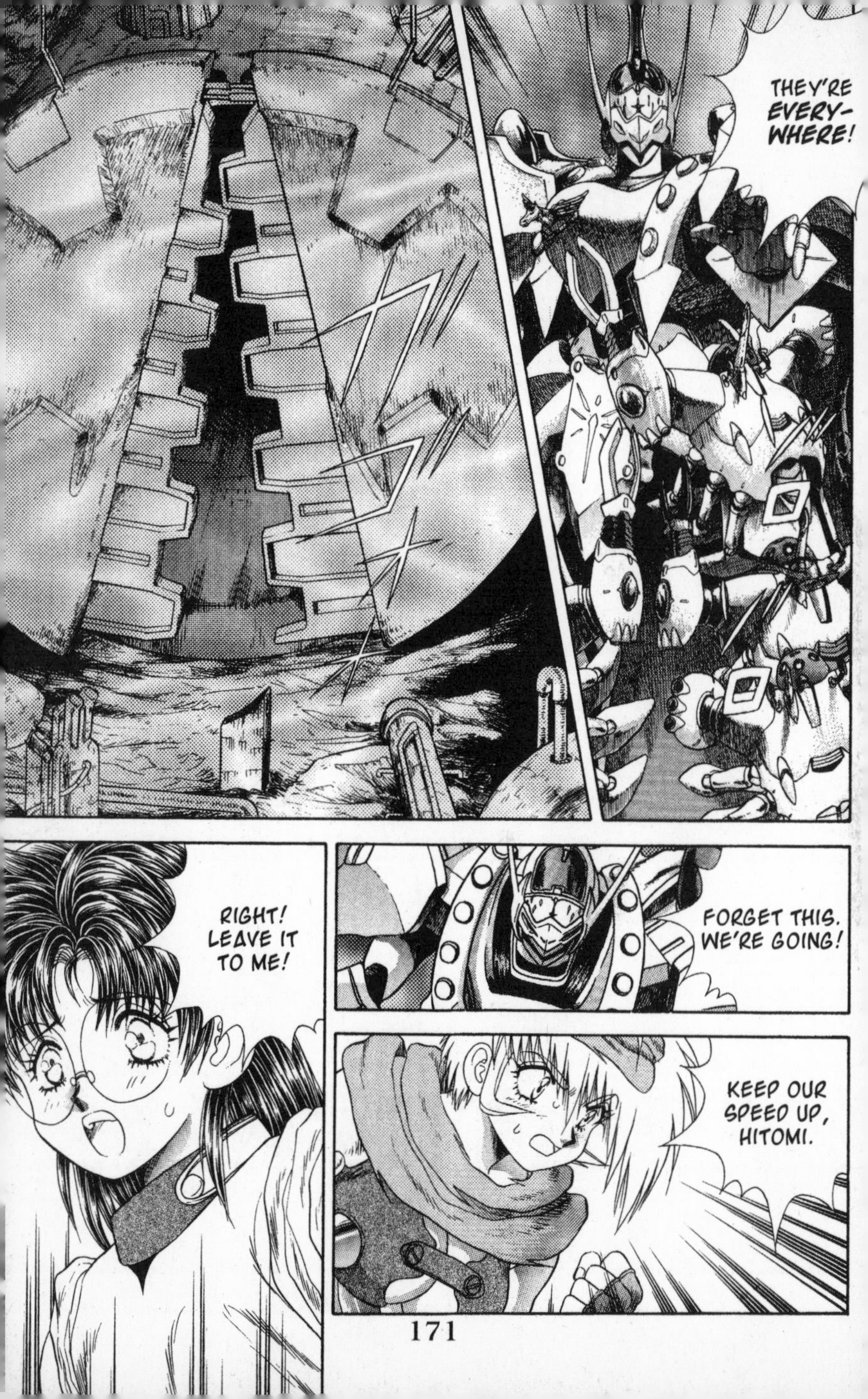
THEY'RE EVERY-WHERE!
FORGET THIS. WE'RE GOING!
KEEP OUR SPEED UP, HITOMI.
RIGHT! LEAVE IT TO ME!

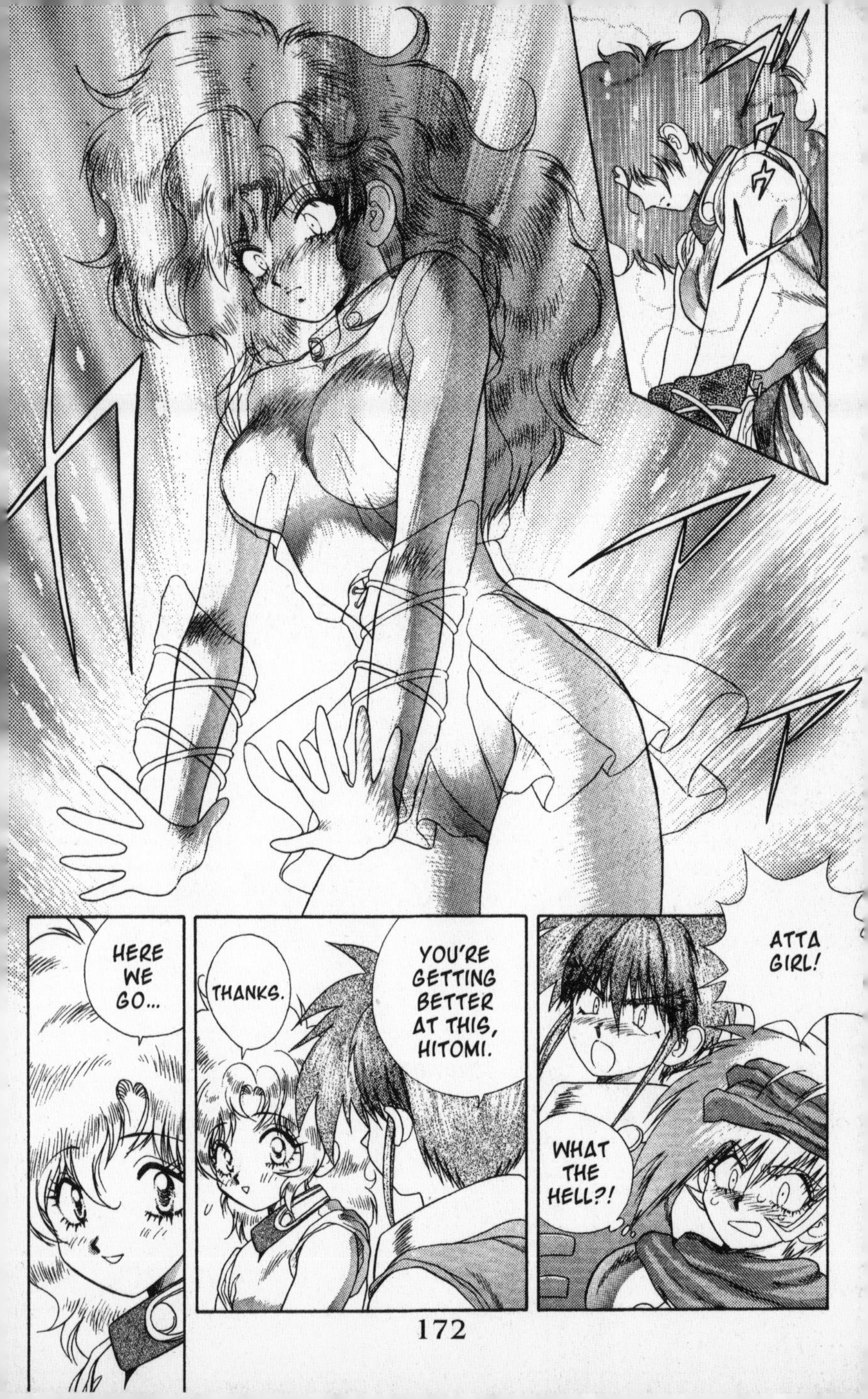
ATTA GIRL!
WHAT THE HELL?!
YOU'RE GETTING BETTER AT THIS, HITOMI.
THANKS.
HERE WE GO...

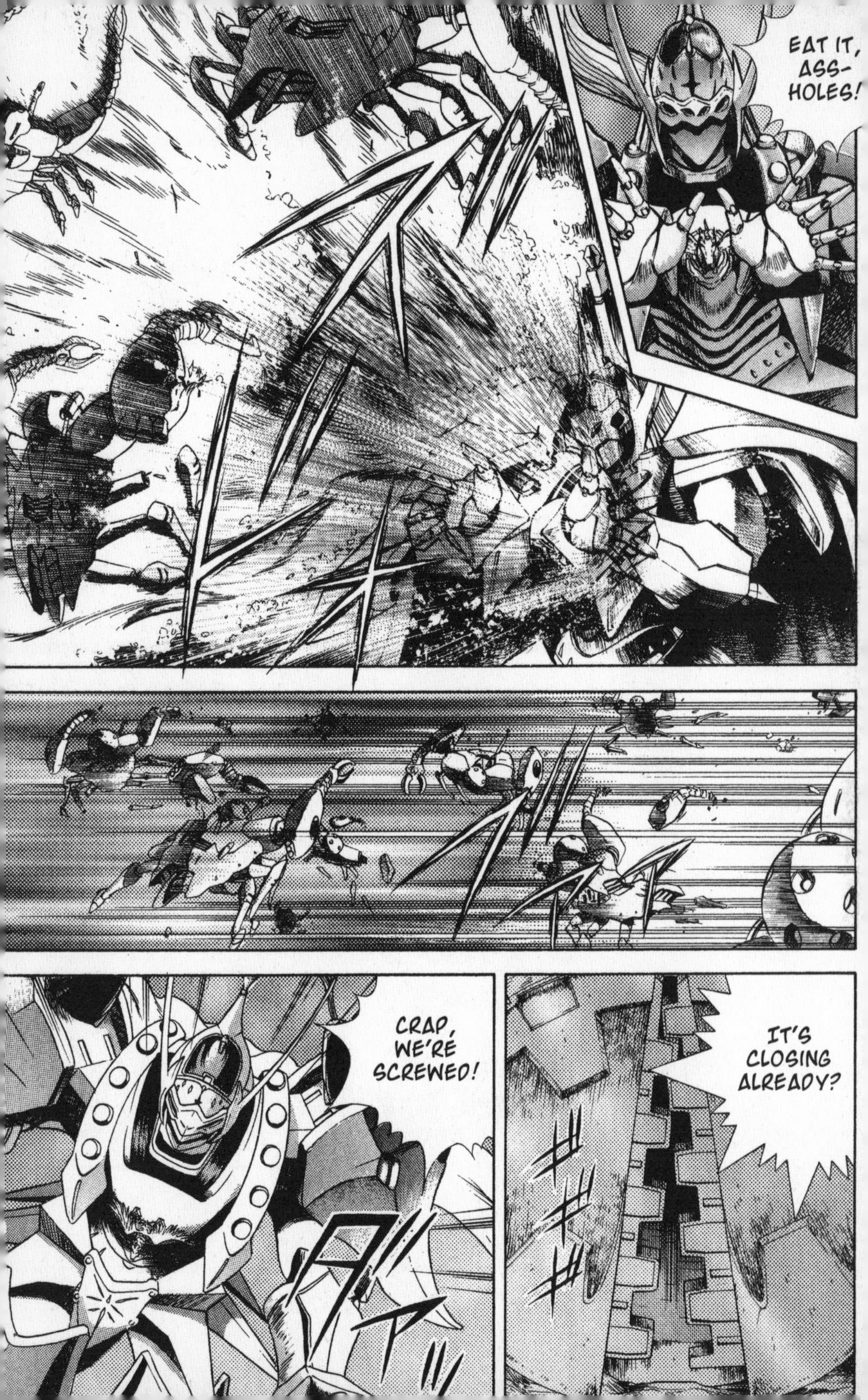
EAT IT, ASS-HOLES!
IT'S CLOSING ALREADY?
CRAP, WE'RE SCREWED!

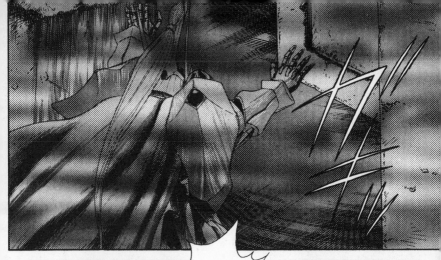

I DON'T THINK WE CAN HOLD IT.

MMN...

HEY, Q-QUIT CLOSING! SHIT!!!

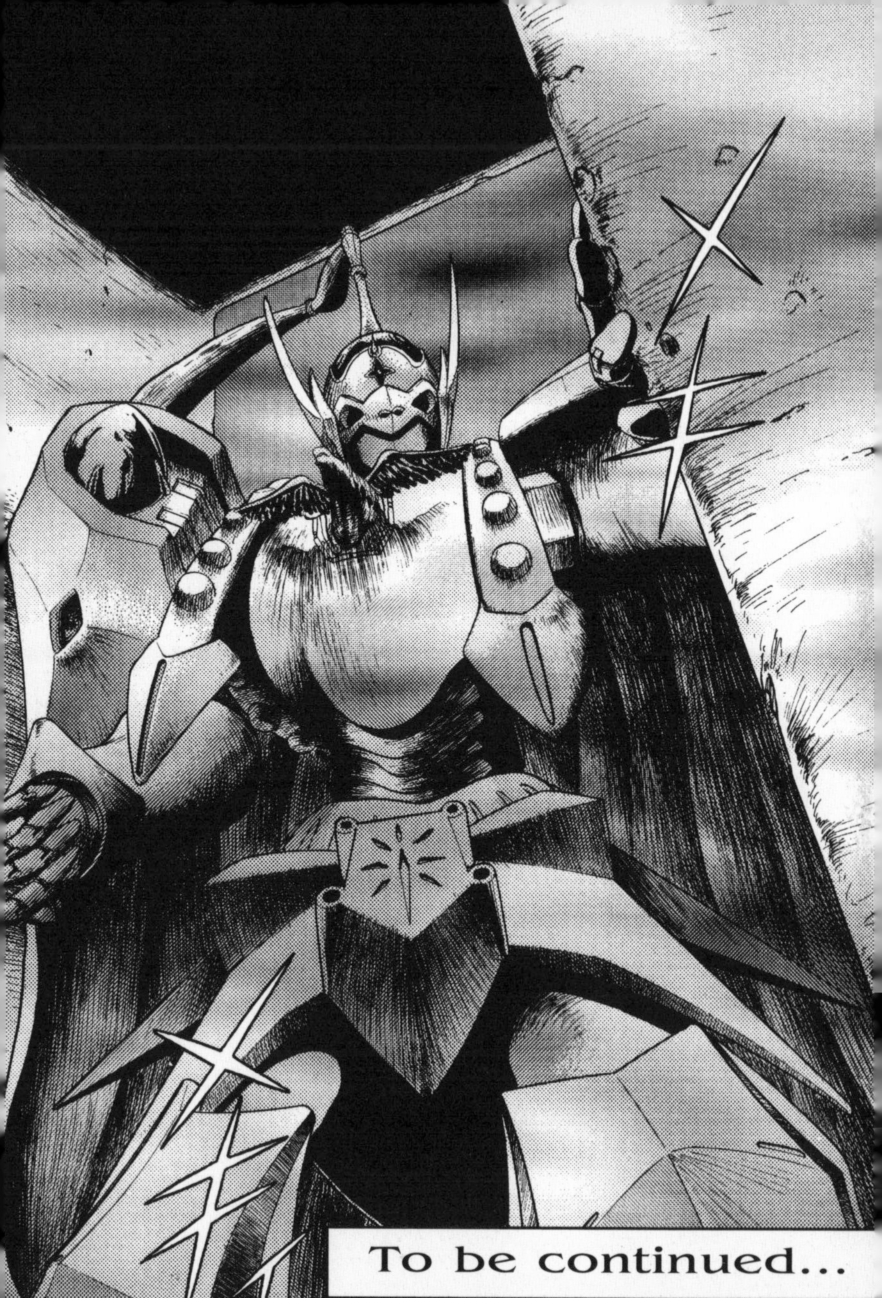
To be continued...

In the next volume of
THE·VISION·OF ESCAFLOWNE

Hitomi, Van, and Shian strike back at Zaibach, but Van's lust for vengeance may cost them their advantage...and their lives. Hitomi struggles to master her mysterious powers while Van races against time to save his captive mother from the sadistic Dilandau.

In the next exciting volume of THE VISION OF ESCAFLOWNE.

On sale soon!

Hey, Katsu Aki here. I hope you're enjoying this manga version of the extensive Escaflowne anime project. Based on the original concepts by Mr. Shoji Kawamori (by the way, sorry for all the trouble Mr. Kawamori), both an anime version and a manga version of Esca have been created; yet those versions ended up creating two separate and distinct worlds (though the mecha designs for the manga were done entirely by Mr. Kawamori). Although this manga's had its difficulties, I'm up for the challenge and intend to go forward at full speed.

Though I guess that's something to be expected and nothing much to be proud of. Hmm...

Anyhow, details follow in the next volume. See you then!

Dec. 1995

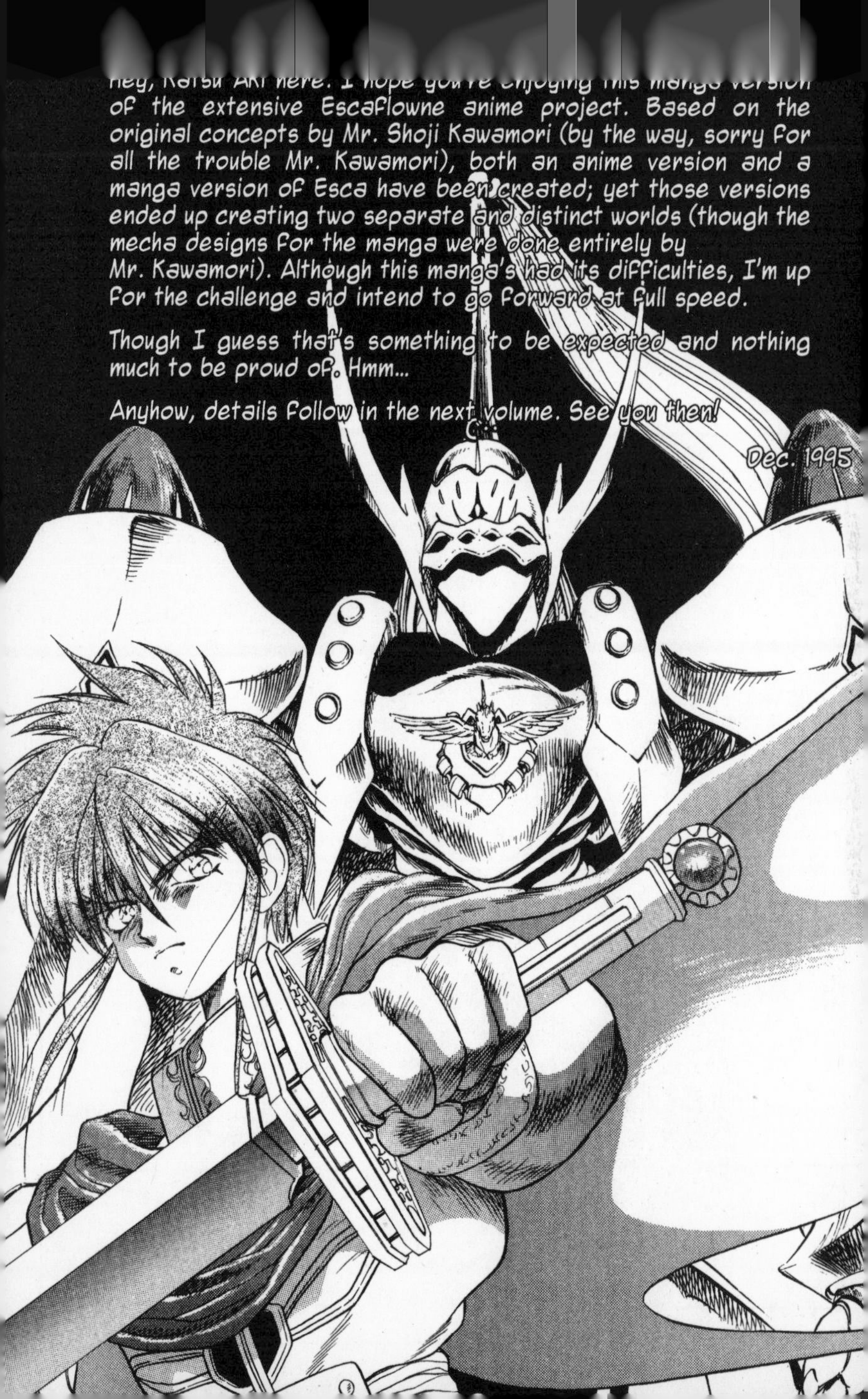

A MESSAGE FROM THE STAFF

FROM THE CONTRIBUTING WRITERS... AND, ALTHOUGH HE'S NOT IN HERE, MR. TERASHIMA (WHO'S ALSO PART OF OUR MAIN GROUP). THANKS!

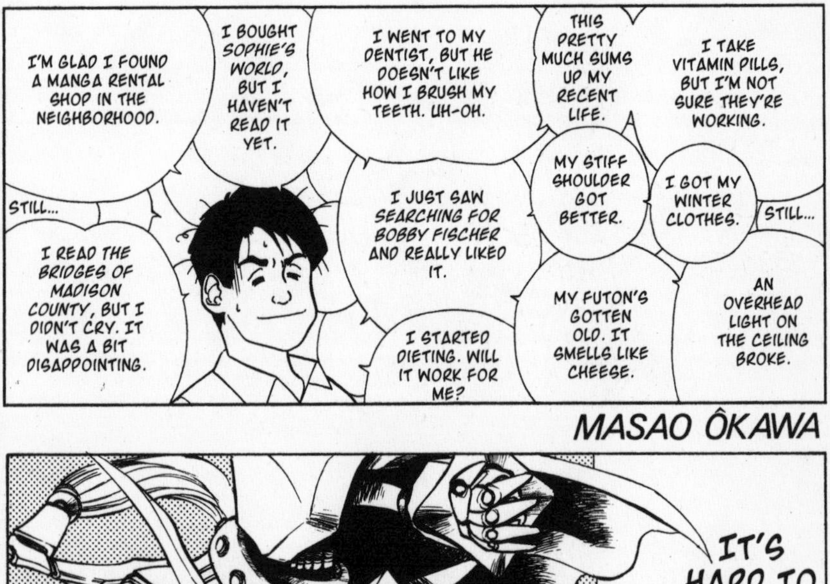
I TAKE VITAMIN PILLS, BUT I'M NOT SURE THEY'RE WORKING.
THIS PRETTY MUCH SUMS UP MY RECENT LIFE.
I WENT TO MY DENTIST, BUT HE DOESN'T LIKE HOW I BRUSH MY TEETH. UH-OH.
I BOUGHT SOPHIE'S WORLD, BUT I HAVEN'T READ IT YET.
I'M GLAD I FOUND A MANGA RENTAL SHOP IN THE NEIGHBORHOOD.
STILL...
I GOT MY WINTER CLOTHES.
MY STIFF SHOULDER GOT BETTER.
I JUST SAW SEARCHING FOR BOBBY FISCHER AND REALLY LIKED IT.
STILL...
AN OVERHEAD LIGHT ON THE CEILING BROKE.
MY FUTON'S GOTTEN OLD. IT SMELLS LIKE CHEESE.
I STARTED DIETING. WILL IT WORK FOR ME?
I READ THE BRIDGES OF MADISON COUNTY, BUT I DIDN'T CRY. IT WAS A BIT DISAPPOINTING.

MASAO ÔKAWA

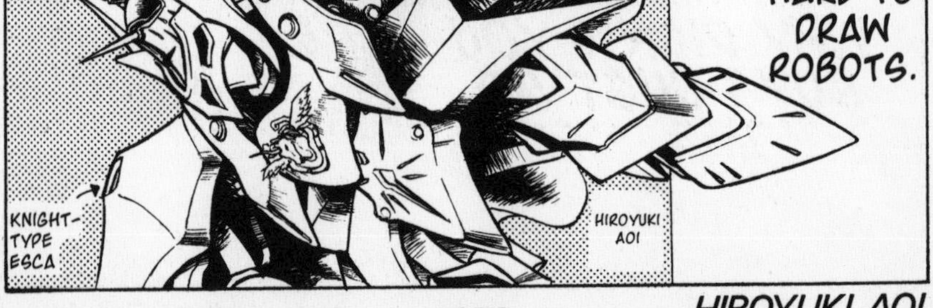
IT'S HARD TO DRAW ROBOTS.
HIROYUKI AOI
KNIGHT-TYPE ESCA

HIROYUKI AOI

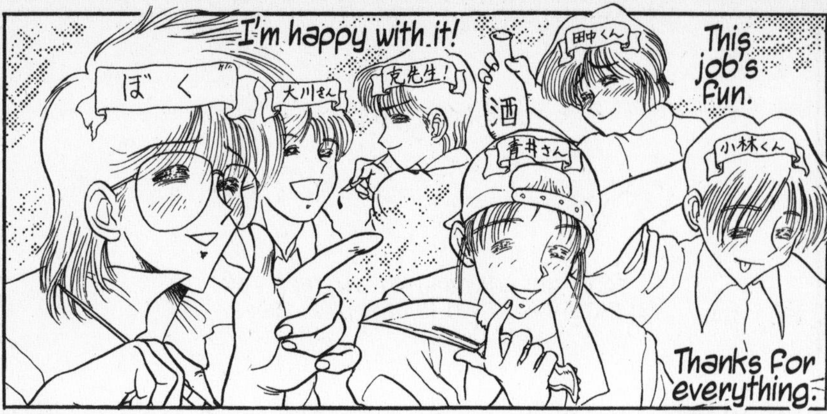
This job's fun.
田中くん
小林くん
酒
克先生!
I'm happy with it!
青井さん
大川さん
ぼく
Thanks for everything.

YÔICHI ITO

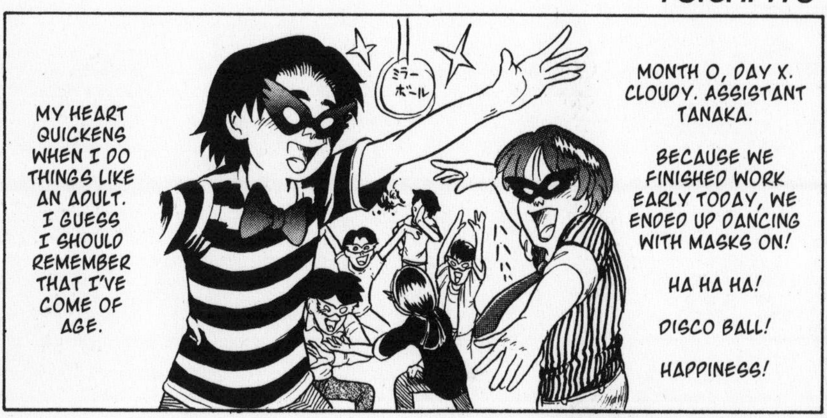
MONTH O, DAY X. CLOUDY. ASSISTANT TANAKA.
BECAUSE WE FINISHED WORK EARLY TODAY, WE ENDED UP DANCING WITH MASKS ON!
HA HA HA!
DISCO BALL!
HAPPINESS!
ミラーボール
MY HEART QUICKENS WHEN I DO THINGS LIKE AN ADULT. I GUESS I SHOULD REMEMBER THAT I'VE COME OF AGE.

OSAMU TANAKA

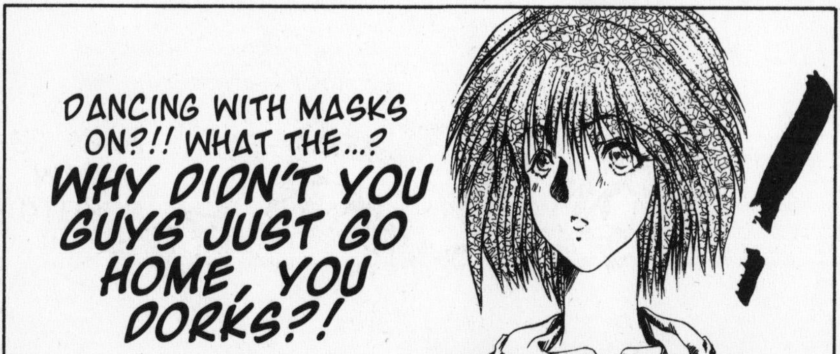
DANCING WITH MASKS ON?!! WHAT THE...?
WHY DIDN'T YOU GUYS JUST GO HOME, YOU DORKS?!

SHÛICHI KOBAYASHI

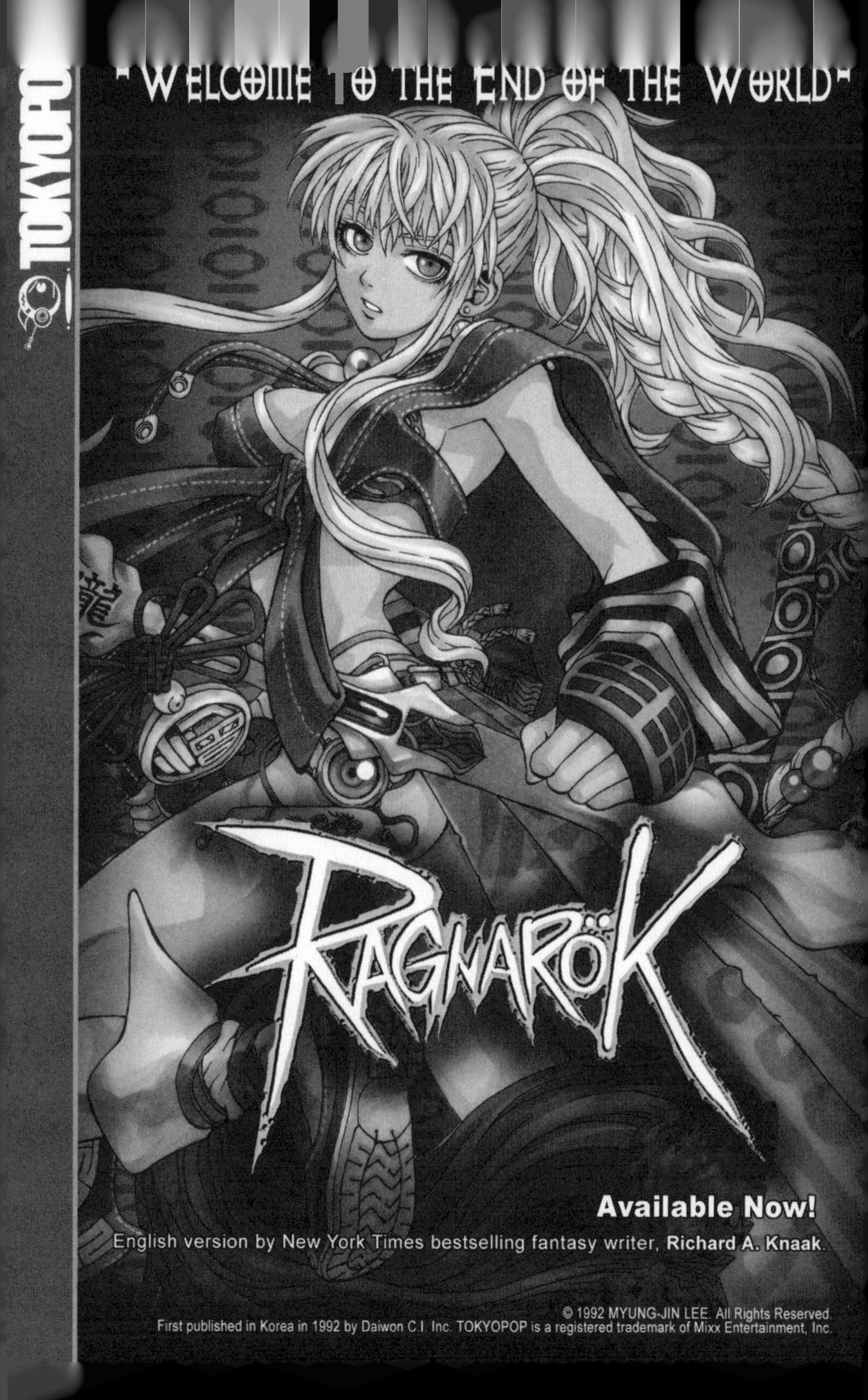
TOKYOPOP
"WELCOME TO THE END OF THE WORLD"
RAGNARÖK
Available Now!
English version by New York Times bestselling fantasy writer, Richard A. Knaak.
© 1992 MYUNG-JIN LEE. All Rights Reserved.
First published in Korea in 1992 by Daiwon C.I. Inc. TOKYOPOP is a registered trademark of Mixx Entertainment, Inc.

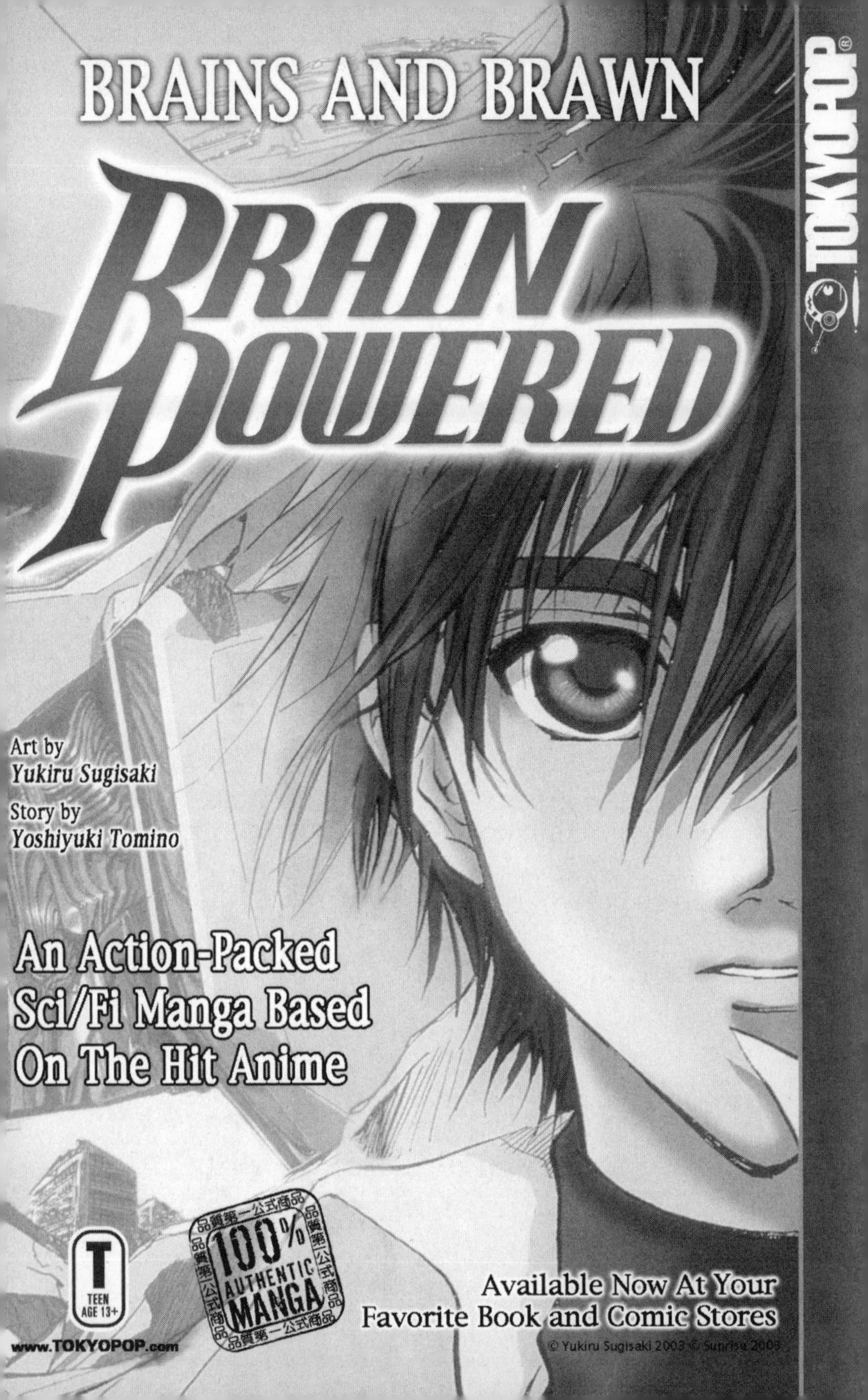
BRAINS AND BRAWN
BRAIN POWERED
TOKYOPOP
Art by
Yukiru Sugisaki
Story by
Yoshiyuki Tomino
An Action-Packed
Sci/Fi Manga Based
On The Hit Anime
T TEEN AGE 13+
100% AUTHENTIC MANGA
Available Now At Your
Favorite Book and Comic Stores
www.TOKYOPOP.com
© Yukiru Sugisaki 2003 © Sunrise 2003

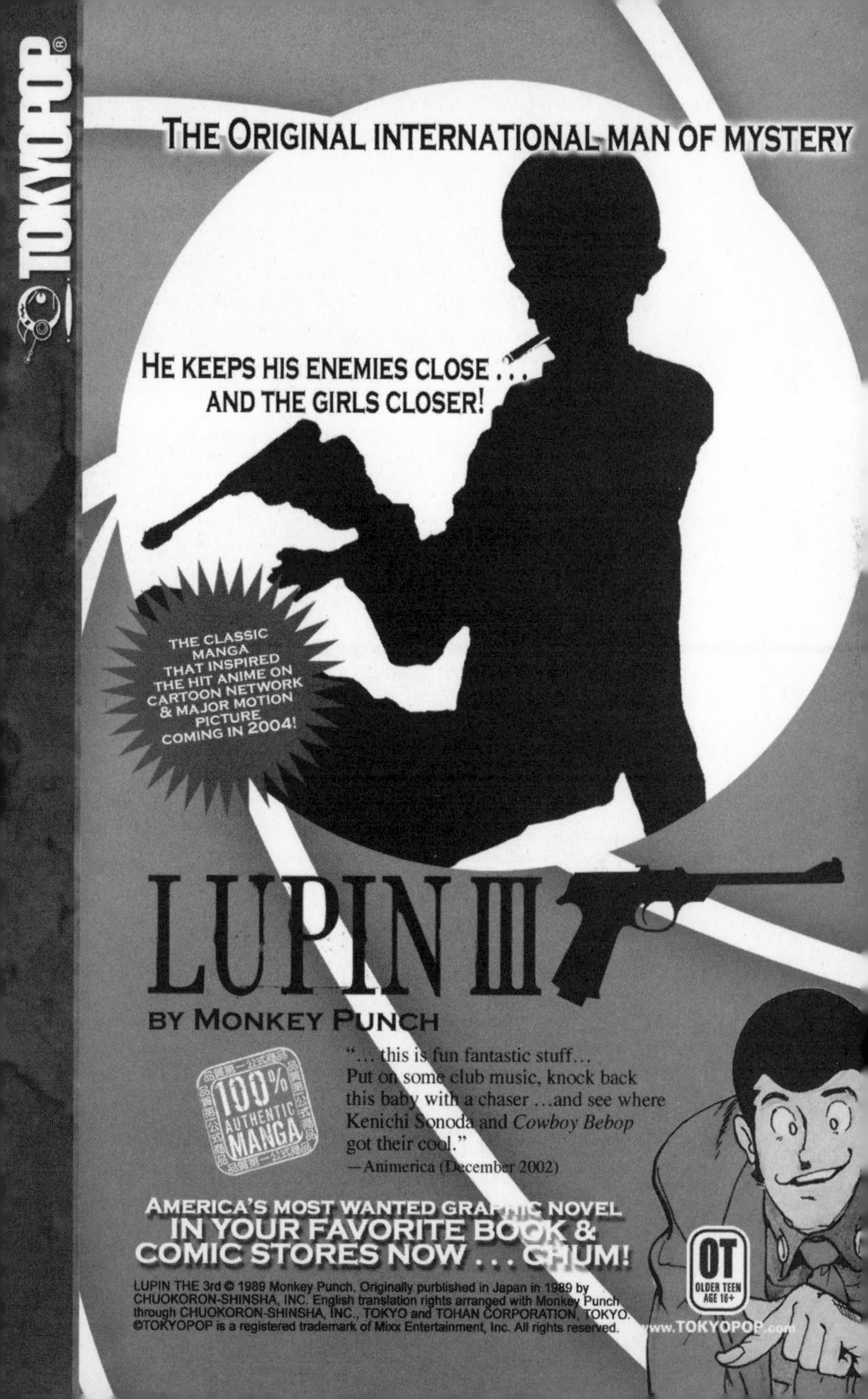
TOKYOPOP®
THE ORIGINAL INTERNATIONAL MAN OF MYSTERY
HE KEEPS HIS ENEMIES CLOSE . . .
. . . AND THE GIRLS CLOSER!
THE CLASSIC MANGA THAT INSPIRED THE HIT ANIME ON CARTOON NETWORK & MAJOR MOTION PICTURE COMING IN 2004!
LUPIN III
BY MONKEY PUNCH
100% AUTHENTIC MANGA
"... this is fun fantastic stuff... Put on some club music, knock back this baby with a chaser ...and see where Kenichi Sonoda and Cowboy Bebop got their cool."
—Animerica (December 2002)
AMERICA'S MOST WANTED GRAPHIC NOVEL
IN YOUR FAVORITE BOOK & COMIC STORES NOW . . . CHUM!
OT OLDER TEEN AGE 16+
LUPIN THE 3rd © 1989 Monkey Punch. Originally purblished in Japan in 1989 by CHUOKORON-SHINSHA, INC. English translation rights arranged with Monkey Punch through CHUOKORON-SHINSHA, INC., TOKYO and TOHAN CORPORATION, TOKYO. ©TOKYOPOP is a registered trademark of Mixx Entertainment, Inc. All rights reserved.
www.TOKYOPOP.com

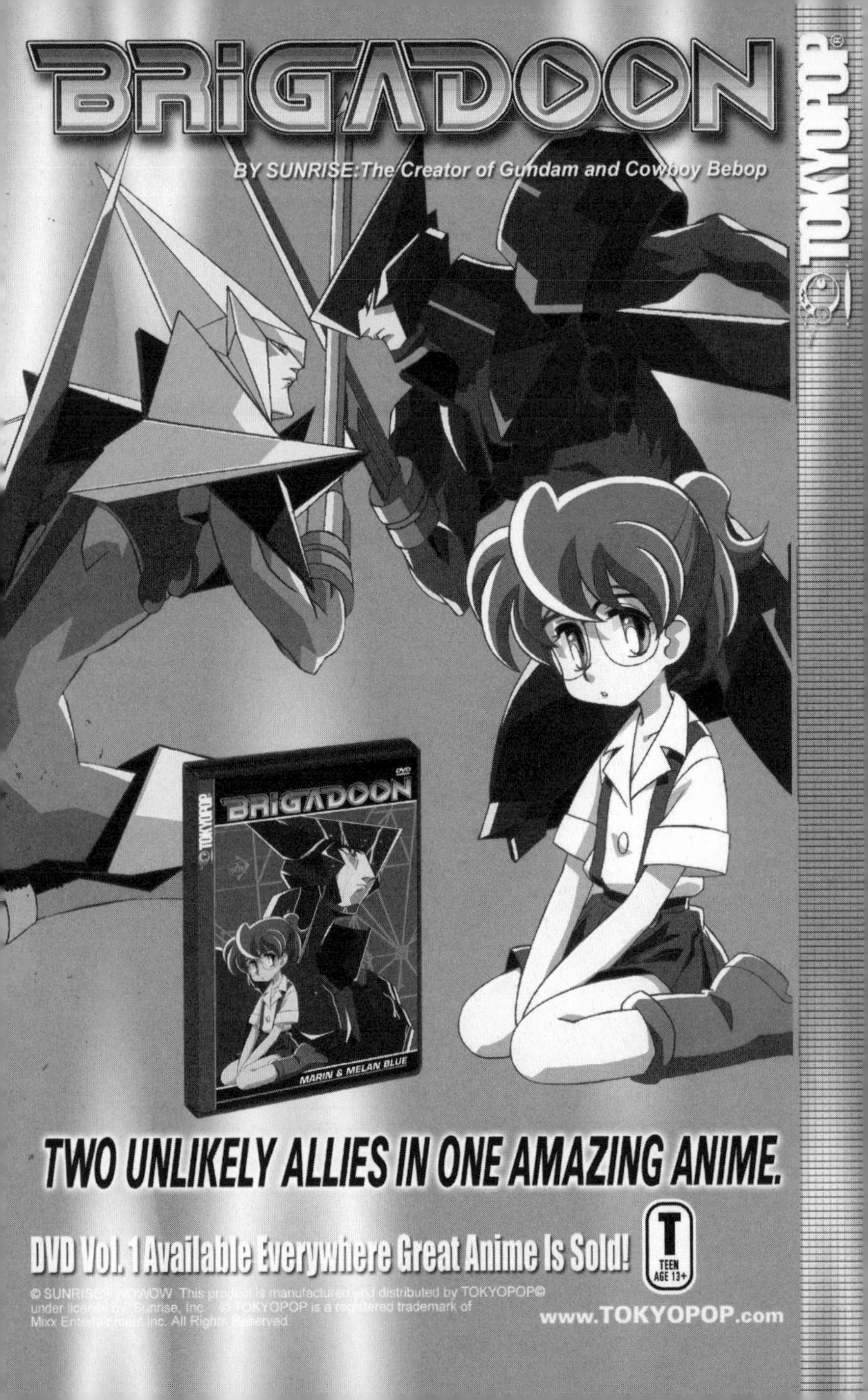

PLANETES

By Makoto Yukimura

Hachi Needed Time... What He Found Was Space

100% AUTHENTIC MANGA

A Sci-Fi Saga About Personal Conquest

Coming Soon to Your Favorite Book and Comic Stores.

TEEN
AGE 13+

www.TOKYOPOP.com

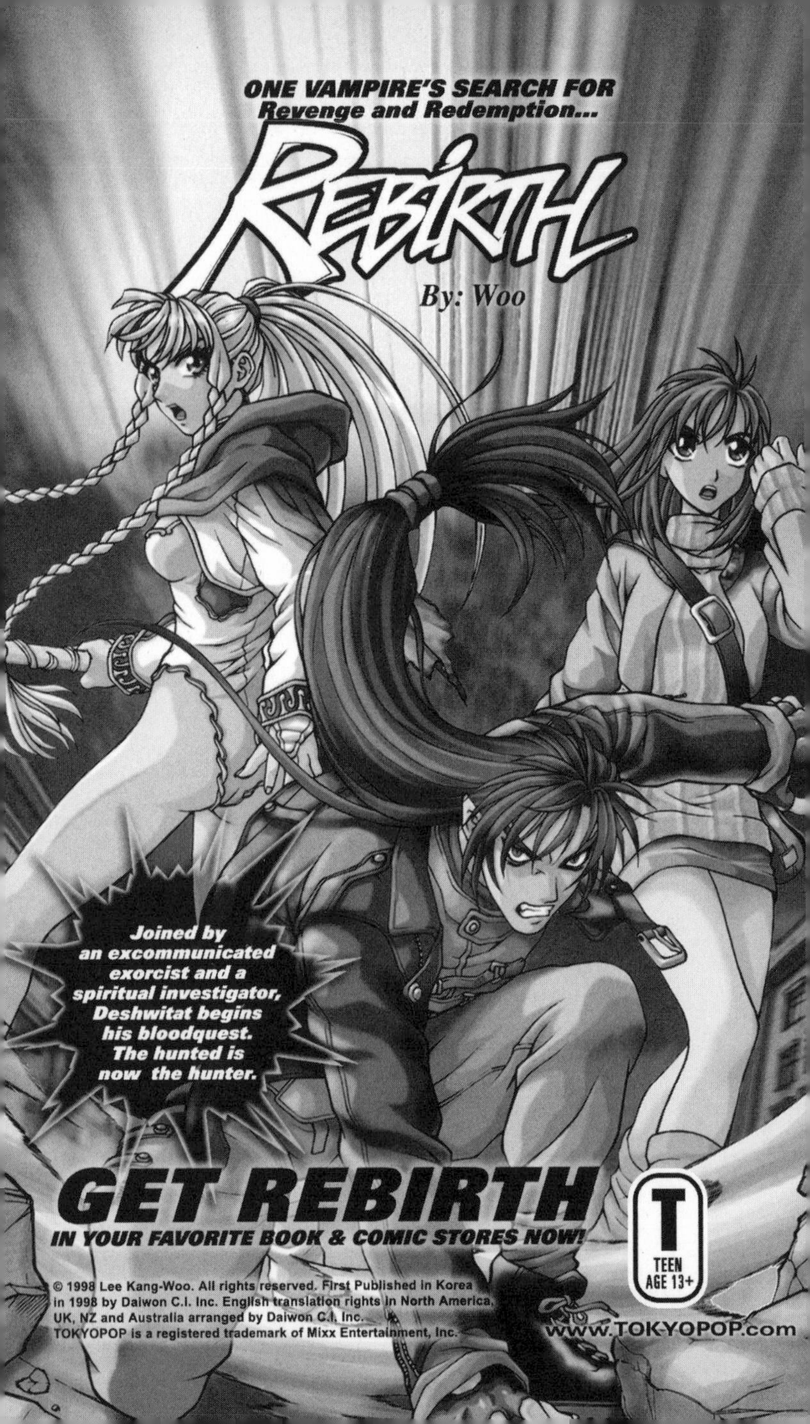
ONE VAMPIRE'S SEARCH FOR
Revenge and Redemption...
REBIRTH
By: Woo
Joined by an excommunicated exorcist and a spiritual investigator, Deshwitat begins his bloodquest. The hunted is now the hunter.
GET REBIRTH
IN YOUR FAVORITE BOOK & COMIC STORES NOW!
T
TEEN
AGE 13+
© 1998 Lee Kang-Woo. All rights reserved. First Published in Korea in 1998 by Daiwon C.I. Inc. English translation rights in North America, UK, NZ and Australia arranged by Daiwon C.I. Inc.
TOKYOPOP is a registered trademark of Mixx Entertainment, Inc.
www.TOKYOPOP.com

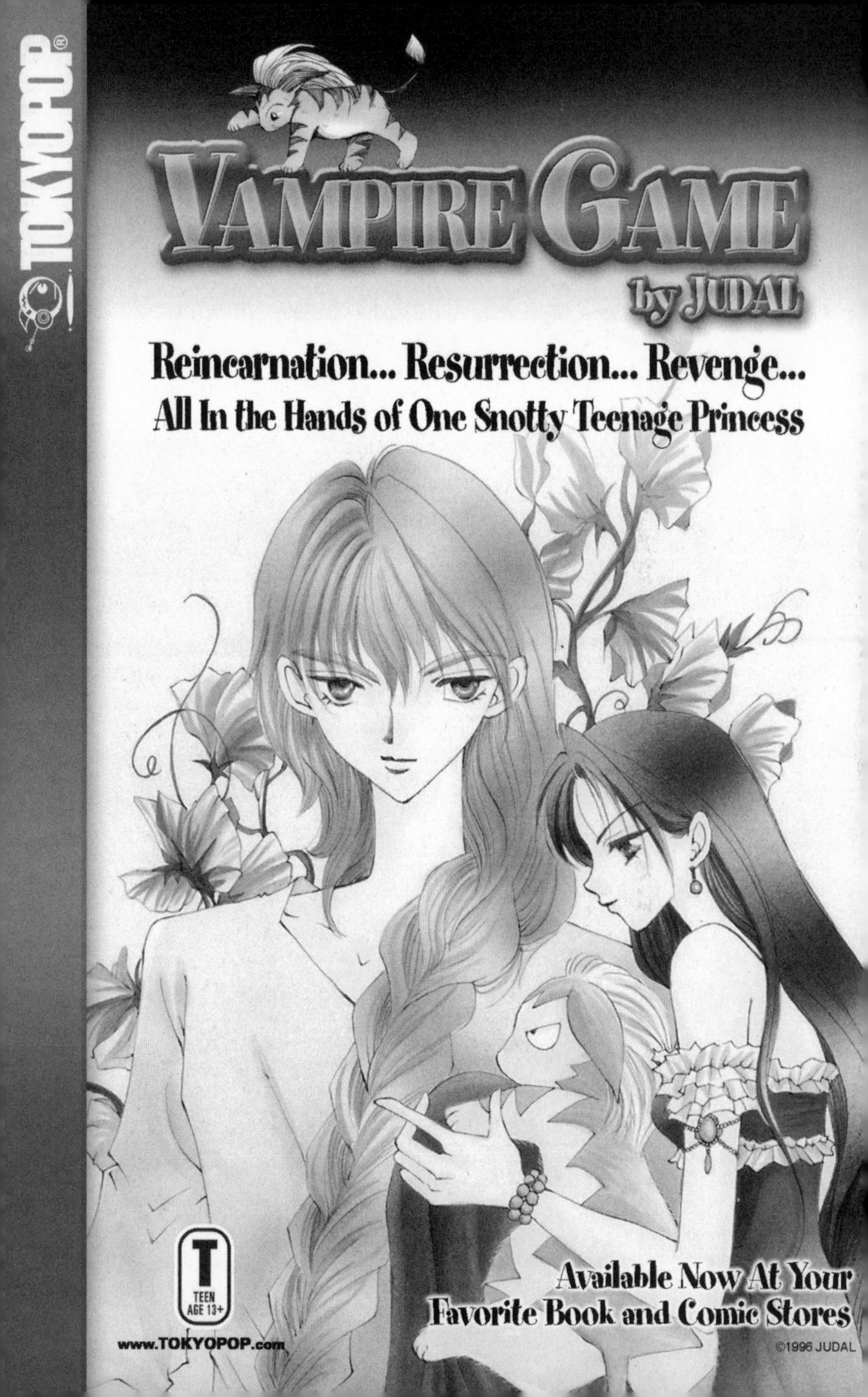
TOKYOPOP®
VAMPIRE GAME
by JUDAL
Reincarnation... Resurrection... Revenge...
All In the Hands of One Snotty Teenage Princess
T
TEEN
AGE 13+
Available Now At Your
Favorite Book and Comic Stores
www.TOKYOPOP.com
©1996 JUDAL

STEALING IS EASY - DECIDING
WHAT TO TAKE IS HARD.

AVAILABLE NOW AT YOUR FAVORITE
BOOK AND COMIC STORES

www.TOKYOPOP.com

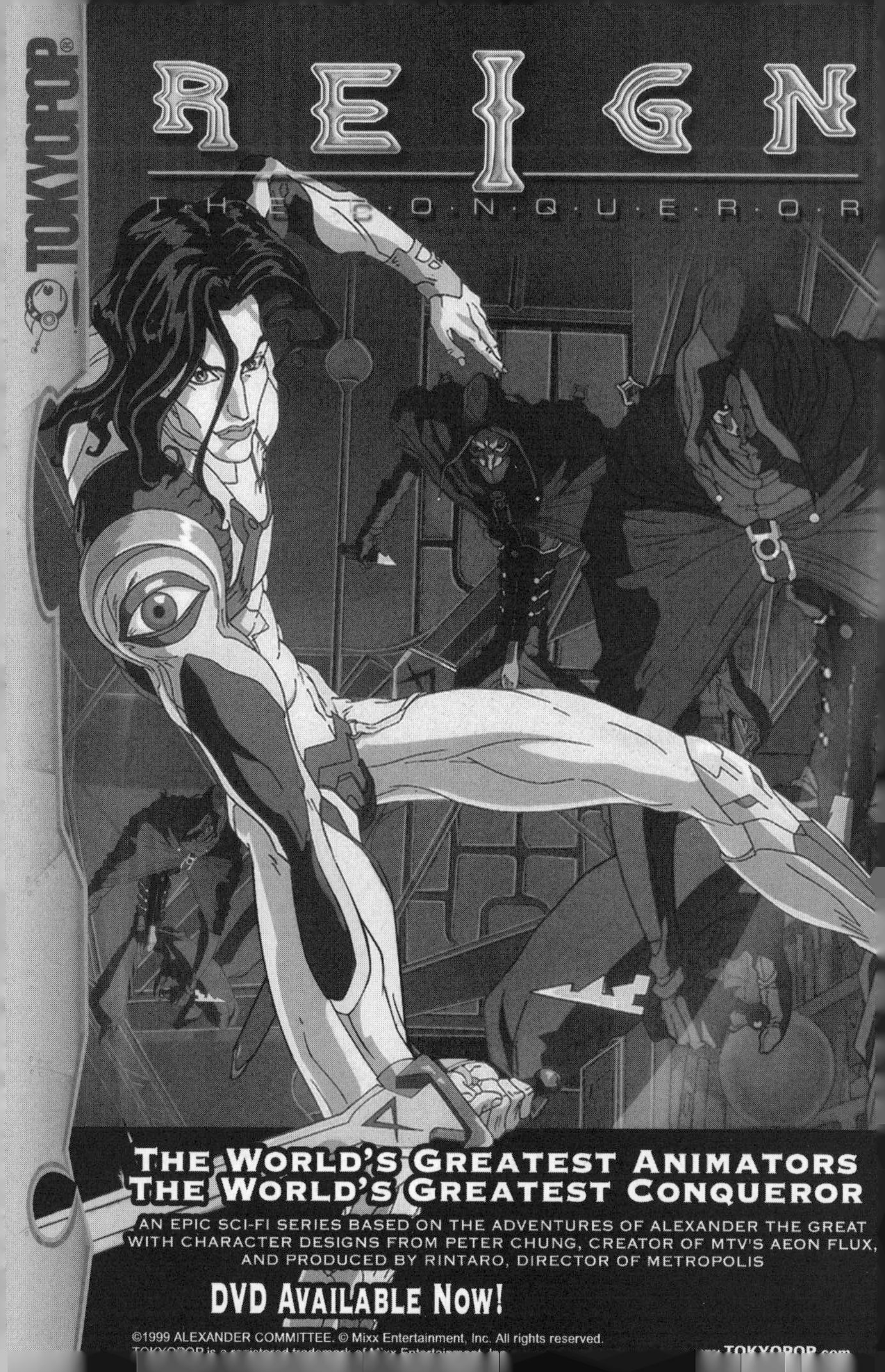

TOKYOPOP®
REIGN
THE CONQUEROR
THE WORLD'S GREATEST ANIMATORS
THE WORLD'S GREATEST CONQUEROR
AN EPIC SCI-FI SERIES BASED ON THE ADVENTURES OF ALEXANDER THE GREAT WITH CHARACTER DESIGNS FROM PETER CHUNG, CREATOR OF MTV'S AEON FLUX, AND PRODUCED BY RINTARO, DIRECTOR OF METROPOLIS
DVD AVAILABLE NOW!
©1999 ALEXANDER COMMITTEE. © Mixx Entertainment, Inc. All rights reserved.
TOKYOPOP.com

STOP!

This is the back of the book.
You wouldn't want to spoil a great ending!

This book is printed "manga-style," in the authentic Japanese right-to-left format. Since none of the artwork has been flipped or altered, readers get to experience the story just as the creator intended. You've been asking for it, so TOKYOPOP® delivered: authentic, hot-off-the-press, and far more fun!

DIRECTIONS

If this is your first time reading manga-style, here's a quick guide to help you understand how it works.

It's easy... just start in the top right panel and follow the numbers. Have fun, and look for more 100% authentic manga from TOKYOPOP®!